God's Apocalyptic Insurrection

God's Apocalyptic Insurrection

A Post-Evangelical Theology of Salvation

RICHARD D. CRANE

CASCADE *Books* • Eugene, Oregon

GOD'S APOCALYPTIC INSURRECTION
A Post-Evangelical Theology of Salvation

Copyright © 2024 Richard D. Crane. All rights reserved. Except for brief quotations in critical publications or reviews, no part of this book may be reproduced in any manner without prior written permission from the publisher. Write: Permissions, Wipf and Stock Publishers, 199 W. 8th Ave., Suite 3, Eugene, OR 97401.

Cascade Books
An Imprint of Wipf and Stock Publishers
199 W. 8th Ave., Suite 3
Eugene, OR 97401

www.wipfandstock.com

PAPERBACK ISBN: 978-1-6667-1222-3
HARDCOVER ISBN: 978-1-6667-1223-0
EBOOK ISBN: 978-1-6667-1224-7

Cataloguing-in-Publication data:

Names: Crane, Richard D., author.

Title: God's apocalyptic insurrection : a post-evangelical theology of salvation / Richard D. Crane.

Description: Eugene, OR : Cascade Books, 2024 | Includes bibliographical references.

Identifiers: ISBN 978-1-6667-1222-3 (paperback) | ISBN 978-1-6667-1223-0 (hardcover) | ISBN 978-1-6667-1224-7 (ebook)

Subjects: LCSH: Salvation—Christianity. | Evangelicalism. | Theology, Doctrinal.

Classification: BR1640 .C73 2024 (paperback) | BR1640 .C73 (ebook)

VERSION NUMBER 101024

Material from the following journal articles is used with permission:

Chapter 11 is a revised version of:
Crane, Richard. "Rethinking the Grammar of Atonement: Forgiveness, Justice and Apocalyptic Recapitulation." *Perspectives in Religious Studies* 46 (2019) 55–78.

Chapters 7 and 8 draw from material first published in:
Crane, Richard. "'Salvation is a 'Group Project': An Ecclesial Soteriological Imagination." *Perspectives in Religious Studies* 38 (2011) 61–83.

Contents

Preface: Do Not Skip This Preface! | vii
Acknowledgments | xiii

Introduction | 1

Section One: What If the Reigning Soteriology Is Part of What We Need Saving From?
Introduction | 25

Chapter One
Problems with the "Plan of Salvation" | 29

Chapter Two
Soteriological Pathologies and Racial Injustice | 45

Section Two: Soteriology and Biblical Narrative
Introduction | 71

Chapter Three
First Testament Soteriological Trajectories | 81

Chapter Four
Setting the Stage for Jesus: The Intertestamental Period, Apocalyptic Literature and Economic Realities in First-Century Palestine Under Roman Occupation | 104

Chapter Five
The Soteriology of Jesus: Messiah, Savior, Inaugurator of the Kingdom of God | 127

Chapter Six
Jesus of Nazareth as Apocalyptic Collision with the Powers of the Present Age | 150

Section Three: A Soteriological Vision

Chapter Seven
A Soteriological Vision, Part 1: Integrating Biblical and Theological Themes | 173

Chapter Eight
A Soteriological Vision, Part 2: Salvation Is Incorporation into and Participation in the Eschatological New Creation | 188

Chapter Nine
Justification and "Personal Salvation" | 199

Section Four: Sin and Atonement

Chapter Ten
What We Need Saving From: Or, We Are All in This Mess Together | 217

Chapter Eleven
The Grammar of Atonement: Apocalyptic Recapitulation, Forgiveness, and Rectification | 238

Section Five: The Struggle for Justice as Participation in the Eschatological New Creation

Chapter Twelve
The Politics of Salvation as Participation in God's Eschatological/Apocalyptic Intrusion | 265

Chapter Thirteen
Eschatological Hope, Apocalyptic Soteriology, and the Struggle for Justice and Human Dignity and Flourishing | 296

Conclusion | 311

Bibliography | 315

Preface
Do Not Skip This Preface![1]

THIS BOOK IS AN "experiment in soteriology."[2] As such, it has been written, in part, to respond to two urgent realities within the life of ecclesial communities in the United States.

First and foremost, the events of the past several years have exposed, or rather, more fully exposed, profound pathologies within American Christianity. It was not support for a Republican candidate but rather the unfathomable enthusiasm[3] for the candidacy, and then the presidency, of Donald J. Trump that have functioned as the proverbial canary in the coal mine. Immediately after the 2016 election, an African-American student at the Christian university at which I taught for twenty years shared how deeply troubled she was. She was not merely upset about the outcome of the election but also the fact that so many of her fellow students, most of whom professed to be Christians, supported Mr. Trump. She was not sure whether the students who supported Donald Trump did so because of his racist rhetoric. But as she pointed out in a classroom conversation, what left her so shaken was the fact that this was not a "deal-breaker" for them!

But what does the doctrine of salvation have to do with any of this? Isn't there a "pure" Christian gospel of salvation, timelessly true, that is not contaminated by the tragic failures of Christians to live up to "other parts" of the Christian faith, such as the imperative to love all of the neighbors? Is not soteriology one area of Christian doctrine that is timeless and

---

1. See the last paragraph of this Preface for an explanation of the non-violent ramifications of the use of the word "insurrection" in the title of this book.

2. I am quite intentionally alluding to Edward Schillebeeckx's subtitle in Schillebeeckx, *Jesus*, 1979.

3. This enthusiasm for candidate and then President Trump was most concentrated among white evangelicals, but was also strong among white Christians generally and was not limited to white Christians.

trans-contextual, the "same" salvation message to all people in all times and places?

The surprising answer to this question is *no!* We neither believe nor embody the Christian faith within a timeless or ahistorical space of pure ideas. Nor is our interpretation and understanding of the faith cordoned off from the past. Each generation of Christians may make modifications within the web of belief or doctrine, ethics, and practice as part of the "traditioning" process, but we also inevitably inherit a theological edifice constructed in the past, which includes serious deformations that are not easy to recognize. As Robert P. Jones argues, "The version of Christianity our ancestors built, and which we inherited, the 'faith of our fathers,' was a cultural force that, by design, protected and propagated white supremacy."[4] Much within our inherited theologies of salvation is the product of ways of thinking about the Christian faith that assumed that being a Christian was compatible with explicit belief in white supremacy and the inferiority of people of color.[5] While most white Christians today, we believe and we hope, would repudiate explicit belief in white supremacy, we often do not see the ways in which the theologies we inherit were forged in this very crucible. Our inherited soteriologies are not innocent of the sins of the past and contribute, even if unwittingly, to the contemporary perpetuation of racial fears, biases, perceptions, and injustices, in part, by an "individualization" of sin and salvation that results in an "inability to see" the ways that racial injustice is embedded in systems that function to produce harmful outcomes[6] even when that is not the intention of participants in these systems.

At the present moment, much that represents itself and understands itself as Christianity in the United States is deeply broken and disfigured. In this situation, I have sought to return to what Karl Barth called "the strange new world within the Bible"[7] and propose a reading of the Bible with a different set of lenses. While still a seminary student, I read Edward Schillebeeckx's *Jesus: An Experiment in Christology*. Where most of the debate generated by this book centered upon Schillebeeckx's arguments about the resurrection and the empty tomb tradition, the book was transformative at the beginning of my theological journey because of the way in which Schillebeeckx situated Jesus in relation to the messianic hopes that had begun to emerge in our book of Isaiah. Schillebeeckx spoke of Jesus as the revelation of the God who is benevolent and anti-evil, the God whose will and purpose

---

4. Jones, *White Too Long*, 234.
5. Jones, *White Too Long*, 234.
6. Emerson and Smith, *Divided by Faith*.
7. Barth, "Strange New World within the Bible," 28–50.

is to overcome and deliver human persons from the powers that afflict and inflict suffering in order that humans might flourish. I have never forgotten Schillebeeckx's pithy phrase, "[Humanity's] cause [is] God's cause."[8]

The second major motivating concern of this book is this post-evangelical or ex-evangelical[9] moment. "Ex-evangelicals" are deeply involved in the "deconstruction" of their inherited versions of the Christian faith. But what is also desperately needed at this moment are theological endeavors designed to "reconstruct," to articulate a more faithful theological vision, to offer pathways forward. When evangelicals find their faith ruptured, many leave evangelical circles but find no expression of the Christian faith to replace what was lost. One of my animating concerns is to contribute to the task, much larger than the aspirations of any one theologian or church leader, of setting forth a rich, meaningful, and hopefully faithful articulation of the Christian faith for persons who have lost their evangelical ecclesial and theological homes. This book is not written only for ex-evangelicals but also others who have, or are close to, jettisoning the Christian faith because it seems hopelessly allied with patriarchy, racism, wealth, and authoritarian social and political impulses.

As a white theologian, I know my limitations when it comes to speaking about racial injustice. I recently read the "Introduction" to Jonathan Tran's *Asian Americans and the Spirit of Racial Capitalism* and was reminded of how much I have to learn. I certainly will not be able to write about race with the erudition and insight of theologians like J. Kameron Carter, Willie James Jennings, M. Shawn Copeland, and Tran. Nevertheless, my hope is that this book makes its unique contribution by addressing the ways in which soteriology may either exacerbate racial injustice or provide a framework that enables Christians to recognize that resisting every form of injustice is not peripheral but rather at the very heart of the gospel. After all, if the atoning work of Christ on the cross was to form a new humanity in his crucified and risen body, then the work of dismantling dividing walls of hostility, especially by those of us who inherited a Christianity which constructed those walls, is integral to what it means to be "in Christ" and to participate in Christ's death and resurrection.

Most theological books and journal articles on "soteriology" tend to focus upon one of the following dimensions of salvation: atonement,

---

8. Schillebeeckx, *Jesus*, 229.

9. I have no personal investment in the category of "evangelical Christian." Absent the current American context that has rendered the word problematic, due to the identification of the word evangelical with a particular species of Republican politics, evangelical is, or used to be, a good word. The word once referred to the good news after all. But the term has been tarnished by its associations.

justification, or *theosis*. I will endeavor to paint a big picture, to sketch a broad vision of soteriology that includes not only atonement doctrine but also questions about justification, *theosis*, the reign of God and an inaugurated apocalyptic eschatology, ecclesiology, discipleship, and an account of participation in the *missio Dei* that includes the struggle for a just and humane world.

In trying to paint a big picture, as I have struggled to write this book, I have felt like the main character in J. R. R. Tolkien's classic short story *Leaf by Niggle*. There is a beautiful and powerful vision of the Christian faith that I have caught a glimpse of, one that feels, to borrow an expression from the prophet Jeremiah, like a fire shut up in my bones (Jer 20:9) that I cannot but seek to articulate in all of its grandeur. And yet, I feel like the character of Niggle. This is a task that is "too large" and "too ambitious" for me and certainly too ambitious for a single book. Indeed, I have accumulated enough research material and have written rough drafts sufficient for three or four book projects.

As deadlines approach, I have come to think about this book as a kind of "volume one" of a larger soteriological project. This book will devote more attention to the crafting of a biblical argument for the soteriological big picture I am attempting to paint. My long-term goal will be to write a second book on soteriology that engages even more deeply with important theological voices in the Christian tradition and one which situates my own project or proposal in relationship to current theological trends and trajectories. But for now, painting a big picture means that some of the "fine-grained analysis" that is present in earlier drafts of almost every chapter had to be trimmed.

This book sits awkwardly on the borderline between academic book and a book written for an audience of persons who are interested in theology but are not theologians in the narrow, professional sense of the word. This book is written in the hope that it will be read far beyond academic circles narrowly defined. I hope it is a book that speaks to pastors, church leaders, persons interested in theology, thoughtful Christians of all kinds, and especially to persons who have been committed Christians but are no longer sure that Christian faith makes sense. At this moment, when Christian nationalism and other toxic expressions of the Christian faith are the loudest public voices, it is easy to "deconstruct" a Christianity that serves to undergird projects of Christian cultural dominance. This book aspires to make a small contribution to the task of articulating a vision of another way to be Christian that might provide theological resources for a more faithful imagination regarding how the body of Christ is called to represent Christ.

In the final analysis, theology matters to the extent that it has an impact upon Christian life and practice. The ultimate goal of this book is an immodest one. I truly hope to have an impact on the way Christians think about what it is we need to be saved from, what it is we are saved for, and what it means to live or embody this gift of salvation. The pathologies of our inherited soteriologies are not the singular cause, but nonetheless they have played a role in the perpetuation of racial and other injustices or, at minimum, to the inability to see the systems that inflict great harm on persons in our society and the body of Christ. Vietnamese-American Theologian Phuc Luu suggests that the demise of Christianity is less likely to be the outcome of an increasingly secular world and more likely to result from the type of Christianity that is predominant. He contends that the most urgent question is not whether Christianity will survive but "*which kind* of Christianity and *whose* Jesus will be passed down to our theological descendants."[10]

Hopefully, our imaginations are not so constrained by the destructive left-right binary oppositions in our society that we think that the only kinds of Christianity are those allied with whatever is the flavor of the day in right-wing politics or left-wing politics. The urgent need is for a Christian vision that is simultaneously contextual and traditional. How do the realities we now encounter impact the way we read Scripture and the ways we appropriate, interpret, and reshape the versions of the faith we inherited. But how do we also seek to read Scripture with an openness to what has been ignored, repressed, or simply "not seen" because our theological lenses, shaped by the soteriological pathologies I will describe in the first section of the book, are not calibrated to see what is in fact integral to the story of salvation the Bible tells?

Finally, I have no illusions regarding this project. This book will not be groundbreaking theological scholarship that transforms the academic guild. My hope is that this book offers something to the theological imagination of Christian leaders and persons struggling with inherited versions of the faith. What I argue, in effect, is that inherited soteriological imaginaries are deeply problematic. In my twenty years of teaching undergraduate students, I often asked the question, "Do we have to think about things in this way, or is there another way to frame the issue?" As humans, and this is certainly the case with respect to any religious faith, we inhabit certain metaphors, imaginaries, and narratives. But sometimes these metaphors, imaginaries, and narratives become dysfunctional, distorted, and distorting. What if there is another way to read the Bible? What if there is another way to put the pieces together in a theological synthesis that is a creative and

---

10. Luu, *Jesus of the East*, 14–15.

faithful imaginative act? In this book, I will argue that the center of soteriology should be Jesus's premium on human flourishing and well-being. My hope is that the result is not a bland, theologically liberal emphasis on being nice like Jesus. Rather, my goal is to suggest that salvation from God draws us into the work that is, apart from God, impossible. This is the task of being conduits of God's apocalyptic intrusion and insurrection against the powers that deal death. To be drawn into a mode of participation in God's healing and rectification of all things is not something humans can do by our own power. It is not a "works righteousness." However, what has been obscured by years of certain Protestant imaginaries that dramatically bifurcate justification and the rest of the Christian life, is that the very gift of salvation is incorporation into the way of life of the eschatological new creation. That way of life involves being conduits of life, the life that flows from God to us through Christ and the Spirit and into the old creation in bondage. And while a creation in bondage to destructive and enslaving powers will fight back, the eschatological new creation keeps arriving and as it does, healing, transformation, and freedom do happen!

The word insurrection is often associated with violence. However, Jesus and the "kingdom" he inaugurates are non-violent in character. Jesus's command to Peter to put away his sword extends far beyond the Garden of Gethsemene. Jesus's followers are not called to advance his Reign with violence or coercion.

In Matt 12:22–29, Jesus describes his mission with a violent metaphor: binding the strong man and plundering his house. However, Jesus's resistance to the powers of evil and the oppressive powers of empire and temple establishment involved no killing. The "weapons" in Jesus's arsenal were creative and aggressive acts of resistance and sometimes scathing truth-telling. Jesus's assault upon the powers that inflict death is non-violent, yet incredibly disruptive. It is this meaning that is intended by the word "insurrection." This meaning will be clarified further in chapters 6 and 9.

Acknowledgments

It is simply impossible to thank the great cloud of witnesses who have influenced my life and Christian faith. First and foremost is my wife, Mary, who has always believed in me and supported me even in the most uncertain and disappointing times. She supported me through my PhD work at Marquette University as we struggled to make ends meet and raise two small children. She encouraged me to teach as an adjunct because it was an "open door," a professional opportunity, even when this was financially stressful and it meant that she would need to continue to work full-time for a few more years. And when I was presented with two job offers twenty years ago, one a permanent position as a campus minister and the other a more precarious one-year faculty position at Messiah College, she encouraged me to take the risk in order to get my foot in the door. For years, Mary was a Roman Catholic lay minister. She is also a great theological mind. We have struggled together to be teachers, ministers, and faithful Christians amid the upheavals of the past ten years.

I am thankful to my children, Rebecca Brandt and Richard Joseph Crane, both of whom have grown up to be compassionate and deeply reflective adults. Hopefully, the day will come when my grandchildren, Colton, age eleven, Ian, age four, and Amoura, two months, are able to read this book.

I owe a significant debt of gratitude to Professor Bradford Hinze, now at Fordham University. Brad was my dissertation director at Marquette University. The encouragement he provided for me as I struggled with anxiety and "imposter syndrome" was crucial as I completed my dissertation. Along the way, I was blessed to learn from many great teachers. As a freshman in high school, Ms. Pat Yates pushed our classes to achieve excellence. I learned grammar and every part of speech. I learned to write! I was introduced to the great literary classics. Her English class opened my world and helped instill in me a love for learning.

Acknowledgments

Multiple professors at Samford University, including W. T. Edwards, Karen Joines, and William Cowley, and at The Southern Baptist Theological Seminary before the fundamentalist takeover, including Molly Marshall and David Mueller, shaped my love for Christian Theology. At Marquette University, I was privileged to learn from Thomas Hughson, SJ, Robert Masson, Christine Firer Hinze, Kenneth Hagen, D. Lyle Dabney, Patrick Carey, and others.

Thanks are in order to Messiah University and, especially, though certainly not limited to, my colleagues in the department of biblical, philosophical, and religious studies. I "retired" after twenty years at Messiah after the 2022–2023 academic year. My life has been enriched by great conversations with Eric Seibert (God and violence), George Pickens (religion, politics, and practical jokes), Sharon Putt (atonement), and Drew Hart (theology, politics, race and theology), David Weaver-Zercher (theology and politics and the Anabaptist tradition), John Yeatts (Anabaptist theological tradition and college football!), and Robin Collins and his wife, Rebecca Adams (conversations at the intersection of theology and philosophy). I am grateful for my other colleagues through the years, including Emerson Powery, Jake Jacobsen, Shelly Skinner, Rebecca Harris, Stephen Gallaher, Mike Cosby, Jay McDermond, Meg Ramey, Brian Smith, Timothy Schoettle, Lareta Finger, Chris Van Gorder, Devin Manzullo-Thomas, and John and Susie Stanley. Additional gratitude is owed to Rick Schaeffer. Rick is a Chemistry professor, but his theological reflections are such that he should have been a theologian as well. I will miss conversations with Todd Allen, Ed Arke, John Fea, Jim LaGrand, and Robin Lauermann. And, of course, there are so many more persons that I have failed to mention. I am also grateful to Dwayne Magee, who took one of my classes and has never ceased to encourage me to finish this book, most often while eating pizza together! I dare not begin to mention the many students whose profound questions, engagement in class, and struggles to make sense of their inherited Christian faith helped me to develop further the ideas and insights in this book.

I owe a debt of gratitude to theologians associated with the National Association of Baptist Professors of Religion Region-at-Large, whose meetings I attended until the intrusion of the demands of law school. Curtis Freeman, Mikael Broadway, Scott Bullard, Barry Harvey, Steve Harmon, Beth Newman, Adam English, Philip Thompson, Mark Medley, and others, as well as theologians who were members of the College Theology Society, were supportive and offered crucial critique and feedback on my work.

When I "retired" from Messiah University, I did not actually retire. I am a lawyer, working for a small employment law firm. This position allows me to be advocate for clients who have experienced discrimination

Acknowledgments

and other injustices in the workplace. I am grateful to Seton Hall University School of Law for the gift of the Distinguished Weekend JD Scholarship, which made it possible for me pursue my JD. I have been blessed to suffer the anxiety of being a non-traditional law school student with some great friends, including Marque Staneluis, Mal Garvin, Marwa Abdelbary, Bill Braunlein, Andrew Simon, Tricia Connolly, Joe Keller, and so many others, too numerous to mention. I have been blessed to learn from great legal minds who combine scholarship, years of legal experience, and deep passion for justice, including Professors Angela Carmella, Claudette St. Romain, John Jacobi, Solangel Maldonado, Abdul Rehman N. Kahn, Richard Winchester, Jon Romberg, Paula Franzese, Jonathan Hafetz, and so many others.

I must include special thanks to a professor at Seton Hall School of Law. Even though I was not able to take one of his classes while at Seton Hall, I was privileged to meet Dr. David Opderbeck before I arrived on campus. Dr. Opderbeck is both a legal scholar and professor, and in his "free time" he earned a PhD in theology. He is a much better theologian than I will ever be. I have been privileged to engage in conversations with David.

I am deeply appreciative of Pastor Max Ramsey, who has been a paradigmatic disciple in his radical commitment and hospitality to the persons Jesus prioritized in Matt 25:31–46. Max is a pastor who combines deep theological wisdom and insight, deep pastoral love for people, and community engagement that embodies so much that I am gesturing toward as faithful ecclesial practice in this book.

There are many who I love and appreciate whose names I will not mention because they would not endorse the viewpoints expressed in this book. Indeed, many persons I love might see the book as an attack on their cherished convictions. Obviously, this is painful since my goal is to engage in faithful theological analysis and evaluation and not to "attack." However, my vocation as a theologian must be, first and always, faithfulness to Christ as best as I can discern. This theological vocation is often painful because it takes us to places we might wish to avoid for the sake of harmony. The call and vocation of the theologian is the vocation of contributing to the repair of patterns of Christian discourse and practice that have become harmful and antithetical to the way of Christ, even if adherents of those understandings may also genuinely desire to be faithful. Nonetheless, there are many persons who would ardently disagree with me who I love and to whom I owe a depth of gratitude.

I could not even begin to mention the names of so many other persons I have been blessed to know in the churches I have attended and so many other arenas of life. The persons who have impacted my life and thought

Acknowledgments

certainly stretch far beyond the names listed here. My fear in compiling this list of names is leaving out the names of so many more remarkable persons who have graced my life!

Introduction

IN 1988, DR. KATIE Cannon raised this question about the racial injustice she encountered as a child:

> How could Christians who were white, flatly and openly, refuse to treat as fellow human beings Christians who had African ancestry? Was not the essence of the Gospel mandate a call to eradicate affliction, despair and systems of injustice?[1]

The answer to Professor Cannon's second question is that, for the most part, white Christians in the United States do not believe that the essence of the gospel is a call to eradicate affliction, despair, and systems of injustice.

Of course, many white Christians and churches have acted in compassionate ways in response to human suffering and need, and very often, across racial lines. Many white Christians would profess, and many seek to live out, a commitment to just treatment and respect for all human persons.

However, the specifically *soteriological* point I am making is that action to alleviate suffering is not widely considered by white Christians to be anywhere close to the "essence of the gospel." This soteriological conviction was stated explicitly by a man who, at that point in time, had been elected to represent evangelical Christians. In 2005, Ted Haggard, then president of the National Association of Evangelicals, stated:

> The African American [evangelical] community has an honorable concern for social justice, and that affects their politics. That concern comes from the Scripture. The Anglo community has a different history, so different Scriptures stand out to them. To the Anglo [evangelical] community, most of their sermons are theological. It's salvation by grace through faith, and other

---

1. Cannon, *Black Womanist Ethics*, 1.

theological points, so social-justice issues don't have the same compelling justification.²

To his credit, Haggard was trying to express appreciation for African-American evangelicals. Yet, he clearly acknowledged that social justice, while having a scriptural basis, is peripheral to "the" gospel, which, according to Haggard, "Anglo Christians" consider to be "salvation by grace through faith." Haggard rather bluntly stated that the African-American concern for social justice lacks "compelling justification" for most white Christians due to convictions at the heart of white (Anglo) soteriology. In the summer of 2019, survey data confirmed Haggard's characterization. The data showed that seven in ten Black practicing Christians (70 percent) reported being motivated to address racial injustice, while only about one-third of white practicing Christians (35 percent) said the same.³

The past eight years have exposed the extent to which racial fault lines in the United States and American Christianity remain deep and damaging. And the dominant soteriological imagination continues to play a significant role in this brokenness along racial lines.

Fall 2016

Between 77 percent and 81 percent of white evangelicals voted for Donald Trump in 2016, as did 60 percent of white Catholics and approximately 50 percent of white mainline Protestants.⁴ Prior to the 2016 election, Donald Trump played a central role in the "birther" controversy. His announcement that he would run for president was accompanied by derogatory comments suggesting that most Mexicans crossing the border illegally were rapists and drug dealers.⁵ During his campaign, he advocated banning all Muslims from entering the country.⁶

Yolanda Pierce, a professor of African-American religion at Princeton Theological Seminary who taught and lectured for years in evangelical churches and schools, most of which were predominantly white, had understood her vocation to be a bridge-builder within the body of Christ. But after the 2016 election, Pierce professed that "something has been broken

---

2. Stafford, "Good Morning Evangelicals!," 42.
3. Barna Research Group, "White Christians"; "Black Practicing Christians."
4. Martínez and Smith, "How the Faithful Voted."
5. Lee, "Fact Checker."
6. Jackson, "Donald Trump's Call for Banning Muslims."

for me ... [the] fragile hope that the work of racial and gender justice will be embraced by the larger church." She wrote:

> Eighty-one percent of white evangelicals and born-again Christians voted for someone who, on tape, mocked a journalist with disabilities ... [and] admitted to sexually assaulting women.... I watched as eighty-one percent of white evangelicals and born-again Christians dismissed his affairs, adultery, multiple marriages, participation in porn subculture, refusals to release his tax returns, failure to donate to charities to which he promised money, ... participation in racist lies about President Obama, ... and still voted for him.[7]

July 2020[8]

While 2020 will be remembered most for COVID-19, this year has featured three high-profile killings of African-American persons: the racially-motivated murder of Ahmaud Arbery,[9] the death of Breonna Taylor in a botched raid by members of the Louisville Police Department, and the murder of George Floyd by Minneapolis police officer Derek Chauvin. This summer has seen protests in cities across the United States, accompanied by calls for reforms in policing.[10] In the meantime, the president has persisted in racially-charged rhetoric, including emphatic support for all things Confederate, such as monuments, names of military facilities, and the rebel flag. On May 29, 2020, he tweeted the phrase, "When the looting starts, the shooting starts." This phrase was originally used by Miami police chief Walter Headley, a man with a long history of bigotry against the black community, in 1967, to describe how he would deal with what he called crime and thugs and threats by young black persons.[11] On June 1, 2020, Donald Trump marched across Lafayette Square to the patio of St. John's Episcopal

---

7. Pierce, "Watching 81 Percent of My White Brothers and Sisters Vote for Trump."

8. This section of the "Introduction" was written in July 2020. This segment reflected my frame of mind at that moment in time. To say that the ground has shifted between the summer of 2020 and early 2023, as I complete this manuscript, is an understatement.

9. Booker, "White Defendant Allegedly Used Racial Slur."

10. It has been estimated that anywhere from 15 million to 26 million Americans participated in protests in the wake of the murder of George Floyd during the summer of 2020. Buchanan et al., "Black Lives Matter May be the Largest Movement in US History."

11. Sprunt, "History Behind 'When the Looting Starts, the Shooting Starts.'"

Church to declare himself "your law and order president," language which harkens back to Richard Nixon's southern strategy dog whistles as well as the rhetoric of ardent segregationist George Wallace. There he posed, holding a book he has little familiarity with, a Bible, in order to convey the impression that his authoritarian gesture finds its moral foundation in the Bible and Christian faith.[12]

To shift from the national to the local, the ministerial experience of a family member, shortly after the video of Derek Chauvin's murder of George Floyd went public and American citizens, black and white, filled the streets, illustrates the tragic failures of much of white Christianity in the United States to even talk about the long history and present reality of racial injustice. This person was a part-time minister at a small congregation in a mainline Protestant denomination in a small Midwestern town. As the events of the summer of 2020 unfolded, as 15 to 26 million persons participated in marches in support of racial justice, the pre-planned summer sermon series on "heaven" continued without modification. The sermon series accentuated the need for a personal salvation experience to ensure one's admission into heaven and in order to avoid hell. This escapist soteriology was accompanied by the pastoral choice simply to ignore the crises of 2020. The issues of race and policing went unaddressed except for a generic prayer for police officers[13] the Sunday after the George Floyd video was released and the first wave of protests occurred across the nation.

Two Sundays after the video of George Floyd's death went public and protests were occurring throughout the country, the chosen text was Jesus's parable of the rich man and Lazarus. The primary point derived from this text by the pastor was that hell is real and, therefore, accepting Jesus as one's personal savior is the key to avoiding it. The issues that this parable raised pertaining to disparities of wealth and poverty, economic injustice, human suffering, and the "damnable" sin of ignoring persons who are destitute,

12. Baker et al., "How Trump's Idea for a Photo Op Led to Havoc in a Park."

13. As Christians, we should indeed pray for the safety of police officers and appreciate the many police officers who seek to do their jobs with integrity and treat the persons they encounter fairly and with dignity. We should recognize the complexities and difficulties police officers may face.

However, the larger issue certainly includes individual police officers who abuse their authority, but it is not merely a matter of individual police officers, but rather, the systems within which individual police officers work. To fail to grapple with questions of larger public policy decisions that involve militarized policing in urban areas, the ways the war on drugs has devastated minority communities, the systems that are often complicit in or condone police brutality and unjustified extra-judicial killings, is to dismiss the claims of our African-American brothers and sisters in Christ that things are not right. To take their testimony seriously is not to be "against the police," but rather, to be on the side of justice and well-being for everyone, including police officers.

vulnerable, and marginalized, were ignored. My "relative" was assigned this text and expected to preach a similar message in the second, smaller congregation over which the pastor served. However, she departed from that script in the effort to be faithful to the parable and the explosive context of the events of the past two weeks. Her sermon emphasized eschatological justice for the people in this world who are destitute and mistreated. My family member included George Floyd among those for whom, like Lazarus, a God of justice has a special concern. To say that this generated discomfort is an understatement.

What happened at this congregation is but a microcosm of significant strands of white Christianity in the United States, whether evangelical, mainline Protestant, or Roman Catholic. For example, Father Bryan Massingale notes that black Catholics are leaving the church in significantly higher numbers than white persons and in greater numbers compared to African-American Protestants leaving their historically black church traditions.[14] One significant reason is that less than one-third of African-American Catholics who worship in predominantly white parishes heard sermons addressing questions of racial justice during the summer of 2020. More than 75 percent of black Catholics say that a commitment to racial justice is an essential or important dimension of their faith, compared to only 13 percent of Catholics overall. Massingale sums up the issue this way:

> The Black exodus from the Catholic Church is due to the fundamental disconnect between what the vast majority of Black Catholics ... see as essential for understanding faith and the concerns being addressed in most white congregations. It is not the whiteness of the Catholic Church that is an issue. It is the unwillingness of the white Catholic community to engage realities that are existentially important for African American believers.... The not-so-subtle message conveyed is that such concerns are irrelevant to the Catholic faith.[15]

Fall 2020 through Summer 2021

During the summer of 2020, I felt some small measure of hope that this could be a *kairos* moment in which a majority, or at least a critical mass, of

---

14. Only 54 percent of Black adults who were raised Catholic continue to identify as Catholic. This compares to 81 percent of Black adults who were raised in African-American Protestant churches, and 61 percent of white Americans who remain Catholics into adulthood. Massingale, "Black Catholics Are Leaving the Church," 40–41.

15. Massingale, "Black Catholics Are Leaving the Church," 40–41.

white Americans might truly seek to come to terms with both the history and present reality of racial injustice. But this hope was short-lived. Large numbers of white Christians were quickly part of a backlash, responding with hostility to African-American concerns about policing and racial justice. These Christians conflated the violent behavior of a small percentage of actors at protest marches with all protest against "extra-judicial" police violence. Framing the issue as "Blue Lives Matter" versus "Black Lives Matter," these Christians articulated their conviction that African-American concerns about policing were simply not valid and were to be dismissed as "anti-police." Amid cries for racial justice, large numbers of white Christians maintained strong support for then President Donald Trump and are now up in arms about a new bogeyman, critical race theory. All of this reveals the depth of resistance to any claims by African-American persons that racial injustice in the United States is real. Ironically, the very people who profess to believe the doctrine of original sin are in fact deeply entrenched within a narrative of their own personal and societal innocence.

Between the 2016 and the 2020 elections, a lot happened! President Trump asked why the United States should accept more immigrants from "shithole" countries such as Haiti and countries in Africa, asserting, "We should bring in more people from places like Norway."[16] After the Charlottesville, Virginia "Unite the Right" rally, organized by white supremacist groups, ended in tragedy, President Trump's response was to claim moral equivalence between the counter-protestors and the white supremacist groups. His words were, "There were bad guys, very fine people, and blame on both sides."[17]

And yet, white evangelicals were just as enthusiastic for Donald Trump in 2020. Between 76 percent (Edison exit polls) and 81 percent (AP VoteCast survey) voted for him.[18] The white mainline Protestant vote for Donald Trump was again almost evenly split, while the white Catholic vote was between 56 percent and 58 percent.[19]

The survey research of Sean McElwee and Jason McDaniel found that either racism, racial bias, racial resentment, or racial fear were central factors in much of the Christian vote for Donald Trump. They concluded that negative racial attitudes toward African-American persons and negative attitudes about immigration, legal or non-legal, were the key factors

---

16. Watson, "Trump Questions Why US Welcomes People."
17. Norris, *Witnessing Whiteness*, 15.
18. Newport, "Religious Group Voting and the 2020 Election."
19. Burge, "2020 Vote for President by Religious Groups—Christians."

associated with support for Donald Trump rather than economic distress or anxiety.[20]

Other studies have uncovered similar and overlapping connections between support for Donald Trump and anxieties about the loss of cultural dominance on the part of white religious persons. A survey conducted by Diana Mutz and another survey, conducted by the Public Religion Research Institute ("PRRI"), arrived at similar conclusions. Cultural anxiety, or perception of threats to white Americans sense of dominant group status, fueled the vote for Donald Trump. The PRRI study noted, "White working-class voters who say they often feel like a stranger in their own land and who believe the US needs protection against foreign influence were 3.5 times more likely to favor Trump than those who did not share these concerns."[21]

Joseph Baker, Samuel Perry, and Andrew Whitehead argued that the strongest predictor for voting for Donald Trump was "Christian nationalism," which has been linked to fear of outsiders, including antipathy toward Muslims and other "ethnoreligious outsiders." Donald Trump was highly successful in tapping into Christian nationalist desires to see Christianity privileged in the public sphere and to return America to a mythic past in which the United States was an overtly "Christian nation." The authors define Christian nationalism as the belief, embedded within an ensemble of narratives, traditions, myths, value systems, and symbols, that America is "[a] distinctively 'Christian' [nation] and that this should be reflected in its public policies, sacred symbols, and national identity."[22] Christian national-

---

20. McElwee and McDaniel, "Economic Anxiety Didn't Make People Vote Trump, Racism Did."

21. Mutz, "Status Threat, Not Economic Hardship, Explains the 2016 Presidential Vote"; Cox et al., "Beyond Economics."

22. Baker et al., "Keep America Christian (and White)," 272–75.
The survey questions utilized to identify Christian nationalism as a strong predictor of support for Donald Trump, using Likert response options ranging from "strongly disagree" (1) to "strongly agree" (4) were:

- The federal government should declare the United States a Christian nation.
- The federal government should advocate Christian values.
- The federal government should enforce strict separation of church and state.
- The federal government should allow the display of religious symbols in public spaces.
- The federal government should allow prayer in public schools.

The survey questions utilized to identify hostility toward immigrants and other ethnoreligious outsiders as strong predictors of support for Donald Trump were:

- Immigrants are more likely to commit crime than US citizens.
- Recent immigrants are more reluctant to assimilate than previous immigrants.

ism was found to be a powerful predictor of intolerance toward immigrants, racial minorities, and interracial families as well as opposition to gay rights, support for harsher punishment for criminals, including the death penalty, support for other authoritarian measures of social control, justification for use of excessive force against black Americans in law enforcement, and to traditionalist, patriarchal gender ideology. The sense of loss of a mythic Christian past is intertwined with assumptions about race, sex, and gender, and a hierarchical ordering of society.[23]

The survey data garnered by PRRI's 2018 American Values Survey confirmed the studies mentioned above. White Christians are consistently more likely than whites who are religiously unaffiliated to deny the existence of structural racism. Yet, the survey found a "robust relationship" between being a white Christian and holding racist attitudes. The more racist attitudes a person holds, the more likely he or she is to identify as a Christian. Religiously unaffiliated white persons are significantly less likely to hold racist attitudes than white persons who identify as Christian. On the Racism Index, with 0.0 as the lowest mean and 1.0 as the highest, the mean for white evangelical Protestants was .78, for white Catholics .72, and for white mainline Protestants .69. By way of contrast, the mean for white persons without a religious affiliation was .42. The mean was .24 for black Protestant Christians. All of the data, Robert P. Jones concludes, suggests that white Christian churches, Protestant and Catholic, have served as institutional spaces for the preservation and transmission of white supremacist attitudes.[24]

- Immigrants are a drain on the economy.
- Immigrants bring diseases to the United States.
- Police should be allowed to raid businesses and homes in order to find undocumented workers.
- Deportation is a good solution to immigration issues.
- Creating a "pathway to citizenship" will encourage illegal immigration.

23. Baker et al., "Keep America Christian (and White)," 275–76.

24. Jones, *White Too Long*, 171, 175–76, 182–85; Jones, "Racism among White Christians Is Higher than among the Nonreligious."

PRRI included controls for church attendance, but found no evidence that higher church attendance has any mitigating effect on racist attitudes. Jones concludes that "whatever Christian formation is happening in churches, it is not positively impacting the racial biases among frequent attenders."

The PRRI survey used a Racism Index composed of fifteen questions related to the history of white supremacy and perceptions of African-Americans. Included were questions about the Confederate flag and monuments, whether the killing of African-Americans by police are isolated incidents or part of a broader pattern of how police treat African-Americans, and whether racial minorities use racism as an excuse for economic inequalities. Other opinion questions, with a scale to register degrees of

Introduction

This survey data is discouraging. The realities behind the data are also incredibly complex. There is always a grave danger of painting with the proverbial broad brush and speaking about "white Christians" or "white evangelical Christians." The world is always more complex than our categorizations. There is a lengthy continuum among persons who count as white with respect to racial attitudes and perceptions. My own experience and sense of things, admittedly anecdotal, is that most white Christians are not motivated by racial hatred. However, it is not the potholes you see that are the most dangerous to your car's tires, alignment, and struts, but the ones you do not see. In the same way, it is not always the overt forms of white supremacy that do the most damage but the powerful undercurrent of fears, biases, and inaccurate assumptions about other groups that are always lurking just beneath the surface, alongside deep, visceral ideal pictures of what the United States is supposed to "look like," that are the most damaging. In addition, as will be discussed later in the book, the endemic individualism of much of white American Christianity renders persons "blind" to systems and institutions and their powerful impact, sometimes contrary to the intentions of persons acting within these systems in accordance with the norms and pressures embedded within these systems.

The racial anger of many white Christians lies with the sense that African-American criticisms of the racism endemic within American society threaten the deep, mostly unarticulated, intuitive sense that many white Christians have regarding the fundamental innocence and purity of the nation and its white cultures. To call attention to past and present racial injustice as deeply embedded within the history, culture, and societal institutions

---

agreement and disagreement, included:

- If blacks would only try harder, they could be just as well off as whites.
- White people in the US have certain advantages because of the color of their skin.
- A black person is more likely than a white person to receive the death penalty for the same crime.
- Racial problems in the US are rare, isolated situations.
- Today, discrimination against whites has become as big a problem as discrimination against blacks and other minorities.

Statements assessing xenophobia included:

- The American Way of Life needs protecting from foreign influence.
- A question pertaining to Donald Trump's efforts to implement a partial Muslim travel ban.
- A question about support for building a wall on the southern border.

of American society threatens the assumption that "our" preferred social order, way of life, and values are fundamentally good or innocent.[25]

2022–2023

In 2022–2023, the cause *du jour* in the conservative outrage media, dutifully mimicked in many evangelical Christian circles, is "anti-wokeness." "Wokeness," in the political rhetoric of its critics, is an amorphous term that can function to label anything the person affixing the label does not like. But it seems that even mentioning or acknowledging past or present racial injustice is "woke liberalism."[26] For example, the singing of the Black national anthem, *Lift Every Voice*, prior to the Super Bowl in February 2023, was decried as "woke liberalism."

African-American protests in the summer of 2020 were the impetus for the "anti-wokeness" backlash, which amounts to a "doubling down" on assertions of white and American innocence. An example was the non-renewal of the contract of Julie Moore, a professor of English at Taylor University, an evangelical Christian institution. Moore's offense was not a classical christological heresy. Her "heresy" was the inclusion of *The Color of Compromise*, a book by Jemar Tisby, an African-American evangelical Christian, on her syllabus. Though Moore had exposed her mostly white Christian students to texts wrestling with issues of racial justice in America for years, under the pressure of student complaints about the "wokeness" of her class and of Tisby's book, it seems that she had crossed an unacceptable line for the powers-that-be at Taylor University.[27] Tisby's book provides a well-argued and well-documented account of what should be uncontroversial and obvious to conscientious Christians: in American history, Christian faith and racism have been intertwined and mutually reinforcing.[28] But his book was deemed, at Taylor University, to be unsuitable for "Christian" consumption.

Something has gone terribly wrong when Christians refuse to listen to other Christians of a different skin color because those Christians truthfully

---

25. A prime example of this mythology of innocence is Rev. Baily Smith's description of the United States as "the country the children of God built." See Smith, "Sin that Seems So Nice," at 28:15.

26. For example, on a college football discussion board, I have seen plenty of "rants" against the NFL placing the words "end racism" on the backs of football helmets as "woke liberalism." In other words, even acknowledging the reality of ongoing racial injustice is just too much!

27. Smietana, "Taylor Professor Julie Moore."

28. Tisby, *Color of Compromise*.

name the racial injustices and failings that are part of our tragic reality. This is no longer a Christianity whose elementary grammar is confession of sin, repentance, and trust in God's forgiving and transforming grace. Rather, this is a Christianity that believes, most fundamentally, in "our" innocence and purity.

What's Salvation Got to Do with It?

But what does the doctrine of salvation have to do with any of this?

Christian support for slavery and colonialism and the construction of a racial hierarchy, which gave sanction to slavery and colonialism, were always intertwined with soteriological convictions. The African slave trade was often justified on the grounds that the capture and enslavement of men and women from Africa resulted in the salvation of souls that would otherwise be lost.[29]

Christian convictions about the soteriological exclusiveness of Christ were deployed in profoundly perverse ways to transform religious difference into racial difference. J. Kameron Carter argues that the first maneuver in the creation of "race" and the development of white supremacy was supersessionism. Israel is displaced from the soteriological center of Christian identity and replaced with white Europeans, who are mapped onto Israel's special relationship with God.[30] Classical Christian convictions about the soteriological exclusiveness of Christ could have inspired a zeal for evangelism animated by a spirit of love for the religious other. Instead, those outside the faith were regarded as enemies of God and Christian civilization. As they encountered non-Christian others who were also darker-skinned, a world viewed through the lens of this supersessionism generated a toxic religious and racial hierarchy.[31]

Willie James Jennings describes the creation of a racial aesthetic, with white flesh as beautiful and black flesh as damaged and ugly, and a racial hierarchy, with white as superior in intelligence, civilization, and capacity for the gospel and black flesh at the bottom of the hierarchy as less intelligent and less capable of being civilized without coercive discipline. Whiteness indicated a high probability of salvation at the top of the hierarchy. But as one moved "down" a sliding scale of darkness, the probability of salvation is

---

29. Jennings, *Christian Imagination*, 15–20.
30. Norris, *Witnessing Whiteness*, 39–41, 46; Carter, *Race*, 4.
31. Norris, *Witnessing Whiteness*, 46; Fletcher, *Sin of White Supremacy*, 27.

lessened, with black bodies being the least likely to be saved, except through force or slavery.[32]

It was a perverse soteriological logic. Religious others are racial others and racial others are religious others and, as such, are enemies of Christ. Therefore, they should be conquered and subdued and, as part of that conquest, converted. Even before Christopher Columbus's voyage, papal decrees had blessed the African slave trade by Portuguese, and later Spanish, explorers, who were also granted full authority "to invade, search out, capture, vanquish, and subdue all Saracens and pagans whatsoever, and other enemies of Christ wheresoever placed, and reduce their persons to perpetual servitude."[33] After Columbus's return from "the new world," Pope Alexander VI issued two papal bulls in 1493, granting Spanish monarchs authority to expropriate any new land not owned by a Christian lord. This theological vision placed white Christians at the top of the scale of being with the mandate to subdue the earth.[34]

In the United States, part of the inherited soteriological imagination was forged to uphold the institution of slavery. Ministers such as Cotton Mather and George Whitefield, out of genuine concern for the eternal salvation of enslaved persons, made a soteriological "deal with the devil." Many slave-owners did not wish to see their slaves evangelized since a long-standing social convention in England had been that a baptized slave, now a sister or brother in Christ, was to be set free. In order to receive the privilege of preaching the gospel to enslaved persons, Mather, Whitefield, and others insisted that salvation of the soul does not entail liberation of the body.[35] This maneuver was the beginning of a long tendency to place concern for racial and for economic justice, of non-white persons and impoverished white persons as well, outside the range of concerns of "the gospel."

Neither a Conservative Evangelical nor a Protestant Liberal Project

In an interview with Nicholas Kristof, published in *The New York Times* the day before Easter 2019, theologian Serene Jones seemed to deny the physical resurrection of Jesus and suggested instead that the real message of

---

32. Jennings, *Christian Imagination*, 15–37.
33. Nicholas V, "Bull Romanus Pontifex"; Norris, *Witnessing Whiteness*, 41.
34. Alexander VI, "Inter Caetera"; Norris, *Witnessing Whiteness*, 41–43.
35. Emerson and Smith, *Divided by Faith*, 25; Broadway, "Preaching What We Practice," 292–94.

Easter is the message that love is stronger than life or death.[36] The next day, terrorist attacks on churches in Sri Lanka resulted in the deaths of hundreds of Christians. Andrew McGowan, dean of Berkeley Divinity School, the Episcopal seminary at Yale, was scathing in his response: "If Easter really meant just that love is more powerful than death, but Jesus didn't rise, how's the love-death score today?"[37]

Episcopal priest and theologian Wesley Hill also wrote in response to Jones's Easter Saturday interview. Hill pointed out that he finds inspiration in the fact that many young mainline Protestants seem to be convinced that a robustly biblical, Nicene, and Chalcedonian orthodoxy is not at odds with a concern for the poor and oppressed and a commitment to action for political change in the direction of social justice. He expresses his conviction that the future of mainline Protestantism will feature a tight connection between concern for the marginalized, radical politics, and the hope of the bodily resurrection. Hill ends his essay with this powerful vignette:

> A few years ago, . . . I was reunited with a friend I had gone to college with. During our student days, my friend had migrated more and more leftward in her political and social commitments, and at the time I wondered whether she might soon decide that a robustly orthodox Christian faith was one more structure of patriarchal and racist oppression that needed to be dismantled. We lost touch after graduation, and years later, when we met up, I expected my friend to tell me she no longer had an evangelical faith. As it turned out, the opposite was true. Having lost none of her progressive political instincts, my friend had become more Christian since when I knew her. "I've realized," she told me, in so many words, "that the world I've been working for is the world God promised when he raised Jesus from the dead.[38]

Overview of the Book

The thesis of the book is that salvation means being drawn into union with the triune God through incorporation by the Spirit into the risen Christ. But this ancient Christian motif of *theosis* should be integrated into a theological account of salvation as incorporation into the eschatological new creation. If Jesus is the savior and the messiah, he is, by definition, the

36. Kristof, "Reverend, You Say the Virgin Birth Is a 'Bizarre Claim?'"
37. Hill, "After Boomer Religion."
38. Hill, "After Boomer Religion."

bringer of the reign of God. Incorporation into Christ, which is inseparable from being drawn into the eschatological new creation, is entirely a divine gift of grace contingent upon the action of Jesus Christ in his life, teachings, deeds of healing and deliverance, crucifixion, resurrection, and enthronement. We have been and are being saved by God and are not saved by our own human agency. But salvation also embraces what we are "saved for." And what we are saved for is participation in the eschatological new creation in its arrival and ongoing intrusion into the world disrupted by the destructive powers of sin, death, and oppression. If God's reign puts all things right, then the gift we receive is the power of the Spirit to participate in the *missio Dei*, God's work of rectifying all things. If this is the case, Christian participation in struggles for justice, deeds of compassion and deliverance, and all actions that engender life, healing, and wholeness in others is not peripheral to the gospel. It is at the very heart of the gospel.

Part One

In the first segment of this book, I address the conventional, popular evangelical soteriology and presentation of "the plan of salvation," but not only for the purpose of joining the expanding chorus of post-evangelical critics who are deconstructing evangelical Christianity. Popular evangelical soteriology is interesting because it is "the American soteriology." It is the intensification of convictions and assumptions shared by most white American Christians (and not only white Christians) in the United States over the past three centuries. The popular soteriological imagination of white evangelicals, liberal Protestants, and Americanized Roman Catholics has much in common because each, in their own ways, are products of a long and shared history that includes the individualization of salvation, the privatization of religion in modernity, the creation of a racial taxonomy, and the particularities of the American experience. This segment will explore how soteriological convictions have played a crucial role in the Christian support for a long history of mistreatment, oppression, and marginalization of African-American persons and, in particular, the normalization of the segregation inscribed into the body of Christ itself.

Part Two

The second segment of the book is an effort to go "back to the Bible" in order to discern a different soteriological trajectory. This soteriological vision is one which is "invisible" to conventional American Christian Bible reading. In these chapters, it will be argued that a central biblical soteriological theme is rectification, putting things right, and that this includes societal justice.

At the heart of this soteriological trajectory is God's covenant relationship with Israel as narrated in the "First Testament." God chooses Israel as the people through whom God's rectification of a disordered world might begin to take visible shape within human history. God calls Israel to be a "counter-imperial" community whose life together embodies Yahweh's justice, which includes special concern for the vulnerable and economic arrangements designed to ensure that all persons have access to the resources of life. The great enemy in this drama is "empire," including, at different points in the story, Egypt, Assyria, Babylon, Persia, and later, the Seleucid and Ptolemaic offshoots from Alexander's Macedonian empire. Yahweh's opposition to the empires, which are characterized by idolatry, wars of conquest, brutality, slavery, and economic oppression, is central to the Bible's soteriological drama. In opposition to the sufferings and injustices in a world dominated by empire, a vision of a future age of justice, peace, and human flourishing begins to emerge in the writings of some of the prophets.

After a brief sketch of the emergence of an apocalyptic imagination within the Judaism of the "intertestamental period," this segment will seek to identify Jesus's mission, purpose, and agenda. Jesus proclaims the "inbreaking" of the reign of God. The Synoptic Gospels feature what has been described as "inaugurated eschatology." In Jesus's own person and deeds, the reign of God breaks into human history. As the inaugurator of the kingdom, Jesus initiates the repair and healing of humanity and all creation. Jesus comes to put things right. He heals broken bodies, restores outcasts to community, and seeks to reorder the life of faithful Israelites around the vision of justice and compassion at the heart of the Torah and the prophets. In doing so, Jesus "inserts" the future kingdom into the present.

Jesus also resisted powers and social systems that oppressed, destroyed, and dehumanized human persons. He attacked the ways in which the purity-codes of the Torah had been "hijacked," as it were, to legitimate the wealth and power of the aristocratic elite who benefitted from predatory economic practices. He was crucified because he spent the last week of his life seeking to undermine the moral legitimacy of the temple because of its predatory economic practices.

Part Three

In part three, I will begin to sketch my "constructive" or substantive soteriological proposal: (1) To be "saved" is to be united with Jesus the Messiah, the inaugurator of the kingdom of God. To be united with the Messiah is simultaneously to be drawn into the eschatological kingdom he inaugurates; (2) To be drawn into the kingdom he inaugurates, the eschatological new creation, is to be drawn into participation in his mission of putting things right, which includes resisting powers and forces of oppression and injustice that crush and dehumanize. Salvation is the very precious gift of being called to be God's agents of justice, healing, and deliverance, especially for the most vulnerable.

One of the ways this book differs from a characteristically Protestant theological imagination is in its emphasis on participation in the *missio Dei* as integral to the meaning of salvation. Participation in the "arriving" reign of God involves yielding ourselves to God, opening our lives to God, so that we might be conduits through whom the eschatological new creation invades the present age in transformative ways. This is part of the very meaning of salvation in that it is what we were "saved for." This may sound to Protestant ears like "salvation by works" because it cuts against the sensibilities of Protestant soteriological imagination that would "locate" matters of discipleship and the mission of the church as theological themes that follow from salvation rather than internal to soteriology itself.

However, in my proposal, works righteousness is excluded. In agreement with Katie Geneva Cannon, I argue that the essence of the Gospel includes the call to eradicate affliction, despair, and systems of injustice. But this is not to be understood as, in any sense of the word, earning salvation. To be drawn into the intrusion of the reign of God through union with Christ is always a gift of grace and never a matter of earning God's favor, nor is it autonomous human construction of a just world.

In the United States, Christianity often bifurcates along a left-right, two-party system that mirrors the American political and cultural wars. Conservative Christians emphasize that salvation is personal and individual, while liberal Christians, or at least those with a liberationist bent, view salvation as this-worldly political liberation. However, I would argue that these two dimensions, in an apocalyptic soteriology, are intertwined. Nothing is rectified on the "macro level" unless individual persons are rectified through divine forgiveness, justification, healing, liberation from bondage, and personal transformation.

The third chapter in this section will reframe the doctrine of justification in a way that preserves the best insights of the magisterial Protestant

Reformation. Justification is indeed entirely an unearned gift of divine love and gracious acceptance of sinners that is not contingent upon any human act or achievement. As the dead have no agency, human persons as sinners have no capacity to put themselves in the right with God. Justification, however, is not merely a legal declaration but is a participation in Christ's resurrection. If we recognize that resurrected life is an eschatological reality, then we can make the connection to recognize that justification is not something separate from being drawn into the space of the eschatological new creation.

Instead of understanding justification as forensic declaration and imputation of Christ's righteousness and then "cordoning off" sanctification and discipleship into another compartment of Christian existence, justification will be interpreted in relationship to *theosis*. "Justification" and "sanctification" are not two entirely separate stages in the order of salvation. Justification is God's entirely gracious act of drawing us into union with God's own life. This union is transformative. Christ's righteousness is not merely legally imputed but truly is a righteousness that transforms our hearts, desires, moral imagination, actions, and relationships.

The Protestant critique was that infused rather than imputed righteousness meant that the Christian could claim this infused righteousness as his or her own rather than professing that Christ is our righteousness. However, if we understand infused righteousness not as the insertion of "created grace" but as ongoing union with God, the transformative righteousness flowing into us through the Holy Spirit is always a "constantly-given gift" in which we participate. Faithful human agency is always inside of God's agency and is never an autonomous response outside of this divine enabling.

However, God's redemptive work is not limited to the salvation of an aggregate of individuals. Each individual's salvation is bound up with God's work of putting all things right. This encompasses the healing of our relationships, the healing and reclamation by God of shattered human lives, *and* the rectification of systems, structures, and institutions that impede human flourishing. To be saved is to be drawn into this "arriving" and intruding eschatological new creation as it engenders ever new and creative patterns of love and justice and as it foments creative resistance to all that kills, steals, and destroys life. Therefore, participation in the intrusion of the eschatological new creation means taking on the social cost of advocating for immigrants and refugees at a moment in which persons fleeing for their lives are regarded, by many in our society, not as Christ *incognito* to welcome (Matt 25:31–46) but as dangerous "outsiders" beyond the boundaries of our care and concern. It includes the fight against mass incarceration, human trafficking, inequitable school funding, and wage theft that harms the working poor. Faithful resistance always includes the creative work of imagining and "piloting" new possibilities. This may look something like support for and fostering of entrepreneurial companies that make a profit and achieve some positive social objective, such as the employment of persons previously incarcerated or youth who are aging out of the foster care system.[39] And, of course, this participation includes the ordinary deeds of Christians who listen when another person shares their deep hurts and struggles, ministries to empower persons to overcome addictions, food pantries, and ministries that embody deep care for homeless persons.[40]

Part IV: Sin and Atonement

While sin involves destructive behavior on the part of the individuals, for which we need divine forgiveness, this chapter will argue that the primary meaning of the word "sin" should be corporate in character. Sin is humanity's "group project," the total "messed-up" human situation. Certainly, one dimension of the human sin situation involves behaviors, habits, vices, and dispositions for which we are individually culpable. But in the Bible, particularly within the Pauline corpus, sin is also a supra-personal power which holds us in bondage, from which we need not only pardon but also deliverance.

While St. Augustine's doctrine of original sin as a biological explanation of the transmission of sin is problematic in light of evolutionary biology, there is a need for a reformulated doctrine of original sin that recognizes the fundamental Pauline insight (Rom 5:12–21) that the human race is bound together in a tragic solidarity of sin and death. Humans are interconnected and our actions impinge upon one another. Sin spreads as every harmful or destructive action has a tragic ripple effect. As such, we are all caught up in one interconnected tapestry of destruction that the human race has woven together.

For example, racism, sexism, and biases against persons due to appearance, age, social class, etc., are perpetuated by internalized social norms, and social sanctions for going against these norms, which shape

---

39. https://www.thecrackedpotcoffeeshop.com/our-shop.

40. See, for example, the work of Streetlife Communities in Milwaukee (https://www.streetlifecommunities.org), which includes the provision of emergency and survival resources for homeless persons, the treatment of homeless persons as persons of great dignity and worth, efforts to connect persons with community and social service resources, outreach to sex workers, most of whom are being trafficked against their wills, and a youth group oriented toward rescue of young persons from gang activity.

our perceptions and behavior. Every generation is socialized in ways that perpetuate oppressive social values. Prior to anyone's self-conscious moral choices, our socialization provides us with the moral values, language, and concepts that serve as the moral and "reality" coordinates that structure our choices. We all inherit a distorted or tilted "moral game board" upon which we make our moral choices.

Over the course of the past fifty years, one of the most important contributions of theologies in the liberationist trajectory has been a strong emphasis on the ways that sin is embedded within and perpetuated by systems, institutions, and social structures. Without a strong doctrine of sin as corporate as well as individual, it is impossible to account for the depth of evil and self-deception within which people who desire to be "good people" are entangled. Without the theological categories to recognize that sin's toxic tentacles are wrapped around everything that is human, we will perpetuate injustices because we have been effectively socialized "not to see" systemic sin but rather to believe, in the words of Barry Harvey, that the basic patterns of our social order, current configurations of family, nation-state, culture, and economy, are not fundamentally damaged or in need of radical transformation.[41]

Of course, soteriology requires an account of the meaning of Jesus's crucifixion. The chapter on atonement will take its bearings from Martin Luther King Jr.'s "lived theology," deeply rooted in the history and theological imagination of the black church, which embodies an implicit "grammar of atonement." King held together love for enemies and the goal of reconciliation. However, King rightly insisted that the precondition for reconciliation is justice. King knew that unjust systems are perpetuated by the self-deception of the beneficiaries of those systems who insulate themselves from "seeing" the injustice and brutality of these systems. King's non-violent campaigns were efforts to strip the façade of legitimacy from unjust systems, exposing their "moral ugliness." Boycotts, sit-ins, and marches were provocations and, indeed, "collisions" with sinful systems. One of the most salient insights that emerges from King's leadership in the American civil rights movement is that powers of evil are defeated by a kind of violently non-violent collision with unjust systems by persons armed only with the power of truth. This willingness to resist and collide with unjust systems is motivated by a very tough love that desires to "crush evil systems" in order to liberate not only the victims of those systems but also those who support and benefit from these systems from their own self-justification, self-deception, and bondage.

41. Harvey, "Into Lands as Yet Unknown," 305–6.

When the reign of God breaks into the present age, conflict with the powers of sin and death is inevitable. The cross is the point of collision, within human history, of the in-breaking reign of God and the concentrated powers of the present evil age. Jesus's mission is to set human persons free from the enslaving powers that destroy and diminish human life. But breaking the power of sin, evil, and death cannot be accomplished by non-confrontational sweetness; rather, it is through courageous and truthful resistance, what Rep. John Lewis once called "good trouble."

This chapter will connect the resistance politics of Jesus with King's activism and St. Irenaeus's recapitulation motif. For Irenaeus, Christ saves us as the second Adam, the inaugurator of a new humanity. Jesus is the one who gets "being human" right by living a life of unreserved love and obedience to God and love for humanity. Jesus's crucified and risen body is the space in which the human situation is rectified. When we are joined to Christ (*theosis*), we are incorporated into this space where creation has been put right. United with Christ, our human nature is healed and transformed. Recapitulation and *theosis* are linked, in this chapter, with the inaugurated apocalyptic eschatology of the Synoptic Gospels and Pauline corpus. That Jesus is the head or inaugurator of a new humanity is inseparable from Jesus's apocalyptic inauguration of the eschatological new creation within human history. And Jesus's inauguration of the reign of God includes conflict with the powers of sin and death that is necessary to break their dominative grip and establish the new mode of existence, life "within" the invading eschatological new creation.

The cross as victory over sin and the powers of evil (*christus victor* motif) is simultaneously the event through which God's forgiveness reaches us (western substitutionary trajectory) in such a way as to initiate the forgiveness, reconciliation, and rectification of individuals as part of God's rectification of all things. Christ bears our sins, not by being punished in our place but by absorbing our sins without passing the contagion of sin on to others. In Christ, God bears our sins by entering into solidarity with humanity and becoming a victim of the chain reaction that is the one human history of sin. Through the cross, God's forgiveness of our sins happens as an event in human history rather than a legal pardon issued from on high. God forgives as one who has been wronged, victimized by humanity, on the stage of human history.

But divine forgiveness is not blanket amnesty that pardons sins in such a way, as Rowan Williams argues, as to jettison the demand for justice and to "shoulder aside" the victims of injustice.[42] God's forgiveness does not

---

42. Williams, *Resurrection*, 16–22.

let offenders off the hook but rather requires us to encounter Christ at the site of those we have wronged. To say yes to Christ is not to receive a formal pardon that lets us "off the hook," but the rectification and transformation of self that calls us to turn toward our victims to seek forgiveness and to make amends in order to heal and rectify the damage of sin.[43]

Part V: Eschatology and Social Action

Christian hope for the life to come is often placed in opposition to passionate struggle for justice in this world. In this portion of the book, it will be argued that hope for an eschatological future need not disable efforts to be agents of healing and transformation in the present.

A "disabling" way that Christians imagine the return of Christ is to imagine that everything will instantly be put right. This might be taken to imply that all human action and struggle for a just world prior to this eschatological culminating event are ultimately irrelevant. On this picture, it is as if all of our efforts to show compassion and kindness, to be agents of repair, healing, and transformation are, when Christ returns, washed away like sandcastles on the beach. On this picture, our actions within the present life have no eschatological purchase. N. T. Wright's proposal that the Christian calling is not to "build the kingdom of God" on earth but to "build for" the kingdom of God provides a better way to imagine our task in the present. Wright argues that whatever we do out of love for God in Christ and for the sake of the neighbor God calls us to love, whether it is feeding the hungry, working for more just and equitable educational systems or the end of mass incarceration, or mentoring of an at-risk child, etc., will last into eternity, will find its way into the New Jerusalem. Our present efforts to be conduits of God's reign of love and justice in the here and now somehow, beyond our ability to comprehend from where we currently stand within an unfinished story, contributes to God's final victory, to the new world of eschatological justice, love, and peace.

To consider the classical questions of "Christ and culture" as a soteriological issue, instead of separating "social ethics" from soteriology, is likely to be considered a "category mistake." Soteriology is conventionally thought to belong to that portion of the Christian life that pertains to the individual's standing with God, while social ethics is deemed to be a subsequent matter, pertaining to the church's "public witness" and public mission in society. However, this chapter will argue that the gift of salvation draws us into the eschatological new creation in its intrusion into the territory occupied by

43. Williams, *Resurrection*, 16–22.

the disordering powers. Therefore, to be saved is to participate in both the church's collision with its social order and its positive and creative engagements for the sake of the "common good."

In addition to the Christian nationalist segments of the "religious right" seeking cultural dominance in order to "take America back for God,"[44] there seem to be three major trajectories within American Christian "social ethics." The first is an Augustinian trajectory that includes the Christian Realist approach associated with Reinhold Niebuhr and the broader category of thinkers that D. Stephen Long describes as neo-Augustinians;[45] the second is the Liberationist tradition; and the third is the Neo-Anabaptist approach. Long describes this latter group as "ecclesial ethicists." Neo-Augustinians and Liberationists emphasize Christian engagement in extra-ecclesial politics. Neo-Augustinians have tended to be more reformist in temperament, affirming of classical liberal democratic norms of American society, and emphasizing conventional political activity. Liberationists, whose ranks include feminist and black theologies as well as a plurality of Hispanic/Latino/Latina/Latinx, Asian, and LGBTQ theologies, have reflected upon American society from a stance as outsiders and construe American society as profoundly diseased, disordered, oppressive, endemically racist, sexist, heterosexist, and economically unjust. Neo-Anabaptists have also articulated scathing critiques of American society and the capitalist economic system but have tended to place more emphasis on the church as an alternative *polis*.

This chapter will have affinities with features of each of these major strands. For white Christians, there is an urgent need to listen carefully to the more radical critique articulated by theologians in the liberationist trajectory, particularly nonwhite theologians who have called attention to the tragic fault lines of injustice when it comes to race, criminal justice, and economics.

On the other hand, I will also appropriate the concerns from theologians who might be categorized as postliberal or neo-Anabaptist. The salvation Christ brings is ecclesial. It involves the formation of a radically new kind of human community, called to embody, in its life together, a "counter-imperial" alternative. This community is called to "do together" the life of discipleship, which entails love of enemies, hospitality, and generosity. This community is called to be a visible and living repudiation of the fallen world's ways of domination, fear, and exclusion of the "other." This

---

44. Not every Christian thinker or leader who is theologically and politically conservative falls into the category of Christian nationalism.

45. Long, *Augustinian and Ecclesial Christian Ethics*.

alternative way of life requires intensive catechesis or formation of character and identity in order to cultivate a "sociologically sectarian" people willing to be a cognitively dissonant minority in at least some significant respects.

The constructive argument to be made in this chapter, in continuity and discontinuity with neo-Anabaptist tendencies, is that an apocalyptic soteriology, which accentuates radical discontinuity between God's eschatological new creation and the world in its current bondage to enslaving powers and principalities, need not lead to an ecclesiology that would promote a principled withdrawal into counter-cultural ecclesial enclaves.

This is because the church's inner life is always already situated on the playing field these powers occupy. There is no quasi-geographical space to which the church can go or withdraw to escape from this "contested terrain." Christians are inextricably entangled in systems and structures and powers in their daily lives of buying and selling, living here rather than there in our society's racially and economically stratified residential arrangements and in our employment situation. Therefore, the eschatological new creation into which Christians are drawn is not "somewhere else" into which Christians might escape from the realities of the world in its current social, cultural, political, and economic realities. Rather, we have been drawn into the reign of God in its intrusion and invasion of this contested space.

Therefore, in faithful continuity with Jesus's own resistance to enslaving powers, participation in God's insurrection against powers that dominate and enslave, dehumanize and oppress, is part of what we were *saved for*, at least within the space and time of this present age. There can be no neat dividing line between ecclesial politics and extra-ecclesial political engagement. The politics of the kingdom of God calls us to cultivate communities that embody Christian virtue within the church's own "internal" life together in such a way that Jesus's prioritization of human well-being leads us to resist whenever and wherever humans are abused and dehumanized.

Participation in struggles for justice, human dignity, and human wholeness will have an *ad hoc* and piecemeal character because the goal is not Christian cultural or political dominance. The point of engagement is tethered to the conviction that the very meaning of God's kingdom is that human beings matter to God. Therefore, God's people are called to stand with and for persons and communities who are threatened, harmed, or abused. Rather than quests for control of the levers of power, Christians should seek to be a constant disruptive presence, exerting a variety of forms of pressure and resistance through truth-telling, participation in both ordinary politics of voting and lobbying, protests and boycotts, and sometimes, outright disobedience to unjust laws.

A broad trajectory of liberation as well as other Protestant theological liberalisms tend to feature an imagination tethered to a model of divine immanence, according to which God is at work in human history within an immanent historical trajectory toward liberation and justice. In contrast, an apocalyptic sensibility will imagine divine action in terms of intrusion and interruption of God's eschatological future and God's power to effect dramatic and often unforeseeable transformations that elude the human ability to plan or achieve. However, in what might be deemed to be a half-turn back in a liberationist direction, it is crucial to insist that apocalyptic discontinuity between the present world order and the reign of God is not, or rarely is, total antithesis. What is fallen is still God's good creation. In addition, social orders and human institutions are never monolithic, internally self-consistent, and self-enclosed systems of values but are sites of contestation.[46] As such, they include creational goodness and possess potential for novelty and transformation. Emphasis on the divine eschatological intrusion into a fallen world must not be construed in such a way as to deny that the eschatological Spirit is also the ubiquitous Spirit who is always at work in the world, drawing the world toward God and God's ultimate eschatological purposes. For this reason, transformation may erupt unexpectedly from within the interstices of the old. This is not the organic or immanent unfolding or development of possibilities latent within the old. God's eschatological new creation remains God's possibility rather than an autonomous human achievement. But apocalyptic transformation is the *transfiguration* of the old as the Spirit makes possible unanticipated transformations. If genuinely positive transformation happens in human history, it is to be attributed to the power of the Holy Spirit opening up new possibilities for human flourishing, reconciliation of enemies, peace, justice, food for the hungry, healing for the sick, and fragments of social justice. Instead of assuming that Christian political engagement requires the requisite cultural dominance to exert influence on the state and control of the processes of social change from the top down, we envision a model of Christian political engagement that is concerned, first and foremost, with faithful, concrete, and locally embodied ecclesial witness that begins with "the least of these" in our midst. This kind of Christian political engagement would be characterized by hope in the possibilities that may be opened up by the God who meets us in the irruption of the eschatologically novel in the midst of the ordinary.

This a quick synopsis of the argument of the book. But according to the popular trope, the proof of the pudding . . .

---

46. This was the argument of Kathryn Tanner in *Theories of Culture*.

SECTION ONE

What If the Reigning Soteriology Is Part of What We Need Saving From?

Introduction

We Christian theologians in the United States work in a house haunted by the ghosts of slavery.[1]

—M. Shawn Copeland

WHAT IF WHAT WE need "saving from" includes our reigning ideas about salvation? What if the ways we imagine salvation are contaminated by the sanctioning of slavery and white supremacy and this contamination rises to the surface in ongoing white Christian indifference to racial injustice? What if this corrupted soteriological imagination has served as a lens through which we read the Bible, rendering us unable to see a more profound soteriological vision in Scripture?

What this means, at minimum, is that theologians, especially white theologians such as myself, should not engage in soteriological reflection as if the question of salvation can be discussed in abstraction from the catastrophic impact of the deformations of Christianity we have inherited and continue to inhabit.

1. Copeland, *Enfleshing Freedom*, 2.

Section One: What If the Reigning Soteriology Is Part of What We Need Saving From?

Less than sixty years ago, Dr. Martin Luther King Jr. struggled to make sense of these disordered moral and soteriological coordinates:

> In the midst of blatant injustices inflicted upon the Negro, I have watched white churchmen stand on the sideline and mouth pious irrelevancies and sanctimonious trivialities. In the midst of a mighty struggle to rid our nation of racial and economic injustice, I have heard many ministers say: "Those are social issues, with which the gospel has no real concern." And I have watched many churches commit themselves to a completely other worldly religion which makes a strange, un-Biblical distinction between body and soul, between the sacred and the secular. . . . I have traveled the length and breadth of Alabama, Mississippi and all the other southern states. On sweltering summer days and crisp autumn mornings I have looked at the South's beautiful churches with their lofty spires pointing heavenward. . . . I have found myself asking: "What kind of people worship here? Who is their God?"[2]

James Cone's final book, *The Cross and the Lynching Tree*, bears further painful witness to our soteriological deformations. White Christians, who claimed to worship and to receive their salvation from a crucified Savior who was hung on a tree and tortured, were the very people who hung and tortured thousands of innocent African Americans on lynching trees between the end of Reconstruction in 1877 and 1950. Most contemporary white Christians have not given much thought to this tragic history. Most white American Christians today have not seen the connection between Jesus's crucifixion and lynching, nor struggled to come to terms with the question of how our Christian ancestors of as little as two or three generations ago could have been on the side of crucifiers, while still viewing themselves as followers of a crucified Lord. What is also striking is the current silence of so many white churches and theologians on matters of race, racism, and whiteness, even amid the resurgence of white nationalism. This is a paradigmatic exemplification of the silence that James Cone called "theology's great sin."[3]

Part of the fault, Cone charges, lies with white American theologians and ministers who, by and large, have not included this history in their theological reflections or preaching on the soteriological meaning of the

---

2. King, "Letter from Birmingham Jail," 292–97.

3. Cone, *Cross and the Lynching Tree*, xiii, 8–9, 30–31; "Theology's Great Sin," 139–52; Norris, *Witnessing Whiteness*, 7; Hughes, *Myths America Lives By*, 98–100.

cross.⁴ In most white atonement theology, the cross is understood in highly abstract ways, disconnected from histories of suffering, injustice, and brutality, as if Christ died for our sins in an ahistorical and "spiritual" sphere of reality.

Robert Jones points out that the norms of white supremacy are woven deeply into white Christian identity. However, these norms operate far below the level of consciousness. Even the most well-meaning white Christians are unaware of the deeply racialized moral and theological imagination which perpetuates racial injustice, racial separation, and an inability even to see systemic forms of racial injustice.⁵

This "inability to see" was evident in survey data from the summer of 2019. Only 38 percent of white practicing Christians believe the US has a race problem, compared to 78 percent of black practicing Christians. In 2019, only 42 percent of white practicing Christians at least "somewhat agreed" that the US has a history of oppressing minorities, as compared with 75 percent of black practicing Christians, and 61 percent of white practicing Christians manifested an individualizing approach, claiming that racial problems largely stem from individual beliefs and prejudices.⁶

This racial perception gap is supported by a white Christian soteriological imagination. Robert Jones points out that white supremacy was, prior to the 1960s, an all-but-unquestioned cultural assumption in America. Until that point, most white persons explicitly believed that African-Americans were biologically and culturally inferior and incapable of assimilating into the American mainstream. For this reason, Christian doctrine and ethics within most Christian groups had to develop in ways that were compatible with, and accommodating of, that worldview. This rendered black claims to justice invisible and illegitimate, protected white economic and social interests, and assured white persons of their own moral purity.⁷

Our churches, by and large, remain segregated. Eight in ten American congregations are composed of an overwhelming majority of members of one race.⁸ The claims of H. Richard Niebuhr in 1929 ring true today.

---

4. Cone, *Cross and the Lynching Tree*, xiii, 8–9, 30–31; Hughes, *Myths America Lives By*, 98–100.

5. Jones, *White Too Long*, 10.

6. Barna Research Group, "White Christians"; "Black Practicing Christians."

7. Jones, *White Too Long*, 70–71, 75, 187; Shelton and Emerson, *Black and Whites in Christian America*, 170.

8. Sociologists identify a single-race church as one with over 80 percent of its membership consisting of a single race. A 2015 study found that only 20 percent of US congregations are racially "mixed," meaning they have at least a 20 percent minority demographic in its membership. Lipka, "Many US Congregations Are Still Racially

American churches, Niebuhr argued, have accepted "the accommodation of Christianity to the caste-system of human society" and have "draw[n] the color line in the church of God."[9]

The very fact that most white American Christians do not deem the *de facto* racial segregation of most American churches to be problematic, or even give this matter much thought, is evidence enough of ecclesiological and soteriological deformations. It is a failure to recognize that salvation includes incorporation into Christ's body, instead construing salvation as primarily or exclusively an individual relationship with Christ. It is a failure to "see" what is central in the book of Ephesians: that a multi-ethnic community that joins together in one fellowship persons from previously divided and hostile ethnic, social class, and gender divisions, is at the heart of the good news and central to Christ's saving work on the cross (Eph 2:11–22).

As Jason Shelton and Michael Emerson argue, the hyper-segregated character of American congregations also means that churches become "echo chambers" in which gatherings of the like-minded reinforce rather than challenge each other on perceptions of race in America. They argue that white and black Christians tend to understand the Christian faith through two distinct lenses. Black Christians tend to have a more social view of the faith and a structural view of success and failure, due in part to the ways black Christians directly experience structural patterns of oppression and privilege. White Christians operate with an individualistic worldview, dependent in significant measure on individualistic accounts of sin and salvation. This, in turn, undergirds belief in personal merit and effort as the primary determinate of success and failure.[10] As Jennifer McBride argues, this makes it difficult for white Christians to see themselves as bearing any responsibility to take action to address racial issues.[11]

Segregated."

9. Niebuhr, *Social Sources of Denominationalism*, 6.

10. Shelton and Emerson, *Black and Whites in Christian America*, 172–75; Norris, *Witnessing Whiteness*, 19.

11. McBride, *Radical Discipleship*, 46.

CHAPTER ONE

Problems with the "Plan of Salvation"

WHAT MANY EVANGELICALS BELIEVE to be "the" plan of salvation is not the only problematic strand of soteriology that is "out there," but it represents a culturally dominant expression of longer-term trends within western and especially American Christianity.

How we conceive of salvation depends upon: some notion of what we need to be saved from (doctrine of sin); what we were created to be or become but have failed to attain (theological anthropology); what we are saved for, and whether that pertains to this life, the life to come, or both (ecclesiology, ethics, eschatology); the character and purposes of the God who saves (doctrine of God); and how God saves or what God does to save (soteriology proper, which includes but is not limited to atonement theology).

Through the ages, Christians have articulated diverse theologies, metaphors, and conceptions of salvation. For Christians in the United States who attend churches identifiable as variants of conservative evangelicalism,[1] a particular picture of salvation has had a powerful grip upon the ways the faith has been imagined and embodied.

Finding problems with this "conventional" account of salvation is as easy as shooting the proverbial fish in the barrel. But the goal is not to "bash" evangelicals, but to understand how conservative evangelicalism is the paradigmatic expression of "the American soteriology." The irony is that even in those theological and ecclesial spaces in which conservative

---

1. Of course, what or who counts as evangelical is a contested matter. Evangelical is a very broad category, or a very big tent, into which have been placed very diverse Christian groups, denominations, and movements. Not every expression of Christian faith that might either claim the label of evangelical or be labeled by others as evangelical embraces this theology of salvation.

evangelicalism is most emphatically repudiated, portions of this soteriological imaginary remain powerful.

For example, many former evangelicals, including ministers, migrate to mainline Protestant congregations, where the preaching and ministry are often shaped as reactions against the pathologies of variants of conservative evangelicalism. For example, liberal Protestantism often is characterized by a therapeutic approach to Christian faith that combines, ironically, both a reactive rejection and retention of elements of conservative evangelical soteriology. For example, reaction against evangelical emphases on hell, divine wrath, and the fear such proclamation engenders is, nonetheless, accompanied by the same kind of individualistic and interior-focused spirituality of evangelical spirituality. The dominance of the therapeutic paradigm in mainline Protestantism, with its assurances of God's complete acceptance and forgiveness, does not actually differ from the therapeutic orientation of evangelical soteriology, which accentuates, at least for those who avail themselves of the offer of salvation, God's complete love and forgiveness and the comfort of knowing one is assured of heaven. Whether God loves, accepts, and forgives only the "truly saved," as in evangelicalism, or pretty much everybody, as in liberal Protestantism, the outcome is much the same: one need not feel any guilt because God loves us in spite of our flaws and failures. Both evangelicals and Protestant liberals are likely to resonate with the old bumper sticker that proclaimed, "Christians aren't perfect, just forgiven." The concept of "grace" operative in both a conservative evangelical and liberal Protestant contexts often leads to a spirituality in which we do not have to do anything but bask in the love of God! With this therapeutic "lived theology," religion is most fundamentally about my individual relationship with God and my inner peace.

What Is "the Plan of Salvation?"

During my seminary years, I was briefly a member of a struggling urban congregation. A mission team from a suburban church was assisting the congregation by hosting a week-long revival designed to revitalize a dying congregation. I joined this mission team as we canvassed the neighborhood, knocked on doors, and delivered invitations to the nightly services. The mission team's strategy was to ask each person we visited the question, "If you were to die tonight, are you 100 percent certain that you would go to heaven?" This question, of course, was designed to set the stage for sharing "the plan of salvation," which offers the proper "technique" for getting there.

Problems with the "Plan of Salvation"

This way of inviting persons to faith in Christ has already defined salvation as an "after-life insurance policy," something that takes effect when we die. "Getting saved" is the technique whereby one secures one's reservation in heaven.

The Christian "gospel" is believed to be encapsulated in a short list of propositions that are often referred to as "the plan of salvation," the ABCs,[2] or the Roman Road to Salvation. While acknowledging the risk of painting with a very broad brush,[3] I will suggest that an accurate summary of this conventional understanding of salvation goes something like this:[4]

1. Everyone has sinned (Rom 3:23). Since God's righteous standard is perfect obedience to his law, we will never be able to achieve this standard.

2. This means that we are in severe trouble because "the wages of sin is death" (Rom 6:23).

3. A righteous God must punish sin. That penalty is eternal separation from God in hell.

4. Thankfully, there is a solution. Jesus is punished in our place so we do not have to go to hell. Since the punishment has been suffered by Jesus, it is possible for God to pardon us for our sins.

5. But each individual must make the personal choice to accept Jesus as savior. It is a free gift, ours for the asking, to be received by faith, which is understood to be an act of trust in the reliability of God's promise of salvation to those who believe. Accepting this free gift typically takes the form of asking God for salvation, praying what is often referred to as "the sinner's prayer." The website of Jack Chick publications, which has played a major role in promoting and popularizing this soteriology, invites persons who wish to "get saved" to pray this prayer:

---

2. The ABCs are: (a) Accept that you are a sinner; (b) believe that Christ died for your sins and rose again; and (c) confess Christ as your Savior.

3. In offering such a broad characterization, one can offer a description that is generally accurate. Nevertheless, different Christian groups that articulate the plan of salvation may offer qualifications and nuances that evade some of these criticisms.

4. A prime example of a presentation of "the plan of salvation" is found on the website of William Frederick (http://thecomingepiphany.com/BookArticles/todie.htm).

J. R. Daniel Kirk points out that the Apostle Paul is seen, erroneously, as primary promoter of this soteriology. Kirk summarizes the so-called "Romans Road to Salvation" in this way: (1) We've all sinned (3:23); (2) wages of sin is death (6:23); (3) Christ died for us; (4) confess Jesus as Lord, believe he has been raised, and you will be saved (allowed to go to heaven when you die) (Kirk, *Jesus Have I Loved, But Paul?*, 31–32).

> Dear God, I am a sinner and need forgiveness. I believe that Jesus Christ shed His precious blood and died for my sin. I am willing to turn from sin. I now invite Christ to come into my heart and life as my personal Saviour.[5]

Those who accept this offer are assured of a future in heaven, stand fully pardoned before God, and are now invited into a personal relationship with Jesus Christ.

Analysis of the Logic/Theoretical Framework of the Plan of Salvation

This "plan of salvation" is nowhere to be found in the Bible. In a typical evangelistic tract, the Bible verses are "cherry-picked" from different parts of the New Testament. If this is "the" plan of salvation, *the* Christian gospel itself, one would expect we would find a clear, step-by-step summary somewhere in the New Testament in the same precise, clear, and systematic fashion in which it is presented in a typical evangelistic tract. "The plan of salvation" is not directly derived from the Bible but rather is the result of a synthesizing interpretation.[6]

---

5. https://www.chick.com/information/general/salvation.asp.

6. Of course, all theology, academic or popular, is the result of complex interpretive judgments and acts of imaginative synthesis. The Bible is a varied collection of writings by different authors and/or communities in different historical and social contexts. To have a theology at all requires the creative and imaginative task of endeavoring to fit the Bible's complex pieces together into some kind of loosely coherent theological vision of the meaning of the faith as a whole. Some ensemble of interpretive decisions about the meaning of the whole are pragmatically necessary if we are to engage in the most basic Christian practices such as preaching, teaching, and engaging in communal prayer and worship.

But this interpretive task should be engaged in with awareness that the Bible does not yield to a systematizing logic that would allow us to capture and articulate *the* Bible's theology. There are no "biblical instructions" regarding how to hold together Scripture's plurality. And while the many critical tools of contemporary biblical scholarship might aid efforts to offer a meticulous exegesis of any particular literary unit in the Bible, the tools of biblical critical scholarship cannot provide a method for how we might construe or interpret the meaning of the Bible as a whole for Christian belief and practice.

This does not mean that theology is arbitrary. Good reasons and arguments can be offered for the ways any particular Christian thinker or group puts the pieces together. But doing so remains a task grounded upon a multitude of interpretive conjectures and decisions, guided by a multiplicity of metaphors and past theological syntheses. And, we engage in this task while navigating the continual disruptions of prior synthetic judgments precipitated by ever new forms of human experience as Scripture is interpreted in ever new situations and contexts.

In my criticisms of what I will refer to as the "conventional"[7] model of salvation, I am not questioning the genuineness of the experiences of salvation that many individuals have experienced when responding to presentations of the conventional version of the plan of salvation. Nor do I wish to denigrate the importance of conversion experiences. As will be pointed out in the conclusion, conversion is indispensable to salvation. In these experiences, humans often experience and encounter God in very powerful and life-transforming ways. At issue in this chapter is how the conventional version of salvation theorizes salvation. I would argue that something much deeper and richer happens when persons entrust their lives to Christ than what is "conceptualized" by this picture of salvation.

Retributive Justice in the Criminal Court as the Organizing Logic

After "establishing" that we are all sinners by way of reference to Romans 3:23, evangelistic tracts and preachers hopscotch over three chapters of Romans to quote 6:23: "The wages of sin is death." One online evangelist offers this interpretation of Rom 6:23 as one of the pivotal propositions of "the plan of salvation":

> Realize that there is a punishment for being a sinner, and that punishment is death. . . . Not only a physical death, but also a spiritual death. The place of spiritual death is called Hell. . . . There is probably no person alive who can say that they never told a lie. We all have sinned and we all deserve the punishment of Hell for our sin.[8]

Romans 6:23 simply says that "the wages of sin is death." There is no explanation of what is meant by the term "death." Paul could have meant the condition of mortality. He could have been speaking metaphorically of a life on earth that is mired in misery, futility, and destruction. To interpret Rom 6:23 to mean that God punishes sin by sending persons to hell is to *interpret* Rom 6:23 in light of a larger set of theological assumptions and a powerful organizing metaphor.

Often, our metaphors take on a life of their own and structure or even compel our thinking in extremely powerful ways. The master metaphor of

---

7. I use the term "conventional" rather than "traditional" because this is not the way Christians through the ages have theorized salvation. In fact, this explanation of "the gospel" is relatively recent in the long span of Christian history.

8. http://thecomingepiphany.com/bookarticles/todie.htm.

conventional American soteriology is derived from the criminal court.[9] The God-human relationship is imagined as a legal one in which sin is like crime and God is the judge, jury, and executioner. Because God is the judge, God must punish sinners unless there is an acceptable way to pardon without compromising God's justice.

Inside of this master metaphor, God's righteousness is construed as retributive justice, defined as "punishment that fits the crime." A retributive concept of justice is the idea that the requirements of justice are satisfied, what is wrong is made right again, only by inflicting some pain or penalty on the wrongdoer that is equivalent or proportional to the wrong committed. Retributive justice has nothing to do with consequences that are a natural or intrinsic part of some wrong action. Retributive justice means inflicting pain on the wrongdoer that is additional and extrinsic to any pain and suffering the wrongdoer causes himself or herself. Retributive justice is also distinct from punishment designed to be educative or character-building. A concept of justice as retributive assumes that there is a moral balance in the universe and that for any wrong done, equivalent pain inflicted on the wrongdoer restores that moral equilibrium, regardless of whether or not the pain inflicted makes any positive difference at all in repairing the damage caused by the wrong.

Conventional views of hell fit this description. God keeps people alive for all eternity in order to inflict pain and torment. There is no other objective to hell on this account except to inflict pain. Persons in hell are not being taught some lesson that will help them do better after they get out of hell. Hell, conceived of in this way, is simply there to inflict endless punishment because, somehow, this is required to satisfy the requirements of justice.

Saved by God from God

In the final analysis, what we are saved from is not really sin but rather punishment. Since God is the punisher, God saves us from God. Salvation means that God's merciful "side" saves us from God's retributive or wrathful "side."[10] Christ's death, understood as substitute punishment, serves as a

---

9. If our salvation metaphors had been drawn from the civil court instead of the criminal court, a very different picture of salvation would have been the result. Salvation would have been pictured in terms of "making amends" and putting a wrong situation right through acts of restitution or restoration. Divine righteousness-justice would have been construed as restorative rather than retributive justice.

10. Evangelist Paul Washer was willing to make this logic explicit when he tweeted, "God saved you for Himself; God saved you by Himself; God saved you from Himself,"

kind of internal divine accounting mechanism whereby God transfers the retributive punishment we deserve to Christ.

The implication is that divine love is pictured as coercive love. God makes a very generous offer: complete amnesty and a glorious future in heaven. But if the offer is rejected, a divinely imposed sentence of eternal conscious torment will be the result. God offers love, but the love will quickly be withdrawn and exchanged for hostility if the offer is rejected. A humorous internet meme[11] illustrates the logic of the conventional version of salvation:

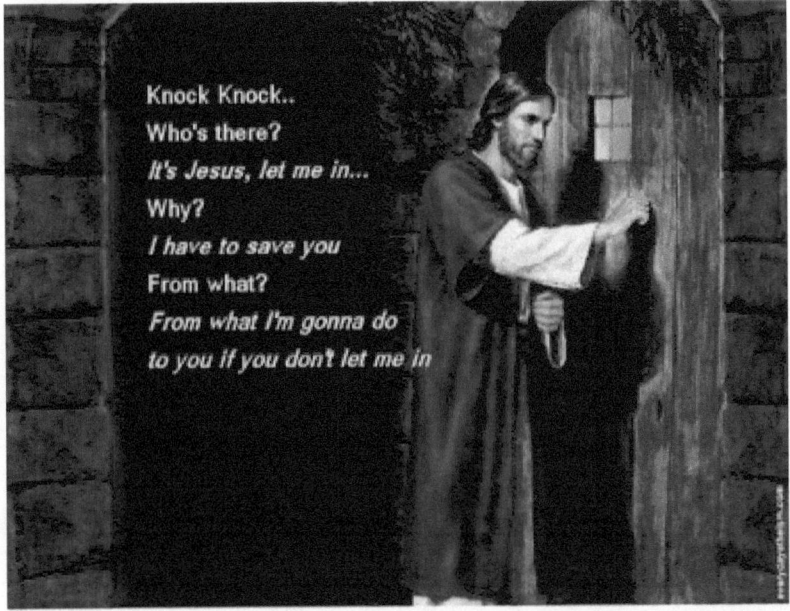

Bondage to sin as something intrinsically self-destructive, enslaving, and harmful to others is inevitably treated as peripheral to "the real problem" from which we need salvation. Our primary need, on this account, is not rescue from oppressive systems and structures that are the sedimentation of past and present sin. The real problem is not bondage to sin. The real problem is the legal situation we find ourselves in because we have sinned. We are guilty and therefore must, at some point, be punished. The fundamental human dilemma is construed as one of guilt and subjection to divine punishment. Therefore, salvation will be construed strictly, or at least primarily, as pardon that gets us off the hook.

January 18, 2019, https://twitter.com/paulwasher/status/1086231884139499525?lang=en.

11. The source or originator of this meme, widely shared on social media, is unknown.

Section One: What If the Reigning Soteriology Is Part of What We Need Saving From?

Individualism and Self-Interest

Salvation is reduced to a strictly individual matter. Every *individual* stands alone before God. Our "sin problem" is not really *our* sin problem at all. This overly individualistic understanding misses all the ways the Bible points to the "corporate" features of human sin and the corporate features of salvation. For example, in Rom 5:21–32, St. Paul depicts sin as a collective problem in which humanity is bound together in a tragic solidarity of sin and death.

What salvation rectifies, on the conventional view, is strictly the individual's legal and personal relationship with God. This is a very narrow picture of salvation. It does not envision any transformation of the world. Perhaps saved individuals have a positive and secondary impact on various aspects of the world, but God's work of salvation, strictly speaking, does not pertain to putting things right in the social or political world.

Of course, evangelical soteriology is but the intensification of American hyper-individualism that conceives of the self as sovereign, isolated, and self-contained, alongside the notion that God is to be found and experienced within the interiority of the self in its solitude, instead of the community of faith. Harold Bloom has argued that this picture of the divine-human relationship is deeply embedded in the imaginative DNA of American society and is "the American Religion."[12] An emphasis on the individual's deep interior connection with God is no less present in much liberal mainline Protestant therapeutic preaching that assures persons that they are loved, affirmed, and accepted by God. While this is anecdotal, I have heard, on more than a few occasions, Catholic priests describe the resistance they have encountered to the "passing of the peace" during mass from parishioners who did not see any connection between worshiping God and greeting the persons with whom they had gathered to worship and receive the Eucharist.

Another danger of the conventional version's way of framing the issue is that accepting the offer of acquittal becomes the ultimate act of self-interest. J. R. Daniel Kirk identifies this conventional version as an escapist, individualistic, and me-centered understanding of salvation.[13] Likewise, Ron Sider laments this impoverished understanding of the gospel as merely forgiveness of sins and personal "fire insurance." Instead of the demand for

---

12. This was the central argument of Bloom, *American Religion*; Guth, *Christian Ethics at the Boundary*, 171.

13. Kirk, *Jesus Have I Loved, But Paul?*, 31–32.

discipleship and radical transformation of the self, we reduce salvation to a consumer commodity, a ticket to heaven.[14]

Another (Better) Way to Think About What We Need Saving From

For persons whose primary Christian formation has been within certain evangelical communities, it is difficult to extricate oneself from this legal-retributive imaginative framing of the issue when one has been catechized to assume that this is simply "the" Christian gospel. In order to recognize the deep logic of the conventional account, it is helpful to offer a comparison to other ways of framing the issue of our sin problem.

On the conventional account, God saves us from what God will otherwise do to us if we do not "come to Jesus." But what if we framed the issue of "what we need saving from" as the terrible mess we, the human race together, have made of God's good world? What if what we need saving from is the horrible things we do to one another and from the damage we inflict upon ourselves and others? God's wrath, on this account, would not be seen as the requirement that retributive punishment be inflicted. Rather, God's wrath would be seen as God's love in its opposition to what destroys the people God created and loves. God's wrath is God's love in action against those destructive powers and actions that destroy God's work of love. On this account, God is not the source of destruction. Human sinfulness is the source of all that is destructive.

Or, what if we reframed how we think about the oft-repeated statement that sin separates us from God. This picture[15] is often found in evangelistic tracts:

---

14. Sider, *Scandal of the Evangelical Conscience*, 56–59.

15. This image is taken from a web site that is designed to present the conventional "plan of salvation" (http://bible.org/article/gods-plan-salvation).

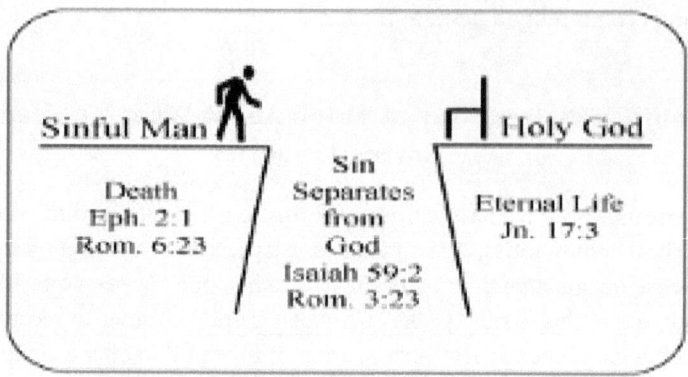

If sin separates us from God, "who" or "what" does the separating? In the retributive account, God does the separating, as an externally-imposed punishment, after we have sinned, by refusing to allow us into God's presence for all eternity. God is one who banishes.

We could reframe the issue. What if, instead, we understood the phrase "sin separates us from God" to mean that when we sin, we are the ones who do the "separating." To sin is to push God away, to turn away from God. In the paradigmatic narrative of Genesis 3, after Adam and Eve eat the forbidden fruit, it is Adam and Eve who hide from God. Adam and Even were banished from the garden, to prevent them from eating of the tree of life in their now fallen and broken state, but they were not banished from God's presence and love. In Genesis 4, after Cain murders his brother Abel, Cain is the one who imposes exile from God upon himself by going away from the presence of the Lord (4:16). God does not banish Cain.

Separation from God is self-inflicted. Sin carries within itself its own punishment. God does not have to inflict an external consequence upon us. By sinning, we turn away from God and then we turn against one another. The wages of sin is death because, by sinning, we reject the God who is the source of life, the source of the truly fulfilling way to be human, and turn toward ways of living that lead to sorrow, death, and destruction. God does not need to add a further penalty. We inflict sin's harm upon ourselves and, tragically, other humans as well.

Faith and Works

The conventional version of the plan of salvation emphasizes that salvation is received by "faith" and has nothing to do with "works." Salvation is believed to happen in a once-and-done conversion experience. Then, one is "completely saved."

Asking Jesus into one's heart is understood to be a matter of faith, defined as believing or trusting God's promises to save the person who firmly believes Christ died for our sins and that he will "save" those who ask. Christian Ethicist David Gushee describes this as soteriology in action. During the musical worship portion of a college chapel service, the worship leader's unscripted theological reflections included the claim that "the only thing required of us is to believe that Jesus's blood saves us. Nothing more."[16]

Salvation is indeed entirely God's gift and is in no sense earned by human effort. This is the crucial insight the Protestant tradition has rightly sought to safeguard since the sixteenth century. But the problem lies with how the conventional version "frames the issue" through its "working definitions" of "faith" as interior and passive and "works" as any activity.

The conventional understanding of the catch-phrase "by faith and not by works" has the disastrous consequence of treating the rest of the Christian life as radically secondary in importance compared to "getting saved." Indeed, since one is already fully saved by faith and not by "works,"[17] discipleship has been stripped of any *telos* or transcendent purpose beyond the mere external expression of gratitude to God. Ethical imperatives found within the New Testament are treated as a random assemblage of "principles for living," which are interpreted as helpful for a happier and more successful life. This results in a profound marginalization of the teaching, message, and practices of Jesus.

Justification: Protestant and Catholic: The Short Version

The problematic features of evangelical soteriology did not develop *ex nihilo* on American soil but rather were developments within a long trajectory within western theology and Christian practice. I will narrate and analyze

---

16. Gushee, "Jesus and the Sinner's Prayer," 72.

17. In Romans 4, what St. Paul "excludes" when he speaks of justification by faith is "works" understood as "earning" (4:4). But language, and how it is made to function by different groups, is a slippery reality. When contemporary evangelicals and other Protestants speak of faith and not works, "works" are erroneously understood as a life with the ethical commitment to live in conformity to the patterns of love, generosity and resistance to enslaving powers exemplified by Jesus

that history in greater depth in a later chapter on justification. In this brief account, I will note that from Origen to St. Augustine to the medieval period and into the present, the Roman Catholic Church, as well as Eastern Christianity to the extent that the language of justification is used at all, has understood justification to be the lifelong process of transformation of the self, made possible by God's grace at work in the life of the Christian. On this account, to be justified is to be transformed, to be made just, righteous, and holy, such that one begins to become a person whose moral character and patterns of activity are conformed to the pattern of Jesus Christ.

For this longstanding theological tradition, our ultimate acceptance by God on judgment day depends upon whether, after baptism and initial justification, we lived lives of Christian faithfulness and obedience, producing good works and good fruit. Protestants in the mainstream or magisterial Reformation tradition redefined "justification" as a divine legal verdict. God declares us to be righteous in his eyes because Christ's perfect righteousness is imputed or credited to us.[18] For the magisterial Reformers, there is nothing that human effort contributes to our justification. It is entirely the work of Christ. Even the faith by which we believe and receive this gift of justification is something God gives to us.

For the magisterial Protestant theological tradition, sanctification is the life-long process of being made holy and transformed into a person whose character comes to resemble that of the generous, life-engendering love of Jesus Christ. Sanctification requires our participation and effort, our active engagement to open our hearts and lives and allow God to transform us. Because the Reformers wanted to emphasize that salvation is entirely God's work and as such, is not contingent upon human choice and effort, sanctification was sharply distinguished from justification and, to some inevitable extent, given the polemical context of the Reformation era, de-emphasized. Our justification was considered to be that which is decisive when it comes to our ultimate acceptance by God.

The Evangelical Revivalist-Conversionist Paradigm

With the frontier revivals of the first and second Great Awakenings in the United States, an emphasis on having an individual conversion experience as the true entry point into the Christian life, rose in ascendancy. Though persons from Presbyterian, Methodist, and Anglican/Episcopalian backgrounds had dramatic religious experiences, those traditions that practice adult or "believer's baptism," were more fertile soil for the shift to the

18. Campbell, *Quest for Paul's Gospel*, 34–35.

revivalist-conversionist paradigm represented by the conventional plan of salvation. Here, the hyper-individualism and the "sanctification of choice" that are part of the American DNA have come to take precedence over the magisterial Protestant understanding of justification as entirely the action and verdict of God that precedes any human response of faith to God's gift.[19] The language of "making a personal decision to accept Christ" would have been, to say the least, alien to the magisterial reformers.

The idea of "justification by faith alone" has slowly morphed into the idea of *salvation* by faith alone, with justification now treated as the entirety of salvation and sanctification as an optional, though certainly desirable, add-on feature. The sharp distinction between justification and sanctification found in the first century of the magisterial Protestant Reformation expands into an even greater separation.

Now, salvation is thought to happen in a one-moment-in-time conversion experience[20] and then, one is completely "saved." This "salvation" is understood strictly in terms of a Protestant construal of justification: we are pardoned for our sins, declared to be righteous in God's eyes, and assured that we will go to heaven when we die. But defining salvation in this way means that salvation and the Christian life of discipleship are located in two completely different and unrelated compartments of the Christian life. Salvation is the most important thing. Sanctification and following Jesus after salvation are something else entirely, important but not indispensable to salvation.

The notion that salvation is "by faith and not by works," especially when the meanings of the terms "faith" and "works" are not carefully scrutinized, produces a great deal of theological and practical mischief. If salvation is by faith and not by works, and if salvation is equated with justification, fully obtained in a single momentary conversion experience, then a person could actually have one sincere moment of believing Christ and experiencing a conversion and then proceed to live a morally rotten life. In my undergraduate classes, I would humorously suggest that this viewpoint means that a person could say the sinner's prayer, take possession of the "ticket to heaven," and then proceed to become a dedicated puppy-kicker, serial killer, or "hitman" for an organized crime syndicate without jeopardizing in the least his or her assurance of heaven. To reinforce this point, I often presented this "false conundrum." If salvation is by faith and not by works, I would ask, do we have the option of accepting Christ as our Savior

---

19. Clapp, "Why the Devil Takes Visa," 22–23.

20. Conversion to Christ and conversion experiences, in all of their variety, are very important, very precious, and should not be deemphasized. At issue is how we understand these experiences theologically.

but politely opting out of accepting him as our Lord? Could we be "saved by faith" by sincerely believing in the reliability of "the plan of salvation," truly trusting that Jesus died for our sins and is willing to pardon our sins and "take us to heaven," and then say the "sinner's prayer?" Is it possible to have this "faith" while also choosing not to allow our lives to be re-ordered and transformed by Christ? To say we must accept Christ as Lord means that we must *do* something. We must hand our lives over to Christ and commit ourselves to a life of obedience and discipleship. In spite of the inevitability of sin and failure within the Christian life, we must in some measure follow through on that commitment. This seems to suggest that saving faith requires "works," an intentional commitment to a life of action in accordance with the way of living exemplified by Jesus.

This theological pathology is enthusiastically embraced by the "free grace" movement. The distinctive belief of this movement is that salvation and the Christian life of practical sanctification are entirely separable. The free grace movement takes the distinction made during the Protestant Reformation and drives the proverbial bus over the cliff. The free grace school asserts that "the sole condition for receiving everlasting life is faith alone in the Lord Jesus Christ." Faith is defined as "the conviction that something is true." "To believe in Jesus is to be convinced that He guarantees everlasting life to all who simply believe in Him for it." Therefore, this movement draws the stunning conclusion that

> No act of obedience, preceding or following faith in the Lord Jesus Christ, such as commitment to obey, sorrow for sin, turning from one's sin, baptism or submission to the Lordship of Christ, may be added to, or considered part of, faith as a condition for receiving everlasting life. This *saving transaction* between God and the sinner is simply the giving and receiving of a free gift.[21]

The "free grace school of theology" takes the problematic tendencies of the Protestant Reformation tradition to their "logical" but nonetheless, theologically pathological conclusion. If "works" means any ethical behavior and if salvation is by faith, defined as the interior act of believing or trusting God's promises, then obedience to Christ is, by definition, irrelevant to salvation. Following Christ in a life of obedient discipleship is *entirely optional* when it comes to salvation.

This conundrum exists because of horrendously flawed working definitions of "faith" and "works." Faith is understood to be what we do on the inside, with our "mind" and our "heart," in an invisible and interior part of

---

21. This is from the website of the Grace Evangelical Society. Italics are mine. See http://www.faithalone.org/about/beliefs.html.

our "selves." Faith is understood as passive believing and trusting. Because it takes place in the invisible and interior recesses of one's soul, faith is assumed to be the opposite of the kinds of activity that we do with our bodies in the visible or public world.

Therefore, when Paul's language of justification by faith and not by works or by "the works of the law," in his letters to the Roman and Galatian churches, is interpreted by persons in imaginative captivity to the conventional account of salvation, that language is construed in terms of this problematic binary logic. Faith is what the self does on the "inside." It is private and subjective. Works comes to be understood as the binary opposite. Works are defined as any visible and public action, activity, or doing. On this binary logic, we "have faith" with our minds, hearts, and soul(s) and we do works with our bodies. This binary logic takes the Protestant Reformation distinction between justification and sanctification and further separates them by placing each, in a dualistic fashion, into completely different "compartments" of the human person. The Christian life of obedience, discipleship, and ethical action comes to be seen as belonging to the exterior life of the individual and therefore secondary, totally unrelated to salvation, or, at best, a mere "external expression" of our interior relationship with God.

Better Definitions of Faith and Works: A Glimpse Ahead

It *is* indeed "theologically correct" to assert that salvation has nothing to do with works *if* by works we mean *human effort to earn and secure God's approval and acceptance*. This kind of "works" is indeed "a bad thing" because it is an effort to enter into a *quid pro quo* relationship with God.

But if we define works as action or activity that is in conformity with the pattern of life exemplified, embodied, and commanded by Jesus Christ, I will argue, then salvation has everything to do with "works," though, as will be pointed out, living in this way is not at all a matter of earning God's favor or even something that is possible apart from the gift of the Spirit who draws us into the way of Christ.

The false "faith-works" binary and "Savior-Lord" conundrum are easily resolved if we offer a better account of the meaning of "faith." The Greek word *pistis*, translated into English as "faith," carries with it the idea of loyalty or faithfulness, not merely interior believing or trusting. This is the argument made by Matthew Bates, who points out that faith has been inappropriately interpreted and nuanced to mean, with respect to the gospel, "trust in Jesus's righteousness alone" or "faith that Jesus's death covers my sins rather than allegiance to King Jesus."[22] Defined in this way, faith is not just a cognitive act but a "whole person" response. Faith means turning toward Christ with one's entire self. As such, it is a believing and it is an activity. To believe in Christ as Savior involves committing oneself to Christ as Lord because one pledges one's unconditional allegiance or loyalty to Jesus Christ as the true sovereign ruler of this world. This means committing oneself to a way of living in conformity with Christ's Lordship.

When Jesus called his first four disciples, all Galilean fishermen, with the words "follow me," the only way they could exercise faith was with their feet. It was impossible to have an interior and private experience of faith in Jesus while remaining on their boats. Faith is allegiance, a whole person, "head, heart, hands, and feet," response to Christ. Faith means the total orientation of our lives, which includes our activity, toward Christ. Faith includes within itself obedience and service to Christ.

Of course, many Christians will object that this is "works righteousness." But this "doing" that is an indispensable component of believing most certainly does not earn God's favor, acceptance, or forgiveness. This obedient loyalty, the faith by which one commits oneself to Christ, is itself a gift from God. The ability to "walk in the newness of life" (Rom 6:1–11) is not something we accomplish by our own agency, strength, or willpower, but is the gift of the Holy Spirit. The effort and action involved in "belief-trust-obedience" to Christ are not human achievements at all. Our human action is entirely "inside of" and made possible by God's prior action of drawing us into union with the crucified and risen Christ by the Holy Spirit. There is nothing we can do to earn this gift of God's love, acceptance, and action of drawing us into God's own life, which is that which empowers and makes possible our allegiance to Christ.

---

22. Bates, *Salvation by Allegiance Alone*, 9.

CHAPTER TWO

Soteriological Pathologies and Racial Injustice

For at least 350 years in the United States, the Christian faith, as lived and believed by predominantly-white Christian groups, coexisted comfortably with a white supremacist social imaginary. Of course, it is easy to see the moral perversity of ante-bellum defenses of slavery by ministers and theologians. But it was the entirety of Christian faith, theology, and practice that was lived and believed as if being a Christian was entirely compatible with, and indeed supportive of, explicit belief in white superiority.[1] Theological convictions were not untouched by white supremacy and cordoned off within a sphere of ideas or beliefs or doctrinal purity.

Today, we may not be able to see clearly the impact of white supremacy upon our inherited theologies. But the doctrinal forms we have inherited continue to function in problematic ways, even if explicit forms of white supremacy are contrary to conscious intentions of many white Christians today.

An Individualized and Vertical(ized) Salvation and the "Flattening" of Sin

The conventional version of the plan of salvation frames the issue of sin as primarily a matter between the individual and God. The "real sin problem" is that sin separates "me" from a holy God and puts me in the crosshairs of divine punishment. Even if, by sinning, we hurt other people, this will be

---

1. Jones, *White Too Long*, 234.

seen as merely "collateral damage." The central issue is the legal trouble sin gets me into with God. If the real sin problem, that which I most need to be saved from, is individual punishment in hell, salvation comes to be seen as whatever exempts "me" from punishment.

To the extent that our "real" sin problem, as well as the "salvation solution" to that problem, is construed as primarily between the individual and God, resisting injustices that distort social and political relationships and endeavoring to put these things right is not really within the scope of "gospel concerns."

In addition, when the imaginative categories for thinking about sin is the legal-retributive framework, the result will be a "flattening" of sin. One popular mantra, particularly prominent among evangelical Christians, is that "all sin is equal in God's eyes" and therefore, "no sin is any worse than any other sin." The rationale behind this mantra is the notion that the primary consequence of sin is eternal separation from God, the price for offending a holy God. Therefore, any sin has the same eternal deadly consequences and therefore, no sin is "worse" than any other.

The result is that grotesque injustice and abusive behavior are no more problematic than any other "sin." On this account, taken to its (il)logical conclusions, rape is no worse in the eyes of God than consensual pre-marital sex. Petty shoplifting is just as damnable as premeditated murder or participation in a genocide. An individual's struggle with alcohol or lust,[2] on the one hand, and grotesque cruelty and social injustices that condemn some people and groups to poverty, poor health, and lives of pain and struggle are, on this analysis, equal in that all sin will condemn the individual to hell. And participation in a lynch mob is no worse in the eyes of God than a small lie to avoid personal embarrassment about why one was late to a doctor's appointment.

Shortly before his death, James Cone wrote *The Cross and the Lynching Tree*.[3] If we consider the horrendous reality of lynching, the conventional approach, with its flattening of sin and individualizing of salvation, lacks the resources to respond and resist. One might imagine a Christian in the grip of the social imaginary of the conventional approach to salvation to say

---

2. The point is not to minimize individual human sin. Great interpersonal and social evils exist because of the sinful "hooks" in human nature that draw us into the vortex of social evils. Individual lust often provides the fuel for sex trafficking that fuels pornography. The "fuel" for the group pride that perpetuates white supremacy and the racial injustices flow from it is individual pride, or, ironically and conversely, flow from the insecurity that motivates persons to seek their self-worth within a racial hierarchy that bestows superior status upon, in this case, white persons.

3. Cone, *Cross and the Lynching Tree*.

something along these lines: "We are all equally sinners in the eyes of God, whether we are white persons then or now or black persons then or now. All sins are equal. The white community's 'lynching problem' is no more sinful in the eyes of God than an individual African-American's personal faults." If sin is flattened in this way, the solution to our sin problem is not God's power that rectifies situations that are wrong and unjust. Rather, the solution, on this account, is that Jesus absorbed the divine wrath and took our punishment as our substitute to make possible a divine pardon that exempts individual sinners from hell. On this conception, the rectification of human relationships characterized by injustice and brutality are outside of or, at best, peripheral to the saving work of Christ.

The way the issue is framed on a conventional evangelical soteriology excludes from the outset Christian theological concern with matters such as the brutalities of lynching and explicit white supremacy. This is because our sin problem is framed as one of individual guilt. Therefore, the solution is substitute punishment and pardon,

But if we read Cone's *The Cross and the Lynching Tree* and then ask what "we" need saving from, we might find ourselves confronted with other possible answers to this question. We might find ourselves compelled to "reframe the issue."

For example, for a people in the grip of white supremacy at the heart of the culture of lynching, there is the need for salvation from the collective idolatry of a group that believed itself to be a superior, who covertly worshiped and valorized their own values and way of life as inherently sacred, who believed themselves and their way of life to be uniquely "God-blessed," as in the "lost cause theology" of the post-Civil War south. Their very identity as a people was a lie. Salvation from idolatry is inseparable from deliverance from group or collective self-deception and self-righteousness, the belief in the purity and innocence of our group. And might we not also insist that African-Americans, whether facing slavery, the evils of the post-Reconstruction era such as vagrancy laws and Black Codes, lynching, or contemporary mass incarceration and extrajudicial killings, need deliverance from injustice and the deep racial biases that make abuses and injustices possible.

Of course, every person needs forgiveness and deliverance from the grip of personal sins. But what conventional soteriology wittingly or unwittingly screens out is the ability to "see" that sin's destructive power also includes what the sins of others do to us. And when the sins of others are amplified because embedded within the normal operating procedures of society, such as the Jim Crow laws or the ways poor and minority communities are often policed in the name of the war on drugs, salvation in its full measure must involve deliverance or "liberation" from the sins of others and the rectification of those arrangements.

The Mutual Resonance of the Individualization of Sin and Salvation and Anti-Structuralist Individualism as Social Imaginary

This individualization of sin has had a powerful impact upon the ways in which many white Christians think about social systems and institutions. All humans inhabit what might be described as a social imaginary, the optic through which we "see" the world and the "reality coordinates" this optic provides. The myriad ways any human person has been socialized shapes what is assumed to be real, true, good, and normal.[4] Christian Smith and Michael Emerson identify the social imaginary of white evangelical Christianity with the interpretive categories of "accountable freewill individualism" and "anti-structuralism." Individuals are assumed to exist independent of structures and institutions, are accountable for the choices they make as moral agents with free will, and are personally responsible for, and fully in control of, their own decisions and destinies. Systems themselves are not seen as corrupted. Injustices tend to be attributed to bad behavior of individuals.[5] In a manner that is incipiently Pelagian, sin is located strictly within the will and choices of self-governing individuals, not in the destructive impact of flawed systems or institutions upon individuals.

"Accountable freewill individualism" and "anti-structuralism," as a social imaginary, are tightly tethered to the "individualization" of sin and salvation in western soteriology. This social imaginary is incapable of recognizing that humans are interconnected and adversely affected by the sedimentation of past sin. Canadian social theorist Henry Giroux has criticized what he calls a characteristically American concept of individual responsibility that is blind to inequalities in power and wealth and their adverse impact on individuals and groups.[6] For example, educational inequalities, the home in which one was raised, and the networks and connections available to persons from privileged homes tilt the economic playing field. As schools are funded largely by property taxes, the ways Americans sort themselves

---

4. Harvey, "Into Lands as Yet Unknown," 298–99, 302–5.

5. This way of making sense of the world is in large measure, the product of certain strands of western individualism, intensified by the American experience. It is not limited to, though it may be highly concentrated among, white evangelicals. Emerson and Smith, *Divided by Faith*, 76–79, 94–101, 110.

6. Harper, "Henry A. Giroux."

residentially by race[7] and economic class perpetuate inequalities from one generation to the next.

Seeing the world through this individualizing and "anti-structuralist" imagination, a significant percentage of white evangelicals are incapable of "seeing" a wide range of distortions of free markets that tip the playing field, such as massive government subsidies to well-connected business enterprises, and instead embrace a version of market fundamentalism. On this individualizing optic, the only plausible differentiating factor between the economically successful and unsuccessful would have to be explained on an individual level. The implication is that economic failure is simply the result of moral failure.

Paul Froese claims that there is a connection between this fervent individualism of American Christianity and uncritical support for a "market fundamentalist" version of free market capitalism. The market is believed to be a fair and neutral system in which individual choices and actions alone determine success or failure. If each individual alone is responsible for his or her eternal salvation, it makes sense that each individual is responsible for his or her economic well-being without government assistance.[8]

Of course, an optic that renders those who inhabit it less inclined to perceive or register the impact of systems and structures will more often than not function to inculcate support for the status quo, since such a social imaginary cannot even imagine the need to evaluate and criticize systems themselves. Calls for justice by those who are unhappy with the current social order, as has been the case with social change movements by African-Americans and other racial and ethnic minorities, or dissatisfaction with current economic arrangements, will be met with incomprehension and anger by those who, in the words of Barry Harvey, believe that the basic patterns of relating within their preferred social order are not fundamentally damaged or in need of radical transformation.[9] If everything that happens is understood to be mostly the result of individual actions, then one simply does not register that there could be ongoing systemic distortions,

---

7. Sachs, *Price of Civilization*, 39–40, 78, 280n14; Shipler, *Working Poor*, 142–73, 201–18. Of course, residential sorting by race is not entirely a matter of economics. As Richard Rothstein and others have clearly documented, a long history of political decisions and public policy intentionally segregated American cities and in particular, confined African-Americans into certain urban spaces while preventing African-American and other minorities from access to suburban property. Rothstein, *Color of Law*.

8. Froese was one of the research team members of the third wave of the Baylor Religion Survey (Dougherty et al., *Values and Beliefs of the American Public*). Froese, "How Your View of God Shapes Your View of the Economy."

9. Harvey, "Into Lands as Yet Unknown," 305.

inequities, and injustices tethered to the sedimentation of past explicit discriminatory policies, including legal segregation, discriminatory federal housing policy, employment discrimination, and a harshly racially biased criminal justice system. As Robert P. Jones uncovered in his survey data, 75 percent of white Christians believe that racial minorities use racism as an excuse for economic inequalities more than they should, and 64 percent of white Christians believe that the killing of African-American men by police are isolated incidents rather than part of a broader pattern of how police treat African-Americans.[10]

Anthropological Dualism: "It's Not a Religion, It's a Relationship"

One of the deep assumptions embedded within the conventional account of salvation is a kind of anthropological dualism. In its more popular rather than philosophical understandings, anthropological dualism describes the latent assumption that there is a sharp division between two parts of the human person. The conventional view of salvation depends upon an implicit assumption that our personhood is sharply divided into an interior spiritual part, which is believed to be the "real" me, and an exterior part, which includes my body and all my visible and public actions.

The problem is not that of making a distinction between the dimensions of our personhood that we might helpfully picture with the metaphors of "interior" and "exterior." For example, my thoughts are inward in the sense that others cannot "see" or know what I am thinking unless I convey at least some dimensions of my thoughts verbally or, quite often, in nonverbal fashion, such as a smile or an angry scowl.

The problem is when this distinction between my "inner" reality and "outer" reality comes to be seen as an extremely sharp separation. In reality, the line between the inner and outer dimensions of life is extremely fuzzy and permeable. The "inner" and "outer" merge or blend into each other in ways that are very difficult to separate. For example, our very ability to have thoughts depends upon learning a language, which is, of course, a reality that is public, social, and physical, rooted in the public world of action and interpersonal communication. Language and the patterns of behavior that are intertwined with language come to us from the "outside." And, of course, to be human at all is to be dependent on our relationships with others from the very beginning of our lives. While our relationships are "matters of the heart," bound to our deepest feelings, relationships depend upon language

10. Jones, *White Too Long*, 165–75.

and physical proximity through sight or hearing or physical contact. Who "I" am on what we call the "inside" is completely dependent on what I have received and appropriated from the "outside."

Harold Bloom has argued that "the American religion" is a variant of the ancient Christian heresy of Gnosticism. Religion is construed as a personal matter between the individual and God. God is to be found within oneself, through inward solitude or when we are "alone with Jesus." Bloom identifies Southern Baptist Christianity as one of the paradigmatic expressions of this gnostic tendency. The Baptist emphasis on knowing Jesus, in a solitary encounter, takes priority over public worship, doctrine, or acts of charity.[11]

The primary location or focal point of the Christian life comes to be seen as the private, inner sanctuary of the "soul" or the "heart." The "really important" part of being a Christian is my personal and individual relationship with Jesus. And this sensibility is not limited to conservative evangelicals. Many American Christians, whether theologically conservative or theologically liberal, view church as optional. It is assumed that we don't need the church or connection with other Christians to "connect" with God. In the privacy of the human heart, each individual has a direct and unmediated access to God.

All that belongs to the Christian life that is visible, public, and embodied is seen as secondary and external expressions of the real, inward, spiritual relationship of the individual and God. This includes public worship, baptism, the life of the Christian community, and obedient discipleship. All too often, even the public worship of many of our churches is designed to enable each individual worshiper to have an intensely private emotional experience of God, even if "we" may all be in the same physical space.

These assumptions represent the fruit of individualistic trajectories within modern Protestantism and, even before the Reformation, the individualization of salvation in medieval Catholicism, which long preceded the American experience.[12] This dualism is pervasive within Protestantism

---

11. Bloom, *American Religion*, 15, 24–25, 32–33, 64–65, 200, 206. What Bloom calls "the American religion" was given classical expression by William James in his definition of religion "as meaning . . . the feelings, acts, and experiences of *individual men in their solitude,* so far as they apprehend themselves to stand in relation to whatever they consider the divine" (James, *Varieties of Religious Experience*, 31).

12. How did we get here? Telling the whole tale would require another book. Long before the Protestant Reformation, there were strands of Christian spirituality that tended to denigrate the body and portray the spiritual quest in terms of a flight from the material to the spiritual.

Another part of this story is tied to the Lutheran wing of the Protestant Reformation. The Magisterial Reformation was dependent on political rulers to establish

generally. German theologian Karl Heim argued that the first principle of Protestantism is that we find God only in a spiritual act that occurs in deep solitude and with full mental clarity. Heim spoke of the sober inwardness of the Protestant conscience "entirely alone with Christ."[13] When this dualistic view is followed to its logical conclusion, salvation is unrelated to the church, which comes to be imagined as an aggregate of individuals who already enjoy their own "prior" relationship with God. As Friedrich Schleiermacher, the father of modern liberal Protestant theology, wrote:

> The antithesis between Protestantism and Catholicism may provisionally be conceived thus: the former makes the individual's

---

Protestantism in their nations, cities or territories. Therefore, the pressure was upon early Protestant thought and practice to be strongly supportive of the power and authority of those rulers. On the Lutheran side, Martin Luther's notion of two kingdoms or two governments was designed to keep the church separate from the governance of society and by doing so, make Protestantism more attractive to rulers than Catholicism, with its history of power struggles between the church and the ruling powers. In making this move, Luther separated body and soul. He suggested that God had ordained worldly government to govern outward and visible human conduct. Rulers have jurisdiction over bodies, while God and the church have jurisdiction over the soul. Of course, Luther did not make an absolute separation here, but his way of framing the issue of the proper sphere of temporal authority helped to set the stage for the idea that the church's sphere of authority is the individual's inner spiritual self, while the government's sphere of authority is the outward and visible life of human persons. Luther, "Temporal Authority," 51–69.

The early years of the Baptist tradition in seventeenth century England featured this spiritualizing move by Thomas Helwys. In his effort to secure religious liberty for Baptists, Helwys maintained that the king may claim authority over bodies but not souls. Helwys, *Short Declaration of the Mystery of Iniquity*, 32–35, cited by Broadway, "Practicing What We Preach," 386, 394.

The separation between the personal and spiritual sphere and the public realm was intensified in the sixteenth, seventeenth and eighteenth centuries. The emergence of the modern nation-state, with its claims to be the supreme sovereign authority within its national borders, was accompanied by a re-positioning of "religion" as something "located" within the sphere of the individual's private and interior self. The community to which one's public loyalty belonged was not the international church, but one's nation-state. Cavanaugh, "Fire Strong Enough to Consume the House," 398–409; Lash, "Church in the State We're In," 123; Milbank, *Theology and Social Theory*, 9–48, 87–98, 104–6, 126–30; Asad, *Genealogies of Religion*, 27–8, 39–42.

In the United States, the earliest trajectory of first amendment jurisprudence with respect to the "free exercise clause" took its bearings from Thomas Jefferson's comments in his reply to questions from the Danbury (Virginia) Baptist Association. Jefferson's comments reflect this dualistic body-soul binary and confinement of religion to the interior self. He wrote, "Religion is a matter which lies solely between man and his god . . . the legislative powers of government reach actions only, and not opinions" (Jefferson, "Letter to the Danbury Baptists").

13. Heim, *Nature of Protestantism*, 79, 104, cited by Yeago, "Christian Holy People," 101.

relation to the Church dependent on his relation to Christ, while the latter makes his relation to Christ dependent on his relation to the Church.[14]

The church comes to be seen as existing to serve the individual Christian in his or her personal walk with God. The church is like a convenience store where we stop for supplies for our individual "road trip with Jesus." We go once a week, find helpful nuggets of advice for our own individual Christian life, and hit the road again alone with Jesus. The church is seen as a helpful aid for living the Christian life but, in the final analysis, it is dispensable. We go to church as spiritual consumers looking for nourishment for ourselves.

Soteriological Dualism Variant One: The Point of the Gospel Is to Change Hearts and Save Souls, Not to Change the World . . .

In the mid-1960s, Jerry Falwell preached a sermon entitled "Ministers and Marches" in which he declared, "Preachers are not called to be politicians, but soul winners." The target of Falwell's criticism was Martin Luther King Jr. and other ministers involved in the civil rights movement. Using characteristically dualistic language, Falwell asserted that the gospel does not clean up the outside but regenerates the inside. Political activity beyond this distracts Christians from their sole purpose: "to know Christ and make him known."[15]

Dualism, Slavery, and Indifference to Racial Justice

Mikael Broadway points out that the effort to justify slavery theologically was aided by the idea that Christian faith pertains to a "circumscribed sphere of spirituality divorced from bodies, economics, and politics."[16] This separation put the bodies of enslaved Africans outside the concern of the church. Christian slaves could be considered brothers and sisters in Christ on the spiritual plane but nevertheless could be brutally whipped, abused,

---

14. Schleiermacher, *Christian Faith*, 103.
15. Of course, this is the "same" Jerry Falwell who became the poster child for conservative Christian politics as one of the founders of the "Moral Majority," How to make sense of his change of mind will be the subject of the next segment of this chapter. Tisby, *Color of Compromise*, 166; Du Mez, *Jesus and John Wayne*, 98.
16. Broadway, "Preaching What We Practice," 388–94.

and treated as property in the social and economic realms of life.[17] This maneuver came in handy as ministers such as Cotton Mather and other clergymen sincerely longed to see slaves evangelized for the sake of their eternal salvation. The problem was that in England, there had been a long-standing convention that an enslaved person, by accepting Christ and being baptized, was to be set free from involuntary servitude. This convention was a grave economic threat in the new world, which was dependent on a slave economy. Therefore, it was crucial to insist that salvation of the soul does not entail liberation of the body. This allowed ministers like Mather and George Whitefield to combine belief in equality in the spiritual domain with support for the institution of slavery.[18]

Rev. Douglas Hudgins, pastor of the prominent First Baptist Church in Jackson, Mississippi, during "Freedom Summer" in 1964, further manifested the pernicious effects of this body-soul separation. As civil rights activists fought for voting rights for African-Americans and white supremacists engaged in acts of violence and brutality to preserve a segregated society, Hudgins preached a gospel of individual salvation, proclaiming that the cross of Christ has nothing to do with social movements or realities outside the church. For Hudgins, the focal point of the Christian life is the inner purity of the individual Christian's soul and its intimate relationship with God. The real battle against evil, he taught, is the inward spiritual struggle against temptation. Hudgins was heavily influenced by Baptist theologian E. Y. Mullin's idea of "soul competency," the notion that each individual has a direct and unmediated experience and relationship with God. Visible and external realities are of no consequence when it comes to the purity and intimacy of the interior relationship of the soul with God. For Hudgins, one does not experience God in the lived reality of everyday life or even in compassionate actions such as feeding the hungry or our relationships with others. God is to be encountered and experienced solely in the individual's "own walk with Jesus in [his or her] private spiritual garden."[19]

17. Broadway, "Preaching What We Practice," 388–94.

18. Emerson and Smith, *Divided by Faith*, 25; Broadway, "Preaching What We Practice," 292–94.

19. Marsh, *God's Long Summer*, 88–90, 106–8, 113–15. While Hudgens did not endorse the extra-legal violence of the Ku Klux Klan, his sermons, as Robert P. Jones points out, were carefully curated to leave white supremacy undisturbed. First Baptist Church of Jackson, Mississippi included in its membership Governor Ross Barnett and Robert and Thomas Hederman, owners of the fiercely segregationist newspaper, the *Jackson Daily News*. Ross Barnett won the governorship by running an overtly segregationist campaign, making statements such as "God was the original segregationist," and "the Negro is different because God made him different to punish him." On the evening before his gubernatorial inauguration in 1960, Hudgins conducted a Christian

Charles Marsh argues that one cannot understand white Christian indifference to black suffering and hostility to the aspirations of African-Americans for justice without also understanding the religion that found expression in the theology of Douglas Hudgins. Hudgins represents a clear and blatant expression of this "spiritual" Christianity that locks the Christian's relationship with God into a spiritual realm that does not really impact the world of bodies, politics, economics, and relationships between people groups. This theology of personal salvation was designed to protect white Christian power and white Christian consciences from black demands for justice and thereby permitted Christians to be blissfully indifferent to injustice and the violence inflicted against African Americans.[20]

Christianity Today adopted the same basic "apolitical" stance. The magazine refused to endorse the Civil Rights Act of 1964 because it was not in keeping with the magazine's evangelical belief that social change came best through personal conversion.[21]

The One Thing: How Dualism Continues to "Disable" Christian Engagement on Behalf of the Marginalized and Obstruct Concern about Racial Injustice and *de facto* Segregation

Most white evangelicals today would emphatically disavow white supremacy. However, the way that we have imagined Christian life as first and primarily a "personal relationship with Jesus Christ" has rendered a long history of racial injustice and segregation either invisible to white Christians or outside the range of genuine Christian concern

These tendencies are on display in a little book entitled *The One Thing*, written by Thom and Joani Schultz in 2004. In this book, the faith-works and soul-body dualisms shape the way the Christian faith is understood. The book's authors have no malicious intentions to cultivate segregated churches. Indeed, their promotional material and the book itself includes pictures of persons from diverse racial and ethnic backgrounds. This book was written out of a sincere and passionate desire to help churches become more faithful to the gospel as the Schultzes understand the gospel. But their apparent obliviousness to the pernicious racialized dynamics in American society and, in particular, American churches, if appropriated,

---

consecration service for Barnett. Jones, *White Too Long*, 40–43.

20. Marsh, *God's Long Summer*, 113–15; Jones, *White Too Long*, 41.
21. Tisby, *Color of Compromise*, 140.

will perpetuate racial separation within the body of Christ and render Christians indifferent to racial injustices in society, in spite of their explicit intentions.

One problem is the way in which the deep imagination of conventional soteriology shapes what they "see" and what they "do not see" as the heart of the Christian faith. This theological imagination also serves as an interpretive filter for how they read and interpret the Bible and for the ways in which biblical texts that do not fit into their paradigm are unwittingly screened out or marginalized.

The Schultzes define the "one thing," that which is the most fundamental and important matter at the center of the Christian faith, as "a heart-to-heart relationship, a close and growing friendship, with God." Jesus's gospel message is interpreted to be simply "believe in [me] and you will have eternal life."[22] The meaning of the phrase "*believe in*" is interpreted to mean not merely knowing about but being in relationship with, to trust, to love.

Taking Luke 10:38–42 as their foundational biblical text, they interpret the story of Mary and Martha as an expression of Jesus's preference for a heart-to-heart relationship over service and activism. Martha misses the point, they insist, by allowing other "things," such as serving Jesus, cultivating righteous motives, observing protocol, and championing justice, to displace a heart-to-heart relationship with Jesus.[23]

The Schultzes are not wrong in their conviction that a relationship with Christ is "the one thing." The problem is their narrow concept of "relationship." "Relationship" is understood to pertain to the sphere of the individual's personal heart-to-heart relationship with God. Visible actions, deeds of deliverance for the needy and suffering, passionate concern for the hungry, impoverished, and oppressed are seen, in the final analysis, as quite secondary to the gift of salvation because salvation pertains to "internal" matters of "belief," "faith," "trust," and "loving relationship." Therefore, the outward and public dimensions of Christian life, such as ethics, obedient discipleship, and social justice, must be pushed to the periphery as, at best, merely external "expressions" of the relationship.

---

22. Schultz and Schultz, *One Thing*, 15–16.

23. Schultz and Schultz, *One Thing*, xx, 15–16. The Schultzes do not consider another plausible reading of this gospel narrative other than a very conventional interpretation of this text as one pitting the cultivation of one's individual spiritual life against a life of activity in service to Christ. No consideration is given to the possibility that the story may be, for example, about Jesus's counter-cultural act of opening the role of disciple to women instead of reinforcing traditional roles for women.

Soteriological Pathologies and Racial Injustice

This interior-exterior dualism is a powerful lens, shaping how they appropriate Jesus's message and example in the Gospels. Discipleship, obedience, and justice are presented as, first and foremost, *dangers* that can distract us from "the one thing." "Jesus clarifies for us that our response to his teachings is very important," they note, but quickly add that "nothing is more important than our *relationship* with him."[24] In this way, the Schultzes relegate Jesus's life, teaching, and practice to the periphery, as matters unrelated to the core matters of salvation:

> To be clear, Jesus certainly advocated feeding the hungry, clothing the naked, tending the sick, and visiting the imprisoned. He beckons us to love others. In doing so, we show our love for him. Our compassion grows out of our relationship with him. Service to others is one of the things Jesus's friends do. But service—even directly serving the Lord—is secondary to "the one thing."[25]

But why must we frame the issue in this manner? Why is serving Jesus by feeding the hungry categorized as something that "flows out of" one's relationship with Jesus instead of being seen as internal to one's relationship with Jesus? The reason the Schultzes frame the issue in this way is that their dualistic, conventional view of salvation confines their interpretive imagination. "Relationship" is assumed to be, primarily, a spiritual and internal reality, while service and action are realities belonging to the external dimension of reality.

If we repudiate this dualism, such actions could be seen as part of the relationship. For example, St. Irenaeus did not separate obedience and relationship. Intimacy with God, knowledge of the Father, and union with Christ come through following Jesus and obeying his commands. For St. Irenaeus, it is in the practical life of discipleship that deep communion with Christ is forged.[26] In Matt 25:31–46, Jesus indicates that these actions, feeding the hungry, clothing the naked, hospitality to strangers, and other deeds of compassion, are indispensable and internal to the relationship itself. How we treat "the least of these" is not an "expression" of our relationship with Christ. It is how we treat *Christ*. If we neglect the least of these, our relationship with Christ is a damaged relationship.

The supreme irony is that the literary context of the story of Mary and Martha, which forms the foundation of the Schultzes theological vision, has been unwittingly screened out. According to the Schultzes, Jesus's gospel

---

24. Schultz and Schulz, *One Thing*, 16.
25. Schultz and Schulz, *One Thing*, 53.
26. Loewe, "Irenaeus's Soteriology," 4.

message is simply "believe in [me] and you will have eternal life." But they can only give this answer because they have interpreted the story of Mary and Martha as if it were unconnected to the story immediately preceding it in Luke's Gospel: the parable of the Good Samaritan (10:25–37). There, Jesus gives a very different answer to the question, "What must I do to inherit eternal life?" There, Jesus recites Israel's Great Shema of Deuteronomy 6:4–5 and adds to the imperative to love God the imperative of loving the neighbor as one loves oneself. When the scribe asks Jesus to define neighbor, Jesus offers an expansive definition of who counts as my neighbor and an expansive account of love as action to rescue my neighbor when he or she is in distress. The kind of right relationship with God that results in "eternal life" is not an interior spiritual matter but involves visible and concrete deeds of rescue and deliverance when the neighbor's life, health, and well-being is threatened.

Though "the one thing" is said to be the *individual's* personal, heart-to-heart relationship with *God*, the book is a comprehensive vision for the ministry and mission of local congregations that is organized around "relationships," not only the relationship of each Christian with God but relationships of Christians with each other. The book goes into great detail about the creation of an atmosphere that facilitates the formation and building of relationships among persons. Their vision for the local congregation is organized around the master metaphor of relationship:

> What if the church prominently fashioned itself around relationship? What if it de-prioritized the distractions of well-intentioned ministries and focused on ending the [relationship] famine in our culture? What if it elevated human relationship building above the rituals we've come to associate with "church?" What if it utilized what we know about building great human friendships to nurture real friendships with Jesus? What if it made *the one thing* the top priority?[27]

This is the point at which the book almost crosses the threshold from a hyper-individualistic Christianity to a more faithful ecclesiology. But ultimately, they cannot escape the grip of the dualistic imagination of the conventional picture of salvation. Relationships with other persons are imagined as signs rather than sacraments, merely pointing to our relationship with God. Friendship with God is imagined as *much like* human friendships.[28]

---

27. Schultz and Schulz, *One Thing*, 33.
28. Schultz and Schulz, *One Thing*, 33.

For St. Paul, the salvation achieved through Christ's death on the cross is not merely an individual heart-to-heart relationship with God, but the creation of a new kind of human community that is the dwelling place of God, where persons formerly divided and hostile to one another are reconciled (Eph 2:11–22). Incorporation into Christ through baptism (Rom 6:3–4; Gal 3:27) inducts us into a community that actively breaks down the divisions and forms of domination and exclusion, including race and ethnicity, sex and gender, and economic class, that divide humans from one another (Gal 3:28; Col 3:11). This Pauline vision of salvation in Christ is at odds with homogenous groups composed of birds of a feather.

But "one thing" churches remain in a "suburban captivity" in which the relationships that are cultivated seem to be mostly between persons who share much the same socio-economic and cultural demographic. Because the Schultzes remain captive to the individualism of the conventional version of salvation, their vision of church functions to screen out the hurts, the sufferings of, and injustices perpetrated against members of the body of Christ who are not visible from their own neighborhoods. Indeed, the book is scathing in its opposition to churches who are "too engaged" in advocacy and activism in pursuit of societal justice. Such concerns for the human sufferings of those outside of our daily experiences are dismissed as peripheral to "the one thing," the individual heart-to-heart relationship with Christ.

Most revealing in this respect is what they "see" as human needs and sufferings to which the church should respond and those human sufferings they define as "distractions." They sharply criticize an unnamed denomination for its consideration, at a district assembly meeting, of denominational responses to a list of social, political, and moral issues including racism, poor and vulnerable populations, federal child nutrition programs, the needs of the elderly, world hunger, homelessness, international debt relief, poverty, and HIV/AIDS. These issues are dismissed as items quite distinct from, irrelevant to, and distractions from the church's role of "growing relationships with Jesus Christ."[29] But even as they dismiss the suffering of persons who are impoverished, malnourished, homeless, or negatively influenced by racism, there is a human hurt that registers on their radar as a matter of great urgency. They call for a relationship-focused church as a spiritual response to our culture's "relationship famine." Due to "our" busy lifestyles, they note, we find it harder and harder to find, establish, nurture, and rely on real friendships. This call for churches to respond to the felt need of so many persons in our culture who are lonely or lack deep and satisfying relationships with others is, in itself, quite commendable. But

---

29. Schultz and Schulz, *One Thing*, 50–51.

the crucial question is why does suburban loneliness, the friendship void of otherwise affluent and successful people, count as a genuine need while engagement with and for persons who suffer because of racism, poverty, and global hunger are defined as distractions from the one thing?

A decisive clue comes from the way *The One Thing* finds a paradigm for relationship building for the sake of evangelism in the advice of Lee Strobel, who makes this suggestion for church leaders who desire to penetrate their communities with the Gospel. Strobel suggests an evangelism strategy in which church members

> build at least one strong, deep, authentic and caring relationship with an unchurched person in [his] community. Golf together. Go to dinner and movies together. Come out for his son's soccer game; invite him to your daughter's piano recital.[30]

Golf, dinner, movies, soccer games, and piano recitals are part of "normal life" for some persons in our society, but certainly not for everyone. What is revealed here is a "suburban captivity" in which the mission of the church is to nurture relationships among affluent persons within mostly homogenous congregations that value comfortable environments featuring gourmet coffee bars and cafes. But why do some kinds of human friendships count as pointers to relationship with God, while nurturing other kinds of relationships are viewed as threats that might derail the church from its mission of nurturing a relationship with God? Why is it that building relationships with the neighbor who plays golf is a wonderful evangelism strategy but the kinds of relationships that might be forged with persons on the margins of society, those who suffer hunger, poverty, and injustice, count as distractions?

That opposing racism is also named as a distraction is deeply disturbing. The overwhelming whiteness of most suburbs is not a demographic accident or merely a matter of self-sorting by economic status. As Richard Rothstein carefully documents in *The Color of Law*, racial segregation in America's cities and suburbs was carefully planned and maintained by government policy at the national and local level.[31] If suburban churches are not actively working to address matters of racial segregation and injustice in both church and society, these churches are, even if unintentionally, perpetuating the deepest divisions and fault lines of our society and as such, are conformed to the patterns of this world (Rom 12:1) instead of being the

---

30. This quotation is from *Outreach Magazine*, cited by Schultz and Schultz, *One Thing*, 92. However, further information is not provided.

31. Rothstein, *Color of Law*.

social space in which dividing lines of hostility are dismantled and alienated people groups are reconciled (Eph 2:11–22).

The One Thing exemplifies the ways in which the conventional view of salvation and the spiritualization of the Christian life as a vertical relationship with God provide a set of blinders that enable many white Christians simply "not to see." As Mikael Broadway points out, racial apartheid remains the primary reality of our mostly racially homogenous churches. That this does not even register as a problem for many white Christians is partly the result of the deep assumption that "what happens in the church is deemed spiritual, and the fact that black and white bodies have been separated by an unrighteous history makes little difference in the perceived spiritual relationship to God."[32] On the conventional version of salvation, one's individual, vertical, heart-to-heart relationship with Jesus is unrelated to the church's own fractures and the dividing walls of hostility that churches tragically maintain. This theology of salvation enables white Christians to treat racial injustice and the racial divisions in society and in the body of Christ as something we need not be overly concerned about.

Soteriological Dualism Variant Two: The Evisceration of Ecclesiology and the Political Activism of the Religious Right

How is it possible for the "same" soteriological imagination to support an apolitical Christianity and also undergird a vigorously engaged political activism?

The answer lies in the ecclesiological implications of treating the heart and center of the Christian life as the individual Christian's personal relationship with Christ, which is the relegation of the church to the periphery of Christian existence.

Humans are social creatures with a fundamental need to belong to some kind of community that bestows personal identity, meaning, and an ultimate and transcendent purpose. If the church has been reduced to an instrumental means to enable individuals to find their own connection with God primarily within an asocial, individual, private, and interior sphere, humans will inevitably look elsewhere for a community that provides a sense of identity and a transcendent purpose.

This "void" has often been filled by an idolatrous nationalism that has replaced the church with the nation as the people of God. American

---

32. Broadway, "Practicing What We Preach," 390–94.

Section One: What If the Reigning Soteriology Is Part of What We Need Saving From?

Christian history is one in which, as Mark Noll, Nathan Hatch, and John D. Woodridge argue, Americans have transferred their ecclesiology from church to the nation as the primary agent by which God is at work in human history.[33] For many, being a Christian is merely a component part of the "larger" identity of being an American. The United States of America becomes a quasi-ecclesial body, a sacred and divinely established order. Allegiance to God and allegiance to the United States are conflated since it is believed that America is God's chosen people, the nation through which God's providential mission in the world is to be realized and, indeed, a nation that is itself a "redeemer-nation." In this way, the social and corporate community which bestows our identity and the corporate project that gives many American Christians a sense of purpose is "America" or, for some, a particularly Christian nationalist ideal for the United States.

In the twenty-first century, evangelical politics, and certainly many other white as well as some non-white Christians, are deeply invested in Christian nationalism, the belief that America is God's chosen nation and must be defended as such.[34] This corporate project, filling in the ecclesial void, is a Christian America. It is this project, the promotion and defense of a preferred vision of "Christian America" and Christian cultural and political dominance, to which many white evangelical and other Christians are devoted. The highest holy day is not Easter but the Sunday closest to the fourth of July, when churches hold patriotic extravaganza worship services.

Andrew Whitehead and Samuel Perry argue that at least 19.8 percent of Americans are staunch Christian nationalists, while many more hold some of the beliefs and attitudes characteristic of Christian nationalism. Christian nationalists strongly affirm that the United States was founded as a Christian nation, that this founding was God's action, and that failure of the nation to acknowledge God and maintain its identity as a Christian nation runs the risk of a withdrawal of the divine blessing from the country. Because these persons emphatically believe that the United States has a special relationship with God, they also tend to believe that the federal government should formally declare the United States to be a Christian nation, return formal prayers to public schools, and allow the display of religious symbols in public places, such as the Ten Commandments in courthouses.[35]

Kelly Brown Douglas traces the link between Anglo-Saxon exceptionalism and today's Christian nationalism. She argues that Christianity was intertwined with "Anglo-Saxon exceptionalism" from before the founding

33. Noll et al., *Gospel in America*, 178.
34. Du Mez, *Jesus and John Wayne*, 4.
35. Whitehead and Perry, *Taking America Back for God*, 25–26, 35–36.

of the American Republic. She describes the mythological and imaginative power of Roman historian Tacitus's admiration for certain Germanic tribes, expressed in his *Germania*, written around 98 CE. Tacitus described them as "free from all taint of intermarriages, brave, of strong moral character, and possessing a peculiar instinctive love for freedom and individual rights." Over time, the English came to consider the tribes described by Tacitus as their Anglo-Saxon forebears, superior in blood, moral qualities, and political institutions. Pilgrims and Puritans brought this myth to America. They considered themselves the Anglo-Saxon remnant, fleeing the Church of England, with its corrupted Norman and Catholic abuses, and, as such, regarded themselves as the bearers of a divine mission. This reverence for Anglo-Saxon superiority was enthusiastically embraced by Thomas Jefferson as the basis for American political institutions. Though hardly orthodox Christians, Jefferson and Benjamin Franklin believed that Americans were chosen by God to implement an Anglo-Saxon system of governing, and they drew deeply upon symbolism of Americans as the new Israelites.[36] The myth of America as a chosen nation because of its alleged Christian founding was intertwined in its origins with racial claims about the allegedly superior purity, morality, and love of freedom of the Anglo-Saxon people.[37]

This kind of American Christian exceptionalism was not limited to contemporary conservative evangelical Christians. White mainline Protestants believed "we" were on the verge of "the Christian Century," when Christian principles would finally begin to shape national policy and world events.[38] In 1909, liberal Protestant social gospel minister Washington Gladden identified the United States as the new Israel.[39] Beginning in the 1940s and 1950s, most white Christians, whether conservative evangelical or liberal Protestants, believed that God had chosen the United States for a special mission in the world. After all, the US had just "saved the world" from Nazi tyranny. In the 1950s, a high percentage of American Christians believed that the United States was a Christian nation, standing for truth and right against "godless Communism."[40]

The 1960s were traumatic for those who believed in the righteousness and innocence of American society and what was believed to be "traditional American values." Challenges to race relations, gender roles, sexual ethics,

---

36. Douglas, *Stand Your Ground*, 3–14.
37. Hughes, *Myths America Lives By*, 20.
38. Jones, *End of White Christian America*, 34.
39. Du Mez, "Os Guinness, Eric Metaxis."
40. Hughes, *Myths America Lives By*, 113–14.

and the conviction that America was always on the side of truth, justice, and righteousness in its military campaigns came as a shock to many white Christians, for whom the 1950s was a golden age of peace, prosperity, and moral rectitude. As the society changed dramatically in the 1960s, white Christians were alarmed by what they perceived as the attempt to "evict God from the public square" and destroy public morality. In particular, Supreme Court rulings in *Engel v. Vitale* (1962),[41] forbidding prayer in public schools, and *Roe v. Wade* (1973),[42] which treated abortion prior to the viability of the fetus as a fundamental right,[43] gave many white Christians the sense that "our country" is being taken away from us.

The rise of the religious right, in response to the massive political, social, and cultural upheavals of the 1960s occurred not in spite but because of an individualizing soteriology with a weak ecclesiology, which made possible the displacement of the church by the nation as the primary identity-bestowing community and social project for Christians. As long as Christians were mostly content with the social order, it was easier for white Christians to imagine and represent themselves as apolitical. But when their preferred vision of America was threatened by criticism and movements for social change, the transition exemplified by Rev. Jerry Falwell makes sense. In the mid-1960s, Falwell insisted that "preachers are not called to be politicians, but soul winners." In 1976, he had changed his mind. He stated that "this idea that 'religion and politics don't mix' was invented by the devil to keep Christians from running their own country."[44] It is this belief that the United States is "our" society that has driven the activism of the religious right.

The agenda of the religious right was reclaiming America as a Christian nation.[45] Pat Robertson expressed this aspiration for Christian cultural dominance quite explicitly in 1991:

> There will never be world peace until God's house and God's people are given their rightful place of leadership at the top of the world. How can there be peace when drunkards, drug dealers, communists, atheists, New Age worshipers of Satan, secular humanists, oppressive dictators, greedy moneychangers, revolutionary assassins, adulterers, and homosexuals are on top?[46]

41. *Engel v. Vitale*, 370 US 421 (1962).
42. *Roe v. Wade*, 410 US 113 (1973).
43. Hughes, *Myths America Lives By*, 113–14.
44. Tisby, *Color of Compromise*, 166; Du Mez, *Jesus and John Wayne*, 98.
45. Hughes, *Myths America Lives By*, 115.
46. Robertson, *New World Order*, 227, cited by Hughes, *Myths America Lives By*, 115.

Soteriological Pathologies and Racial Injustice

As Robertson's statement illustrates, protecting their preferred vision of a Christian America has meant evangelical hostility toward and fear of those deemed to be threats: communists, feminists, liberals, secular humanists, homosexuals, the United Nations, the government, Muslims, immigrants,[47] and, most recently, the bogeymen of "critical race theory" and "woke liberalism."[48]

If anyone is to be associated as the public face of conventional evangelical soteriology, it would be Billy Graham. Even though Billy Graham did not play a prominent role in the rise of the religious right in the late 1970s because, in large measure, he was reticent to get involved in politics immediately after he had been burned by his association with Richard Nixon, Graham's career embodied this same Christian nationalism which interprets the United States as a sacred order and bearer of God's cause. Graham proclaimed:

> Our founding fathers believed in God and they meant that America should always be dependent on him. . . . In the Mayflower Pact, Christ was acknowledged and was given his rightful place, while nearly every state constitution of the thirteen colonies recognized God.[49]

In Graham's messages, one finds an intriguing symbiotic relationship between individual conversion experiences and the identification of America as God's country. As a paid evangelist for Youth for Christ, Graham

---

47. Du Mez, *Jesus and John Wayne*, 11–13.

48. Robert P. Jones renders a much harsher judgment. He argues that the real underlying motivating factor was defending a white supremacist status quo. When white supremacy was still safely ensconced in the wider culture, he argues, white evangelicals argued that the Bible mandates a privatized religion. This served to delegitimize the work of black ministers and Christians fighting for racial justice. But as these forces gained power, white evangelical Protestants "discovered" a biblical mandate for political organizing and resistance. Jones, *White Too Long*, 103–4.

Jones's critique clearly applies to Jerry Falwell. Even when Falwell was proclaiming that the church must stick to "saving souls" and staying out of politics, Falwell was not actually staying out of politics. During the 1950s and 1960s, Falwell, then an avowed segregationist, helped lead local efforts to resist school integration. In 1958, he preached a sermon entitled, "Segregation or Integration: Which?" In the sermon, he condemned the decision in *Brown v. Board of Education*, proclaiming that "if Chief Justice [Earl] Warren and his associates had known God's word and had desired to do the Lord's will, the 1954 decision would never have been made. . . . [Schools] should be separate. When God has drawn a line of distinction, we should not attempt to cross that line." Like many other white evangelical churches, especially in the South, Falwell's congregation responded to the *Brown* decision by establishing a segregationist "Christian" academy. Du Mez, *Jesus and John Wayne*, 98–99; Hughes, *Myths America Lives By*, 102.

49. Graham, "Americanism."

preached a gospel of heroic Christian nationalism in rallies that featured patriotic hymns, color guards, and veterans' testimonies. Even while claiming to preach a privatized gospel of personal salvation, Graham sought to ensure that born-again Americans embraced Americanism, the idea that America was a nation ordained by God to save the world. He proclaimed that "Communism is a religion that is inspired, motivated, and directed by the devil," who had declared war against God. In this war, America was on God's side.[50]

Graham stressed the importance of personal salvation for resistance to communism, linking the power of Christianity to love for America. "The most effective weapon against communism to be a born-again Christian . . . because you will never find a true born-again Christian who is a communist or a fellow traveler."[51] In his "Americanism" radio address, Graham insisted that it all begins with the individual making a personal decision to invite Christ into his heart. But he connected this to the civil rather than ecclesial project. "I'm asking you to receive Jesus Christ . . . as our forefathers did who made our nation great. . . . When you make your decision for Christ, it is America through you making its decision for God." Graham identified the positive outcome of individual conversion as America's recovery of its worldwide prestige in the battle for hearts and minds between America, democracy, God, and freedom and godless communism. Turning to God in great numbers would lead to the recovery of this prestige as the divorce rate would decline, strengthening the home, the race problem would be solved, and crime statistics improved. All of these social changes are envisioned as the direct result of a critical mass of individual conversion experiences.[52]

To his credit, Graham often desegregated his evangelistic crusades. He seemed genuinely to desire positive race relations. On one occasion, he invited Dr. Martin Luther King Jr. to pray during one of his crusades. But Graham's "God and country" Christian nationalism and his individualist soteriological imagination shaped the way he reacted to the civil rights movement. Graham could only think about the issue in individualist terms. He stated that "the heart of the problem of race is in loving our neighbor" and he believed that race relations would improve gradually, one conversion and one friendship at a time. In this way, Graham avoided coming to terms with any sharp critique of racial injustice as deeply embedded within American history, society, politics, and law. Graham did not walk with protestors or call for open housing or desegregated churches. His response to

50. Du Mez, *Jesus and John Wayne*, 25–26; Butler, *White Evangelical Racism*, 42–43.
51. Du Mez, *Jesus and John Wayne*, 25–26; Butler, *White Evangelical Racism*, 42–43.
52. Graham, "Americanism."

Martin Luther King Jr.'s "I Have a Dream Speech" was to say that "only when Christ comes again will little white children of Alabama walk hand in hand with little black children."[53]

Yet, Graham was willing to call for changes in government policy in response to the Watts riots and other urban uprisings in the 1960s. King, who was adamantly opposed to the resort to violence of these riots, insisted that we recognize riots as the language of the unheard. However, Graham could only see anarchy and the unraveling of the fabric of the nation. He said that the nation needed "tough laws" to crack down on such flagrant disregard for authority. This "law and order" rhetoric resonated with white evangelicals.[54]

Graham could not embrace the civil rights movement, nor could he recognize deep and endemic racial injustice embedded into the laws, institutions, and fabric of the nation because of his commitment to America as a sacred and divinely instituted order with a messianic mission to save the world from godless communism. With these commitments, a critique of the nation beyond individual moral failure was not possible.

Where Did Jesus Go (WDJG)?

Since, on the conventional account, salvation is by faith, which is implicitly or explicitly understood to be passive, interior believing or trusting, how we ought to live is construed as a totally separate issue from the question of salvation. "Living" the gospel is a peripheral matter because the gospel is believed to pertain to a realm of hearing and believing in an interior, spiritual "space." When it comes to Jesus, the implication is that, except for his crucifixion, the rest of Jesus's life, his example and practice, his parables, his healings, his confrontations of the wielders of unjust power, and his preaching of the kingdom of God, as narrated in the Gospels, are not relevant to salvation. At most, Jesus is understood to be offering "practical advice or principles for living." This theology places Jesus's own teachings, example, healings, table fellowship, parables of the kingdom of God, and preaching of the kingdom of God on the backburner as secondary matters. What Jesus commanded and exemplified, such as loving enemies, not laying up treasure on earth, refusing violent retaliation, caring for and including the most

---

53. Tisby, *Color of Compromise*, 134–35, 140; Butler, *White Evangelical Racism*, 34.

54. Tisby, *Color of Compromise*, 134–35, 140, citing Martin, *Prophet with Honor*, 320–21.

marginalized persons, feeding the hungry, clothing the naked, and visiting those in prison can be set aside as peripheral to salvation.[55]

The political priorities of politically conservative evangelicals as they emerged in the late 1970s and 1980s revealed an agenda that bears little resemblance to the priorities of Jesus. Jerry Falwell's Moral Majority supported prayer and the teaching of creationism in the public schools, and opposed the Equal Rights Amendment, gay rights, and the US-Soviet SALT treaties.[56] This Christian political agenda promoted free enterprise, patriotism, and an aggressive militarism, while opposing "welfare" and reliance upon government instead of "turning to God." The Moral Majority was staunchly against the Domestic Violence Prevention and Treatment Act in the name of protecting the rights of parents to use physical punishment as a mode of child rearing. Kristin Kobez Du Mez chronicles the evangelical cultivation of an ethos of militant masculinity, which glorifies a patriarchal gender order in the home and an aggressive militaristic foreign policy. A father's rule in the home is linked to heroic leadership on the national stage. "By the time Trump arrived," she argues, "conservative evangelicals had already traded a faith that elevates compassion for 'the least of these' for one that derides gentleness as the province of wussies."[57] Evangelicalism's pantheon of heroes, she notes, included William Wallace as portrayed by Mel Gibson in *Braveheart*, Oliver North, Teddy Roosevelt, Generals McArthur and Patton, and John Wayne.[58]

In the 1980s and 1990s, the main agenda was family values and, in particular, defending the patriarchal and authoritarian institution of the nuclear family. For the "Christian family guru," James Dobson, the agenda was the preservation of the patriarchal family for the sake of a preferred political vision, and for the sake of the order, discipline, and security of the nation.[59] Of course, the importance of sexual integrity within marriage, which was of paramount importance during the Clinton administration, ceased to be quite so important when it came to support for Donald Trump!

---

55. Of course, we should affirm the centrality of the cross. The problem is when we abstract Jesus's death on the cross from the rest of his life, teachings, and practices.

56. Hughes, *Myths America Lives By*, 115.

57. Du Mez, *Jesus and John Wayne*, 2–3, 97.

58. Du Mez, *Jesus and John Wayne*, 4. What strikes me as amusing in the high admiration for John Wayne is the fact that Wayne was an actor. Wayne was not a cowboy, nor was he a real Green Beret. He pretended to do those things while the camera was rolling and recording scripted action. He didn't actually do the things for which he is often regarded as a great American hero.

59. Du Mez, *Jesus and John Wayne*, 81–83.

Kristin Kobez Du Mez notes that more than any other religious demographic in America, white evangelical Protestants support preemptive war, condone the use of torture, and favor the death penalty. All of this stands in great tension with the Jesus who was unjustly killed through the death penalty and who commanded Peter to put away his sword. White evangelical Protestants have more negative views of immigrants than any other religious demographic, and 68 percent do not think the US has a responsibility to accept refugees.[60] Evangelical fears of and hostility toward the economically desperate immigrant and the refugee seeking asylum, fleeing for their lives, is out of alignment with the Jesus who once suggested that the difference between the eschatological sheep and goats was not whether or not one had said the sinner's prayer, but whether or not hospitality was shown to strangers.

---

60. Du Mez, *Jesus and John Wayne*, 3–4.

SECTION TWO

Soteriology and Biblical Narrative

Introduction

Is there is a "soteriological story-line" in the Bible? Perhaps a better way to frame the issue is to ask whether, amid the overlapping, intersecting, developing, and converging narratives, themes, and motifs present in the Bible, there is "something" identifiable that might offer resources for a very different soteriological vision. This raises the question of the unity and diversity of Scripture. Over the course of the past seventy or more years, biblical scholars and theologians have been engaged in robust conversations as to whether we can speak of the unity of Scripture at all.

Pitfall: Imposition of a Neat Master Narrative Upon the Christian Canon

Any attempt to speak of an identifiable narrative configuration or story-line in the Bible is fraught with peril. Walter Brueggemann cautions against the imposition of a neat master narrative upon the Christian canon which will inevitably function to suppress the diversity, tension, and conflict within this collection of texts. Taking the one-line drama of salvation, which moves from creation to fall to redemption and new life, as the core of the biblical faith "is excessively systematic and is imposed upon the Bible out of a scholastic grid by those who have never read the Bible closely, or who have not the patience to linger over the troublesome specificity of the biblical text."[1]

There are multiple voices in the Bible's choir and some do not sing in harmony with others. The Bible is not, simplistically speaking, a singular, seamless narrative. No one telling of the tale could capture all of the plotlines, wisdom, truth, richness, and complexity of this collection of ancient writings gathered together as our sacred Scripture. Richard Hays echoes Brueggemann in his acknowledgment that the Bible seems to fall apart into a cacophony of disparate voices:

> Even an elementary acquaintance with the contents of the Christian Bible shows that it is a multilayered collection of texts composed by many human authors in different locations in the Near East and the ancient Mediterranean world, across the time-span of a millennium. How then could its testimony about God possibly be a unified theological whole?[2]

In an article written more than thirty years ago, Bradford Hinze articulated similar concerns about the classical *Heilsgeschichte* movement, associated with names such as Oscar Cullman, Gerhard von Rad, and G. Ernest Wright, that came to prominence in the mid-twentieth century. This sensibility was characterized by a strong emphasis on the unity of Scripture, tethered to the Bible's recital of God's mighty acts in history. This perspective gave expression to the idea that the Bible's narratives disclose an order in history, the plan of God unfolded in a schema of creation, fall, election, exodus, covenant, monarchy, and exile within a distinctively Hebraic conception of history as dynamic, linear, and futurist. In the New Testament, the divine plan of salvation within human history unfolds from the life, ministry, death, and resurrection of Jesus to the nature and mission of the Church until the end of the world. In this way, salvation-history offers a grand plot for interpreting biblical and world history. The two testaments are related through a promise and fulfillment motif. While the New Testament takes up the trajectory of salvation-history from the Old Testament through transformative new interpretations, this fluidity reaches closure with the formation of the canon. Since Christ is the definitive revelation of

---

1. Brueggemann, *Texts Under Negotiation*, 69–70.

2. Hays, "Can Narrative Criticism Recover the Theological Unity of Scripture?," 197–200. Though acknowledging this reality, Hays ultimately argues that the Bible does offer a coherent, even if complex, dramatic narrative.

God, revelation is now closed and time is homogeneous from Christ to the end of the world.[3]

Hinze questions whether God's revelation, attested in Scripture, actually provides us with such a unified story-line. He agrees with those who criticize salvation-history for imposing an alien order onto the biblical canon. Salvation history represses discontinuities and unresolved conflicts within the biblical witness in the interest of identity, harmony, and continuity. Hinze asks whether an interpreter can feasibly isolate or posit "the" narrative of salvation in the Bible without, in fact, imposing the interpreter's own construction, shaped by his or her theological interests.[4]

Salvation-History vs. Apocalyptic

One of the more interesting theological conflicts of the early twenty-first century has been fought primarily on the terrain of Pauline studies, though theologians have followed biblical scholars into the fray. The conflict has been between a more nuanced salvation-historical sensibility and an approach that has appropriated the label of apocalyptic. Apocalyptic readings of Paul emphasize the "radical invasiveness of the Christ-event" and, therefore, the discontinuity between the advent of Jesus Christ and Israel's history and covenant relationship with God, the law, and Israel's sacred Scriptures. Salvation-historical readings emphasize the continuity between the Christ-event and Israel's history.[5] Edwin Van Driel points out that thinkers associated with this new apocalyptic sensibility view the salvation-historical approach as compromising the singularity of the gospel of Christ's coming as God's apocalyptic invasion of this world by presenting Jesus as the climax of God's covenantal relationship with Israel, such that Jesus's story is only a subplot in the story of Israel. But advocates of this more recent salvation-historical sensibility argue that the new apocalyptic seems to view God's act in Christ as abrogating the previous salvific presence of God in and through the covenant with Israel.[6]

---

3. Hinze, "End of Salvation History," 229; Miller, "Dragon Myths and Biblical Theology," 38.
4. Hinze, "End of Salvation History," 234–36, 244.
5. Rose, "Paul, Christ, and Time."
6. Van Driel, "Climax of the Covenant vs Apocalyptic Invasion," 7–8.

Section Two: Soteriology and Biblical Narrative

Apocalyptic

For scholars associated with this new apocalyptic sensibility, God breaks into history in Jesus Christ independent of God's age-old promises tied to Israel's history.[7] In his commentary on Galatians, J. Louis Martyn argues that for Paul, Jesus Christ represents God's liberating invasion of an enslaved cosmos. Martyn sees Paul's argument as one in which Christ's death on the cross is the "dissolution" of the cosmos and, indeed, Martyn seems to suggest, creation itself, represented by the elemental spirits of the cosmos (Gal 4:3, 9) to which humans are enslaved. The cross and resurrection thereby introduce into the continuity of human history a fissure that marked the beginning of an entirely new eschatological reality.[8]

Douglas Campbell acknowledges that the starkness of this apocalyptic reading of Paul seems to produce a "scandal of discontinuity" that cuts the Christian community off from the narratives of Israel.[9] For Martyn, Christ brings about the death of the old order, not the climax or renewal of Israel's covenant. Martyn places great weight upon Galatians 3 for his particular version of an apocalyptic theology. Martyn finds Paul's identification, in Galatians 3, of Christ as the singular seed of Abraham, rather than the people of Israel as the collective/plural seed of Abraham, to be highly significant. For Martyn, Paul sees a radical discontinuity between God's promises to and covenant with Abraham and his covenant with Israel, featuring the law mediated to Moses. The continuity runs from the covenant with and promises to Abraham to Christ, but through the discontinuity of God's covenant history with Israel, which includes the law. For Martyn, this spells the end of *Heilsgeschichte* as a linear history of the people of God prior to Christ, since the law is one of the enslaving powers.[10]

Salvation-History

On the more recent salvation-historical approach associated with N. T. Wright and Richard Hays, among others, there is a single continuous narrative of Scripture which moves from Adam through the stories of Abraham and Israel until it reaches its climax in Jesus the Messiah. In response to a world gone awry, given expression in Genesis 3–11, God called and entered

---

7. Tillig, "Paul, 'Apocalyptic' and 'Salvation-History' Approaches."

8. Davis, "Challenge of Apocalyptic to Modern Theology," 38, 40–42; Martyn, *Galatians*, 125–40.

9. Campbell, *Quest for Paul's Gospel*, 63.

10. Rose, "Paul, Christ, and Time," 9; Martyn, "Events in Galatia," 174.

into covenant relationship with Abraham and his descendants, the people of Israel. Through this people, God would rescue the world from its plight and bring blessing. However, Israel could not live up to God's purposes; therefore, the task of Jesus the Messiah would be to offer God the obedience Israel should have offered. Jesus becomes the faithful Israelite through whom God's single plan of salvation can continue and the blessing which comes through Israel reaches the nations of the earth.[11]

In this new salvation-historical approach, there is a greater emphasis on continuity, with Christ viewed as a completion of previous frameworks deemed anticipatory or unfulfilled. Christian Scripture is unified, Richard Hays argues, because the New Testament reaffirms Israel's *Shema* by bearing witness to one God: the God of Abraham, Isaac, and Jacob, and the God and Father of Jesus Christ. Hays argues that Scripture can be understood in light of the church's rule of faith as a complex but finally coherent dramatic narrative. For example, in a recent essay, Hays argued that attention to the narrative pattern found in the book of Hebrews, the Johannine corpus, Paul, and Matthew reveals a theological and narrative coherence in their understanding of the purpose and effect of Jesus's death on the cross as an act of radical faithfulness to God's redemptive purpose and that Jesus's act of faithfulness provides a normative paradigm for the ongoing narratively shaped identity of those who trust Christ as Savior and follow him as Lord.[12]

Critique of the Apocalyptic Trajectory Associated with J. Louis Martyn

It is tempting to suppose that one may identify one's theological perspective as an apocalyptic sensibility only if one follows the line of Pauline interpretation associated with J. Louis Martyn. But, as Benjamin Blackwell, John K. Goodrich, and Jason Maston point out, "There is little consensus regarding what the label 'apocalyptic' actually suggests about Paul's theological perspective."[13]

Michael Bird argues that the negation of Israel's history proposed by Martyn is certainly not a feature of actual apocalyptic literature, which is concerned with the fulfillment of what God has planned for Israel. Israel's election is never questioned. Israel is essential to the drama of redemption.

---

11. Wright, *Justification*, 104–6, 114; *Paul and the Faithfulness of God*, 117, 120; Van Driel, "Climax of the Covenant vs Apocalyptic Invasion," 9–10.

12. Hays, "Can Narrative Criticism Recover the Theological Unity of Scripture?," 193, 200.

13. Blackwell et al., "Paul and the Apocalyptic Imagination," 3–5.

The seers who wrote the apocalypses were convinced that Israel's traditions could be reinterpreted and rehearsed in new imaginative, and sometimes very strange ways, but it is always centered on what God is going to do with Israel. Apocalyptic is driven by the conviction that God would save his people, vindicate them, and make them great among the gentiles.[14]

Sometimes, Douglas Campbell adopts a more mediating position between the two allegedly opposing readings of Paul. Though he qualifies this acknowledgment by stating that it is not the central component of Paul's thought, Campbell acknowledges that there is a "salvation-historical" component to Paul's theology, with narrative continuities between the Old and New Testaments. Adam, a generic figure, is deceived by the evil intelligence of sin itself, and thereby sin enters creation permanently, taking up residence within the very constitution of humanity, "the Flesh." With sin, death also arrives. Sin and death produce the fundamental human condition of slavery within a kingdom ruled by evil forces. All of creation, human and non-human, has been joined to humanity's enslavement (Rom 8:19–22). Though the law is not itself sinful, it deepens the tragic human and cosmic situation and is impotent to alleviate it. Paul's deeply pessimistic account of human incapacity has similarities to 4 Ezra. The solution is that God's son, Jesus Christ, enters into the oppressed state of humanity, in obedience to God the Father, assumes its enslaved nature, and dies. But he is raised to new life by the divine, life-giving Spirit and exalted to the Father's right hand, where he now reigns, judges, and intercedes.[15]

The narrative continuity is highlighted as Campbell argues that Paul has fused together two Jewish narratives into one christological narrative of descent and ascent. The first is a narrative of debasement and execution drawing on martyrological notions. The second is that of royal enthronement and glorification that is messianic and eschatological. This narrative synthesis results in this narrative of salvation: Jesus entered into a state characterized by the story of Adam, dies obediently within this state as a martyr in accordance with God's will, and is raised to new life and enthroned on high as Israel's king. The Pauline text in which the fusion of these two narratives is most evident is Philippians 2:5–11, which draws on the martyrological tradition of the atoning value of the martyr's death, an idea that is present in 2 Maccabees 6 and 7.[16]

---

14. Bird, "Invasive Story."
15. Campbell, *Quest for Paul's Gospel*, 27, 57–58.
16. Campbell, *Quest for Paul's Gospel*, 58.

Introduction

Conclusion: A Way to Think About the Bible's Continuities and Discontinuities

Hinze proposes the replacement of the category of salvation-history with that of the economy of salvation. The manifold testimonies in the Scriptures, as well as early Christian writings, witness to the one economy of salvation. We have good reasons, biblical, liturgical, and creedal, for affirming the universality of God's salvific design. There are indeed recurring and interrelated references to key episodes in the narratives about Israel and Jesus and the community of disciples that are constitutive of the economy of salvation insofar as they construe and convey God's salvific purpose. Hinze insists that Christians must speak of the life, death, and resurrection of Jesus as the core and norm of the Christian faith, but this does not require isolating one singular grand plot for this story, whether deemed to be present in or above or below the text, which is stable in design or reception. This sort of claim betrays the richness and diversity of the biblical witness. A unified plan, whether linear or labyrinthine, is beyond human ken.[17]

Hinze suggests that the Bible offers us fragments or traces of an economy of salvation. These fragments and traces are given in the intratexual web of the Scripture world and, as such, the Scriptures can be understood as a fragmented whole. However, this implies that there remains an indeterminacy and openness in the Bible and in the history of its reception.[18]

When it comes to interpretation, there are a variety of ways of construing and receiving these narratives. Within the Bible itself, certain narratives are sometimes repeated, at other times revised or reconfigured, in order to draw out further implications of a narrative tradition in a new situation or sometimes even subverting earlier claims within the received tradition. Drawing on Jewish scholar Michael Fishbane's work on the rabbinic tradition of interpretation, Hinze notes that in the "traditioning" process, continuities and discontinuities are intertwined. The development and reform of a tradition are often supported by arguments claiming that a given change will enable the community to remain in continuity with other aspects of the tradition. Developments or reforms that are discontinuous with some facets of inherited tradition often yield deeper continuities.[19]

Hinze insists that the Bible's meaning is not merely a product of the Bible's internal or "intratexual" web of meaning but also a product of its interpretation and reception, which always takes place in intertextual ways

---

17. Hinze, "End of Salvation History," 242–43.
18. Hinze, "End of Salvation History," 242–44.
19. Hinze, "End of Salvation History," 235–36; Hinze refers to the work of Fishbane, *Biblical Interpretation in Ancient Israel*, 408, 435–40.

and therefore, in different social and cultural spheres of production of meaning. Both in the production of the various biblical texts and in the interpretive reception of these texts, there is no isolated and pristine process of revelation. These texts are revelatory precisely within a complex set of cultural and social relationships.[20]

Hinze maintains that the Bible testifies to God's economy of salvation, but this economy is not a comprehensive map of human history. God is always calling his people into uncharted territory. This pilgrimage must be guided by the Bible, but interpreting the Bible for faithfulness to Christ in ever new circumstances is more than re-description of the world of the Bible. In this spirit, Brad Hinze suggests that in the church's ongoing traditioning process, the Holy Spirit might lead God's people down paths that are in faithful continuity with God's revelation in Jesus Christ but not clearly indicated within the Scripture's own narratives and other sacred texts.[21] Hinze concludes:

> [Christian theology] cannot abandon protology, teleology, and eschatology. Rather it is the responsibility of Christian theology not only to transmit cherished narratives, but also to reconfigure them in a manner that is faithful to the biblical witness and responsive to the present situation. In this task, theology is properly understood as contextual, practical (as in phronesis), and rhetorical.[22]

My own argument is tethered to an apocalyptic soteriology, but does not posit the more radical discontinuity between Jesus Christ and God's covenant relationship with Israel associated with J. Louis Martyn and others. In making this argument, I will seek to appropriate Bradford Hinze's arguments in an apocalyptic sensibility as well.

One the one hand, the New Testament attests to Jesus Christ as the Alpha and the Omega (Rev 21:6; 22:13), the one in whom all things hold together, the one through whom and for whom all things have been created, the sovereign Lord of the cosmos, the one whose death and resurrection were for the purpose of reconciling all things to himself (Col 1:15–20). Jesus Christ is the meaning of the narrative of salvation. God's revelation in Christ is unsurpassable in that Jesus Christ is God's eternal self-utterance in the flesh (John 1:1–5, 14).

---

20. Hinze, "End of Salvation History," 243–44.
21. Hinze, "End of Salvation History," 238–39, 245.
22. Hinze, "End of Salvation History," 242–44.

However, Jesus is the not only the Alpha, the agent of creation, not only is he the divine self-utterance incarnate in human history, but he is also the Messiah, the Omega, the one whose reality is eschatological.

Even though Jesus is the one in whom the fullness of God dwells bodily (Col 1:19), *our human* theological understandings of the full meaning of Jesus's life, death, resurrection, ascension, enthronement, and return remain radically incomplete. A kind of apophatic reserve is appropriate. Since the eschatological future remains future, we have not been given a finished narrative of salvation within Scripture but rather one that remains open to a future that will be Christ, but whose full contours and dimensions are unknown to us who, for now, see through a glass darkly. Precisely how eschatological judgment, the eschatological healing and transfiguration of all things, the dead are raised, and all things are put right remain enigmas to us. We do not know precisely how, in all of its details, all things will be finally seen truly in relationship to Christ. We do not know exactly how all things will be reconciled to Christ or how his cosmic Lordship will be realized eschatologically.

The biblical narrative itself is one characterized by extraordinarily surprising twists and turns from a God who always turns out to be ever greater than previously imagined. We should also anticipate that the eschatological future might be "wilder than we could ever imagine" and characterized by so much that is presently "unanticipatable." Of course, our faith that Christ is who Scripture says he is, the one who is the very self-expression of God, the one who embodies God's purposes, means that this future will be in radically faithful continuity with God's revelation in Christ as attested in the New Testament. Yet the shape of that continuity may be unbelievably surprising.

Jesus's first followers asked the risen Jesus Christ whether he would *at this time* restore the kingdom to Israel. They were simply told, "It is not for you to know." Instead, they were commissioned to bear witness (Acts 1:6–8). This post-resurrection vignette indicates that the unfolding of the ongoing narrative of salvation is not one in which we have been given a comprehensive roadmap. How human history will unfold between Christ's resurrection and God's eschatological future remains unrevealed, and the meaning of what has already occurred between roughly 33 CE and the present moment in history is not yet illuminated with the fuller light of the eschatological unveiling of the truth about the totality of human history.

A narrative that *anticipates* an eschatological fulfillment is not a narrative in which there is closure because the eschatological fulfillment has not yet happened. How the story will continue to unfold in human history, and how that continual unfolding will shed light upon the canonical narrative, is open to further acts of interpretation and performance.

Here, Bradford Hinze's argument that the Bible itself does not offer closure, does not offer an "intratextual" world of meaning, is crucially important. The Bible's meaning is not confined to "the Bible" itself but emerges in ongoing acts of interpretation in ever new cultural settings. The reality gestured toward in Acts 1:6–8 parallels Hinze's point that God is always calling his people into uncharted territory and that the Holy Spirit might lead God's people down paths that are in faithful continuity with God's revelation in Jesus Christ but not so clearly indicated within the Scripture itself.[23]

The Bible, the ecclesial community, and ever new circumstances mean that the story continues and is unfolding in ways that may be in faithful continuity with, but are not entirely circumscribed by, the Bible itself. We interpret the Bible, praying for the Spirit's illumination, in light of our efforts to evaluate where we have been and where we believe we are called to go in light of present realities, struggles, and sufferings. It is in this way that we open ourselves to God to continue the story through God's people as we encounter novel realities.

---

23. Hinze, "End of Salvation History," 238–39, 245.

CHAPTER THREE

First Testament Soteriological Trajectories

OFTEN, THE BIBLE'S "STORIED framework"[1] is described as a "creation-fall-redemption-eschatological fulfillment" schema. But these terms, standing alone, are open-ended abstractions, a blank theological page that might be filled in with a wide array of interpretive understandings. Attempts to specify "the" narrative configuration of Scripture are always interpretive conjectures that inevitably highlight and "foreground" some narratives and texts of the Bible and inevitably deemphasize or "background" other narratives and texts.

With these caveats in mind, I will seek to identify certain lines of development, trajectories, continuities, and reinterpretations within Scripture itself. Within the pages of the Bible, one finds a "traditioning" process in those biblical texts that provide interpretations and reinterpretations that develop further certain motifs found in earlier texts and traditions. Here, it is important to point out that I am reading the First Testament from the vantage point of my interpretation of the New Testament.

In the next several chapters, I will propose that there is a soteriological vision that appears, reemerges in different variations, and which provides the frame of reference for most of the writings of the New Testament. As important as the motifs of creation and fall are, I will start with the theme of empire. The primary focus in this chapter will be upon four motifs: empire, covenant and justice, God's justice and Israel's monarchy, and the emergence of what is almost, but not quite yet, eschatological hope.

---

1. I am using this term cautiously, in light of the considerations I raised in the introduction to section 2.

Empire

The Bible is obsessed with politics and economics. Even very serious readers of the Bible miss this because they are not looking for it. In our day, we are accustomed to thinking that religion and politics belong in separate compartments of reality, and since the Bible is about God, it must be about religion. However, a central theme in the Bible is God's people living either under the threat, or directly under the dominative boot, of empire. The Bible considered as a whole is a counter-imperial document. Throughout the Bible, God's people wrestle with how they are to order their communal life together in ways that model an alternative to empire. In the First Testament, we encounter Egypt and, later, the Assyrian empire, which invaded, conquered, and ended the Northern kingdom of Israel somewhere between 740 and 732 BCE. The southern kingdom of Judah and the city of Jerusalem fell, in the early sixth century BCE, to the Babylonian Empire. The temple was destroyed and many of the people were exiled and resettled in Babylon. The return from exile, around 538 BCE, followed soon upon the heels of the defeat of the Babylonians and the emergence of the Medes and Persians as the new imperial power in the region. Alexander the Great ended the imperial dominance of the Medes and the Persians and the Jewish Maccabean revolt took place during the reign of Antiochus Epiphanes, an heir to a portion of Alexander's empire. And of course, the entire New Testament takes place on the terrain occupied by the Roman Empire. These empires are not merely decorations on the stage on which the biblical drama is played out. They are central to the unfolding of the story. Empire is God's great adversary. In fact, as belief in Satan emerged in Jewish faith, Satan was understood as the animating spirit of imperial oppression.

Salvation in the Bible has a lot to do with the defeat of this world's imperial powers, who falsely and idolatrously claim to be the objects of ultimate allegiance but are, in reality, purveyors of injustice and oppression.

Egypt

Toward the end of Genesis, we find the fascinating story of Joseph, one of the twelve sons of Jacob and, indeed, his favorite son. Because of his father's blatant favoritism, Joseph internalized a sense of superiority to his brothers. When he foolishly and arrogantly told his brothers of overnight dreams of a future in which Joseph would rule over his eleven brothers, who would bow down and pay him homage, his resentful brothers sold him to Egyptian slave traders. Joseph was imprisoned when he was falsely accused of making an improper sexual advance on his owner's wife and languished for years without reasonable hope of release. But his divinely given gift of interpreting dreams took him to the royal palace, where he successfully interpreted two of the Pharaoh's dreams after Pharaoh's magicians, prophets, and diviners were unable to do so. Joseph was elevated to second in command in the Egyptian empire, where his wisdom, foresight, and planning saved the Egyptian people from starvation during the seven year famine that was anticipated in Pharaoh's dream.

This story has all the elements to keep an audience's attention: sexual intrigue, family dysfunction, betrayal, pride, a rise to power from the depths of misery and defeat, and, best of all, family reconciliation after Joseph forgave his brothers and the entire family was reunited and saved from starvation.

But lost to many readers, because Joseph is seen as a Bible hero, is a more sinister imperial underside to this story. On the positive side, Joseph had the foresight to store food by requiring the Egyptian people to contribute a percentage of their crop's yield during the seven years of bounteous harvests in preparation for the seven year famine. However, Genesis 47 tells us that during the famine, he extracted all of the money from the Egyptian people in exchange for the food that they themselves had provided to the ruling powers for storage. After their money was gone, Joseph exploited their hunger and desperation by requiring them to exchange their livestock, which, of course, represented future production of food for small farmers. When Pharaoh's kingdom had acquired all of the livestock, Joseph required the people to purchase their survival by trading their land for food. Now, the royal household and the Egyptian priestly class owned all of the land. The people were allowed to farm the land they once owned, essentially as tenant farmers, with seed purchased from Joseph, on the condition that twenty percent of their harvest belonged to the government. Here we see the insidious economy of empire. Land ownership and wealth are concentrated in the hands of the few. Most of the people are reduced to the status of landless peasants, day laborers, or tenet farmers, who work the land but retain only enough to keep themselves alive at a subsistence level.

A few generations later, the Hebrew people become the victims of empire. Seeing their rapid reproduction rates, a new pharaoh became apprehensive. Here we see the "scapegoating" mechanism that often comes into play when rulers and people groups are motivated by fear of an ethnic "other" in their midst. In the name of "national security," Pharaoh enslaved the Hebrew people in an effort to preempt the remote possibility that they might ally themselves with an enemy nation in a future war. Ruthless

Section Two: Soteriology and Biblical Narrative

imposition of harsh labor was followed by an attempted gradual genocide when Pharaoh commanded every Jewish male baby to be killed.[2]

Exodus one celebrates the courage, cunning, and "civil disobedience" of two Hebrew midwives, Shiprah and Puah, who, because they feared God, refused to carry out Pharaoh's orders. They used clever deception to thwart his plans. When summoned by Pharaoh to explain why they had not killed male infants, they "reported" that Hebrew women are so healthy that they give birth before the midwives arrives. While truth telling is usually the morally right thing to do, in this extreme situation, their deception was praiseworthy because they saved the lives of the innocent. God blessed them for their willingness to resist Pharaoh (Exod 1:15–21).

The exodus story introduces a theme that runs throughout the Bible: God's opposition to and conflict with empire. The powerful ancient near eastern empires were both oppressive political orders and religious systems. Ancient Egypt was a sacral order. Society, state, culture, nature, cosmos, and religion, Gerhard Lohfink points out, were bound together into a unity personified in the person of the pharaoh and his relationship with his divine patron, Horus. Pharaoh was the divine king, whose relationship to the pantheon of deities was thought to have secured the prosperity and security of Egypt and even of the cosmos itself.[3]

The Exodus story repudiates this ancient religious and political imagination. God is not aligned with the powerful empires and other political powers that rule this world in abusive ways. God identifies instead with the people who are mistreated by this world's powerful. This God hears the cries of those treated as non-persons. As Walter Brueggemann points out, Yahwism celebrated the God who broke the bow of the mighty and placed the poor on thrones (1 Sam 2:1–10; Exod 15:1–18).[4]

In the ancient near east, what happens on the cosmic level, the sphere of deities and other sorts of "spiritual" beings, was believed to be reflected by "on-the-ground" political and social realities. God's deliverance of the

---

2. Exodus chapter one should serve as a perennial warning about God's opposition to racial and ethnic fear and hatred. A tragic pattern throughout human history has been the tendency of people groups to fear, scapegoat, vilify, and inflict violence on minority groups in their midst.

3. Lohfink, *Does God Need the Church?*, 68; Hanson, *Political History of the Bible in America*, 159.

4. Brueggemann, *Theology of the Old Testament*, 178–79; Grimsrud, *Instead of Atonement*, 22; Hanson, *Dawn of Apocalyptic*, 14–15; *Political History of the Bible in America*, 145–46; Verhey, *Remembering Jesus*, 355.

Israelites from economic slavery and the defeat of the gods of Egypt (Exod 12:12) were understood to be two dimensions of the same reality.[5]

Throughout the Old Testament, God's acts of deliverance were seen as divine victories over disordering powers, including politically oppressive powers. Ancient Near Eastern mythological imagery of divine victory over the sea or sea monsters or dragons, along with symbolism of the underworld, death, chaos, and nothingness, are found throughout the First Testament to articulate Israel's conviction that YHWH alone overcomes chaotic forces and brings life-affirming order. This theme is powerfully present in the story of the parting of the waters of the Red or Reed Sea (Exod 15). YHWH saves his people by delivering them through the sea, an ancient near eastern symbol of chaos, from Pharaoh's armies and chariots and therefore, from Egypt's death-dealing imperial order.[6]

This theme of God's opposition to and ultimate victory over empire reappears throughout the biblical canon! In the apocalyptic texts that find their way into the canon, God's defeat of empire is the culminating act of human history prior to the establishment of God's new order of peace and justice on earth.

Covenant

It is highly significant that in Israel's foundational narrative, God identifies Godself as the God who liberates from oppression, the God who delivered the Israelites from mistreatment at the hands of an evil imperial power (Exod 20:2). Who is God? God is the one who delivers from oppression and bondage so that God's people might flourish! Israel's core confession of who God is and what God has done is articulated in Deut 26:5b–9a. God is the God who acted when the Egyptians mistreated and oppressed the Israelites, delivering the Hebrew people with a mighty hand and then gave the people possession of a fertile land upon which they could flourish.

God's response to the threat posed by human rebellion and wickedness to God's good creation was to call forth a people to live in covenant relationship with God, who would provide a testimony to divine righteousness, goodness, and compassion as the true hope for humanity.[7]

In the book of Exodus, rescue from Egypt is followed by the giving of the covenant at Mt. Sinai. The form of the covenant resembled ancient

---

5. Brueggemann, *Theology of the Old Testament*, 179.
6. Lohfink, *Does God Need the Church?*, 68.
7. Hanson, *Political History of the Bible in America*, 486.

Hittite suzerainty treaties.[8] This kind of treaty was usually far from equitable or just. Typically, the dominant party, the king of a nation who has conquered or is threatening military action to conquer, sets the terms for the weaker covenant partner, the vassal. Or sometimes, the vassal king and his nation have been threatened by one powerful nation and seek protection from another powerful nation at the price of a relationship of subordination to a dominant nation. In either case, the vassal king must abide by the terms of the covenant, which typically involved paying a hefty tribute of taxes, valuable raw materials, and sometimes the nation's own citizens as slaves or conscripted laborers as well as providing military support when the dominant nation goes to war.

The point of appropriating the cultural form of the suzerainty treaty was to emphasize that YHWH alone is the one true king to whom Israel owed absolute allegiance and obedience (Exod 19:5–8). The keystone of the covenant is the first commandment in the Decalogue, to worship YHWH alone (Exod 20:3–5; 23:13; 34:14). But unlike the typical suzerainty treaty, this relationship is not exploitive. Israel was liberated from a false and oppressive ruler in order to be bound to the world's true sovereign, a good Lord who wills for his people to flourish. The foundation of the covenant is God's own love and faithfulness (*hesed*). God's commands, unlike Pharaoh's, produce dignity, true freedom, and well-being.[9] God's will is not to diminish Israel by extracting their resources and enslaving them (e.g., Lev 25:42). It is the false gods and their imperial representatives on earth who enslave. As the servant to God, Israel must not be a slave or servant to anyone else (Lev 25:42). God's purpose is blessing, protection, and the gift of the land upon which they might dwell in peace, security, and corporate prosperity.

In stark contrast to the economies of empire, land was broadly distributed. In an agrarian society, land is capital. Land meant access to the resources needed to live and flourish. After Israel's narrated conquest of the land of promise,[10] land was divided between the tribes, with the exception

---

8. Mendenhall, *Law and Covenant in Israel and the Ancient Near East*.

9. Brueggemann, *Theology of the Old Testament*, 182–83.

10. Of course, the narratives of Israel's violent conquest of the land of Canaan, including, in some cases, the genocidal practices of *herem* warfare, have troubled Christian interpreters of the Bible for thousands of years. Recent scholarship on Israelite origins has led many First Testament scholars to argue that many of the violent scenes, especially in the book of Joshua, were not actual historical accounts but rather, gave expression to aspects of Israel's theological self-understanding. Significant evidence, much of it archeological, suggests that the vast majority of the tribal groups that came together to form the Israelite people did not enter the land of Canaan from the outside, but were groups who had long lived in the land. Evidence includes artifacts like pottery, as well as lack of evidence of a massive invasion and displacement of the original

of the Levites, who were given cities to inhabit throughout the territories of the other tribes. Within each tribe, the land was divided among the clans and families, guided by the ideal of access to land for everyone (Josh 13–21).

Covenant faithfulness was to be embodied in a communal way of life characterized by social and economic justice and compassion of the people for one another. If the poor are being trodden upon, Yahweh is no longer being properly worshiped (e.g., Isa 58).[11]

The covenant and its law codes were meant to be the charter for a new social project, a "counter-imperial" social order. Economic justice was one of the central preoccupations of the Torah, as well as the prophets. There are a wide range of economic justice provisions, some of which were designed to provide a safety net for those who did not own land or for persons at risk of losing land through indebtedness. Israelites were commanded not to

---

inhabitants of the land that would be incompatible with reading the book of Joshua as a factual account. The story of Moses's leadership of the escape from Egypt may well have been the product of the authentic memory and experience of a portion of the people who joined up with the other tribes composing the people of Israel, but not of the whole people who became the Israelites. As diverse tribal groups came together to form one people, they likely appropriated the stories and experiences from each group as their own, as stories belonging to the whole people of God.

The majority of the tribal groups who formed the people of Israel were likely Canaanites who asserted independence from the kings of the Canaanite city-states and broke away by fleeing to the hill country to form their own village-based ways of life. In doing so, they also broke from the idolatrous faith of their neighbors. One of the classical accounts of Israelite origins, though far from the last scholarly word on the topic, is Gottwald, *Tribes of Yahweh*.

All of this suggests that the narratives of a massive military invasion of the land, resulting in the slaughter or expulsion of the people who previously inhabited the land, should actually be read as stories with the theological purpose of teaching the Israelites to understand themselves as recipients of the gift of the land from a gracious God and therefore, bound in covenant to worship Yahweh alone, instead of seeking agricultural success from Canaanite fertility deities such as Ba'al and Asherah. Jerome Creach argues, for example, that we should look to the way the book of Deuteronomy functioned to support King Josiah's religious reform program. Josiah's reform program included the destruction of pagan sanctuaries, alters and priests. Deuteronomy's accounts of the complete elimination of the people groups who worshiped these deities were intended to inspire, not acts of genocidal warfare, but complete devotion to the task of eradicating all pagan elements from Israelite society (2 Kgs 23:4–20). Creach, *Violence in Scripture*, 97–111.

Of course, some of the portrayals of God in Deuteronomy and Joshua are troubling whether these events happened or not and the issues raised cannot be resolved here. For some good introductory scholarship that wrestles with the complex questions of Israelite origins and the meaning of violent portrayals of God, in addition to the books mentioned above, see Seibert, *Disturbing Divine Behavior*. For a different perspective, see Copan, *Is God a Moral Monster?*.

11. Lohfink, *Does God Need the Church?*, 8; Brueggemann, *Theology of the Old Testament*, 184.

reap the entire harvest of their fields, but to leave the edges unharvested so that the poor and the resident alien could gather food for themselves and their families (Lev 23:22; Deut 14:28–29; 24:20–21). Lending with interest to the poor and destitute was forbidden (Exod 22:25; Lev 25:35–37; Deut 23:19–20) in order to minimize a major source of impoverishment and misery among the peasant class, the inability to pay back loans incurred in purchasing basic essentials such as clothing, food, and seed for next season's planting. Israelites were not to burden debtors with interest nor hold essential goods, such as a poor person's cloak, which doubled as his or her blanket at night, as collateral.[12]

The Jubilee year occurred every fifty years (Lev 25). If a household had economic setbacks sufficient to require the head of the household to sell the land in order to survive, the land could not be sold in perpetuity because God is the true owner of the land and dwelling on the land is God's gift (Lev 25:23). Instead, the land was sold only for the number of years between the date of its purchase and the next Jubilee year. Then, the land was to be returned to the family that originally owned it. The sale price was to be adjusted in accordance with the amount of time the new owner would possess the land because God's will is that the Israelites do not take advantage of each other but instead deal justly and fairly (Lev 25:17). The social and economic objective of this provision was to prevent the concentration of land, over the course of a few generations, in the hands of fewer and fewer families, creating both a landed aristocracy and increasing numbers of landless peasants.

Every seventh year is the Sabbatical year (Deut 15:1–11; Lev 25:1–6, Exod 23:10–11). Persons forced to sell themselves into indentured servitude to survive were to be set free and sent away with sufficient resources to allow them to get back on their feet again (Deut 15:12–15). Unpaid debts were to be forgiven every seven years. The book of Deuteronomy also closes a loophole. God's people are called to be generous in lending to those in need and are warned against refusing to lend to their poor neighbors when the Sabbatical year of debt forgiveness was near (Deut 15:9–10).

These law codes were designed to provide a safety net for the poor, destitute, and economically vulnerable. Yet, as Gerhard Lohfink points out, even though these laws are meant to prevent grotesque inequalities, they also realistically account for and seek to mitigate the continual drift of any society into rich and poor, masters and slaves:

> For example, if a farmer gets into trouble through bad harvests or bad management and needs a loan in order to be able to

12. Hanson, *Political History of the Bible in America*, 151.

continue farming, the law in Deuteronomy 15:7–11 steps in, urging fellow Israelites to provide an interest-free loan. However, if the debt is too great and the debtor is forced to work for someone else as a day-laborer, the law in Deuteronomy 24:14–15 secures the worker a daily wage. If the person in question is still not able to pay back the debt, Deuteronomy 24:12–13 requires a humane way of dealing with the deposit given: For example, if a poor man has given his cloak as a deposit, it must be returned to him at sundown so that he can cover himself in the cold hours of the night. If the debt becomes so enormous that the result is seizure of the person, that is, debt slavery, one of the most commonplace and yet severe institutions found everywhere in the ancient Near East, according to Deuteronomy 15:1–6 this may not be imposed during a Sabbatical Year. And if this enslavement for debt occurs outside the sabbatical year, according to Deuteronomy 15:12–18 the debt slavery must end in the next sabbatical year, and the freed Israelite must . . . be equipped with cattle and seed in order to build a new life.[13]

A motif that runs through the entire Bible is God's special concern for persons who are economically vulnerable. Compassion for the economically vulnerable was central, not peripheral, to Israel's vision of what it meant to be in right covenant relationship with God. The extremely high number of texts in which God commands his people to take care of those who would otherwise be destitute indicates that this is a matter precious to the heart of God.[14] Throughout the Old Testament, the Israelites are enjoined to take measures to ensure access to livelihood and food for the widow, the orphan, and the resident alien. Of the non-Israelite residing in Israel, Lev 19:33–34, echoed by Exod 22:21–23 and 23:9, enjoins God's people to "love them as yourself." Humane treatment of the outsider is what faithful Israelites should do because this behavior mirrors God's compassion when Israel was an alien people treated inhospitably in Egypt. And the God who responded in mercy to the cry of Hebrew slaves abused by Egyptian taskmasters will not ignore the cries of widows and orphans in Israel who are victimized by members of their own community (Exod 2:21–24).[15]

If we read the Torah in search of soteriological insight, we just might see the beginnings of a vision of the meaning of salvation. God not only

---

13. Lohfink, *Does God Need the Church?*, 83–84.

14. For example, see Exod 22:21; 23:9; Lev 19:33; Deut 10:18; 24:17–18; 26:12; 27:19; Ps 10:14; 68:5; Isa 1:23; 10:1–2; Jer 7:4–12; 22:3; Zech 7:9–10; Mal 3:5.

15. Hanson, *Political History of the Bible in America*, 150–51; Grimsrud, *Instead of Atonement*, 22.

delivers from oppression but establishes for himself a people who live together in ways designed to promote justice and compassion for the needy and destitute. Salvation *is* this communal quality of life given powerful and paradigmatic expression in Isaiah 58. What does it mean to be God's people, living in covenant relationship with God? It means devotion to mutual care and concern, a love for neighbor going far beyond legal obligations. At issue in Isaiah 58 is what it means to know, seek, and please God. When the people complain about what they perceived as God's lack of response to their day of fasting, the prophet identifies the hypocrisy at the heart of their worship and invites them to a form of worship pleasing to God. The Israelites are upbraided for exploiting their workers and fist-fights with one another on the very day in which they claimed to be involved in a national fast to seek God's favor. Through the prophet, the people are informed that the kind of fasting God desires includes breaking the yoke of injustice and oppression to set oppressed persons free, feeding the hungry, clothing the naked, and providing the wandering homeless person with shelter.

The Covenant (and the Prophets): God Is a God of Justice

God commands his people not to take bribes and pervert justice that is due to the poor in civil court (Exod 23:6; Deut 16:19–20), not to take a widow's garment as collateral for a loan, since a widow who would offer her garment as her only collateral is clearly destitute (Deut 24:17). In Deuteronomy, provisions are made for the protection of runaway slaves (23:15–16), against the seizure of a poor person's property as equity for a loan (24:10–13), and for prompt payment of wages to the poor (24:14–15).[16] God's very character is justice, and God expects this justice to be reflected in the actions and political arrangements of his people. God is not partial, does not take bribes, executes justice for the widow and orphan, loves the foreigner, and provides food and clothing for the foreigner in need (Deut 10:17–19). For God, the treatment of the widows and orphans is a litmus test of righteousness and justice (Isa 1:17).[17]

The writings of the prophets reveal a God who is a relentless opponent of oppression and abuse. The books of Amos, Micah, Hosea, Isaiah, and Jeremiah feature words of judgment against economic injustices and the accumulation of great land-holdings by the wealthy. Amos railed against those who sold the needy into debt slavery for a debt no greater than the cost of a "pair of sandals," thereby trampling the heads of the poor into the

16. Brueggemann, *Theology of the Old Testament*, 188–89.
17. Brueggemann, *Isaiah*, 22–23.

dust (Amos 2:6). He spoke scathing words of judgment against the wealthy living in great luxury and indifferent to the plight of their poor fellow Israelites. More specifically, Amos condemned those who reclined on beds of ivory and was ruthless in his criticism of the wealthy and greedy women of the Northern Kingdom, calling them, in unflattering language, "fat cows of Bashan" (Amos 2:6-7).

Prophets railed against merchants who cheated the poor (Hos 12:7-9; Amos 4:1-3; 6:1; Mic 6:11). They condemned corrupt judges, who took bribes from the powerful in exchange for judgments in their favor as they cheated the poor (Isa 5:23; 10:1-4; Ezek 22:12; Amos 5:10-15; Mic 7:3).[18] Micah 2:12 condemned those who engaged in fraud to acquire land unjustly. Isaiah 10:1-2 condemned those who enacted laws and rendered legal decisions designed to perpetuate injustice against the poor, especially the economically vulnerable widows and orphans.

Ambiguities of Monarchy

Israel was originally a loose federation of tribes and kinship networks. This was an "anti-imperial" alternative to the city-state system of ancient agrarian civilizations, in which the people were required to yield up a percentage of their crops as tithes and offerings to the deities and, of course, to their political representatives on earth. Israel's early rejection of these oppressive arrangements is an integral dimension of their foundational stories, including the Exodus story of liberation from hard bondage in Egypt.[19]

Nonetheless, Israel's tribal confederation ultimately failed. The book of Judges ends with the sobering observation that in the absence of a king, there was no overarching moral or legal structure and everyone did what they deemed to be right in their own eyes (21:25). To this moral chaos was added a new threat to the security of Israel's tribes. The Philistines, who had settled on the eastern shore of the Mediterranean, possessed vastly superior military technology. In response to these two crises, support grew for a king and a powerful and centralized authority that could better organize and mobilize for national defense.

The Bible does not speak with one voice on this matter. The Bible includes both pro-monarchy and anti-monarchy perspectives. On the anti-monarchy side, 1 Samuel 8 is paradigmatic. Samuel, who functioned as the *de facto* leader of the Israelites in his roles as priest, prophet, and judge,

18. Verhey, *Remembering Jesus*, 368.

19. Hanson, *Political History of the Bible in America*, 128-45; Horsley, *Jesus and the Powers*, 12-15; Verhey, *Remembering Jesus*, 355.

was approached by leaders of the tribes, who made their request so that the Israelites could "be like all the nations." God's message to Samuel identified this request as another sad chapter in Israel's history of idolatry and as a rejection of YHWH as their true king (1 Sam 8:7–8).

Walter Wink argued that this request was displeasing to God because monarchies in the ancient near east were built on dominative and hierarchical power relations, economic inequality, oppressive politics, patriarchy, aristocracy, taxation, standing armies, and war.[20] Samuel's message to the Israelites makes this fundamental point. If you choose monarchy, a king will conscript your sons to fight in his wars, conscript your sons and daughters to labor in his fields and kitchens, will tax your harvest, and take sizable portions of your land away from you. A monarchy will centralize power and require a huge bureaucratic and military apparatus. Through taxation of the harvest and livestock, Samuel warns, you will find yourselves in economic slavery. The request for a monarchy represented a half turn back to the kind of imperial economy from which God had delivered his people in the first place (1 Sam 8:8–10).

Soon enough, Samuel's warning proved accurate. The reign of King Solomon featured a proliferation of administrators and burdensome conscription for forced labor for Solomon's building projects (2 Sam 20:24; 1 Kgs 4:1–19; 5:13–18; 12:1–19). Jerusalem and the royal court prospered while the poor, laboring under the heavy tax burden, lost possession of their land. A royal census eliminated the old tribal boundaries in favor of districts that were more efficient for the purposes of taxation and conscription (2 Sam 24; 1 Kgs 4:7–19).[21] The people's resentment boiled to the surface. Solomon was the last king of the united monarchy. The ten northern tribes rebelled and broke away from the Davidic monarchy after Solomon's son, Rehoboam, announced at his coronation that he would intensify these oppressive measures.

Yet, alongside the sharp criticisms of the monarchy, one finds voices that are enthusiastic about the positive prospects of kingship under God's ultimate sovereign rule. The Deuteronomic historian also included the voices of those who saw the monarchy as God's means of deliverance of his people from the Philistine threat (1 Samuel 9–10).

Perhaps there was truth in both perspectives. The desire for a king was, in large measure, a failure to trust Yahweh alone for security and to turn, instead, to trust in military might. But on the other hand, God works in the world to achieve God's purposes through people who are flawed

---

20. Wink, *When Powers Fall*, 4–5.
21. Verhey, *Remembering Jesus*, 366–67.

and imperfect. Even though the institution of the monarchy fell short of God's ideal will, God worked providentially through the monarchy once it was in place. The focal point of these hopes was the Davidic dynasty. God blessed King David and promised him an enduring line of descendants on his throne (2 Sam 7:15-16; Ps 89:35-37). Psalm 72, a coronation psalm, is a powerful expression of this hope that Judah's kings would rule in accordance with God's will and purposes. Such kings would represent God by presiding faithfully over a just society and protecting the poor and vulnerable. This psalm articulates the hope that the king would be endowed with YHWH's justice. YHWH's justice is a justice that is particularly concerned for the needy and afflicted who have no advocates and are thereby threatened with death, oppression, and violence.

If we read Psalm 72 canonically in relationship with Psalm 146, the connection between YHWH's justice and the justice that is to be enacted by the king is even more pronounced. In Psalm 146, the God identified as the creator of all things is also the God who feeds the hungry, sets prisoners free, opens blind eyes, lifts up persons who have been beaten down, is especially concerned with widows, orphans, and aliens, and, in all of these ways, is a God who brings about justice for the oppressed. According to Psalm 146, this is who God fundamentally is!

The First Testament emphatically rejects ancient near eastern royal ideology that would grant absolute authority to kings on the assumption that the actions of kings are, without question, divinely sanctioned by the deities who are the patrons and protectors of the king. Instead, ultimate and absolute sovereignty belongs to YHWH, Israel's divine sovereign. Human kings are obligated to rule in accordance with God's rule as revealed in the Torah.[22] Thus, we find limitations placed upon monarchical power in Deuteronomy 17.

One of the amazing features of the First Testament is the confrontation of kings by God's prophets when kings abused their power and exploited, murdered, and trampled upon people. In many ancient societies, prophets functioned to validate the agenda of kings and to offer religious sanction to their programs and actions. This phenomenon also occurred with the "court prophets" of some of Judah's and Israel's kings (1 Kgs 22). But the First Testament celebrates those prophets who operated independent of royal control and, when necessary, reminded the king that he was in violation of God's will and purposes. This was the case with Elijah, who brought a scathing word of denunciation from God to King Ahab after he and his wife Jezebel murdered Naboth by framing him for a crime he did

---

22. Hanson, *Political History of the Bible in America*, 199-200.

not commit, complete with false witnesses who had been bribed, resulting in his execution by stoning. Then, they seized the vineyard and ancestral land of Naboth, who had refused to sell it in the name of faithfulness to the Torah's command not to sell the land in perpetuity (1 Kgs 21:19–20).

The prophet Nathan confronted King David after David abused his power and sought to cover up his adulterous behavior by commanding his general, Joab, to participate in the murder of Bathsheba's husband, Uriah the Hittite, by abandoning him on the battlefield (2 Sam 11:1–12:1–4). When King Jehoiakim built his royal palace with conscripted laborers he did not compensate, thereby exploiting and enslaving those without social power, the prophet Jeremiah brought words of harsh divine judgment (Jer 22:15b–17).

Exile

Our First Testament is a remarkable document. The Israelites do not tell a propagandistic story about their own greatness or innocence. Unlike some recent voices in current American political debates, they did not seek to erase the telling of those parts of their history that are painfully honest about their own injustices. Rather, the tale that is told is of God's faithfulness in spite of Israel's persistent disobedience.

The northern kingdom fell in 722 BCE to the Assyrian empire. The southern kingdom fell in 586 BCE to the Babylonians. The city of Jerusalem, along with the temple, was destroyed and many of the people were exiled and resettled in Babylon. It seemed that all was lost. The promise of the covenant was that the people would dwell securely in the land if they were faithful to God. Now, every feature of Israel's faith and hope had been stripped away as they lost their land, their political independence, the monarchy, and the temple. The hopelessness and bitterness, the raw emotions of despair and rage, of the first few years of life in exile in Babylon are on full display in Psalm 137, where the psalmist asks the rhetorical question, how can we sing the Lord's songs while in a foreign land? The answer was assumed to be obvious: "We can't." The obvious answer turned out to be the wrong answer!

If the Israelites had succumbed to typical sociological dynamics, exile should have resulted in their assimilation into the dominant Babylonian culture and the loss of their unique religious, ethnic, and cultural identity. Yet, this did not happen. Instead, the Israelites made crucial adjustments to maintain their unique identity and sense of mission as God's chosen people.

The exile led to the rebirth of the people of God.[23] They faced and came to terms with what they saw as their failures to live up to their calling as God's covenant people. They rededicated themselves to their unique identity and mission. Paradoxically, it was the recognition that their tragic situation was the result of divine judgment that provided the grounds for the transition from despair to the hope that judgment was ultimately in the service of their restoration to their mission as the people of God.[24]

Once the exile had occurred, the message of God's prophets shifted to a message of future hope. In the middle portion of the book of Isaiah, written during the Babylonian exile, we find an intensification of the message of hope (e.g., 40:1–2; 54:9–10).[25] Prior to the fall of Jerusalem, Jeremiah had been the prophet of doom and gloom, bringing a message of "terror on every side" (20:3). But once the exile had occurred, Jeremiah's message shifted to one of hope. To the people who had believed that it was impossible to sing the Lord's song in a strange land, Jeremiah, in effect, encouraged the exiles in Babylon to do just that. He encouraged them to make a life in Babylon: to build houses, plant gardens, and see to it that their children married so that the Jewish people might increase. Jeremiah offered hope for a return to the homeland after seventy years and a regathering of God's people from all over the globe (29:4–14).

Judgment is not God's last word since God is enduringly faithful to God's covenant. In the prophets of the exilic and post-exilic periods, one finds not only hope for restoration to the homeland but also of a new intimacy of God with Israel (Jer 32:28).

The Theological Contradiction

These prophetic hopes for a return to the homeland became reality when the Medes and Persians conquered Babylon and became the new imperial power in the region. Persian imperial policy allowed exiles to return to their homelands. The city of Jerusalem and the temple were rebuilt.

On the positive side, this experience validated for the Israelites that God had been faithful in spite of Israel's infidelity (Ezra 9:7–9). But there was also the painful reality that exile was not entirely over. Though they

---

23. Lohfink, *Does God Need the Church?*, 105.

24. See, for example, the prayer of repentance in Daniel chapter nine, as well as the powerful and poetic prophetical oracles found in Isaiah 40–55.

25. Isaiah 40–55 is often referred to by scholars as Second Isaiah. This portion of Isaiah is attributed to an unknown prophet, in the "school" or "tradition" of prophecy that began with the pre-exilic prophet Isaiah.

were home, they were not an independent nation, ruled over by Yahweh and a restored Davidic dynasty. Nehemiah also identified status of the Israelites as slaves, ruled over by foreign overlords who extract a disproportionate percentage of the people's harvests and livestock (9:36–27). While the exile is over, the new boss is still an oppressive foreign overlord. Israel continued to be ruled politically by idolatrous rulers who are not in subjection to Yahweh.

The Jewish people faced a question that intensified as their history unfolded. Why is the world dominated by imperial powers that are idolatrous, cruel, violent, barbaric, imperialistic, and politically oppressive? If YHWH is this world's true sovereign ruler, why is the world dominated by anti-God powers that produce suffering and injustice contrary to God's good purposes for humanity?

In the ancient near east, the defeat of any nation was imagined and assumed to be the manifestation on earth of what was happening in the heavens: the defeat of the conquered nation's patron god by the god of the conquering nation.[26] Therefore, there is an incredible sense of dissonance between political realities "on the ground" and Israel's core affirmation of YHWH's kingship. Psalm 47 is but one example among many that could be cited as an expression of Israel's core faith in Yahweh's sovereign rule. YHWH is worshiped as a great king over all the earth, the one who reigns over the nations. But this core affirmation was difficult to reconcile with the subjugation of the Jewish people to the succession of mighty empires.

Barry Harvey frames the issue this way:

> Israelites profess that there is no king but Yahweh, whose dominion over creation admits no rivals and no partners. Yet, everywhere they looked in their daily lives, they saw a vast array of worldly powers/authorities claiming privileges/ prerogatives reserved for God alone. . . . These principalities challenged divine sovereignty, claiming that the constellation of institutions, events, and peoples over which they presided was the real, true, and rational order of things; that there was no choice but to act in accordance with it.[27]

The Beginnings of Messianic Hope

The experience of a world so disordered, ruled by ungodly and idolatrous powers that produce the miseries of war, famine, disease, suffering,

26. Hanson, *Political History of the Bible in America*, 199.
27. Harvey, *Can These Bones Live?*, 60.

economic oppression, and slavery, represented a crisis for Israel's faith. However, the divinely inspired theological imagination of Israel's prophets led them to conclude that these realities cannot be the final state of affairs.

This contradiction generated hope in a glorious future in which this world would finally be brought into alignment with the truth that YHWH reigns. The language, imagery, and symbolism used to articulate this hope draw deeply from the well of the Torah, of God's promises that, if faithful to the covenant, God's people will dwell securely in the land and flourish within a just social order where everyone has access to food and livelihood. Israel's faith in YHWH's kingship took the form of an emerging and developing hope that the final chapter of human history will be one in which this world is brought into alignment with God's good purposes. This hope is not initially an eschatological hope, if by eschatological we mean hope for an afterlife or a cataclysmic ending of human history. These eschatological and apocalyptic dimensions develop later. Initially, it is simply the hope for a future in which God's good purposes are brought to fruition on earth.

During the period of the exile, prophets begin to articulate the hope for a future return to the homeland (Isa 43:1–6; Jer 29:14; 31:8–11; Ezek 11:14–17; 20:41–42; 34:11–16; 36:1–36; 39:24–28; Zeph 3:19–20; Zech 10:9–10).[28] When God returns his people to their homeland, there will be flourishing and prosperity, with abundant harvests (Jer 31:4–14; Ezek 36:29–30). In this glorious future, God will pour out his own Spirit (Isa 44:1–5) so that his people will be transformed, given new hearts and made capable of truly obeying God. Both Jeremiah and Ezekiel speak of a new and transformed heart (Jer 31:31–34; Ezek 36:26–30).

When God delivers the people from exile and returns them to their own land, the nations will see God's action and know that Israel's God is truly God (Ezek 36:22–24). This will glorify the God in the sight of the nations so that they, looking on the transformed and restored people of God, will be drawn to worship Israel's God (Isa 56:1–8; 60:1–22).[29] The Israelites will embody God's purpose to be a light to the nations (Isa 49:6) and, by doing so, fulfill the promise to Abraham to bless all peoples through his descendants. Israel will so powerfully and persuasively display the superior wisdom of God's ways that all the nations of the world will stream to Jerusalem to know God's ways of peace (Isa 2:2–4).

A related theme that reverberates throughout the segment of the book of Isaiah written during the exile is the confident affirmation that Israel's

---

28. See also the vision of the valley of the dry bones in Ezekiel 37 as a promise for the restoration of the nation after the exile.

29. Kirk, *Jesus Have I Loved*, 13–14, 56–57.

God is one true God who created all things (42:5–6; 45:12–13). This was not an easy affirmation to make while under the dominative thumb of imperial Babylon, where it was assumed, as a matter of "common sense," that political power relations on earth mirrored the patterns of power in the "heavens."[30] But in the teeth of this pervasive assumption, the Jewish people boldly proclaimed that the idols of the nations are nothing but useless works of human hands (40:12–26; 41:21–24, 29). One day, all nations and peoples will acknowledge YHWH as the one true God, bow down to God and swear allegiance to this God (Isa 45:21b–23; see also Zech 14:9). In a glorious future, the knowledge of the Lord will fill the earth as the waters cover the seas (Isa 11:9). When God's presence so saturates creation, when God is rightly worshiped, honored, and obeyed as the sovereign Lord, every dimension of life on earth will be rectified, healed, and brought into alignment with God's good purposes, which are to bless. Then, this world will be rightly ordered, humans will flourish, and there will be social justice and peace and access to the resources of life will be available to everyone rather than hoarded by the few.

These hopes for a world completely rectified are tethered to hope for the restoration of the Davidic dynasty. Through this righteous king, God's justice will prevail. God will dwell among God's people and there will be peace, agricultural abundance so that food is available for all, and the powerful will not oppress or abuse the less powerful (Ezek 37:24–27).

These streams of hope begin to flow together and merge. A new king from David's line will rule God's people faithfully and lead them to faithfulness. The restoration of the Davidic monarchy will be accompanied by peace, security, liberation from bondage and oppression by foreign overlords, abundance of food, a just social order, and right relationship with God. The future envisioned is one in which all things are put right and God's good purposes are finally realized. These hopes begin to coalesce into what will later become messianic hope. A divinely chosen and Spirit-endowed deliverer and ruler will be God's agent to put the world right. These hopes are given powerful expression in the book of Isaiah in texts that came to be read as messianic texts by many faithful Jews and, years later, the early Christian movement.

In Isaiah 9, we find an anticipation of a future of liberation from foreign oppressors and of peace and justice presided over by a descendant of David. In 9:3–7, joy is associated with God's act of breaking the rod of Judah's oppressor. Endless peace and justice will be the result. The same theme of a restored Davidic dynasty is sounded two chapters later. This time, the

---

30. Brueggemann, *Theology of the Old Testament*, 149.

king will rule justly and protect the poor and the meek and will do so because he is endowed with the Spirit of YHWH (11:1–5).

What is crucial in these texts is a little noticed connection, one that threads its way throughout the entire book of Isaiah, between the Spirit of God, the future Davidic king, and societal justice. Endowed with the Spirit of the Lord, this future king will be a just judge who will not be biased in favor or the rich, powerful, and well-connected. He will be an advocate for the socially and economically vulnerable. The rule of this future king will be associated with deliverance from oppressors, the regathering of Israelites in their homeland, and peace and security. He is the Prince of Peace whose reign will secure everlasting peace. This vision is also present in Jer 23:1–6.

Isaiah 42:1–4 repeats this motif in the first of the "servant of YHWH" poems in "Second Isaiah." It is not entirely clear whether or not this servant is a king, the whole people of Israel, or some other figure. However, this servant of the Lord is endowed with the Spirit of God and he will establish justice on earth, characterized by compassion for the vulnerable. Not only the Jewish people but the nations will look to his teaching for guidance.

In Isa 61:1–4, we see the same pattern of a Spirit-endowed figure associated with justice and peace and restoration to the homeland, but this figure is not explicitly identified as a king or ruler. The original setting of Isa 61:1–4 is after the Israelites have returned home from exile to a land in ruins. Here, the one who is endowed with the Holy Spirit is not said to rule as a king but to proclaim, the role of the prophet.[31] The ambiguity in this text as to the identity of the speaker, prophet or king or both, is due to the presence of the metaphor of anointing, which has its origins in the ritual of anointing a new king. What is proclaimed, by the one anointed with the Holy Spirit, is God's purpose of liberation for the oppressed, the "captives," the Israelites under the thumb of Persian oppression. He proclaims "the acceptable year of the Lord," which is the Jubilee Year of economic redistribution. There is an unspecified reference to God's vengeance, presumably against the foreign overlord oppressors who cause misery. And echoing other texts in Isaiah, there is a reference to joy.

Isaiah 61:1–2a was taken up by Jesus himself as his "mission statement" early in his ministry (Luke 4:16–21). Jesus identifies himself as the fulfillment of the first seven lines of this prophetic oracle, stopping after the proclamation of "the year of the Lord's favor." These hopes for a glorious future age grow out of the Torah's vision of Israel as God's faithful covenant people who embody his ways and by doing so, flourish, reflect

---

31. According to Paul Hanson, This Spirit-endowed messenger may be the prophet in the school of Isaiah who is responsible for this third section of Isaiah or it may be a group or movement within Israel. Hanson, *Dawn of Apocalyptic*, 65.

God's glory, and display God's purposes for the world to see. If we compare the texts from Isaiah with Psalm 146, we discover that Israel's hoped-for future is simply the realization on earth for everyone of what faithful Israelites already know about God's good purposes for human flourishing. God wills justice for the oppressed and vulnerable, food for the hungry, human health, and liberation from bondage!

At points, expressions of exuberant hope in the book of Isaiah push the boundaries of the imagination. Numerous texts in Isaiah have utopian resonances that are excessive vis-à-vis ordinary human hopes. Early in the collection of Isaiah's prophetic oracles, we find a powerful utopian vision in 2:2–4. With God reigning from Jerusalem and settling all international disputes, there is no need for instruments of war. These will be converted into farming implements. Instead of imperial armies coming to Jerusalem to make war, to conquer and plunder, the nations will stream to Jerusalem to learn the ways of peace. When we consider that war is and has so often been a cause of famine, this is a vision of a world in which people flourish and prosper and have plenty to eat. This identical prophetic oracle is found in Mic 4:1–4, which supplements the original by the additional claim that everyone will sit under their own vine and fig tree. There will be no more fear that foreign invaders will seize homes, lands, gardens, and orchards. The evils of war that so disorder our world will be eliminated.

The anticipated future king is the Prince of Peace whose reign will secure everlasting peace (9:6–7). Isaiah 11 conveys a powerful metaphor of a future of cosmic peace that extends to the non-human creation. Poisonous snakes are no threat to humans and wolves, leopards and lions do not devour sheep and cattle. This vision transcends anything imaginable within the present order of things. What makes this all possible is a world saturated with the knowledge of God (11:6–9).

In Isaiah 25, we find another eruption of exuberant hope. Though found in the first segment of Isaiah, this prophetic utterance is likely to have been written in the post-exilic period.

In a world that knows starvation, hunger, and malnutrition, we are offered a beautiful picture of a future in which God provides a joyous feast in Jerusalem to which all the people of the world are invited. This day of joy and feasting is linked to the idea of "salvation," what God has done for his people Israel, taking away their disgrace. Banquets and feasting and wine are associated with joy and celebration and human community. God will wipe away the tears from every eye. This image is taken up in Revelation 21, a text that ties this joy explicitly to the future age when the New Jerusalem comes to earth and all of the horrors of history that cause sorrow are things of the past (21:1–4). It is also a vision of peace since sharing a celebratory meal with all nations is what is done when people groups are in positive rather than hostile relationships with one another. Though this text does not yet reach a hope for a life beyond the boundaries of death, it does speak of a final defeat or final overcoming of death on the part of God.

Isaiah 35:5-6 anticipates a future characterized by healing and physical heath and wholeness for persons with physical impairments.

Isaiah 65:17-25, which is also from the period after the exile, offers expressions of hope for a restored Jerusalem, but it, too, erupts into exuberant hopes for a future beyond human possibilities. In this future of abundant and fulfilling life in Jerusalem, God's people will be secure. There will be no fear that foreign invaders will seize their homes and properties. Jerusalem will be a place of joy. All will enjoy long life and there will not be infant mortality. But this text is sandwiched with language that anticipates the later development of apocalyptic eschatology. God will create a new heavens and a new earth. This suggests a kind of radical discontinuity with the present, a future in which God does something radically new beyond imaginable human possibilities. Once again, we hear of God's purposes for a world of cosmic peace, where even the bloodshed that characterizes the non-human world will come to an end and nothing in all of creation is violent.

Salvation Is . . .

What is "salvation" as it is articulated in these prophetic texts? Salvation is envisioned as a future age, on this earth, where all that currently plagues, destroys, and distorts life is eradicated in this future age of societal justice and peace. Humans will flourish due to the intimate presence of God. Every person will know that Israel's God is the one true God, the Creator and sovereign ruler of this world. The God who is righteous, faithful to his covenant, merciful, and sovereign will not only deliver Israel from exile and re-establish the nation but will extend the blessing so that God's promise to Abraham will be fulfilled as Israel becomes the conduit of blessing to all peoples! In this future, God's good purposes are realized. Humans flourish. There will be justice, peace, joy, and a fair distribution of land such that everyone can eat and have security. Physical ailments and disabilities are no more. When these things come to be, God's will is done "on earth as it is in heaven." This, of course, was the prayer Jesus taught us to pray, where he connected God's reign and God's will being done on earth. Then it will be clear for every eye to see: Israel's God reigns because God's good and loving purposes have prevailed. God's will is blessing, human flourishing, *shalom*, wholeness, and well-being for everyone in every dimension of human existence.

God's ultimate act of salvation is not the rescue of individuals from this world. Rather, salvation is the healing, repair, and transformation of this world so that it truly reflects God's sovereign rule. Salvation is not merely a "spiritual" matter. It involves what we typically speak of as physical, social, and political realities. It is indeed "spiritual" in that it is the whole world knowing God. But the result of knowledge of God is also food for the hungry, healing for the sick, economic justice, political freedom, world peace, social justice, even creation at peace with itself. Salvation, in its "cosmic and eschatological dimensions," is a very big salvation indeed: all things are rectified. As this idea is taken up in the New Testament, we are told that God's ultimate plan is to reconcile "all things" to himself through Jesus Christ (Col 1:20).

Theme of Eschatological Judgment

The prerequisite for the coming of this age of justice and peace is the eradication of the oppressive and idolatrous empires that conquer and dominate, as well as the judgment that purifies God's own people Israel. God will reduce the rulers of this world to nothing (Isa 40:23). Isaiah 47 is an oracle in which God proclaims his coming judgment on the Babylonian empire for their mistreatment of Israel, just as Isaiah 10 had earlier spoken of God's intention to bring judgment upon the Assyrian empire.

Preceding the emergence of messianic hope was the idea of the Day of the Lord, a decisive future moment when both God's chosen people and the Gentile nations would be called to account by God. While popular Israelite religion sometimes envisioned the Day of the Lord as a time in which God's judgment will fall upon Israel's enemies alone, the prophets reminded Israel that this day of judgment includes God's people (e.g., Isa 26:21; Joel 2:11; Amos 5:18–20). For Israel, this will be an event of painful purification, compared to a refiner's fire (Mal 3:1–5). The day of the Lord is envisaged as a trial scene, with special judgment upon those within Israel who have acted unjustly or neglected the poor (e.g., Mic 6:2ff).[32] This idea is prominent in Isa 3:13–15, where God calls the leaders of Israel to account for mistreating the poor.

Modern western persons find this theme of judgment to be unpleasant. But as N. T. Wright points out, God's coming judgment, while terrifying, is a good thing. Wright writes:

---

32. Rutledge, *Crucifixion*, 309.

In a world full of systematic injustice, bullying, violence, arrogance, and oppression, the thought that there might come a day when the wicked are firmly put in their place and the poor and the weak are given their due is the best news there can be. Faced with a world of rebellion, a world full of exploitation and wickedness, a good God *must* be a God of judgment.[33]

---

33. Wright, *Surprised by Hope*, 137.

CHAPTER FOUR

Setting the Stage for Jesus

The Intertestamental Period, Apocalyptic Literature, and Economic Realities in First-Century Palestine Under Roman Occupation

JESUS'S ACTIONS, PARABLES, TEACHINGS, conflicts, crucifixion, and resurrection only make sense if we understand something about the social, historical, religious, and political stage on which they took place. We need some knowledge of the pieces on the proverbial game board on which Jesus made his appearance and how those pieces were set up in first-century Palestine.

Intertestamental Period: A Quick Sketch of the Political Realities of Judah's Post-Exilic Life

We can date the intertestamental period, roughly, as including the years between the middle of the fourth century BCE until the time of the birth of Jesus Christ. These are the years in which, with the one exception of the book of Daniel, no books were written that are included in the Protestant First Testament canon, which is itself based upon Jewish rabbinic decisions made in the second century CE.

After the Babylonian exile, the Jewish people were allowed to return to their homeland and many, but not all, did so. Israel's homeland was much smaller in size, reduced to the province of Judea. The second temple was built in 515 BCE with the permission of their Persian rulers. The temple brought the people together on a regular basis for Israel's great festivals, such as the Passover, forming the theological center that undergirded the identity of the people as God's covenant people. In Ezekiel 40–48, the temple was portrayed as the center of a renewed society under God's rule. Unlike the temple of the pre-exilic period, it was no longer under the supervision of a king. The priesthood became politically powerful. The high priest assumed organizational and political functions, even becoming the representative of the whole of Judea. To finance the sacrificial cult and salaries of the priests, the temple demanded a relatively high burden of taxes.[1]

Two hundred years of Persian rule were relatively peaceful for the Jewish people. Under Persian rule, the Jewish people sought to live peaceably with their imperial overlords with a *modus vivendi* of accommodation, according to which the Jewish people were compliant when it came to matters like taxation and other imperial policies, while the Persian rulers gave wide latitude to Jewish leaders to govern local matters, including religious practice and ordinary community relations, according to Jewish law. In other words, fealty on the part of the Jewish vassals to their Persian overlords was effectively exchanged for Persian tolerance of Jewish religion and law.[2]

That began to change with the rise of Alexander the Great, who conquered Judea in 332 BCE as part of his conquest of the territories previously held by the Persian Empire. After Alexander died in 323 BCE, his empire was divided between four of his generals, Cassander, Ptolemy, Antigonus, and Seleucus, who were referred to as the *didichoi*. The opening of the book of 1 Maccabees narrates the events of Alexander's conquest of Judea, his death, and the division of his kingdom among his generals. In continuity with the First Testament, 1 Maccabees interprets imperial power as evil and opposed to God and describes Alexander in unflattering terms as proud, arrogant, and an oppressor who plundered the wealth of nations by conquest and taxation. Alexander's successors are described as bringing misery on the world (1 Macc 1:1–9). As is typical of empire, they established administrative structures designed to extract resources from conquered territories, enforcing the levy of tribute and the requirement of service from subjugated peoples.[3]

---

1. Albertz, *From the Exile to the Maccabees*, 448–49; Lohfink, *Does God Need the Church?*, 113.
2. Hanson, *Political History of the Bible in America*, 409–11.
3. Portier-Young, *Apocalypse Against Empire*, 50–51.

The Hellenistic era was a time of constant violence for the Judeans. Alexander's successors were regularly at war with one another, challenging each other for dominance and control over regions each king claimed as part of his rightful territory. The land of Judea was contested territory, claimed by both Seleucus I and Ptolemy I as well as their successors. The region the Greeks designated as Coele-Syria, which included Judea, experienced six wars between the Ptolemies and Seleucids between the years of 274 and 168 BCE. Daniel 11:2–29 referred to them as the King of the South and the King of the North. Jerusalem was seized three times during the course of these wars and suffered extensively. Battles fought in and around Jerusalem resulted in casualties, injuries, and damage to public buildings, homes, and fields. The impact of the armies was horrendous, including pillage, destruction, and mass enslavement as the "collateral damage" of war. Conquest and plunder in warfare guaranteed pay for their troops and fueled the imperial economy.[4]

The author of 1 Maccabees described the last of the Seleucid rulers, Antiochus IV Ephiphanes, as an offshoot of the same militaristic, prideful, and rapacious stock of those who preceded him. When Antiochus IV Epiphanes ascended to power, some Jewish leaders allied themselves with him in accordance with the pattern of accommodation that had worked well with their Persian overlords and often with Ptolemaic and Seleucid overlords as well. Unlike previous foreign overlords, Antiochus's intensive program of forced Hellenization, enforced by terror and brutality, was not tolerant of local religious practices.[5] Antiochus prohibited circumcision and replaced Jewish sacrifices with Greek sacrifices, including the sacrifice of pigs on an alter to Zeus erected in the temple.[6] Copies of the Torah were burned and anyone caught possessing a copy was executed, as were women who had their children circumcised and anyone who refused to eat unclean foods (1 Macc 1:51–54, 60–63).

Nonetheless, many Jewish political and religious leaders were willing to collaborate and accommodate. Jason, and then Menelaus, purchased the office of high priest from Antiochus and collaborated with Antiochus's program of forced Hellenization. They permitted him to plunder the temple treasury. A Greek-style gymnasium was built in Jerusalem as part of this strategy of accommodation (1 Macc 1:10–15). In spite of these efforts to curry Antiochus's favor, he entered Jerusalem after his defeat of King

---

4. Portier-Young, *Apocalypse Against Empire*, 50–51, 54–55, 67–68, 70–71.

5. Portier-Young, *Apocalypse Against Empire*, 54–55; Hanson, *Political History of the Bible in America*, 410.

6. Nichols, *Death and Afterlife*, 25.

Ptolemy in Egypt and ransacked the temple, taking many of the sacred and valuable golden vessels.[7]

This precipitated the Maccabean revolt, resulting in the defeat of Antiochus IV in the middle of the second century BCE, which secured independence for the Jewish people for almost one hundred years until 63 BCE. Under the Hasmoneans, Judea achieved territorial expansion approximating that of David's kingdom.[8] However, Jewish independence ended in 63 BCE with the invasion of Roman armies led by Pompey.

From Prophetic to Apocalyptic Eschatology

The years between 515 BCE and the first century BCE were periods of bitter disappointment as the prophetic dream of a golden future of justice and peace, in which God's people flourished on the land, ruled by a descendent of King David, was not realized. In these years, the Jewish community struggled to make theological sense of the loss of nationhood and continuing foreign domination and oppression.[9] As hopes for fulfillment of the vision of Yahweh's restoration of his people in a smooth and continuous process of development were crushed, Paul Hanson argues, circumstances convinced many faithful Jews that the historical-political realm was so dominated by powers of evil that the people of God had no control over the direction of history. The human situation is so tragic and insoluble that the only hope is from outside the human sphere altogether. Between the present and a utopian future, YHWH will unleash a cosmic upheaval, a shaking and overturning of the present order of things.[10] Walter Brueggemann identifies the key feature of the shift from prophetic to apocalyptic eschatology as the idea that the novelty intended by YHWH does not emerge from within the present historical and public processes. Rather, the "sovereign incursion" of YHWH is something utterly new. YHWH's initiative alone will bring about

---

7. Portier-Young, *Apocalypse Against Empire*, 54–55; Hanson, *Political History of the Bible in America*, 410.

8. Lohfink, *Does God Need the Church?*, 112

9. Hanson, *Dawn of Apocalyptic*, 4–6, 8–9, 27–28; Brueggemann, *Theology of the Old Testament*, 172; Rutledge, *Crucifixion*, 140.

10. There are proto-apocalyptic elements already developing within post-exilic Judaism and reflected in several prophetic texts. A prime example of proto-apocalyptic dimensions of some prophetic eschatology is found in Isa 13:9–13, which anticipated the fall of Babylon and spoke of the "day of the Lord" in the language of cosmic catastrophe. The sun and the moon will not give light. The earth will be shaken out of its place.

the blessed transformation (Isa 60:1). All of this will be fulfilled, not by human effort, but because YHWH will act directly on behalf of his people.[11]

According to Paul Hanson, early Jewish apocalyptic eschatology concerns God's "final saving acts" and these final divine saving acts involve "deliverance out of the present order into a new transformed order" of reality. Hanson detects the beginnings of the emergence of apocalyptic eschatology in the imaginary of a new heavens and a new earth in Isaiah 65:17.[12] This expected new order of reality is not conceived, as it typically was in prophetic eschatology, as a rehabilitation or reconfiguration of the present social and political order but as the termination of the present order of things and its replacement by something racially novel.[13]

General Characteristics of Apocalyptic Literature and the Apocalyptic Imagination

Defining the term "apocalyptic" is a matter of scholarly dispute. John J. Collins defines an apocalypse as

> a genre of revelatory literature with a narrative framework, in which a revelation is mediated by an otherworldly being to a human recipient disclosing a transcendent reality which is both temporal, insofar as it envisages eschatological salvation, and spatial insofar as it involves another supernatural world.[14]

In 1997, Collins updated his earlier definition with greater emphasis on eschatology and judgment as integral to apocalypses. He wrote:

> [The two kinds of apocalypses, historical and cosmological] are presented as supernatural revelations, mediated by an angel or some heavenly being, and they invariably focus on the final end of life and history. This final end usually entails the transformation of this world . . . but it also involves the judgment of the individual dead and their assignment to eternal bliss or damnation.[15]

---

11. Hanson, *Dawn of Apocalyptic*, 24–28, 32–33, 36–37, 44, 73–75; Brueggemann, *Theology of the Old Testament*, 172; Rutledge, *Crucifixion*, 140, 350.

12. Hanson, *Dawn of Apocalyptic*, 30.

13. Collins, "From Prophecy to Apocalypticism," 129–61.

14. Collins, *Apocalyptic Imagination*, 5.

15. Collins, *Apocalyptic Imagination* [1998], 3, cited by Murphy, *Apocalypticism in the Bible and Its World*, 8.

Writings typically characterized as Jewish apocalyptic works, or at least books that include apocalyptic segments, include the book of Daniel, 1 Enoch, 4 Ezra, the Sibylline Oracles, 2 and 3 Baruch, 2 Enoch, the Apocalypse of Abraham, The Assumption of Moses, the Testament of Abraham, Testament of Levi, and Apocalypse of Zephaniah. First Enoch is a collection of five apocalypses. Two of these, the book of the Watchers (chapters 1–36) and the Astronomical Book (chapters 72–82), date to the third century BCE, shortly after the imposition of Hellenistic rule after Alexander's conquests, and are the earliest extant Jewish apocalypses. Another major portion of 1 Enoch was written about the same time as the book of Daniel, approximately 165 BCE.[16]

Collins contends that there are identifiable commonalities and assumptions shared by the apocalypses. The world is mysterious and revelation must be transmitted from a supernatural source. The form of an apocalyptic writing typically includes a narrative framework describing the manner of revelation, the main means of which are visions, dreams, communication of mysteries by angels, and otherworldly journeys. There is a hidden supernatural world of angels and demons that is directly relevant to human events. The human recipient is typically a venerable figure from the distant past, whose name is used pseudonymously. Some apocalyptic writings feature an elaborate interpretation or review of history, including prophetic anticipations of a future time of crisis and eschatological upheaval. There is a final judgment after death, which involves justice beyond the boundaries of history and the destruction of the wicked. It is this culmination of history beyond the boundaries of death that differentiates apocalyptic from prophetic eschatology.[17] Martinus de Boer contends that the eschatological dualism of the two ages is the defining characteristic apocalyptic eschatology. This idea is stated explicitly in 4 Ezra 7:50 and there are scattered references to "this age" and/or "the age to come" in other apocalyptic writings (cf. 1 En. 71:15; 4 Ezra 7:112, 119; 2 Bar 44:8, 15; 83:4, 9).[18]

---

16. Murphy, *Apocalypticism in the Bible and Its World*, xvii, 3.

17. Collins, *Apocalyptic Imagination*, 2–8, 11; Murphy, *Apocalypticism in the Bible and Its World*, 7. Apocalyptic elements, including eschatological judgment on the resurrected dead, visions, and heavenly journeys, are also present in intertestamental Jewish writings that are not apocalypses.

18. Boer, "Apocalyptic as God's Eschatological Activity," 50.

The Resurrection of the Dead and a Final Judgment

During the intertestamental period, hope for an afterlife developed. Many, though not all, faithful Jews came to believe that the messianic age will include not only the last generations, but all of the righteous dead, who will be raised from the grave and restored to embodiment (e.g., 1 En. 25:4–6).[19] After the resurrection, there will be a final judgment (1 En. 1:7). All will be judged, and if righteous, vindicated by God and rewarded for faithfulness and obedience. The wicked will be shamed, punished, or destroyed (e.g., 1 En. 1:8–9).

This conviction is bound up with the core belief that God's purposes for Israel will not be thwarted.[20] According to Deuteronomistic[21] theology, the defeats and sufferings of Israel were consequences of infidelity to the covenant (see esp. Deut 28). Obedience brings divine protection from enemies, rain, fertility of cattle and fields, and economic prosperity. Disobedience brings the curses of drought and infertility, disease, and defeat at the hands of Israel's enemies. But during the persecution under Antiochus IV Epiphanes, many Israelites suffered because of their Torah obedience. The incompatibility between Deuteronomistic theology and the experience of the persecution, death, and suffering of those Israelites faithful to the covenant was a theological crisis. What about those who were persecuted for their steadfast refusal to break God's laws, who died because they "forget themselves for the sake of his laws?" (2 Macc 7:23). The earthly suffering of the righteous raised serious questions about divine justice. Either God was faithless and unjust or God's justice would need a new arena in order to be fully worked out. The rise of belief in a future resurrection provided that arena for full and final justice and the vindication of God's faithful people. This is also, most fundamentally, about God's own righteousness in light of God's own covenant promises. If, in this life, the wicked prosper with impunity and the righteous suffer without vindication or relief, there must be something more if God is truly just.[22]

In continuity with the proto-apocalyptic anticipation of a "new heavens and a new earth" in Isa 65:17, the development of resurrection hope was accompanied by the articulation of belief in *creatio ex nihilo*, first expressed in 2 Macc 7:23. The God who created all things out of nothing is the God

---

19. Kirk, *Unlocking Romans*, 19–20; Nickelsburg, "Judgment, Life-After-Death, and Resurrection," 149–51.

20. Kirk, *Unlocking Romans*, 29–30.

21. The Deuteronomistic theological interpretation of Israel's history is to be found in the books of Joshua, Judges, 1 and 2 Samuel, and 1 and 2 Kings.

22. Kirk, *Romans Unlocked*, 12, 15–19, 23.

who re-creates life out of the nothingness of death.[23] After being tortured in unspeakable ways after refusing to eat pork, one of seven faithful Jewish brothers professed his profound conviction that God will raise him and his brothers from death and bestow eternal life upon them for their faithfulness to God's laws.[24]

First Enoch 1:8–9 depicts the end of history as a time in which all will be judged, with the wicked destroyed and the righteous receiving peace and blessing.[25] One of the authorial voices in 1 Enoch maintains that in this lifetime, the righteous receive no reward and sinners escape punishment. But there will be a future resurrection and God's justice will be dispensed in a post-mortem judgment that is universal and cosmic in scope. The righteous will be rewarded in resurrected bodies (25:4–6). Similar arguments about the function of resurrection can be found in 4 Ezra (5:41; 7:31–32) and the Apocryphon of Ezekiel. Chapters 2 and 3 of the Psalms of Solomon indicate that resurrection life is the blessing that comes to those who fear the Lord. God's eschatological judgment will glorify the humble and humble the self-glorifying (2:31).[26]

Reference to a final judgment and exclusion and punishment of the wicked occurs in 1 Enoch 10 and 38, both in the book of the Watchers, and in chapter 108. In 1 En. 10:6–7, the wicked fallen angel Azazel is cast into the fire. All of the Watchers and their children, the Giants who have devoured and destroyed the earth, making it uninhabitable for humans, will be led into and confined forever in the Abyss of fire (10:11–16). The wicked will be destroyed, cast into the fire, and their names blotted out of the book of life (108:2–3). But those who loved God and, for the sake of faithfulness to God, were tortured and persecuted will be vindicated and honored (108:8–13). In the book of the Watchers (chapter 22), Enoch sees chambers inside a mountain where the "spirits of the souls of the dead" are kept to await judgment. Chapter 26 describes the tree of life, whose fruit will be given to the righteous after the judgment.[27]

Daniel 12:1–3 speaks of the resurrection of the dead and a dual destiny, depending on whether each individual is righteous or wicked. John Goldingay draws attention to the theme of eschatological reversal in Daniel: those brought down to the earth (11:35) by the one who exalted himself as a god (11:36) are exalted like the heavenly hosts while the self-exalting one is brought down in shame and contempt. Resurrection is a cosmic and

23. Ormerod, *Creation, Grace, and Redemption*, 4–5.
24. Kirk, *Unlocking Romans*, 17–18.
25. Beaton, "Messiah and Justice," 13–15.
26. Kirk, *Unlocking Romans*, 23–25.
27. Collins, "From Prophecy to Apocalypticism," 138–39.

eschatological reversal of conditions on earth. It functions to secure justice, providing an arena in which the "especially good," including the seer himself (12:13) and the "especially bad," can be justly recompensed.[28]

A Future Messianic Age

Accompanying the hope for the resurrection of the dead and the final judgment is the further development of the hope that emerged in prophetic eschatology for a future age of justice and peace. In the book of the Watchers, after the powers of evil are destroyed, there will be on earth an age of flourishing and wholeness in which all that is evil and destructive is no more (1 En. 10:18–22; 11:1–2). Life lived in resurrection bodies is not necessarily eternal; it is, however, exceedingly long (25:6). Following judgment, God restores humanity to the primeval state through God's gift of the fruit from the tree of life (24:4–25:7). In the book of Dream Visions of 1 Enoch, sheep metamorphose into snow white cows in the final moments of the last judgment, symbolizing the reconstitution of resurrected Israelites into the original Adamic condition (85:3; see also 1 En. 24–25; 61).[29] Other Jewish writings which feature the restoration of creation together with an embodied humanity include 2 Baruch (4:1–7; 6:9; 32:1–7), Psalms of Solomon (14:3–5), the Apocalypse of Moses (28, 41, 43), and Qumran texts such as 1QS (4:22–23) and 4Q521.

The book of Dream Visions of 1 Enoch 83–90, probably written in the late 160s BCE of the Maccabean period, foretells the coming of the Messianic period. The New Jerusalem at last comes and with it God's Messiah. The final period of history will see the triumph of the righteous, the banishment of evil, and the creation of an age that will have no end.[30] In the Psalm of Solomon 17, the messiah's rule is characterized by a general state of justice and righteousness, compassionate treatment of the nations, the exposure of corrupt officials, empowerment by the Holy Spirit, faithful and righteous shepherding of the Lord's flock, and the abolishment of oppression.[31]

In Daniel 7, the culmination of human history is "one like a son of man" coming with the clouds of heaven. To him is given by God, the Ancient of Days, authority, glory, and sovereign power, and all of the world's nations and peoples will worship him.[32] The kingdom established is an

---

28. Goldingay, *Daniel*, 308–9.
29. Kirk, *Unlocking Romans*, 29.
30. Russell, *Divine Disclosure*, 40.
31. Beaton, "Messiah and Justice," 13–15.
32. In 1 Enoch 37–71, the figure of the Son of Man comes to refer to all the faithful.

everlasting dominion that will not pass away and will never be destroyed (7:13–14). As Daniel's vision is explained to him, he is told that the sovereignty, power, and greatness of all the kingdoms which usurped God's sovereign kingship will be taken away and transferred to "the holy people of the Most High." The humane rule of justice given to the saints of the Most High (7:10–14, 17–18, 22) is in sharp contrast to the brutal and monstrous rule of the empires.[33]

A Final End to the Oppressive Imperial Powers: The Theme of God v. Empire Continues and Intensifies

These first two themes are closely bound up with a third theme, the overthrow of all earthly conditions in a great cosmic catastrophe as the climax of a predetermined course of history. Apocalyptic literature tends to be profoundly pessimistic about "the present moment" because evil powers are in control of the world. Hope lies not in possibilities latent within the present moment for progress and improvement but rather with God's interruptive future action.

For example, Daniel 7–12 depicts foreign rulers as agents of chaos, who, after their final season of wanton cruelty, are destined to be annihilated. Together, the apocalyptic writings reflect the belief that the time was rapidly coming when the forces of evil would be confronted by the forces of good in a great show-down in which the cosmos itself would become embroiled. The powers of darkness would be destroyed and the sons of light would receive victory at the hands of God. Apocalyptic writers shared the certainty that the current structures of domination will, in the future, be shattered (Daniel 2), uprooted (The Apocalypse of Weeks), and replaced with a just order (Dan 7:13–27; 1 En. 90:28–38; 91:12–17; Testament of Moses). But, for the apocalyptic mindset, there is no gradual transition to the messianic age. Catastrophe will precede the future messianic age of justice and peace.[34]

The terms "elect" and "righteous" are used in both the singular, as titles for the Son of Man, and in the plural, as attributes of the faithful. The Son of Man is a corporate figure and the exaltation of Enoch as a son of man in 1 Enoch 71 means that Enoch is a paradigmatic figure. The exaltation of the Son of man as eschatological judge and ruler is the corporate future of all the righteous. Georgi, *Theocracy in Paul's Praxis and Theology*, 10–11.

33. Portier-Young, *Apocalypse Against Empire*, 28.
34. Russell, *Divine Disclosure*, xix–xx, 10; Nichols, *Death and Afterlife*, 29; Hanson, *Political History of the Bible in America*, 408.

Section Two: Soteriology and Biblical Narrative

In order to encourage God's people not to give in to the despair, not to see the present order as the permanent state of the world, some apocalyptic literature, including the book of Daniel, the Apocalypse of Weeks, and the book of Dreams in 1 Enoch, feature a historical review. The point is to affirm that the temporal powers are not inevitable or omnipotent, but transient and finite. This historical view affirms God's governance of time, reassures that God's plan in history is being worked out, and sets forth hope for a transformed future rule of God.[35]

For example, Daniel 2 features King Nebuchadnezzar's dream of a frightening image and its destruction. As Daniel interprets the dream, we learn that this imposing figure represents a succession of great imperial powers. According to Carol Newsome, the gold head represents Babylon, the silver the Medes, the bronze the Persians, and the feet of iron and clay most likely represents the empire initiated by Alexander and inherited by his successors, the Ptolemies and Seleucids.[36] Daniel 2:44–45 proclaims that God will destroy these kingdoms and put into place an entirely different social order.

Daniel 7 also links together eschatological judgment, the destruction of the oppressive and idolatrous kingdoms of this world order, and the eschatological establishment of God's kingdom or reign. Daniel's vision of four great, terrifying, and violent beasts that rise up out of the sea alludes to the monstrous nature of the empires. These monstrous empires are portrayed as possessing a ravenous appetite for human flesh (7:5, 7).[37] The final beast had ten horns, representing the different sub-kingdoms of the remnants of Alexander's empire. One of the horns, speaking boastfully, represents Antiochus IV Ephiphanes. This horn was waging war against the saints, speaking blasphemous words against God, and, for a time, prevailing. But a future is coming, readers are assured, in which all of the beasts are destroyed by God's action. Then, we see a scene of final judgment unfold in which the dominion of these empires is taken away and delivered to God's people. In this future, all people worship God, who establishes a dominion that will never be destroyed (7:9–14, 26).

John Collins argues that the messiah, as imagined in significant segments of Second Temple Judaism, is the one who will smite the nations, slay the wicked, and restore the Davidic dynasty, thereby ushering in an era of peace and justice.[38] This theme is reflected in the New Testament book

---

35. Portier-Young, *Apocalypse Against Empire*, 27–28.
36. Newsome, *Daniel*, 17–18.
37. Portier-Young, *Apocalypse Against Empire*, 28.
38. Collins, *Scepter and the Star*, 67, cited by Beaton, "Messiah and Justice," 13.

of Revelation, where the imperial powers that persecuted God's people are destroyed (Rev 19:11–21). This apocalyptic imagination is not peripheral in the New Testament. In 1 Cor 15:24–25, St. Paul proclaims that the final act of human history will be the destruction of all dominion, authority, and power as Christ subdues all of his enemies and hands over the kingdom to God the Father.

Satan and a Kingdom of Evil (Spirits)

Satan, "the Adversary," is a title rather than a name. This character makes few appearances in our Old Testament (Job 1–2; 1 Chr 21:1; Zech 3:1–2). The concept of evil spirits and a unified kingdom of evil presided over by Satan developed during the intertestamental period. These malignant and malicious spiritual forces come to be conceived of as powers that exercise some degree of rule, though it is an illegitimate rule, over the present evil age. In this apocalyptic idiom, the whole of history can be narrated in terms of a conflict between God and those who would illegitimately lay claim to God's royal throne (Dan 7; 1 En. 14; T. Levi 5; 2 En. 20–21; Apoc. Ab. 18).[39]

The book of the Watchers in 1 Enoch features God sending his archangels to defeat and destroy the fallen watchers and their illegitimate children, the Giants, who were half human and half angelic. The source of evil in the book of Jubilees is also traced back to the "Watchers" and the giants. From the bodies of these giants came demonic spirits who were presented as the cause of disease and tragedy of every kind. The book of Jubilees has a developed dualism in which demonic agencies feature prominently. Satan appears as "Mastema," prince of evil spirits, who are responsible for the evil in the world. But Mastema and the demons and fallen angels will in the end be destroyed.[40]

Apocalyptic as Resistance Literature

Anathea Portier-Young draws upon Antonio Gramsci's account of hegemony and Pierre Bordieu's concept of the *doxa* to analyze the totalizing narratives of empire. Hegemony refers to the non-violent forms of social control exercised in all of the ways in which existing realities are imagined and portrayed as normative and universal when in reality, such social orders and practices are but particular and contingent ways of viewing the world

---

39. Russell, *Divine Disclosure*, 25, 36.
40. Russell, *Divine Disclosure*, 36, 50.

and mapping the universe and humanity's place in it. The way of life and cosmology undergirded by hegemonic discourse and practice, or the *doxa*, is that which appears to be necessary and absolute, self-evident and natural, that which goes without saying and is beyond questioning. Such discourse and social imaginary function to limit the range of plausible thought and action.[41]

An example of the hegemonic discourse of Hellenistic rulers after Alexander can be found in imperial iconography on coins and statues, architecture, and the royal cult. Seleucid coins reinforced imperial ideology through the very instrument, money, by which the Seleucids facilitated the payment of tribute from subject peoples. The coins portrayed the king as mighty conqueror, favored by the gods. These included images of Athena, goddess of war, Zeus, the god of thunder and ruler of the Greek pantheon, and Apollo, believed to have appeared to Seleucus in a dream that presaged his military victory and rise to kingship. On one coin is an image of *Nike* (Victory) lifting a laurel wreath or victory crown, flanked by the inscriptions "Seleucus" and "king." The royal ideology of Seleucus as victorious king was perpetuated by his title, *Nickator* (Victor). After his death, Seleucus would be divinized as an incarnation of Zeus *Nickator*, inaugurating the ruler cult wedded to the military persona of the powerful warrior-king.[42]

Anathea Portier-Young argues that resistance to hegemony requires a counter-hegemonic discourse that opens up new parameters for thought and action. Systems of domination easily perpetuate themselves if the structures of domination are invisible. Apocalyptic writings sought to make oppressive structures visible as such by characterizing them as monstrous or demonic. The early Jewish apocalypses were written to resist imperial claims to possess the authorization and power to order the world, which it exercised through force, but also propaganda, ideology, values, and cosmology. Apocalypses countered the totalizing narratives and empire's claims to ultimacy with an even grander total vision of history, the cosmos, and the reign of God. Apocalyptic literature sought to reassure Israelites that ultimate power and authority rest with God. Proclaiming that the empires will be held accountable by divine judgment served to articulate a limit to their power and authority (Dan 2; 7; 1 En. 89:59—90:25).[43]

---

41. Bourdieu, *Outline of a Theory of Practice*, 78–79, 166, 168, cited by Portier-Young, *Apocalypse Against Empire*, 11–13. For her appropriation of insights from Antonio Gramsci, Portier-Young draws upon Mitchell, "Everyday Metaphors of Power," 553; Femia, *Gramsci's Political Thought*; Miller, "Limits of Dominance," 63–79.

42. Portier-Young, *Apocalypse Against Empire*, 52–54.

43. Portier-Young, *Apocalypse Against Empire*, xxii, xxiii, 11–13, 34–35, 52–54; Russell, *Divine Disclosure*, 18.

In the earliest Jewish apocalypses, one finds the use of mythical images to expose and counter the mythologies that fund imperial power. The binary nature of hegemonic construction of reality (inside/outside, center/periphery, good/bad, civilization/barbaric, normal/aberrant) creates possibilities for resistance through critical inversion. The categories are retained but turned upside down, making it possible to imagine the world as ruled not by empires but by God.[44]

The book of the Watchers is a loose allegory for the cultural crisis brought on by the advent of Hellenism, which entailed the spread of information and new ideas about morality that were scandalous to traditional Jews. First Enoch's use of Greek gigantomacy mythology is an example of "critical inversion." In Greek civilization, the "gigantomacy" was a powerful political allegorical myth, which mapped Greek victories over "barbarian" enemies onto the defeat of the giants by the Olympian gods. By the fifth century BCE, the violence and disorder of the giants and other monsters had come to represent the violence of "uncivilized" peoples. These people groups appear within this *mythos* as the antithesis of the "civilized" values of moderation, virtue, and piety. The defeat of the giants served as mythic paradigm for the defense of law, moderation, and self-control and the punishment of *hubris*. The conquests of the Hellenistic kings and the spread of their culture, religion, and forms of civilization, were imagined as a reenactment of the gigantomachy myth.[45]

First Enoch inverts the allegory by identifying the giants with the Hellenistic rulers themselves. The Watchers abandoned their place in heaven to live among and have intercourse with human women and begat monstrous children, giants who were characterized by brutality and voracious appetites. They devour all of the food produced by humans until there is no food left. Then, they devour people (1 En. 7:3–4). It is the giants, now symbolizing the *Diadochi*, not the people they have conquered, who violate the ideals of moderation, law, and order. The angel Gabriel receives the commission to destroy them, but the irony is that their destruction will come through their own lack of self-control in their destructive wars against one another (1 En. 10:9). Rainer Albertz notes that the readers of the book of the Watchers would have easily recognized the not-so-veiled reference to the battles of the *Diadochi* and the never ending chain of Syrian wars.[46]

---

44. Portier-Young, *Apocalypse Against Empire*, 15–17.

45. Portier-Young, *Apocalypse Against Empire*, 18–20.

46. Nickelsburg, "Apocalyptic and Myth in 1 Enoch 6–11," 383–405; Albertz, *From the Exile to the Maccabees*, 579; Portier-Young, *Apocalypse Against Empire*, 7, 18–20.

Section Two: Soteriology and Biblical Narrative

The Roman Empire as the Setting for Jesus's Ministry

As we "fast-forward" from the second century BCE to the period of time that is the setting for the New Testament Gospels, we find God's people once again under the thumb of idolatrous, oppressive, and brutal imperial overlords. The Roman Empire was a "theo-political" entity. After his victory finally ended more than a decade of empire-wide civil war between rival warlords, Octavian, Julius Caesar's adopted son, took the name Augustus, meaning revered and highly honored. The Roman Senate awarded him a ceremonial golden shield, celebrating him as the very embodiment of valor (*virtus*), mercy, justice, and dutiful devotion to the gods, his ancestors, and his posterity (*pietas*). He was acclaimed throughout the empire as the "Savior" who had brought peace and prosperity to the whole world. The word translated in our New Testament as gospel (*euangelion*) was used to refer to an imperial proclamation. The imperial gospel was the good news of a savior, Caesar Augustus, who had established peace and security throughout the Mediterranean world. The Priene Calendar inscription, dated to 9 BCE, identifies the birth of Caesar Augustus as the beginning of a new era and proposed that the calendar should begin with his birthday. He is referred to as savior, the greatest benefactor of all, and a god. The full inscription is:

> The providence which has ordered the whole of our life, showing concern and zeal, has ordained the most perfect consummation for human life by giving it to Augustus, by filling him with virtue for doing the work of a benefactor among men, and by sending in him, as it were, a savior for us and those who come after us, to make war to cease, to create order everywhere. . . . The birthday of the god [Augustus] was the beginning for the world of the glad tidings (*euangelion*) that have come to men through him.[47]

Augustus was worshiped as "equal to the Beginning (*arche*) of all things."[48] In cities in Greece and Asia Minor, this took the form of shrines, temples, and citywide festivals, during which sacrifices were offered to honor this "savior" and his successors, also considered divine. Statues of the emperors were erected beside those of the traditional gods. The "Accomplishments of the Divine Augustus" that were inscribed on monuments in most cities of the empire and included a lengthy list of peoples subjugated, hostages taken, and regions conquered. The imperial cult sought to bestow

---

47. The full inscription is published in Dittenberger, *Sylloge Inscriptionum Graecarum*, 458.

48. Dittenberger, *Sylloge Inscriptionum Graecarum*, 458.

an aura of supernatural legitimacy on the emperor as the visible embodiment of cosmic order and divinely ordained to secure prosperity for the human race. After his death, he was accorded divine honor by the Roman Senate as one had ascended into the Olympian heaven.[49]

Contrary to Rome's propaganda portraying the empire as a bringer of peace, prosperity, law, and civilization, the Roman Empire expanded by brutal forms of conquest and maintained control in the "less civilized" areas of the empire through ongoing military violence. Initial Roman conquests of new people groups and nations often entailed devastation of the countryside, burning of villages, pillage of towns, and slaughter and enslavement of the populace. A Caledonian chieftain, Calgacus, was quoted by Tacitus:

> [The Romans are] the plunderers of the world. . . . If the enemy is rich, they are rapacious, if poor they lust for dominion. Not East, not West has sated them. . . . They rob, butcher, plunder, and call it "empire." They make a desolation and they call it peace. . . . our goods and chattels go for tribute; our lands and harvests in requisitions of grain; life and limb themselves are worn out in making roads through marsh and forest to the accompaniment of gibes and blows.[50]

The ancient Romans obsession with honor drove them to conquer with extreme brutality in order to extract *fides/pistis* (loyalty, i.e., submission and deference) from subjugated peoples. The Romans viewed their relationship with other peoples as a competition for honor. Rome asserted its superiority by humiliating its enemies. Any sign of weakness on Rome's part, such as failure to avenge a defeat in war or to punish a revolt with sufficiently fierce violence, they feared, would undermine Rome's dominance and honor. The Romans reacted with brutality and often genocide, even to minor breaches of treaty and other threats to the order they had imposed. After viewing

---

49. Horsley, "General Introduction," 3, 14, 16; *Jesus and Empire*, 20–24; Elliot, *Arrogance of Nations*, 29–30; Murphy, *Apocalypticism in the Bible and Its World*, 229; Carter, *Matthew and Empire*, 20–21.

50. Tacitus, *Life of Cnaeus Julius Agricola* 30.3—31.2; Carter, *Matthew and Empire*, 15. Tacitus also quoted the rallying cry of another Briton, the rebel Boudicca, from her war chariot where she stood with her two daughters, like her, violated by Roman soldiers: "I am not fighting for my kingdom and my wealth. I am fighting as an ordinary person for my lost freedom, my bruised body, and my outraged daughters. Nowadays, Roman rapacity does not even spare our bodies. Old people are killed, virgins raped." Tacitus then recited the speech in which the Roman commander urged his soldiers to massacre the "unwarlike, unarmed" Britons, who offered defiance, killing some 80,000 people, not sparing even the women. In Tacitus's eyes, this was a glorious victory. Tacitus passes these accounts along with no qualms about the justice of Roman conquest. Tacitus, *Annals* 14.35.

Section Two: Soteriology and Biblical Narrative

the awful scene of corpses in a city destroyed by the Romans, the historian Polybius wrote, "It seems to me that they do this for the sake of terror." Crucifixion, mass slaughter, enslavement, and massacres of entire towns were purposeful attempts to terrorize subjected peoples.[51]

The glory of conquest was pervasive throughout the empire in literature, art, coins, epigraphy, and public monuments. Over three hundred triumphal arches survive or are known from coins or other inscriptions. "Victory" was personified prominently on Roman coins. Rome's victory parades were "civil religious" festivals glorifying the military might of the victors and the humiliating defeat of the vanquished.[52]

The Roman Empire was designed to concentrate wealth and power in the hands of the patricians in Rome. Pre-modern and pre-industrial agrarian civilizations were powered by human labor on arable land. To expand their wealth, they had to expand the amounts of land and labor ruled over. The costs of conquest were borne by the slaves, peasants, and laborers who produced the wealth Rome appropriated through taxation, whereas the profits accrued to a small circle of wealthy and powerful individuals. The bulk of grain and other food imported to Rome was extracted from subject peoples, disproportionately North Africa and Egypt.[53]

Rome's values were power, ruthless resolve, honor, security, revenge, deterrence by terror, the commitment to be seen as invincible, scorn for other peoples, and contempt for manual labor and manual laborers. Service and duty, maintaining one's honor, and acquiring glory were fundamental elite values. Elite persons gained prestige and honor from publicly beneficial acts. Acts of patronage and civic beneficence, such as financing a statue or fountain or a food handout, were avenues for expressing those values. Wealth was not for investing or accumulating, since there was always a continual supply through exploitation of peasants working the land. Wealth was for conspicuous consumption and display through buildings, clothing, jewelry, military acts, food, celebrations, entertainment, clients and servants, and beneficent civic gestures, all of which maintained the distance between the aristocracy and the peasantry and reminded the peasants who they were and who they were not.[54]

James C. Scott has proposed the concepts of the "public transcript" and the "hidden transcript." The hidden transcript is what both dominant

---

51. Horsley, *Jesus and Empire*, 15, 27–28, 30–31.

52. Horsley, *Jesus and Empire*, 26–27.

53. Horsley, *Jesus and the powers*, 25–27; Elliot, *Arrogance of Nations*, 30–31, 132–33.

54. Carter, *Matthew and Empire*, 13, 16.

and subordinate classes say candidly among themselves, out of earshot of the other. In the public transcript, which is the direct communication and interaction between the dominant and subordinate classes, Roman rhetoric displayed the typical assurances regarding their altruism and beneficence, which Jesus himself noted when he criticized the ideological façade designed to cloak domination when he observed that "the kings of the Gentiles lord it over them" while nevertheless calling themselves benefactors (Luke 22:25).[55]

A brutally unjust imperial system must represent itself as legitimate in the eyes of conquered peoples. Walter Wink points out that empires are in a permanent crisis of legitimation.[56] Managing this crisis, Neil Elliot points out, requires a rhetorical arsenal of themes of inevitability, beneficence, and consent. Imperial propaganda portrayed Roman imperial rule as established "according to reason," according to the law of nature that the strong should always rule over the weak.[57] Edward Said, commenting on modern empires, observed that the rhetoric of power seeks to produce an illusion of benevolence when deployed in an imperial setting.[58] One coin portrayed the Roman conqueror extending one hand in alliance with a spear in the other, to be wielded in protection of Rome's allies. *Fides* and *amicitia* (friendship) were the euphemisms through which Rome represented to subject peoples that their subjection and willing obedience would be rewarded by the protective care of their conquerors.[59]

According to Davina Lopez, Roman imperial ideology relied upon an imagined hierarchical ordering of reality that functioned to represent relationships of domination as natural, inevitable, and universal. This structuring of hierarchical reality featured dominant-subordinate pairings such as male and female, active and passive, high and low, conqueror and conquered, order and threat, law and lawlessness, civilization and barbarism, city and country, colonizer and colonized, Greek and barbarian, and cosmos and chaos, among others. Lopez argues that the Romans portrayed themselves as conquerors and their conquests as natural, in terms of these patriarchal and hierarchical power relationships. Roman is to the other nations as male to female. Conquest is portrayed as a penetrative sexual act. Romans narrated and artistically portrayed themselves as the masculine master race and the conquered as the inferior feminine races. The nations

---

55. Scott, *Domination and the Arts of Resistance*, 5, 28.
56. Wink, *Engaging the Powers*, 93.
57. Elliot, *Arrogance of Nations*, 32–33.
58. Said, *Culture and Imperialism*, xvii.
59. Elliot, *Arrogance of Nations*, 38.

are semantically identified or associated with the "lower" values of female, passive, low, conquered, threat, lawlessness, barbarism, country, colonized, land, and chaos. These interlocking systems of signification reveal a construction of reality undergirding the Roman imperial ideology of divinely ordered conquest and rule without end over all the nations.[60]

Judea and Galilee Under Roman Occupation and Rule

Pompey invaded Palestine around 63 BCE. Once there, he invaded the temple and plundered the treasury. He also laid the Jewish people under tribute, a standard Roman punitive as well as revenue-generating measure. The Romans viewed the Jews as "good for nothing but slavery" and despised them as superstitious and exclusive.[61]

Julius Caesar and Marc Antony chose the ruthless military strongman Herod to control Palestine. He was designated "king of the Judeans" by the Roman Senate. He ruled with an iron fist, allowing no dissent and requiring demonstrations of allegiance to his own and Roman rule. Herod ensured the flow of taxes and tribute to Rome and also taxed heavily for his own projects. He confiscated and redistributed estates and extracted as much as he could from the peasant base. Judean, Samaritan, and Galilean peasants who had previously lived under only one set of rulers, the Hasmonean high priests, were suddenly subject to three layers of rule and the economic demands of all three: tribute to the Romans, taxes to Herod, and, on top of required tithes and offerings, an annual tax to the "temple-state." In order to secure the ongoing approval of the emperor, he sponsored massive building projects throughout his realm in honor of Augustus. His extravagant expenditures for building programs, his own lavish court, and his "generosity" to imperial family members exhausted his people economically during his long reign. When Herod died, the nation was impoverished, with as much as 80 percent of the population estimated to be at subsistence level.[62]

After Herod's death in 4 BCE, Herod's three sons were given territories not as kings but as tetrarchs and, for Archelaus in Judea, the title of ethnarch. Philip was given the region across the Jordan River. The emperor installed Antipas to rule over Galilee. The Herodians were Antipas's supporters. They

---

60. Lopez, *Apostle to the Conquered*, xiii–xiv, 1–2, 20–21.

61. Horsley, *Jesus and Empire*, 11, 21, 31–32; *Jesus and the Powers*, 24; Storkey, *Jesus and Politics*, 18; Herzog, *Jesus, Justice, and the Reign of God*, 90–91.

62. Horsley, *Jesus and Empire*, 11, 21, 31–33; *Jesus and the Powers*, 24; Storkey, *Jesus and Politics*, 18; Herzog, 90–91, 99; Barrera, *Biblical Economic Ethics* 133–34.

were the beneficiaries of lucrative deals due to Herodian patronage, including grants of huge plots of land.[63]

Herod the Great had retained the high priesthood and temple apparatus as part of his regime. After eliminating the last members of the Hasmonean family, he installed high-priestly families, imported from the Jewish diaspora, of his own choosing. He arrogated to himself the power to depose and appoint high priests. Eventually, four high priestly families managed to monopolize appointments to the office (houses of Boethus, Ananas, Phiabi, Kamith). They were widely viewed as illegitimate because of their lack of descent from the family of Zadok. These families controlled the temple and its institutions, especially the Sanhedrin and temple treasury. After Archelaus was deposed by Rome in 6 CE, Judea was converted to a sub-province of the province of Syria, overseen by a prefect (Pontius Pilate) responsible to the Legate (or governor) of Syria. After the removal of Archelaus from power, the Romans left the high-priestly rulers in place under the watchful eye and political-military backing of Roman governors in Judea and Samaria. The governors held the power to appoint their own nominee to the high-priestly office. Therefore, the high priests were directly beholden to the governors. The long tenures of Caiaphas and Pilate suggest a close working relationship. Archeological explorations indicate that during Herodian and early Roman times, wealthy high-priestly families built ever more elaborate mansions for themselves on the hill overlooking the temple from the west. This is evidence that they became increasingly wealthy during these decades.[64]

Economic Realities

The goals of Roman political rule were to maintain order and collect the tribute and taxes they imposed on subjugated peoples. Since the empire did not have the structure or personnel to rule each colony directly, it was Roman custom to co-opt provincial aristocracies to achieve these goals. It was typical for aristocratic empires to leave local forms of rule intact. Therefore, the interests of local aristocracies would be aligned with the interests of the empire. Rome and other ancient empires simply added themselves to the top and used the already existing administrative machinery, incorporating the local aristocracy into their system of rule. Tax collection was contracted out to the urban elite who served as tax brokers or as tax and toll collectors.

---

63. Storkey, *Jesus and Politics*, 26–27, 44; Horsley, *Jesus and Empire*, 11, 33; *Covenant Economics*, 86–87.

64. Horsley, *Jesus and Empire*, 11, 21, 31–33; *Jesus and the Powers*, 24; Storkey, *Jesus and Politics*, 18, 27; Herzog, *Jesus, Justice, and the Reign of God*, 90–91;

What they took for themselves beyond that basic requirement was left to the discretion of the collaborators. The Romans allowed them to exploit their people so long as it did not jeopardize stability.[65]

Palestine in Jesus's day was an advanced agrarian society in which wealth was based on control of the land. Seventy percent of the land was used for agriculture and ninety percent of the population engaged in farming. In Jesus's day, the majority of the population would have been economically marginal peasants, living in villages. The peasantry included small landowners who were always on the edge of losing their lands due to heavy imperial taxation. Most landowning families engaged in subsistence agriculture, producing primarily for their own consumption rather than for exchange. At the bottom rung of the economic and social classes were the landless peasants, some of whom had lost their lands due to debt and some who had inherited nothing. These persons worked as tenant farmers or day laborers or were reduced to begging, especially if their health conditions rendered them unable to work.[66]

A small percentage of Israelites belonged to the economic elite, including the high priestly families in Judea and Herodian families or other members of the aristocracy, who effectively ruled and governed on the emperor's behalf. These members of the ruling class were rewarded with grants of land, had great power and privilege, and were kept in their positions by the Romans. Throughout the empire, a retainer class of bureaucrats was created by the governing class to assist in governance. They were elevated above the common folks and shared in the benefits of rule, including significant power, status, and wealth. This class included leading Pharisees and scribes. Jesus was in constant conflict with these groups.[67]

Roman occupation brought with it an imperial economy. Increasing amounts of the peasants' produce was siphoned upward into the control of the wealthy, further augmenting their political and economic power. Both literary and archeological evidence point toward a concentration of land ownership in the hands of the few and ever larger estates. Ordinary people were often harassed by Herod's underlings for bribes and gifts. Under the burdens of Roman taxation, peasants often found it necessary to borrow to feed their families, typically at unmercifully high rates of interest. The motivation to lend, on the part of the wealthy, was the hope of foreclosing and taking possession of a small landowner's land if the debt was not paid

---

65. Goodman, *Ruling Class of Judea*, 127–33; Herzog, *Jesus, Justice, and the Reign of God*, 102–3; Hanson, *Political History of the Bible in America*, 488.

66. Horsley, *Covenant Economics*, 88; Barrera, *Biblical Economic Ethics*, 127–29.

67. Horsley, *Covenant Economics*, 88; Barrera, *Biblical Economic Ethics*, 127–29.

off. There was a significant rise in the number of landless peasants. Heavily indebted peasants were often forced to become sharecroppers on their own land or were forced off the land to become day laborers.[68]

The Sabbatical provision in Deuteronomy for the forgiveness of unpaid debts every seventh year was cleverly circumvented by scribes and rabbis with a loophole called the *prosbul*. Because the elites refused to lend within the year or two years prior to the Sabbatical year, which was direct disobedience of the admonition to do so (Deut 15:9–11), Rabbi Hillel introduced the *prosbul*, a public declaration by the man seeking a loan that he would forego the Sabbatical year cancellation of his debt and repay the money even after the advent of the seventh year.[69]

The goal of the ruling class was to accumulate as much land as possible, with peasants furnishing the labor, mostly under great compulsion through a combination of slavery, *corvee*, or obligations to a patron. Living in the cities, these absentee landlords extracted produce from the countryside through heavy taxation, burdensome rents, usurious interest, or outright theft. The aim was to draw as much surplus from the peasants as possible, leaving them just enough to stay alive and work the land. Taxes and religious impositions alone absorbed 28 to 40 percent of the peasants' produce. After covering costs of farm production, peasants had about 8 to 20 percent of their harvest left for their subsistence. A similar situation obtained with fishermen, with imperial Rome and the ruling elite able to extract the produce of this industry as well. In this precarious economic situation, indebted peasants were threatened with loss of their land and livelihood and the threat of destitution and perpetual malnutrition that came with the life

---

68. Ancient court documents and tax receipts recorded on papyri and ostraca in Egypt, also under Roman occupation in the first century, provide a glimpse of the brutality of Roman taxation. There were over one hundred different types of taxes, from the head tax to taxes on artisans and land, to imposts at harbors and tolls, to levies on some contracts and market transactions. Soldiers were used to coerce the population. The burdens of taxation became heavier for the ordinary peasant because the soldiers were abusive and demanded bribes for themselves. The brutality of the entire system is evident in the beatings and murders by which the Romans and their tax farmers extracted all that could be taken from provincial peasants. Those unable to pay their taxes became fugitives. So burdensome were these impositions and so poor was the countryside that those who were in arrears for a year or two in the payment of taxes were as numerous as those who were able to pay on time. Goodman, *Ruling Class of Judea*, 57; Horsley, *Covenant Economics*, 88; *Jesus and the Powers*, 29; Barrera, *Biblical Economic Ethics*, 132–36; MacMullen, *Roman Social Relations*, 44–45.

69. Horsley, *Jesus and the Powers*, 29; Goodman, *Ruling Class of Judea*, 57; Barrera, *Biblical Economic Ethics*, 132–33.

of a day-laborer. Most of the peasantry was left landless and ended up as tenants, day laborers, or beggars. Some resorted to banditry.[70]

On top of all of the other oppressive taxes and levies, the annual half-shekel temple tax, collected from every observant Jewish male, plus tithes and fees for making sacrificial offerings in the temple, was at least 13 percent of the income of peasants in Palestine. This was an additional layer of burdensome demands upon the resources of the peasantry. Peasants who were unable to pay the temple tax were not eligible to receive the benefits of the temple. They were not able to offer a sin offering and receive forgiveness, and one who did not have the requisite sacrifices performed on his or her behalf was also in a constant state of being ritually unclean.[71]

As we read the Gospels, it is crucial to be aware that a high percentage of the people Jesus addressed were poor persons on the edge of utter destitution. It was no metaphor when Jesus taught his followers to pray, "Give us this day our daily bread."[72] This prayer was a request to survive each day.

---

70. Barrera, *Biblical Economic Ethics*, 132–33, 138–39.

71. Herzog, *Jesus, Justice, and the Reign of God*, 90–91, 121–23, 136–37; Horsley, *Covenant Economics*, 85–86; *Jesus and Empire*, 11, 21, 31–33; *Jesus and the Powers*, 24; Barrera, *Biblical Economic Ethics*, 128; Storkey, *Jesus and Politics*, 18.

72. Horsley, *Covenant Economics*, 81.

CHAPTER FIVE

The Soteriology of Jesus
Messiah, Savior, Inaugurator of the Kingdom of God

Characteristics of the two Ages[1]

Present Evil Age	Messianic Age
	Holy Spirit—Messiah—justice and peace
Empires	God's rule/Messiah rules/ empires defeated
Satan/evil spirits inflict misery on humans	Expulsion of evil spirits/they harm no more
Sickness and death	healing/wholeness/life/resurrection
Injustice and oppression	Justice (especially for the vulnerable)
Economic injustice/gross disparities of	Jubilee: economic justice; all have
wealth and poverty	access to land
hunger/starvation	plenty of food

1. This is the social imaginary as it appears in multiple biblical texts. Over time, these images coalesce in the theological imagination of many, though not all, of the different expressions of the Jewish faith between the fourth century BCE and the time of Jesus and the first centuries of the early Christian movement.

Warfare and violence	peace/swords to plowshares
Poverty/infant mortality	long life (life with no more death)
The thief comes to steal and kill and destroy	But I (Jesus) came to give life/abundant life
	= Human flourishing in every dimension (John 10)

Jesus Saves: But What Does that Mean?

Jesus Messiah is the Savior! On this claim, one finds a solid Christian consensus through the years. But to understand what it means to say "Jesus saves," we must look to the narratives of his healings, conflicts, teachings, and actions. From many of the prophetic writings preserved in our First Testament, through apocalyptic and other writings of the inter-testamental period, many faithful Jews looked forward to a glorious future, often referred to as the messianic age or the age to come, as God's ultimate act of salvation. What does it mean for God to save? It means that God will put all things right, overcoming sin and death, political and economic injustice, war, suffering, and disease. In this glorious future, the knowledge of the Lord will fill the earth as the waters cover the sea, and when that happens, there will be global peace, plenty to eat, long life, healing, and joy. The book of Revelation reveals that this future hope for an earth that is healed and redeemed, a world from which evil and suffering have been banished, was not left behind by the early Christian movement. The book of Revelation imagines and anticipates a future in which tears, death, and mourning are no more (21:3–4).

As Savior and Messiah, Jesus initiates, in the here and now of the present evil age, this coming age of justice and peace where all things are put right. Where Jesus goes, things that were wrong are rectified. Lepers are cleansed and restored to community. Blind eyes are opened. Oppressive, purity-driven religion is resisted. The outcasts are included in the fellowship around the table. Debts are forgiven, the hungry are fed, and economic injustice is resisted. Jesus calls together a community of disciples and calls them to join him in the struggle to resist oppressive situations, include those who were formerly excluded, to love enemies, to show hospitality, and share resources. As we will suggest later in this book, discipleship is not something that is good to do after one is saved. Rather, discipleship, which includes participation in God's mission of putting things right, is central to what we were saved for. The *missio Dei*, the assignment we have been given, the project in which we are engaged, is not something we do to earn or attain salvation. Rather, being drawn into this eschatological new creation, still to come but already invading the present, to be invited and empowered to join God's cause, is part and parcel of the gift of salvation!

The Reign of God Is at Hand

In the Synoptic Gospels,[2] Jesus preaches and teaches about the kingdom of God. In our first two Gospels, he comes out of the gate preaching the nearness of the kingdom of God (Mark 1:14–15; see also Matt 4:17).

What is this kingdom[3] Jesus proclaimed?

One line of interpretation draws the wrong conclusion from Jesus's refusal to seek political power by leading a violent insurrection to drive the occupying Roman imperial officials and military presence out of the land, re-establish Israel's political independence, and restore the Davidic monarchy. Many Christians have denigrated these Jewish hopes, as if such dreams of national liberation were a misunderstanding of their own Scriptures. But these hopes made perfect sense in light of First Testament convictions about God's sovereign rule. Indeed, when Jesus's disciples ask, after his resurrection, "Lord, is it at this time you are restoring the kingdom to Israel" (Acts 1:1–8), Jesus does not rebuke them for asking the wrong question.

There is a popular, but disastrous, misinterpretation of Jesus's refusal to lead an insurrection and assume the throne of a restored Davidic monarchy. This misinterpretation is intertwined with the conventional version of salvation. This is the notion that Jesus was a "spiritual" rather than a political messiah, that his kingdom is an interior, spiritual kingdom in which God rules inside the heart of the Christian believer.[4] Or, "the kingdom of God" is

---

2. The Gospel of Matthew typically substitutes the phrase "kingdom of heaven" where the Gospels of Mark and Luke use "kingdom of God."

3. A note about language: Many have objected to the language of the kingdom of God as patriarchal and as language that valorizes absolutist political authority. For example, a popular substitution is to speak of the Kin-dom of God. I will persist in using the language of kingdom at times because of the kind of kingdom Jesus inaugurates and the kind of king or Lord that he is. This language functions as critique of all human domination, whether patriarchal or political. The language of kingdom is the language that authorizes humans to resist the absolutist claims of any government or human entity to absolute allegiance and obedience. It is language that authorizes forms of resistance when any human authority abuses that authority to exploit, oppress, mistreat, or kill human beings. If we are subject to another kingdom, this relativizes, destabilizes, and reorders our obligations to human authorities.

4. Through the widespread use of the Scofield Reference Bible, the product of one of the theologians of the "lost cause," C. I. Scofield's interpretation of the kingdom of

thought to refer to "heaven," which is supposed to be "up there," "out there," anywhere but this earth. Christians in the grip of this misinterpretation have said things such as, "Jesus did not come to bring world peace but rather inner peace and spiritual peace between God and saved individuals." Jesus's declaration to Pilate that "my kingdom is not [of/from] this world" (John 18:36) is thought to clinch this theological position. Jesus's kingdom must be in heaven. On this interpretation, Jesus came to save our souls, to rescue us from planet earth, so that when we die, we can live forever somewhere else. He did not come to transform this world.[5]

But it would be a catastrophic error to draw this conclusion. While Jesus did not come to establish a *conventional* political kingdom, based upon coercion and violence, with a centralized government and bureaucracy, a standing military, and police, courts, and jails, this does not mean that he did not come to inaugurate a real, even if a dramatically different kind of, social order, a genuinely "political kingdom" on this earth!

To interpret Jesus as a spiritual messiah is, to employ a creative metaphor, to give away the whole farm. A spiritual messiah is not a messiah at all. The messiah, *by definition*, is the one who inaugurates and presides over a world put right, a social order of justice, peace, and human flourishing on this earth. A "messiah" who saves souls for heaven but does not heal, repair, and transform this world is not a messiah at all. If Jesus is the messiah anticipated in the First Testament, then he did not come to rescue us *from* planet earth. Rather, he came *to rescue planet earth* and bring about God's purposes for humanity and all creation!

The Gospel of Mark begins with the good news of Jesus Messiah, the Son of God. "Christ" is the Greek translation of the Hebrew term "Messiah," which means literally, "anointed one." Messiah is a royal title derived from the ritual of anointing new kings with oil at the coronation ceremony. Mark's readers know "the secret," from the opening line of Mark's gospel, that Jesus is the messiah. His actions should be interpreted through the lens of Israel's messianic hopes, and these hopes should not be spiritualized away. In addition, Mark 1:1 draws from Psalm 2, a royal enthronement psalm, which identified the king as the Lord's anointed one and links this with the title "Son of God." While I affirm Nicene christological orthodoxy, this royal title does not function at the beginning of Mark's Gospel as a

---

God as primarily an interior, spiritual kingdom has exercised profound influence on evangelical thought. Grimes, "Racial Ideology of Rapture," 211–21.

5. A more faithful interpretation of "my kingdom is not of this world" is that the source of Jesus's kingdom is not this world's political ways of power and domination and violence. This phrase does not mean that Jesus's kingdom is, geographically speaking, somewhere else.

direct affirmation of Jesus's divinity but rather serves to identify Jesus as the ultimate fulfillment of God's promise to David of an enduring dynasty (2 Sam 7). In the Gospel of Luke, when the angel Gabriel appears to Mary, she is informed that God will give to her son the throne of his father David and he will reign over the people of Israel forever, echoing language of Daniel 7:14 (Luke 1:31–33).

The phrase "kingdom of God" assumes the foundational First Testament conviction that Yahweh is the world's true sovereign ruler. The association of the reign of God and gospel, good news, is linked with the joyful anticipation of return from exile in Isa 53:7.

The Greek words *euongelion* and *basileia* also had a long history of political usage in the Greco-Roman world.[6] *Basileia* was the word commonly used to refer to empires like Rome's, just as the term *Basileus* was used to denote emperors. As William Herzog points out, proclamation of the kingdom of God would be unsettling in a world of Roman imperial rule as well as Herodian client kingship and the temple-state in Judea, all of which were beholden to their Roman imperial overlords for their own security, status, and wealth. Proclaiming an arriving kingdom was, in effect, a criticism of the existing kingdoms as illegitimate.[7]

Inaugurated Eschatology

However, as Christians, we are faced with a serious theological crisis. If Jesus is the messiah, and if the messiah, by definition, is the one who inaugurates, brings about, and presides over the messianic age of peace and justice, Jesus seems to have been a colossal failure. After all, Jesus died a humiliating death on a cross, which certainly seems to be not the triumph of God's kingdom but of Rome's. Even if God raised him from the dead, Jesus left the scene of our human history and the world remains as it ever was, a realm of sin and death, political oppression and injustice, abuse, and human suffering. If Jesus is the messiah, why did he not put the world to rights? The messiah is supposed to bring the world entirely into alignment with God's good purposes, such that God's presence, power, and rule are manifest for every eye to see. More than most Christians recognize, this is a formidable challenge to the credibility of the gospel.

---

6. Friedrich, "*euangelion*," 722–25, cited by Elliot, *Arrogance of Nations*, 188; Murphy, *Apocalypticism in the Bible and Its World*, 229.

7. Herzog, *Jesus, Justice, and the Reign of God*, 203; Carter, *Matthew and Empire*, 5; Miller, "Wrestling with Rome," 283.

For this reason, the hope for Christ's return or "second coming" is not just something tacked onto the Christian hope for salvation. It *is* indispensable to the Christian hope of salvation. Jesus is only the Messiah and Savior if he brings the kingdom of God, the future age of justice, peace, and human wholeness, to this earth and fully brings all of God's creation into alignment with God's good purposes.

The meaning of the resurrection of Jesus is not merely a "super-miracle" confirming that Jesus is divine. The resurrection of Jesus is connected to the belief in the resurrection of the dead in the future messianic age, an eschatological day of justice in which God sets the record straight about the truth of the entirety of human history as well as of each individual life. That Jesus was raised from the dead prior to the end of human history was understood to be God's vindication and validation of Jesus as the Messiah and the "eschatological judge" who will judge all of humanity. That Jesus is the "first fruits from the dead" (1 Cor 15:20) means that our eschatological destiny is bound up with this Jesus and his resurrected body (1 Cor 15:20–23).

But if Jesus did not bring God's kingdom in its fullness and put all things right, what did he do? Part of the answer to this question lies in an interesting plot twist in the previous two-age eschatology, according to which human history is composed of two distinct and non-overlapping ages: the present evil age and the messianic age to come.

In Matt 11:2–5, the setting is the period of time shortly after John the Baptist was imprisoned by Herod Antipas. John sent his disciples to Jesus with a question. In effect, the question was, "Are you the Messiah?" Jesus does not provide a straightforward *yes* or *no* answer to John's question. Instead, he points to what is happening, to acts of deliverance, healing, and transformation. Jesus's deeds are significant because his actions bring about the wholeness or well-being associated with the messianic age: sight to the blind, the ability to walk to those who cannot walk, and hearing to persons who had been deaf are linked to Isa 35:5–6. Good news to the poor, along with another reference to "sight to the blind," was proclaimed by the messianic prophet of Isa 61:1. Multiple expressions of hope for a future Davidic king (Isa 11:1–5) anticipate that he will ensure justice for the poor. The raising of the dead is the hope associated with the messianic age during the intertestamental period.

The meaning of these mighty deeds of healing and deliverance is that the future messianic age is already breaking into the present. Wherever Jesus goes, the messianic age starts happening, even though it happens in bits and pieces rather than all at once. According to much of the apocalyptic literature of the intertestamental period, the present evil age comes to an abrupt and cataclysmic end as a crucial prerequisite for the messianic age to begin. But the Synoptic Gospels offer a "plot twist" in the two-age scheme of history. With Jesus's public ministry, the future age of justice and peace is inaugurated before the cataclysmic end of the present evil age. The full and complete arrival of the messianic age remains a future event. But with Jesus's life, death, and resurrection, the messianic age has already been *inaugurated*. This future age has invaded the present order of things. Scholars have sometimes characterized this vision as "inaugurated eschatology." The kingdom of God is both already here and not yet here. In Jesus's life, death, and resurrection, and then in the outpouring of the Holy Spirit, who gathers humans into Christ and thereby creates a new kind of human community, the kingdom of God has taken root in the present age and will be brought to completion in a glorious future victory of Christ. Exactly how Christ will "come again," to complete the work he started and put all things right, remains a mystery, as Jesus implied in response to his disciples's question as to whether Jesus would establish the kingdom in Israel shortly after his resurrection (Acts 1:1–8).

In Jesus's parable of the mustard seed, he gives expression to this inaugurated eschatology through a metaphor of small and inconspicuous beginnings and slow, organic growth. The reign of God is said to be like a mustard seed, tiny and insignificant. But from such a tiny seed, the mustard plant spreads everywhere and provides a refuge for the birds of the air, which was, in Jesus's day, also an idiom used to describe the most vulnerable persons in society (Mark 4:30–32). Instead of the messianic age beginning immediately after a final battle to overturn imperial power all at once, the kingdom of God begins small. But from such inconspicuous beginnings in the ministry of a wandering Galilean peasant, this movement will grow until it becomes something massive and unstoppable.

Matthew 12:22–29 also features inaugurated eschatology, but this time the metaphor switches from organic growth to a more violent metaphor of "home invasion" and incapacitation, through binding or "tying up," the Evil One. Jesus expels an "evil spirit" from a man who has been made blind and mute by the malicious action of that evil spirit. This was a benevolent action on Jesus's part, delivering this man from a situation of suffering and social death. By virtue of his condition, he is locked out of the ability to communicate and interact with others. But after delivering this man, Jesus was falsely accused by a group of Pharisees of casting out evil spirits by the power of evil, named here as Beelzebul, the prince of demons. In response, Jesus's dramatic and powerful declaration is that "if it is by the Spirit of God that I drive out demons, then the Kingdom of God has come upon you," or, as some translate the Greek into English, "the Kingdom of God is in your midst."

To understand this text, we must remember that the book of Isaiah constantly associates the Spirit of YHWH with the Messiah. The Holy Spirit *is* the eschatological Spirit, who is the power of the "age to come." As the messiah, Jesus is the bringer of good news and deliverance to the poor, destitute, and desperate. Jesus announces that the delivering power of the Holy Spirit at work in his actions means that the future messianic kingdom of God is already present in Jesus's own person and his actions. One might say, as did early church father Origen, that Jesus is the kingdom of God in the flesh, the *autobaselia*.[8] The kingdom Jesus proclaims and inaugurates is all about delivering human persons from bondage, from destruction, from misery, and putting right that which has been disordered by sin and evil.

The flip side of this inaugurated eschatology is conflict and resistance to the powers of evil. Jesus describes the intrusion of the reign of God into the present age not only positively, as deliverance for the afflicted, but also as an invasion, an assault upon the powers that bind and enslave and destroy human persons (Matt 12:29).

What if Everything Jesus Says and Does Pertains to Salvation?

The "working hypothesis" of this chapter is that since Jesus is the Savior, then everything Jesus says and does pertains to the meaning of salvation, not only his death on the cross. And, if Jesus is the Messiah and Savior, Jesus's messianic mission of putting the world right is identical to his salvation mission. What might we "see" if we read the Gospels with that assumption? In this chapter and the next, I will identify several key points to be made about Jesus's mission and ministry as a messianic salvation mission:

(1) What Jesus does as the inaugurator of the kingdom is to initiate the total repair and healing of humanity and all creation. Jesus comes to put things right by inserting or planting the future kingdom into the present. Jesus's mission was not merely to save souls as the personal savior of a small percentage of human persons. He came to rectify the world, not to provide an escape route from the world.

(2) In putting things right, *who* does Jesus prioritize? Jesus certainly loves everybody, but he shows special concern for the poor, the vulnerable the downtrodden, and the social outcasts. He focused much of his energy on persons whose lives, livelihood, and well-being were profoundly threatened by the realities of life under Roman occupation.

---

8. Origen, *Commentary on Matthew* 14.7 (793).

(3) Jesus healed the sick and those with other physical ailments. This action of Jesus is connected with both points one and two above. When Jesus healed sick or broken bodies, he was putting things right. N. T. Wright contends that Jesus's healings of broken bodies and broken lives are a miniature, up-close-and-personal picture of the healing God intends for all humanity. Healings are the first fruits, the sneak preview of what is yet to come. But they were also intrusions of that future into the present. Since sickness and disability were attributed to the stranglehold of Satan upon the present evil age, Jesus's healings were understood as acts of deliverance from bondage to those powers that have illegitimately usurped God's rightful rule (see esp. Matt 12:22–29). These healings signal that the new order, the reign of God, is already dawning in Jesus's actions. William Herzog argues that Jesus's healings and expulsions of evil spirits were in faithful continuity with the God of the exodus, who delivered the people from slavery with a mighty hand (Exod 32:11; Deut 4:33–34). Whenever God's people were in bondage to Satan (Luke 13:10–17) or his demonic minions (Mark 1:21–28; 5:1–20), Jesus searched them out to liberate them.[9] He is the one who makes whole those whose lives have been shattered.

(4) Jesus formed a new kind of human community and social movement. In this community, there is supposed to be mutual love, economic support for the neediest members, welcome for the outcast, and a refusal of practices of domination that mirror the domination hierarchies that were integral to Rome's patronage social order and imperial logic.

(5) Jesus resists every power and social system that oppresses and beats down human persons. He opposes the misuse of God's law to justify economic oppression, and he is killed because he spent the last week of his life seeking to undermine the moral legitimacy of the temple due to its predatory economic practices.

(6) Jesus calls us to participate in what Jesus is doing, as described in points 1–5. Jesus called disciples to follow him and to continue his mission. To be "saved" is to be united with the Messiah, the inaugurator of the kingdom of God. To be drawn into this "eschatological new creation" is to be drawn into the *missio Dei*, God's mission of putting things right and resisting powers and forces of oppression and injustice that crush and dehumanize. To be drawn into this new creation is

---

9. Herzog, *Jesus, Justice, and the Reign of God*, 208–9.

to be God's agent of healing and deliverance, especially for the most vulnerable.

Scot McKnight offers a succinct statement about Jesus that summarizes well much of what was said in my points 1–6:

> Jesus's mission/vision of the kingdom is about restoring the blind, making lame to walk, healing lepers, raising the dead, making sure the poor are cared for by restoring them to their proper social location. Jesus's mission is healing, justice, the ending of disease, dislocation, and oppression and the creation of a covenanted community where the covenant God's will is lived out for each and every person. The work of God in Jesus/the kingdom is to include the marginalized, to render judgment on the powerful, and to create around the marginalized an alternative society where things are put to rights.[10]

What if all of this is not about a secondary domain of ethics or "the Christian life," but is the very shape of salvation, of what we are saved for?

Jesus's Special Concern for the Poor and Destitute, the Social Outcast, and Persons on the Edge of the Abyss of Destruction

In Luke 14, Jesus is invited to a very prestigious dinner party hosted by a wealthy and prominent Pharisee. After going out of his way to offend his host and the guests by healing a very sick and physically disfigured man on the Sabbath, Jesus proceeded to criticize the status-driven behavior of the guests. Jesus continued his "outrageous" social behavior by criticizing the host. The kind of dinner party one should have, Jesus insisted, is not one motivated, like this party, by the quest for power and status. Instead, one should give a banquet and invite all of the "losers," those written off as persons whose lives do not matter, those considered by the respectable members of society as the "lowest of the low." Invite the poor, the physically disabled, the blind, all of whom were all too often abandoned and left to economic deprivation and status degradation (Luke 14:12–14). God's priority and, therefore, the priority of those who accept and understand Jesus's invitation into the reign of God will be those who are presently excluded, oppressed, of low social status, and destitute in this present order.[11]

---

10. McKnight, *Community Called Atonement*, 12–13.

11. This text is entirely consistent with the thrust of the First Testament. The economic justice provisions of the Torah contained provisions to protect the widow,

The Soteriology of Jesus

Mary's *Magnificat* in Luke 1:46–55 is modeled on Hannah's song of praise in the book of 1 Samuel. The *Mangificat* identifies God's redemptive intent as exalting the humble poor and de-elevating the powerful, pulling rulers from their thrones. God is faithful to Israel, and that faithfulness will involve creating a social order in which the poor have enough to eat.[12]

In the last judgment scene of Matt 25:31–46, the criterion for inclusion in the kingdom of God at the final judgment is care for those Jesus describes as "the least of these" who were hungry, thirsty, naked, in prison, and strangers or aliens.[13] Jesus raises from the dead the son of a widow who would be economically vulnerable since her only means of support, her only adult son, is dead (Luke 7:11–16). Jesus heals lepers, who were required to leave their villages and live apart in a state of perpetual quarantine and, as a result, economic destitution (Luke 17:11–19). Of course, in each of Jesus's healings of persons who were blind, mute, or lame, he not only restored persons to physical health but to a state of ritual purity, a pre-condition for being included in their families and villages.[14]

Roman propaganda proclaimed that abundant life and salvation came from an emperor who lived in luxury, exercised near boundless political power, and was glorified as a conqueror. The peace and prosperity bestowed by this empire and emperor primarily benefitted those of wealth, high social status, and political power. The *basileia* inaugurated by Jesus is diametrically opposed to these values and practices. The good news of the kingdom is paired not with conquests and domination but with healings and exorcisms that bring life to the people of low social status. The Beatitudes (Matt 5:3–12; Luke 6:20–22) make clear that the kingdom of God belongs to the poor and persons of low status in the Roman hierarchy. In opposition to Roman values that glorified wealth, domination, violent conquest, and using

---

orphan, and foreigner and others who were in economic need. Jesus's words are consistent with the priorities of God as signaled in Psalm 146 and Psalm 72. And texts such as Isaiah 11 and 61 indicate that God's rule places special emphasis on justice for the poor.

12. McKnight, *Community Called Atonement*, 10.

13. We may quibble over who, precisely, were "the least of these" were in the context of the Matthean community. Some have proposed that the text is a reference to itinerant missionaries in the first century of the Christian era. However, it would be difficult to argue that indifference to any of this world's destitute is consistent with the whole tenor of Jesus's message and ministry.

14. That Jesus shows special concern for the most vulnerable and those considered social outcasts does not mean he does not care for persons who may be socially prominent or powerful. This was the case with Jairus, the leader of the synagogue. His daughter was near death and died while Jesus was on the way. She, too, though born into a more privileged position, was on the edge of death and Jesus prioritized delivering her from death.

debt as leverage to enslave or control others, the values of Jesus's kingdom include welcoming the poor, relinquishing wealth to lift up the poor, and forgiveness of debts. In opposition to the Roman value of competition for status, Jesus repudiated efforts to acquire honor by elevating oneself over others (Luke 14:7–11) and, indeed, taught that greatness in God's reign meant putting service to others as a higher priority than self-advancement (Matt 20:24–28; Luke 22:24–30).[15]

Contemporary Examples of Discipleship that Embody God's Special Concern for Persons Considered as Non-Persons and Those on the Edge of Destruction

What might Christomorphic discipleship look like today if Jesus's special concern for the destitute, the social outcast, and persons on the edge of the abyss of destruction was at the forefront of the church's agenda? Bryan Stevenson, a committed Christian and leader of Equal Justice Initiative (EJI), embodies this kind of discipleship in his legal work. Even though churches may lack the resources to do all that an organization now well-funded and staffed by attorneys is doing, churches can forge relationships with organizations like EJI, with the persons for whom Equal Justice Initiative fights, and with whom the persons in this organization walk. EJI has offered legal counsel to persons on death row and has contributed to the exoneration of several persons, including Walter McMillan and Ray Hinton, wrongly convicted and sentenced to death.[16]

In this segment, I will focus on EJI's political advocacy against the sentencing of juvenile offenders to life in prison without the possibility of parole.[17] In 2008, approximately 2,225 persons were serving sentences of life in prison without the possibility of parole for crimes committed under the age of eighteen. Some of these persons had received this sentence for crimes committed at the ages of 13 and 14 years old.[18] Juvenile offenders sentenced to life in prison are persons who have been treated by one of the

---

15. Miller, "Wresting with Rome," 288–90.
16. Stevenson, *Just Mercy*; Hinton, *Sun Does Shine*.
17. The culmination of this advocacy was the holding of the Supreme Court in *Miller v. Alabama*. Stephenson was successful in his argument before the court on behalf of the petitioners. The court held that the Eighth Amendment's prohibition against cruel and unusual punishment forbids the mandatory sentencing of life in prison without the possibility of parole for juvenile homicide offenders. *Miller v. Alabama*, 567 US 460 (2012).
18. EJI, *Cruel and Unusual*; Rovner, "Juvenile Life without Parole."

most powerful institutions in American society, the criminal justice system, as persons beyond redemption.

There are some cruel injustices behind this reality. First, the adolescent brain is anatomically undeveloped in parts of the cerebrum associated with impulse control, regulation of emotions, risk assessment, and moral reasoning. As a result, young teens are vulnerable to stress and peer pressure and lack the same kind of control possessed by adults to resist impulses and risky behavior. This is not to deny moral responsibility for wrongdoing, but adolescents are not as responsible as adults, especially when they come from dysfunctional, abusive, and dangerous home environments. Children and youth subjected to trauma, abuse, and neglect suffer from cognitive underdevelopment, lack of maturity, decreased ability to restrain impulses, and susceptibility to outside influences greater even than those suffered by "normal" teenagers. Normal adolescents cannot be expected to transcend their psychological or biological capacities in order to operate with the level of maturity, judgment, risk aversion, or impulse control of an adult. But a fourteen-year-old who has suffered brain trauma, a dysfunctional family life, violence, or abuse cannot function even at standard levels for adolescents.[19]

Most of the children sentenced to die in prison for crimes committed while they were juveniles come from violent and dysfunctional backgrounds. These young persons are some of the most vulnerable persons in our society. They have often been physically and sexually abused, neglected, and abandoned; their parents are often prostitutes, drug addicts, alcoholics, and crack dealers; they grew up in lethally violent, extremely poor areas. Several of these children endured years of sexual abuse and rape. One youthful offender who came into contact with EJI had been repeatedly sexually assaulted, beginning when he was just four years old. Another young person, Ashley Jones, was repeatedly threatened at gunpoint by her parents, sexually assaulted by her stepfather, forced into crack houses by an addicted mother, physically abused by family members, and abducted by a gang shortly before her crime.[20]

The racial disparities in the imposition of juvenile life without parole are significant: 62 percent are African American, 23 percent of juvenile

19. EJI, *Cruel and Unusual*, 6–10, 16; Rovner, "Juvenile Life without Parole."

20. EJI, *Cruel and Unusual*, 16–18. In 2012, The Sentencing Project released findings from a survey of people sentenced to life in prison as juveniles and found that 79 percent had witnessed violence in their homes regularly, 32 percent grew up in public housing, 47 percent were physically abused, and 80 percent of the female juvenile offenders had been physically abused and 77 percent had been sexually abused. Nellis, "Lives of Juvenile Lifers."

arrests for murder involve an African American suspected of killing a white person, 42 percent of juvenile life without parole sentences are for an African American convicted of this crime. White juvenile offenders with African-American victims are only about half as likely (3.6 percent) to receive this sentence as their proportion of arrests for killing an African American (6.4 percent). Six juveniles, all of them children of color, were sentenced to die in prison for crimes in which no one was killed.[21] Alongside and often intertwined with racial disparities are economic disparities. Most of EJI's clients are from poor families and did not receive adequate legal assistance to challenge their convictions and sentences. Many had never filed post-conviction appeals. In many of these cases, court-appointed trial and appellate lawyers failed to challenge the sentences imposed on their adolescent clients.[22]

The work of Equal Justice Initiative, to walk alongside and advocate for an end to the abandonment of some of the most vulnerable persons in our society, is a contemporary analogue of Jesus's call to give a banquet and invite the poor, the crippled, the lame, and the blind.

Another organization seeking to embody Jesus's vision of prioritizing those who have been written off as outcasts is Homeboy Industries, one of the largest gang intervention, rehabilitation, and re-entry programs in the world. According to Father Boyle, "We work with those who have been left behind without hope." He started this organization after he became the pastor of Dolores Mission Congregation in Los Angeles in 1986 in an area with the highest concentration of gang activity in the city. The majority of the former gang members who are clients of Homeboy Industries have experienced serious trauma of some kind, whether abandonment as a child, sexual or physical abuse, or a history of family violence and drug abuse.

Father Boyle points out that one of the deepest sufferings of the poor is a toxic shame, a sense of the failure of the entire self. Boyle tells the painful story of Carmen, a gang member, heroin addict, and occasional prostitute. One day, she stepped into Boyle's office, seven minutes before a scheduled baptism, plopped down in a chair, and stated, "I need help." She then narrated her story of graduating from a Catholic high school, falling into a heroin addiction, and trying to stop but failing. Then, bursting into tears, she uttered the words, "I am a disgrace."[23]

The mission of Homeboy Industries is to disrupt the notion that "there may be lives that matter less than other lives." Boyle calls us to disrupt

---

21. EJI, *Cruel and Unusual*, 24; Rovner, "Juvenile Life without Parole."
22. EJI, *Cruel and Unusual*, 22.
23. Boyle, *Tattoos on the Heart*, 42–43.

demonization in order to stand with people considered disposable "so that the day will come when we stop throwing people away."[24]

Jesus Saves = Jesus Rectifies/Puts Right What Is Wrong

The mission of Jesus Messiah, the inaugurator of the reign of God, is to initiate the healing and repair of creation and the totality of the human situation. Jesus comes to mend, heal, restore, renew, transform, and transfigure everything. This *is* Jesus's saving work. Therefore, in our theology of salvation, it is essential that we take into account what Jesus was doing even before his redemptive death on the cross. And it is essential that we understand his redemptive death in terms of his mission of putting all things right.

The first act of Jesus's public ministry in the Gospel of Luke is his identification with the messianic prophet of Isaiah 61, whose mission is to bring good news to the poor, freedom for captives, sight for the blind, liberation from oppression, and the restoration of the economic justice and access to the resources needed for flourishing represented by the year of Jubilee (Luke 4:16–21).

In Mark 3:1–6, Jesus healed a man with a withered hand on the Sabbath. Jesus defiantly announced that the point of the Sabbath is "to do good and save life." Jesus acted with authority as a rabbi interpreting the Torah and redrawing the boundaries of Sabbath observance to involve, as the highest priority, doing good and showing mercy to others rather than avoiding scribal definitions of work. By doing so, Jesus threatened the power and prestige of the scribes and Pharisees as the officially authorized interpreters of the Torah and their authority to classify and define who is and is not pure. This is Jesus putting things right. He came to undermine a form of religious faith that, by its very attempts to order and control the social world, was in fact a disordering power at odds with God's compassionate purposes. Jesus rightly claimed the sovereign authority to act as the mediator of the God of the covenant who restores and recreates rather than rejects and excludes.[25]

The Gospel of Matthew makes a strong and emphatic connection between Jesus's ministry of compassionate healing and the messianic age vision of the establishment of justice and human wholeness where all is put right. Immediately following the narrative of Jesus's healing of the man with the withered hand on the Sabbath, Matthew cites Isa 42:1–3a in order to identify Jesus's action with the servant of the Lord in Isaiah.

---

24. Boyle, "On Radical Compassion." See also https://www.homeboyindustries.org.
25. Herzog, *Jesus, Justice, and the Reign of God*, 180–81.

The Greek term in Matthew's citation of Isa 42:1–3a, translated into English as justice, is κρίσιν, which in turn is the translation in the Septuagint[26] of the Hebrew word *mispat*. *Mispat* has a range of associations and meanings, but its foundational usage seems to be in reference to the judgment of a judge in a court. Since Israel's God is the ultimate king and judge, "mispat" came to be associated with the day of the Lord as God's final act in preparation for the messianic age. The primary connotation of *mispat* is not so much punishment but the justice that rectifies, with judgment against the wicked and oppressors as means to the end of putting all things right. Richard Beaton argues that *mispat* is most fundamentally a salvific term referring to God's justice-making that involves defending the fatherless, looking out for widows, and delivering the oppressed (see Isa 1:17, 21; 51:3–6; Jer 22:3; Zech 7:9; Mic 6:8; Hos 6:6).[27] The citation of Isa 42:1–3 at the end of this segment in the Gospel of Matthew is an identification of Jesus's actions of compassionate deliverance with the servant in Isaiah, who is the one through whom God's righteousness goes out to the nations. In his actions and words, Jesus is the Messiah establishing a just order.[28]

Perhaps one of the most powerful and beautiful stories in the Gospels, in which he rectifies a situation that was deeply wrong, is Luke 13:10–17. In this story, Jesus is teaching in the synagogue on the Sabbath when he heals a woman who suffered a physical ailment that left her stooped over and unable to stand up straight. This condition was attributed to an evil spirit. To attribute her physical ailment to Satan is to identify her condition as something contrary to God's good purposes for human flourishing. Therefore, it is important to recognize that Luke interprets the situation to be one in which Jesus is the power of the Rule of God setting right tragic realities that are contrary to God's will and purposes!

There are so many layers of deliverance from bondage in this story. And it is important to attend to the play upon the words "binding and loosing" that weaves its way through this entire story. According to the retribution theology[29] that was embraced by some, but not all, of the Jewish

---

26. The Septuagint was the Old Testament translated into Greek for Jewish persons in the Greco-Roman world who could not read the Hebrew language.

27. Beaton, "Messiah and Justice," 8–12.

28. Beaton, "Messiah and Justice," 12–15.

29. Retribution theology is the notion that God unfailingly punishes the wicked and rewards the righteous in this life. Examples of the significant currents of retribution theology in the First Testament include Deuteronomy's blessings and curses in chapter 28, portions of the wisdom literature, Psalm 91, and Psalm 73, in which the psalmist struggles with the fact that, all around him, he sees the wicked prosper and the righteous suffer.

people in Jesus's day and widely embraced by many of the powerful people in society, illness and disability were thought to be divine punishment and, therefore, were accompanied by social stigma. Since a person with a serious ongoing physical condition or disability was also considered ritually impure, it is likely that this woman faced social exclusion and marginalization. By naming her condition as Satan's action, Jesus puts right the flawed theology that attributed cruelty to God and wounded the soul of persons who had been taught, by this theology, that God had rejected them. By healing this woman, Jesus delivers her from this social stigma and the emotional pain of rejection by others. Given the popular retribution theology, it is likely that this woman would have believed that God had rejected her. When Jesus healed her, her immediate response was to stand up straight and praise God. Jesus thereby sets her free from a toxic view of God as one who had written her out of God's beloved covenant people. Jesus puts this situation right theologically in that he repudiates a toxic view of God and embodies, in his action, love, healing, and graciousness, a living picture of God as a God of delivering compassion for the vulnerable and suffering.

In a shame-honor culture, she is a person marked for shame and, therefore, a person not highly valued. In open defiance of the social consensus that this woman deserved contempt as one unclean and cursed by God, Jesus called her forward, to the front of the synagogue, which was a place of honor. He called her a "daughter of Abraham," asserting her worth and value in the eyes of God. By asserting her dignity in this way, Jesus placed her back where she belonged, as a cherished member of God's covenant people, from which she had been excluded by the dominant definition of purity.

One of the powerful stories told by Father Gregory Boyle, that echoes Jesus's affirmation of the woman in this story as a daughter of Abraham, involved a former gang member named Mario, who Boyle described as one of the most tattooed guys he knew. Mario worked in Homeboy Industries' café, selling baked goods at the counter. Everyone who knew Mario would describe him as the kindest, most gentle soul they knew. When he was invited to speak to students and faculty at Gonzaga University, Boyle took Mario with him to share his story. During the question and answer period, a woman in the audience asked Mario what advice he would give his own children who, at the time, were approaching their teenage years. Mario, still in the grip of toxic shame, hesitated and then blurted out, in great anguish, "I just don't want my kids to turn out to be like me." After several seconds of silence, the woman, speaking into the microphone, said, "Why wouldn't you want your kids to turn out to be like you? You are loving, you are gentle, you are kind, and you are wise. I hope your kids turn out to be like you!" At that moment, the audience stood and clapped. In the same way that Jesus made the emphatic point that the woman in the synagogue was a daughter of Abraham, treasured by God, this woman's response to Mario affirmed him as someone who was treasured. She saw past the ways the dominant society might consign him to the category of "the wrong kind of person" and instead called Mario to see himself in light of God's transforming work in his life and the blessing to others that his life had become.[30]

In Luke 13:10–17, there is a parallel act of deliverance for the people present in the synagogue. The play in this text on the terms "binding and loosing" requires some background information. The task of interpreters of the Torah, especially rabbis, was to bind the people to a particular practical interpretation of the Torah or to "loose" them from a particular obligation. When it comes to the law governing the Sabbath, binding and loosing pertained to the detailed specifics of what one could and could not do on the Sabbath. The synagogue ruler objects to Jesus's act of healing on the Sabbath and accuses Jesus of violating the commandment to "remember the Sabbath day and keep it holy." According to the ruler of the synagogue, it is shameful to heal on the Sabbath because healing is work.[31]

When the ruler of the synagogue sought to shame Jesus, Jesus assumed the role of rabbi, an authoritative interpreter of the Torah. Jesus called out the ruler of the synagogue and his allies as hypocrites. Rabbinic teaching had rightly "loosed" people to "loose" their farm animals on the Sabbath in order to provide the animals with food and water. Jesus agrees with this compassionate treatment of animals but excoriated the ruler of the synagogue and the rabbinic tradition for forbidding compassionate treatment of human beings who, Jesus insisted, are even more valuable in God's eyes. Whereas the synagogue ruler construed the key to the law as ritual purity, Jesus interpreted the Torah through the lens of the priority of love and compassion. The book of Exodus interprets the significance of the Sabbath in terms of resting on the Sabbath as Yahweh did. Deuteronomy does not contradict Exodus, but it puts a strong emphasis on compassion as a further implication of the principle of Sabbath rest. The Sabbath is about "loosing" or freeing people and animals from endless toil. The logic of the Sabbath is also manifested in the Sabbatical Year, which features "loosing" from the bondage of indentured servitude and indebtedness. Jesus kept the Sabbath holy by his faithfulness to the Sabbatical principle of loosing by setting this woman free from bondage and suffering so she could participate in the praise of Yahweh, which was also one of the central purposes of the Sabbath.

---

30. Boyle, "One of the Most Inspirational Speeches."
31. Herzog, *Jesus, Justice, and the Reign of God*, 118–20, 183–84.

The Soteriology of Jesus

There is an intentional parallel between Jesus's healing of the woman who could not stand up straight and Jesus's reinterpretation of the Torah to prioritize compassion over ritual purity. Satan is the oppressive power that bound the woman so that she could not stand up straight. Jesus is the one who looses from Satan's grip so that the woman could flourish, stand up straight, praise God, and take her rightful place as a daughter of Abraham. Similarly, the purity-driven interpretation of the Torah was an enslaving power that was excessively burdensome to ordinary Jewish peasants. It was extraordinarily difficult to follow all of the proliferating purity rules about handwashing, ritual washing and preparation and consumption of food, and other meticulous rules of purity if one was a peasant, working from dawn to dusk just to survive. Just as Jesus broke Satan's control over the woman's body, so he also broke another power of the present evil age: a burdensome interpretation of God's law in one segment of the rabbinic tradition. Jesus returned the law to God's compassionate purposes for human well-being and freed the people from the life-destroying control this purity-driven religion had exercised.[32]

The purity religion was also burdensome because it functioned to define God's people as composed of those who count in the dominant social order as the right kind of people. This impulse to create forms of religion as mechanisms for excluding and condemning whoever is seen as the wrong kind of person is a powerful human religious impulse. It is also diametrically opposed to the way of Jesus Christ. Father Boyle tells the story of a man still trapped within the "moral imagination" of purity religion:

> Once a man drove by the church and stopped to talk to me. He was a Latino who had become very economically successful and drove a nice car.... He waxed nostalgic about having grown up in the projects and having been baptized and making his first communion there. The man took in the scene at the church: gang members gathered by the bell tower, homeless men and women being fed in great numbers in the parking lot, folks arriving for the AA and NA meetings and the ESL classes. It was a "Who's Who of Everybody Who Was a Nobody": gang member, drug addict, homeless, undocumented. The man shook his head in disgust and said, "You know, this used to be a church."[33]

Boyle's response was, "You know, most people around here think it's finally a church."[34]

---

32. Herzog, *Jesus, Justice, and the Reign of God*, 185.
33. Boyle, *Tattoos on the Heart*, 73.
34. Boyle, *Tattoos on the Heart*, 73.

Section Two: Soteriology and Biblical Narrative

Putting the World to Rights in Fragments

Every time the labors of the Innocence Project or Equal Justice Initiative lead to the exoneration of a person wrongfully convicted of a crime, a little piece of the eschatological future happens in the present because what was wrong has been partially rectified. When the American civil rights movement overcame legalized, "Jim Crow" segregation, something in the world was rectified and brought at least a step closer to God's purposes as signaled in biblical texts about the eschatological future. When addicts are delivered or childhood poverty rates are lowered, these changes are in sync with God's purposes.

We should not fall into the trap of playing the healing and transformation of individuals off against social change that takes aim at unjust systems. Within the confines of his social, cultural, and political context, Jesus did both. The Gospels include powerful stories of Jesus's encounters with individuals who were healed and transformed by their encounters with Jesus. Jesus offered a powerful love and acceptance that empowered persons to open their lives to God's love and be transformed. One thinks of the way in which, as narrated in John 4, Jesus treated the Samaritan woman, a person marked for shame. He took her seriously as a person. He listened to her. In this encounter, she was drawn into the overflowing love and goodness of God and received the life-giving power of the Spirit that Jesus described with the metaphor of living water. At the end of the story, she is the evangelist who is no longer hiding in shame[35] but is boldly pointing others in her village to Jesus.

Luke's story of Zaccheus (19:1–10) is another story of transformation. Zaccheus is morally corrupt. As a tax collector whose personal wealth was gained through dishonest means, he collected more taxes for Rome than was owed and pocketed the difference. As a collaborator with the hated empire, he was the rare wealthy person who was nonetheless seen as shameful. The paradox of Luke 19:1–10 is that Jesus invited himself to Zaccheus's house and yet, in doing so, Jesus was the one "hosting" Zaccheus through Jesus's loving acceptance of Zaccheus. In the presence of Jesus's overflowing divine grace, love, and power, Zaccheus found himself transformed and drawn into the way of the kingdom. With joy, the one who was greedy and grasping and willing to gain wealth by exploiting others is converted to the way of generosity. Zaccheus pledges to give half of what he owned to the poor and to repay times four all that he had taken by fraud and deception.

---

35. Contemporary readers should not jump to conclusions that the Samaritan woman was immoral. Perhaps, instead, she had experienced rejection or abuse and had fled toxic relationships. We do not know the background story.

The Soteriology of Jesus

In the presence of Jesus, Zaccheus's is "put right." Zaccheus is restored to life, community, joy, and to a participation in the overflowing generosity of God.

Jesus Forms a New Kind of Human Community/Jesus Initiates a Social Movement

At the heart of Jesus's mission is the creation of an alternative community, a regathered and reconstituted Israel. In opposition to the hierarchical, exploitative, and exclusionary community maintained by Rome's ruling elite and their aristocratic Jewish collaborators, the community called into the kingdom of God is supposed to be characterized by forgiveness, reconciliation, and mutual sharing. In God's Reign, the first shall be last and the last shall be first (Matt 19:30).[36]

Throughout the Roman Empire, patron-client networks were part of the stratified and hierarchical structure of power through which imperial society operated. Patronage was a mode of political administration that created social relations of dependency. Jesus directly articulated his opposition to these arrangements and identified the values of his alternative community in Mark 10:35-45. Jesus "deconstructed" the façade of beneficence projected by Roman imperial officials while, in fact, the mode of Roman rule was domination. Jesus calls his followers to be a counter-imperial community in which domination is rejected and greatness is measured by service rather than "lording it over" those who are ruled (Mark 10:42-44). In this alternative community, the quest for power and wealth as markers of personal status is renounced. This community is to be one in which all willingly and mutually take on the status of marginal servants to one another. Each person in this new community is called to act in order to secure the well-being of others. Jesus called his followers to repudiate the self-assertion and quest for dominance that the Empire's ruling elite held to be honorable. Jesus's social vision was one of open and generous sharing based on need.[37]

Jesus's new community was one in which the members take care of one another by radical economic sharing. This characteristic of the community and movement Jesus started is reflected in the earliest Christian practices as narrated in Acts 2:44-46 and 4:32-35. In the early phases of the Jesus movement in Jerusalem, the community members shared everything in common, ensured that the basic needs of every person were met,

36. Cox, "Gospel of Matthew and Resisting Imperial Theology," 35.

37. Carter, *Matthew and Empire*, 10; Herzog, *Jesus, Justice, and the Reign of God*, 211–13; Horsley, "General Introduction," 5.

and shared meals together. These practices were in continuity with those of Jesus and his disciples, who had a common purse (John 12:6; 13:29) from which their own need for provisions was provided and sometimes for disbursements for the poor (see Mark 14:4–5). Jesus commanded his followers and potential followers to engage in this radical economic sharing.

Jesus called his people to an alternative way of life designed to provide a cushion against the destructive economic impact of imperial Rome's excessive taxation. What made Roman oppression worse was all the ways people in occupied territories exploited their own people to maintain economic security and gain social prestige and power. Far too many Israelites, up and down the patronage hierarchy, were lending money with interest, contrary to the Torah. This practice plunged fellow Israelites deeper into indebtedness and destitution.[38] Jesus called his followers to forgive debt rather than using debt as leverage either to gain power or to dispossess persons of their lands (Matt 5:42; Luke 6:34).

The premium Jesus placed upon both forgiving sin and forgiving economic debt, and the ways he seemed to conflate rather than sharply differentiate the two, is evident in the parable of the unmerciful servant. After a king mercifully forgave his servant's colossal debt that would have been impossible to repay over a single lifetime, this same servant refused to show the same kind of compassion to one of his own servants, further down the patronage hierarchy, who owed him a very small debt. Instead, he had the man thrown into debtors' prison. This enraged the king who had forgiven his servant's overwhelming debt (Matt 18:21–35). What we should recognize is that this parable does not use an economic metaphor, forgiveness of debt, in order to explain a spiritual reality, forgiveness of sin. Rather, for Jesus, forgiving debt and pardoning offenses are connected. Forgiving debt, in first century Palestine, had literal life and death implications. A person who could not repay a debt might lose their land and become a day laborer, which was a precarious economic existence, almost always leading to destitution, malnourishment, disease, and premature death. By forgiving debt, Jesus's followers could rectify some of the damage to human lives caused by Roman imperial policies.

This is a community that also includes and values those who are social outcasts and the ritually impure (Luke 14:12–14). This vision of a community that welcomes the outcast was lived out by Jesus in his table fellowship with ritually unclean persons, including tax collectors. Shared meals expressed a bond of hospitality and acceptance. Jesus dramatized, in his table fellowship, God's gracious welcome and forgiveness (Matt 9:9–13), and by

---

38. Horsley, *Jesus and Empire*, 14; Herzog, *Jesus, Justice, and the Reign of God*, 107–8.

doing so, called into existence a different kind of human community. Jesus rejected the priestly model for purity and the table at the temple as the blueprint for the table in the village. He rejected the emphasis on ritual purity as the heart of God's law, which stigmatized his table companions as unclean and, therefore, outside the fellowship of the true Israel. Jesus's table companionship with toll collectors and sinners was an intentional and provocative act that publicly repudiated the Pharisees' interpretation of the Torah and their prioritization of ritual purity in ways that many of the Pharisees viewed as blasphemous. Jesus declared that toll collectors and prostitutes are going into the reign of God before the chief priests and scribes (Matt 21:31). Both of these groups were composed of desperate people who had to prostitute themselves in order to survive in unjust systems. As victims of exploitation, they will go into the reign of God ahead of the defenders of the status quo, who stigmatized the poor and the degraded them rather than seeking justice for them.[39]

---

39. Herzog, *Jesus, Justice, and the Reign of God*, 153–54, 221–22.

CHAPTER SIX

Jesus of Nazareth as Apocalyptic Collision with the Powers of the Present Age

MATTHEW 12:22–29 SHEDS CRUCIAL light upon the soteriological mission of Jesus and its continuity with the apocalyptic and eschatological hopes that emerged in intertestamental Judaism. In this narrative, Jesus heals and delivers a man who was blind and mute, which rendered him unable to communicate and, therefore, unable to interact relationally with others. As such, he was cut off from community and rendered economically vulnerable and socially isolated. His life was shattered and destroyed by this condition in his particular social context and point in history. The Gospel attributes his condition to an evil spirit. After Jesus expels this spirit, an act the Gospel of Matthew recognizes as one of beneficence and compassion, Jesus encounters opposition from some of the Pharisees, who accuse him of being in league with Satan. But Jesus counters their accusations by identifying his actions as the work of the powerful eschatological Holy Spirit, who sets humans free to flourish. If it is by the power of the Spirit that evil powers are broken and lives are made whole, Jesus proclaims, the future reign of God is already invading the present order, already happening here and now in and through Jesus's acts of delivering compassion.

As the apocalyptic tradition in Judaism takes up and further interprets the hopes for a future messianic age of peace and justice, the present evil age is depicted as this world disordered and in the stranglehold of anti-God, idolatrous, and destructive powers. These powers include both empires and other oppressive political arrangements and Satan or the Evil One. The Evil One is understood as the source of human misery and suffering. Satan's illegitimate rule within God's good creation is not imagined to be something

Jesus of Nazareth as Apocalyptic Collision with the Powers of the Present Age

distinct from the empires, cordoned off within a non-material and apolitical "spiritual realm." Rather, Satan is the animating impulse behind the idolatry, lust for dominion and power, and brutality of the empires.[1] As noted in previous chapters, the end of the ordinary course of human history and the inauguration of the messianic age is associated with a final and cataclysmic battle against the accumulated powers of evil and the defeat of empire and the malignant spiritual powers that have disordered God's good world with oppression, economic exploitation, brutality, and abuse of human persons.

While the kingdom Jesus inaugurates is about healing, putting things right, and delivering humans from bondage so that they might flourish, Jesus's messianic mission takes place in a world still in the stranglehold of anti-God powers. Matthew 12:22–29 narrates the in-breaking of the reign of God as involving intense conflict as the kingdom of God invades the territory illegitimately possessed by the powers of the present evil age. Jesus describes the reign of God with a violent metaphor of a home invasion in which the occupant of the home is taken hostage. But this home was illegitimately occupied; therefore, the "strong man" is not the rightful owner.

In the apocalyptic strands of first-century Palestinian Judaism, everything destructive of human life and well-being, including oppressive social and political arrangements as well as illness and disability, were interpreted as results of Satan's malicious stranglehold.[2] Just as the apocalyptic tradition envisions a final battle and defeat of the powers of evil, including Satan, evil spirits, and the empires that have usurped God's rightful rule of creation, so Jesus defines his mission here as act of aggression against Satan's stronghold. He comes to bind Satan and reclaim human beings whose lives have been mangled, shattered, destroyed, and harmed by the powers of evil. By doing so, Jesus was re-asserting God's sovereign Lordship over creation. But instead of one quick and final defeat of evil, the Synoptic Gospels envision a more prolonged period of apocalyptic warfare with the powers of the present evil age, an apocalyptic struggle in which Christ's followers will

---

1. Schillebeeckx, *Jesus*, 183–84; Grenz, *Theology for the Community of God*, 289–92. As Ched Myers points out, the kingdom of Satan, within this apocalyptic imagination, is a symbolic accentuation of the negative experiences of earthly rule. Myers, *Binding the Strong Man*, 165.

2. Sometimes, illness and disability were attributed to divine punishment for sin or ritual impurity by some segments of first-century Palestinian Judaism. Jesus's actions and words consistently attribute the causes of suffering to malign powers rather than to God. Jesus's understanding is rooted in Jewish apocalyptic traditions. In Jesus's day, as is true in the present with regard to both Judaism and Christianity, there was no singular version of Judaism. Obviously, there were different currents of thought in first century Palestinian Judaism.

participate,³ though not with conventional weapons of warfare (e.g., Eph 6:10–17).

As noted in the previous chapter, this text features an inaugurated eschatology. The eschatological new creation has invaded the territory illegitimately occupied by anti-God powers of destruction. As the power of the age to come, the Spirit's work is deliverance of human persons from the powers of the present evil age. To hear this text today, in our context, we might say that Satan's power is being broken whenever persons are delivered from destructive forces and powers such as systemic racial biases, addictions, patriarchy, or cultural glorification of wealth and conspicuous consumption, all of which harm and destroy human lives and undermine human relationships and communities. When we think about the ecclesial mission today, we should also think about opposition and resistance to destructive powers, whether we speak of mass incarceration, the racial injustices of the past that persist into the present (such as *de facto* residential segregation), implicit biases that shape hiring decisions, sentencing disparities by race, or grotesque economic inequality. Powers that destroy include bullying, whether physical or in cyberspace, addiction to technology, political echo chambers that make possible widespread belief in conspiracy theories, and destructive media messages about body image, beauty, and attractiveness. Until humans are completely liberated from the plethora of disordering, oppressive, and destructive powers of the present age, the reign of God takes shape in our world as resistance to these powers and forces. This resistance is not a violent frontal assault but creative and resourceful resistance.

---

3. Schillebeeckx, *Jesus*, 183–84. Frederick Murphy points to a theme in apocalyptic literature, according to which, the prelude to the coming of God as judge and the full arrival of the messianic age is a period of unprecedented suffering as good and evil collide. This theme is implicit in the Gospel of Mark. In 1:14, John the Baptist is arrested, handed over (*paradidoi*) to Herod. This is the same word used when Jesus is handed over to the authorities and ultimately executed. Jesus's followers will also be handed over (13:9–13). These all die as martyrs because they oppose Satan and his human collaborators. After his baptism, Jesus is driven into the wilderness by the Spirit to be tempted (*peirazomenos*) by Satan. *Peirazomenos* occurs frequently in eschatological contexts. As the end draws near, the faithful are tested in multiple ways. Jesus begins his own career by undergoing this initial eschatological testing on Satan's own turf, the wilderness. Murphy, *Apocalypticism in the Bible and Its World*, 231–33.

Jesus and the Reign of God: Against the Rulers, Powers, Systems, and Forces that Oppress, Dehumanize, and Destroy

In the temptation narratives of Matthew 4, Satan offers to Jesus "the kingdoms of the world and their glory" (4:8). Here, the Gospel of Matthew depicts Satan as the power behind the world's dominative kingdoms. Of course, in Jesus's day, that was Rome. In this text, in other words, Rome's exercise of domination, oppression, and brutality is named as satanic, a connection also made in the book of Revelation. The word used by Satan in his invitation to this perverse act of worship is the Greek word *proskuneo*, the same word used to describe the act of prostration or bowing in submission before a ruler or emperor. Here, allegiance and submission to Rome and to Caesar, the glorification of Rome's power and values, is tantamount to worship of Satan.[4]

Another narrative that depicts the sphere of the demonic in the social imagination of the Synoptic Gospels, as manifest and, indeed, perversely incarnate in the oppressive power of imperial Rome, is Mark 5:1–15. There, in gentile territory, which would have been regarded as ritually unclean, Jesus encountered a man living in the tombs, the place of the dead. The impurity of dead bodies (e.g., Num 19:10–14) intensified the ritual impurity of the situation. But the horror is intensified exponentially because this man is possessed by "an impure or unclean spirit," which drove the man to self-harm by cutting, cries of anguish, and an emotional state in which he was so out of control that he could not be subdued by anyone. Reading this text today, one wonders whether Mark 5 is describing the suffering of a man who has experienced severe trauma.

When Jesus asked the man his name, the evil spirits identify "themselves" as Legion. No one reading this text in the first century would have missed the obvious political reference. A unit of anywhere from four thousand to six thousand Roman soldiers was a "legion." The reader is invited to see the correspondence between: (1) the demons, described as "unclean," that occupy and destroy this particular man's body and person and (2) the "possession" of the land and its defilement by what is unclean, Roman troops, who enforce imperial Rome's brutal policies of taxation and exploitation. This possession had such a destructive impact on the Israelites and their neighbors, plunging so many persons into poverty, slavery, misery, and death. This man's possession by evil spirits and the "possession" of the land by an evil empire are woven together tightly as two sides of the same

---

4. Cox, "Gospel of Matthew and Resisting Imperial Theology," 34.

proverbial coin. What the evil spirits do to this man through the violent and destructive occupation of his body, Rome is doing to the people whose land Rome occupies violently.

The text dramatizes a symbolic expulsion of the occupying demonic power represented by Rome. As the demons were expelled from the man and allowed to enter the ritually unclean pigs, they were so destructive that they caused the pigs to destroy themselves by running into the sea. One cannot miss the clear indictment of Rome as a power that is diabolical and destructive. And, to accentuate the Bible's anti-imperial stance, there is an intentional echo of another defeat of an empire, the drowning of Pharaoh's army in the Red Sea.

Those who might argue that Jesus was the apolitical messenger of an entirely "spiritual" salvation fail to see all of the ways that Jesus criticized and opposed the institutions, power relations, and exploitive practices that left the common people poor, hungry, and in debt.[5] For example, both Jesus and John the Baptist (Matt 14:3–4; Mark 6:17–18) were harsh critics of Herod Antipas, the puppet king in Galilee. Jesus called Herod a fox, which in its first-century Palestinian Jewish context might mean someone who is deceitful and untrustworthy, or it may be a way of calling him an insignificant person (Luke 13:32). Comparing Herod and John the Baptist, Jesus praised John as a prophet and spoke of Herod as a "reed swayed by the wind," a person without convictions who adjusts to what is expedient (Matt 11:7–11; Luke 7:24–28).

Richard Horsley argues that we err if we interpret the story of Jesus with the flawed and very modern either/or: if Jesus did not foment a revolt, he was politically acquiescent or innocuous. That Jesus rejected violent insurrection against Rome as the route to God's new social order is often allowed to obscure the degree to which the Synoptic Gospels portray the reign of God in conflict with and opposition to the old. Each of the Gospels, after all, are a story in which the main character is crucified, a distinctly Roman form of imperial brutality and terror designed to remove troublesome threats to the empire. Throughout the Gospels, the political leaders oppose Jesus and finally arrest, try, and execute him. Matthew Cox identifies the foundational anti-imperial nature of Jesus's ministry in the Gospel of Matthew:

> From beginning to end, [Matthew] repeatedly and programmatically presents Jesus as offering an alternative to the death-wielding structures of imperial Rome. The three chapters in which Roman presence is most palpable (2, 14, and 27) are the

---

5. Horsley, *Covenant Economics*, 56.

chapters in which Herod slaughters innocent children, Herod Antipas executes John the Baptist, and Pilate oversees the abuse and crucifixion of Jesus. . . . Matthew closely links imperial power to the power of death, particularly the execution of the innocent. That Jesus constitutes a radical alternative is signaled by the application to Jesus of these rulers' titles. In chapter 2, both Jesus and Herod are called "king," a startling juxtaposition that places the reign of Jesus and that of the empire on a collision course.[6]

Purity Codes and the Religious Sanctioning of Wealth Accumulation in a Predatory Economy

In light of the long and tragic history of Christian antisemitism, it is always important to remind ourselves that everything Jesus said and did was a theological maneuver within the faith of Israel. Jesus was not the opponent of Judaism, just as Christians who criticize the theological vision or practice of other Christians are not against Christianity. All religions are likely to spawn perverse expressions of the particular faith when a religion becomes allied with quests for power, dominance, and wealth.

Jerome Neyrey, drawing upon the work of anthropologist Mary Douglas's book *Purity and Danger*, points out that people groups almost always structure their worlds according to some system of order and classification. Humans draw lines and create rules, whether formal or informal, that tell us what and who belong when and where. "Purity" rules map and structure life for a given social group and embody the group's values system.[7] In other words, the Jewish people in the first century were not unique.

Neyrey argues that we see these purity boundaries in the Gospels. These purity maps were made to function in such a way as to legitimate and reinforce the social structure and power dynamics of Jewish society in the first century prior to the Jewish Revolt. For those Israelites invested in the purity system, which is not to be confused with the entirety of Judaism, there is a hierarchy or ranking system. Gentiles are not on the map of God's covenant people (see Acts 10:28; 11:3), nor are Samaritans (John 4:9). The ranking system, from lowest to highest, seems to be:

1. Dead Israelites: concern over Jesus's dead body (John 19:31);

---

6. Cox, "Gospel of Matthew and Resisting Imperial Theology," 33.

7. Douglas, *Purity and Danger*, 38–39; Malina, *New Testament World*, 25–27, 124–26; Neyrey, "Idea of Purity in Mark's Gospel."

2. Morally unclean Israelites: tax collectors and sinners (Luke 15:1–2; Matt 9:10–13);

3. Bodily unclean Israelites: lepers (Mark 1:40–45; Luke 17:11–14), persons who are poor, lame, maimed, and blind (Luke 14:13; see Lev 21:18–21), and menstruants (Mark 5:24–34);

4. Israelites who do not live in meticulous observation of the purity system's requirements: Peter and John (Acts 4:13); Jesus (John 7:15, 49);

5. Israelites who are meticulous in their observation of the purity system's requirements: the rich young man (Mark 23:50–51); Joseph of Arimathea (Luke 2:25–38);

6. Pharisees (Mark 7:3–5; Luke 18:11–12);

7. Scribes and Priests (Luke 10:31–32);

8. Chief Priests (John 18:28; Heb 7:17–28).[8]

Holiness and purity mean, first of all, wholeness. The lack of wholeness of persons with damaged bodies was believed to indicate a corresponding lack of holiness. Persons with damaged family lines are also impure because their wholeness is defective. The highest echelons of holiness have to do with one's standing vis-à-vis the temple. Further classifications are found. In Acts 4:13, Peter and John are classified by the observant elite as "uneducated, common men," that is, *amme ha-aretz*, who neither knew the Law and its purity concerns nor cared about them. The chief priests and Pharisees distinguish themselves from the crowds who are impressed by Jesus but were said to be accursed because they do not know the law (John 7:47–48).[9]

Public sinners, such as tax collectors and prostitutes, are, at best, on the margins of the covenant map. Also on the margins are physically unclean folk, such as lepers, menstruating women, the blind, and the lame. According to the Lev 21:16–20, persons with a blemish, the blind and the lame, persons with a mutilated face or a limb too long, a man with an injured hand or foot, hunchbacks and dwarfs, or a man with an itching disease, scabs, or crushed testicles are excluded as unwhole and unholy Israelites. Such persons are marginal, residing on the fringes or borders of Jewish society. There are, then, those who have put themselves on the perimeter of the purity map (sinners) and those who find themselves put there because of their physical lack of wholeness (sick, deformed).[10]

---

8. Neyrey, "Idea of Purity in Mark's Gospel."
9. Neyrey, "Idea of Purity in Mark's Gospel."
10. Neyrey, "Idea of Purity in Mark's Gospel."

The purity codes of the Torah were rooted in the creation story and the command in Leviticus to the people to be holy as God is holy (20:26). Just as the Genesis 1 creation account narrated God's acts of separating light from darkness, day from night, and water from dry land, the purity codes are about the separation of what are deemed to be incompatible pairs, such as clean and unclean animals. The community of Israel follows the demands of the purity codes to avoid the threat of contamination, the mixing of what should be separated, and the dissolution of creation order back into chaos. Their positive function was to remind the Israelites of their distinctiveness as God's chosen people and, therefore, to remind them to separate themselves from the idolatrous ways of their neighbors in the ancient near east.[11]

However, the purity codes also functioned to exclude or marginalize persons such as Samaritans, persons with obvious physical ailments or disabilities such as lepers, and persons unable to maintain the state of ritual purity due to the inability to pay the annual temple tax or the other fees associated with the temple sacrificial system.[12]

In spite of significant theological differences between members of these groups, the temple establishment, Sadducees, the scribes, and many of the Pharisees, some of whom were also scribes, prioritized the purity codes in their vision for Israel. *Halakha* was the oral Torah, a set of further restrictions added to the law codes of the Torah. The original purpose of this rabbinic interpretive tradition was to interpret the law and to make discerning judgments about the details and specifics of how to apply the law to everyday conduct. But these regulations proliferated, alongside an overemphasis on ritual purity over human compassion, and had become an extremely burdensome set of practices.[13]

According to Jacob Neusner, the Pharisees in the first century were a table-fellowship movement that required keeping everywhere the laws of ritual purity that normally applied only in the Jerusalem temple. They ate private meals in the same condition of ritual purity as did priests during their sacrificial rituals. This was their vision for fulfilling Leviticus's call to be a kingdom of priests and a holy people. Daily fulfillment of this project involved a meticulous keeping of the laws of purity as well as the scrupulous tithing of all food. The Pharisees' goal was to replicate the level of purity or holiness required by the priestly caste in their everyday lives, with the goal being that all Israel must achieve this kind of purity. This goal can be achieved only when each member of the community is scrupulous in

11. Herzog, *Jesus, Justice, and the Reign of God*, 156–57.
12. Herzog, *Jesus, Justice, and the Reign of God*, 156–57.
13. Beaton, "Messiah and Justice," 16.

observing the tradition of the elders. In the case of meals, it means tithing all food purchased, preparing it in pure vessels, serving it in clean dishes, and eating with pure hands. According to Neusner, the setting for law observance was the field, kitchen, bed, and street. The occasion for observance occurred every time a person picked up a common nail, which might be unclean, or purchased a *seah* of wheat, which had to be tithed.[14] However, keeping the Pharisaic oral Torah imposed perpetual, rigorous, and burdensome ritualization of daily life.

Alongside the purity codes was an emphasis on justice and compassion in the Torah and the prophets. These laws look to the exodus and the conviction that the land belongs to Yahweh alone. The land was extended to the Israelites as a gift and, as such, was meant to be a source of life and blessing for all of the people of God. The basic principle was the principle of extension, of sharing and generosity. For example, every third year, the people tithed for the benefit of the Levites, aliens, orphans, and widows that they might eat their fill (Deut 26:12). The same principle undergirds the Sabbatical and Jubilee years, the purpose of which was to facilitate a broad distribution of land, to prevent endemic indebtedness, and to prevent the rise of a ruling class and landed aristocracy with huge estates and the power to exploit a landless peasant base.

While his opponents read the Torah through the priestly eyes of the purity codes, Jesus read the Torah through the eyes of the prophets and those strands of the Torah that most emphasized compassion and justice, especially for the most vulnerable members of the community. In the interpretation of the Torah as a vision for life as God's people, one of these strands or motifs will be given priority over the other. As William Herzog argued, whoever controlled Torah interpretation defined reality. Therefore, the struggle to make an interpretive vision prevail was as much a political as a religious struggle with enormous economic and social consequences. Poverty, interpreted from the viewpoint of the purity codes, is the result of uncleanness. Those who respect the quest for purity will experience blessing and life. The temple authorities, whose legitimation rested squarely on the purity codes, blamed the victims of their own exploitation by portraying them as unclean (the *amme ha-aretz*). But from the viewpoint of the Torah's emphasis on justice and compassion, poverty is the result of the covetous greed of the aristocratic elite, which violates God's will and is opposed to the justice of the reign of God.[15]

---

14. Neusner, *From Politics to Piety*, 67–80, 89–90; Herzog, *Jesus, Justice, and the Reign of God*, 148, 153, 172–73.

15. Herzog, *Jesus, Justice, and the Reign of God*, 149–50, 153, 157–58.

This conflict was also a clash of core values that defined the character of God. The Pharisees' core value was purity. Jesus's core values were forgiveness and compassion because he viewed God as a God of mercy: "Be merciful as your heavenly Father is merciful" (Luke 6:36). The debate was whether the Torah is to be interpreted through the lens of Jesus's prophetic hermeneutic or through the lens of the "tradition of the elders." Each reading is rooted in a conflicting understanding of God. For the upholders of the "tradition of the elders," which prioritized ritual purity, God is most fundamentally the God of the temple, who defines and orders, demands purity and holiness, and draws boundaries. For Jesus, God is the God who liberates, provides, and shows mercy and forgiveness. Of course, William Herzog notes, these alternatives are, in some measure, a false binary, but the issue is over which one is focal and which one is subsidiary.[16]

Jesus clearly adopted the latter approach. He was a harsh critic of the wealthy of his society. In his parable of the rich fool (Luke 12:16–20), he excoriates the wealthy who hoard their resources in pursuit of a life of comfort and security and, by implication, do not consider how to share their resources with the poor and destitute all around them. In his encounter with a rich young man (Matt 19:16–30; Mark 10:17–31; Luke 18:18–30), Jesus reveals the priorities of the kingdom in his answer to the rich young man's question, "What must I do to inherit eternal life?" Jesus tells him to sell everything he has, give the proceeds to the poor, and to follow Jesus.

When Jesus indicated that the way to eternal life is to keep the commandments, William Herzog argues, the young man's answer revealed a narrow understanding of the true meaning of the commandments. According to the standards of his social class, he was Torah-obedient and a living embodiment of the Deuteronomic view of life: the wicked perish but the righteous prosper. But in Galilee and Judea in the early first century under Roman occupation, the only way to become rich was to exploit others. Jesus did not see wealth in this context as a sign of divine blessing but as the result of being a social predator. When the ruling class to which the rich man belonged came to power and used their power to exploit the peasants, they abolished the sabbatical year provision for the cancellation of debts, abolished even the thought of keeping Jubilee, and abandoned the Torah's vision of a land from which poverty had been banished. The ruler's confidence that he has kept the commandments is because he belonged to a faction that interpreted the commandments through the demands of purity. Through this lens, keeping the covenant means keeping a kosher table and eating only acceptable animals, properly slaughtered so that blood is never

---

16. Herzog, *Jesus, Justice, and the Reign of God*, 175–78.

consumed. Most likely, he tithed all that he purchased, married a woman from a house with pure bloodlines, and had abstained from adultery. He no doubt offered appropriate sacrifices, supported the temple with his tithes, and cleansed himself after contracting impurity. He construed his wealth to be a sign of God's blessing and the poverty of others to be God's judgment.[17]

But the principle way one could gain wealth at the time would have been at the expense of the peasant producers, either through fraud, in collecting taxes and tithes, or through lending to peasants having trouble meeting their obligations and then foreclosing and repossessing their land. With regard to his keeping of the commandments, it has likely not occurred to him that, while he never murdered a man face-to-face, he had most likely degraded peasant farmers to the status of day-laborers. From the time a peasant becomes a day laborer, devoid of the safety net of the village and with nothing left to sell but his labor, to the time he dies of malnutrition, is a matter of a few years at most. Every time he alienated a peasant family from their land, he pronounced a death sentence upon them.[18]

The parable of the rich man and Lazarus (Luke 16:13–15, 19–31) is another example of Jesus's scathing criticism of the wealthy. The evangelist situates the parable as Jesus's response to the Pharisees, who were lovers of money and who scoffed at Jesus's claim that one cannot serve God and wealth. Jesus told the story of a profound eschatological reversal of the common assumption that the wealthy have God's stamp of approval and the poor and destitute are cursed and rejected by God. The rich man, who failed to show compassion to Lazarus, who was hungry, destitute, sick, and dying, discovered after death that his life displeased God when he died and found himself in Hades. Here, we see Jesus as the scathing critic of the wealthy for their indifference to persons who were destitute in Judea and Galilee. In addition, Jesus repudiated the retribution theology that defined wealth as a sign of divine blessing and poverty and sickness as a sign of God's punishment. When Abraham, in the parable, told the rich man that his brothers would not listen to one who had returned from the dead if they were not already listening to Moses and the prophets, we recognize that Jesus sees the message of both the law and the prophets to involve active compassion for the needy in society. Here, we see Jesus's resistance both to the economic injustices that have produced such disparities of wealth and poverty and also to an interpretation of Scripture that functioned to justify economic injustice.

---

17. Herzog, *Jesus, Justice, and the Reign of God*, 161–65.

18. Herzog, *Jesus, Justice, and the Reign of God*, 161–67; Horsley, *Jesus and the Spiral of Violence*, 248–49.

Jesus also went out of his way to contest the ways that ritual purity functioned as an ideological support for the wealthy and cudgel to club the poor. When Jesus healed on the Sabbath, dined with ritually impure persons, and disregarded the proliferation of purity regulations, such as those governing ritual handwashing, in the rabbinic oral Torah, he did not "get caught" doing these things. Rather, he went out of his way to do these things publicly in order to provoke his adversaries: to generate conflict through highly public performances designed to contest their interpretation of the Torah and, by doing so, undermine their religious authority and power.[19] In other words, these were intentional provocations, performances of resistance.

In the Gospel of Matthew, the Pharisees are excoriated as poor leaders, the blind guiding the blind (15:14), and shepherds not caring for the sheep (9:36) because of their insistence upon strict *halakha* standards.[20] One of Jesus's skirmishes with the Pharisees came after they criticized his disciples for deficient handwashing practices. Jesus attacked them as harsh, unmerciful, and unjust oppressors of the people. In Matt 23:23, he accused them of forgetting the weightier matters of the law—mercy, justice, and faithfulness—and instead binding heavy burdens upon the common people, offering no assistance as the people struggled to keep such burdensome provisions. It is in this light that we should interpret Matt 12:1–14.

Jesus's citation of Hos 6:6, "I desire mercy and not sacrifice," is a foundational accusation that the Pharisees' insistence on strict adherence to *halakha* is based on a faulty understanding of God. This leads them to "condemn the innocent" because this insistence added to the suffering of the common people. For Jesus, human need takes precedence over laws pertaining to ritual purity. By referring to the disciples as the innocent, Jesus depicted them as representative of the oppressed and downtrodden. By way of contrast, in Matt 11:28–30, a text that sets the stage for the conflicts of chapter 12, Jesus proclaims that his yoke is light compared to the burdensome yolk imposed by *halakha*.[21]

In Matt 9:13, Hos 6:6 was also cited in response to the Pharisees' criticism of Jesus's practice of eating with sinners and tax collectors, the marginalized outcasts. From Matthew's perspective, the Pharisees have misperceived the law and its connection to justice, mercy, and faithfulness. The healing of the man with the withered hand on the Sabbath also pertains to regulations over Sabbath observance. The refusal to allow a crippled man's

---

19. Herzog, *Jesus, Justice, and the Reign of God*, 189–90.
20. Beaton, "Messiah and Justice," 16.
21. Beaton, "Messiah and Justice," 16–20.

healing, due to heavy-handed wielding of the Torah, is viewed by Matthew as unjust. The point is not whether Jesus believes in keeping the commandment regarding the Sabbath. The point is whether it is God or human tradition that requires one to wait until after the Sabbath for healing. Matthew cites and interprets Isa 42:1–3 as a messianic text and identifies Jesus as a messianic figure who brings justice to victory through compassionate healings and resistance to the injustices of the Pharisees. In this way, Matthew identifies Jesus as the Messiah who has already initiated the messianic age of justice, which is being made manifest through healings and deliverance of the poor and downtrodden from a burdensome interpretation of the law.[22]

Quick Excursus: The Religious "Invention" of Race as Purity Code

If Mary Douglas is correct, purity is a broad human phenomena. Purity systems can indeed protect from danger and sustain a group's meaningful identity. But purity systems can also function to exclude in ways that are unjust, harmful, and cruel. It is when purity systems classify some humans as less than fully human, as intrinsically dangerous or unclean, and when these classifications are yoked to systems of domination, that purity systems become evil.

A crucial caveat is that making comparisons across great historical and cultural divides is fraught with peril. What is in some respects alike is always in other respects different. But surely, it is not entirely off the mark to see something akin to a religious purity system in the western Christian and modern creation of race and a racialized view of humanity.

If we limit ourselves to the American experience, racial injustice was tethered to a religious purity system that is manifest in the white fear of miscegenation. After the abolition of slavery, the twin pillars of purity logic, pollution and danger, were projected by the white imagination onto the black body, especially the black male body. Black men were seen as carnal and beastly and a threat to the purity of white womanhood. Accusations of rape or fear of the alleged sexual aggression of black men functioned, perversely, to justify the evils of the lynching.[23]

The purity logic is evident in the persistence of miscegenation laws until 1967, when the landmark Supreme Court case of *Loving v. Virginia* banned miscegenation laws as unconstitutional.[24] Prior to the appeal that

---

22. Beaton, "Messiah and Justice," 16–22.
23. Hopkins, "Construction of the Black Male Body," 205–19.
24. *Loving v. Virginia*, 388 US 1 (1967).

found its way to the US Supreme Court, the judge in the Loving's criminal trial suspended their sentence on the condition that the Lovings agreed to accept banishment by leaving Virginia for twenty-five years and never returning to the state. The judge made this theologically pernicious statement:

> Almighty God created the races, white, black, yellow, malay, and red, and he placed them on separate continents. And but for the interference with his arrangement there would be no cause for such marriages. The fact that he separated the races shows that he did not intend for the races to mix.[25]

In miscegenation laws, with their obsession with purity of blood, we see the purity logic of fear of contamination. In the trial judge's comments, we witness the logic of keeping separate what he regarded as "incompatible pairs."

The logic of purity, with its twin fears of danger and contamination, sustains vitriolic rhetoric against persons crossing the southern US border. In a comprehensive study, Otto Santa Ana identified the metaphors used in the media and public discourse over the years which have profoundly shaped our society's collective perception of undocumented immigrants from south of the border. These images include a "rising brown tide" that will wash away Anglo-Saxon cultural dominance along with depictions of immigrants as animals, weeds that must be uprooted, pathogens, enemies, criminals, and tax burdens.[26] When he announced his intention to run for president, Donald Trump stated:

> When Mexico sends its people, they're not sending their best. . . . They're sending people that have lots of problems, and they're bringing those problems with us. They're bringing drugs. They're bringing crime. They're rapists. And some, I assume, are good people.[27]

Once again, we see the logic of purity. These "others" are dangerous, a criminal element, and a threat to our security. And what was the effort to build a wall along the entire length of the Mexican border but an effort to "quarantine" the impure element, to keep it separated.

---

25. *Loving v. Virginia*, 388 US 1, 3 (1967).

26. Santa Ana, *Brown Tide Rising*, 78, 86, 253–54; Heyer, *Kinship across Borders*, 18; Nevins, *Operation Gatekeeper and Beyond*, 152–53.

27. Lee, "Fact Checker."

Section Two: Soteriology and Biblical Narrative

Jesus and the Temple

The conflict which led to Jesus's crucifixion was his opposition to the temple establishment. We easily miss how politically charged the last week of Jesus's life was because we think, in modern categories, of the temple as a "religious" institution. But the temple was, in fact, an institution resembling, to compare it to contemporary realities in a somewhat anachronistic fashion, a major corporation with significant political connections. Roman domination and control of occupied territories depended upon the authorization of local authorities to carry out certain administrative tasks. Temple personnel, under the oversight of the high priest, were responsible for the collection of the revenue owed to Rome.[28]

Due to the annual half-shekel tax owed by every observant Jewish male, the temple rapidly accumulated large amounts of money. Revenues of the temple and priesthood also included tithes, offerings, and sacrifices. All priests, regular as well as aristocratic, received a portion of their support from these tithes and offerings. Certain choice cuts from the sacrificial animals were reserved for the priests. The pilgrimage festivals, such as Passover, during which Judeans, Galileans, and Jewish persons residing in many other parts of the world came to the temple, meant considerable additional income for Jerusalem generally as well as for the temple and priesthood in particular. The references to money changing in the temple suggests the monetization of the temple economy. This pertained mainly to Jewish persons traveling a distance to Jerusalem, who brought coins instead of animals and exchanged money for sacrificial animals for Passover. Wealth was stored in the temple in the form of precious metals, such as gold and silver, all under the control of the high priesthood.[29]

William Herzog has argued that Jesus sought to free peasants from the iron grip of the temple. The peasants' dilemma was that of being perpetually indebted to the temple, by virtue of not paying their tithes and the annual temple tax, which barred them from effective participation in the benefits, such as the fertility of the land, of the sacrificial system. If peasants were no longer bound to the temple, with its incessant demands for tithes and offerings, they would be better able to maintain the kinship networks of village life on which their survival depended. They would be able to assist one another and prevent fellow Israelites from losing their land due to indebtedness. While Jesus did not forbid payment of the temple tax and even instructed his disciples to pay it on his and their own behalf, Jesus

---

28. Hanson, *Political History of the Bible in America*, 491.
29. Horsley, *Covenant Economics*, 85–86.

proclaimed the non-necessity of doing so when he proclaimed that the sons and daughters are free in Matt 17:24–27. The temple system of tribute-taking, modeled after Roman taxation practices, was not based on the Mosaic law but had been established by precedent. By declaring peasants free of the temple's annual tribute, Jesus is liberating them from this economic burden imposed by a false theology, fashioned in the interests of the rulers at the expense of the people of the land.[30]

While the charge that Jesus threatened to tear down the temple, levied against him at his trial, was either an exaggeration or based upon Jesus's obvious hyperbole, the charge did reflect the reality that Jesus's movement was a profound threat to the temple establishment. If Jesus's movement succeeded, it would seriously undermine the authority and prestige of the temple. By calling the legitimacy of the temple into question, Jesus threatened the most powerful group in Judea. With their precarious hold on power, they would have been particularly sensitive to any challenges to their authority.[31]

Jesus was crucified in Jerusalem during Passover Week, the remembrance and celebration of God's mighty act of delivering the Israelites from bondage to and oppression by an idolatrous empire. The Passover intensified the peoples' yearning for freedom under their true, divine king. Yet, these festivals were presided over by high priests who were client-rulers beholden to Rome. These factors made Judea a powder keg waiting to explode. A prophet like Jesus who criticized the temple could expect to receive a hostile response from a ruling class already under great pressure.[32]

Jesus's adversaries in the temple establishment recognized his actions and words as a threat and a challenge to their authority, power, and honor. They asked Jesus, "By whose authority are you doing these things?" (Mark 11:27–33; Matt 21:23–27; Luke 20:1–8). This loaded question was premised on the assumption that if the high priests, elders, or their functionaries did not authorize Jesus, then his claims to authority are illegitimate. The high priests and elders had ascribed honor, owing to their noble birth. The scribes had acquired honor, owing to their literacy, achievements in interpreting the Torah, and association with the temple authorities.[33] Jesus's creative response to their trap was to force them to answer a question they did not wish, nor were they prepared, to answer. Jesus demanded that his inquisitors answer the question of whether the authority of John the Baptist was from God or merely of human origin (Mark 11:29–30).

30. Herzog, *Jesus, Justice, and the Reign of God*, 192–93, 208–17, 220–21.
31. Herzog, *Jesus, Justice, and the Reign of God*, 237–38, 241.
32. Horsley, *Galilee*, 146; Herzog, *Jesus, Justice, and the Reign of God*, 104–5.
33. Herzog, *Jesus, Justice, and the Reign of God*, 235–36.

This put the scribes in a quandary. There was a long tradition according to which the God who ordained the authority of the priests also ordained the authority of the prophets to bring a word of divine rebuke to priests or kings who abused their authority. John was a recent example of this long prophetic tradition. John baptized and preached a baptism of repentance for the forgiveness of sins—a brokering of God's forgiveness without reference to the temple and its claim of a "spiritual" monopoly. Like Jesus, John had posed a threat to the temple's hegemony. But if they acknowledged, in response to Jesus's question, that John's baptism was of divine origin, they would have conceded that they do not exercise unconditional control over the channels of divine authority and would have opened the door to Jesus's claims of prophetic legitimation. But it would have been disastrous to the scribes to declare publicly that John's baptism was anything less than ordained by heaven since the people believed that John's prophetic ministry and his baptism had been authorized by God.[34]

Understanding the economic role of the temple is crucial for understanding Jesus's action of disrupting the commercial activity in the temple courts as well as his other activities and scathing words during the final week of his life. As the temple amassed wealth, the people of the land were getting poorer. To be rich in that society meant extracting from the poor what belonged to them—whether through extortion, fraud, or oppressive foreclosure. The temple played a crucial role in forcing the poor into more debased forms of dependency. They lost their land, family, and honor.

Wealthy priests and other wealthy aristocrats gained more wealth by making loans at hefty rates of interest. It has been reasonably surmised that the resources coming into the temple from the Diaspora communities as well as from local revenues created a surplus of funds. High priestly families and others with access to such funds drew upon them to make loans to villagers who were struggling to feed their families after meeting their obligations for tribute, tithes, and offerings. From the interest charged and from foreclosures on the loans, well-positioned families increased their wealth.[35] Evidence that this is the case lies in the fact that when the Zealots took control over Jerusalem in 66 CE, they burned the archives, located in the temple, containing the debt records.[36]

The money-changers were the "street-level representatives" of the banking interests of the temple. They were essential operatives in the

---

34. Herzog, *Jesus, Justice, and the Reign of God*, 236–37.

35. Horsley, *Covenant Economics*, 86; Herzog, *Jesus, Justice, and the Reign of God*, 142.

36. Josephus, *Jewish War*, 2:427, cited by Verhey, *Remembering Jesus*, 471–74.

collection of the temple tribute. Accompanying Jesus's disruption of their activities, overturning their tables and forbidding commercial activity, was Jesus's declaration that the temple was meant by God to be a house of prayer for all nations but it had been made into a den of thieves (Mark 11:17).

This statement is a composite of Isa 56:7 and Jer 7:11. Long before, Jeremiah had been called by God to stand in the temple gate to denounce the predatory elite who oppressed the alien, orphan, and widow and who shed innocent blood (Jer 7:5-7). Jeremiah sharply criticized the ruling class for their assumption that their participation in the temple sacrificial system secured God's favor. The ideology of the temple as a divine guarantee of Jerusalem's and Judah's perpetual security, no matter how oppressive the powerful became, was functioning to legitimate oppression. When we look at Jesus's use of the imagery of robbers or bandits and the fact that the members of the ruling class viewed the bandits of Jesus's day as deviant outlaws, Jesus was cleverly suggesting that the real social bandits were not hiding in the caves of the Judean wilderness but were the chief priests.[37]

Against the ethnocentrically narrow restoration program of Ezra (9:1-2; 10:11) and Nehemiah (9:1-2; 10:28-31; 13:1-3), Isa 56:1-8 included eunuchs and foreigners in its vision of Yahweh's in-gathering of the outcasts of Israel. Jesus's ministry to the outcasts and marginal persons is situated within Isaiah's vision. Jesus welcomed and included persons who, because of their uncleanness and cultic impurity, were either banned from the community of Israel or pushed to its margins. Since Jesus had assumed the role of broker of God's forgiveness by reincorporating outcasts into the people of God, he had come to believe that the temple was no longer necessary. As Jeremiah's sermon foretold destruction for the temple by recalling the fate of Shiloh (7:12-15), Jesus symbolically acted out the destruction, not the "cleansing," of the second temple as a prophetic sign of God's impending judgment on what had become an oppressive institution.[38]

In Mark 12:38-44, Jesus condemned the scribes, part of the temple elite, for their status-driven behavior and for "devouring widows' houses" while maintaining a façade of piety by uttering long prayers. The practice Jesus was referring to was the appointment of scribes to serve as guardians or administrators of the widow's estate. The administrator would receive a percentage of the value of the estate, but sometimes an administrator would abuse the role and take more from the estate than was warranted. Once the administrator was appointed and in charge of the deceased's estate, he

---

37. Herzog, *Jesus, Justice, and the Reign of God*, 138-43.
38. Herzog, *Jesus, Justice, and the Reign of God*, 138-43.

would "consume" or "eat away" the estate through exorbitant fees and costs. This practice was described figuratively as "eating up" widows' houses.[39]

Mark 12:41-44 is often read in isolation from Mark 12:38-40, as if it were a nice moral lesson on "stewardship" and sacrificial giving to the Lord's work. But the fact that this episode follows Jesus's condemnation of the scribes for "devouring widows' houses" suggests that we should read verses 41-44 in light of Jesus's condemnation of the scribes for their exploitive and predatory behavior. And we should read Mark 12:41-44 in light of what comes next: Jesus's prediction that the temple, due to God's judgment on the institution, will be completely destroyed (Mark 13:1-2).

While Jesus praises the widow for giving everything she had to live on, Jesus is in fact articulating a scathing criticism of the temple establishment. The temple treasury was supposed to support widows and orphans. Instead, the temple has become an institution that extracts their last copper coins.[40] Since this episode is situated immediately after Jesus's denunciation of scribes for devouring widows' houses, it is reasonable to infer that Mark intended his readers to understand that this widow is so destitute precisely because she has been the victim of the predatory mismanagement of her inherited estate by a scribe who was part of the temple bureaucratic apparatus. Jesus's point is that the temple's ruthless predatory practices are such that it will not stop until it has pried the last penny from the hands of the most economically vulnerable persons in Judah and Galilee. In the Gospel of Mark, these were Jesus's final words in the temple.

Soteriology is incomplete without some account of the atonement, how Christ's death on the cross saves us. This will be the subject of a later chapter. However, it is important to recover what has been forgotten and neglected in much atonement theology. Jesus was crucified because of his activities in the temple during the last week of his life. The temple authorities rightly perceived Jesus as a threat to their political, social, and economic interests. If the people had broadly accepted Jesus's message, the temple would have been abandoned by a large segment of Jewish persons and the flow of money into the temple treasury would have been diminished significantly. From their perspective, he had to be eliminated!

When we think about the meaning of Christ's death on the cross for our sins, we need to connect the meaning of the cross for our salvation to Jesus's week of resistance to the predatory economic behavior of the temple establishment. On the conventional version, Jesus's resistance to economic justice could only be seen as peripheral at best or, more likely,

---

39. Malick, "Poor Widow Who Gave at the Temple," 9.
40. Herzog, *Jesus, Justice, and the Reign of God*, 189.

simply irrelevant to Christ's death on the cross. But if Jesus is the Messiah who came to put all things right, then resisting the predatory economic behavior of the temple establishment makes sense as integral to God's saving purposes. The point of the cross includes putting right the injustice that destroys human beings. The cross includes, as part of its significance for our salvation, God's opposition and call to resistance of the disordering of God's world that we find concentrated in places where power is abused and humans are exploited.

SECTION THREE

A Soteriological Vision

CHAPTER SEVEN

A Soteriological Vision, Part 1

Integrating Biblical and Theological Themes

THE TASK OF THEOLOGY is interpretive, imaginative, and synthetic. I am using the word synthetic to refer to the task of making interpretive judgments. But his does not pertain merely to interpretive judgments about how particular biblical texts are to be interpreted. Rather, the theological task is the imaginative and interpretive one of teasing together multiple strands of biblical material to articulate a theological vision of how things "hang together." The Bible is not, after all, a singular literary unit with a singular and systematic body of "ideas." It is a complex ensemble of narratives, metaphors, motifs, and theological threads that run through several biblical "books" and are, at points, amplified, reworked, and given new meanings that are both in continuity and discontinuity with previous ones. In the New Testament there is, of course, Johannine, Pauline, synoptic, and Petrine material, and even within these bodies of New Testament literature there is plurality, such as that between the pastorals and the letters, that are more clearly from St. Paul's hand. And, of course, our interpretation and appropriation of this material is profoundly shaped by a long history of diverse theological traditions and trajectories of biblical interpretation.[1]

---

1. These reflections bear a relationship to the questions asked and the tentative proposals of David H. Kelsey in *The Uses of Scripture in Recent Theology*. Kelsey explored the diversity of ways in which theologians appeal to Scripture to authorize their proposals. Kelsey suggests that the answers to these questions are tied to what he characterizes as a "discrimen," a configuration of criteria that are "in some way related to

This synthetic task never achieves closure in a perfect synthesis that captures a "biblical vision" or a "biblical worldview." Inevitably, all theological proposals that seek to articulate the Christian faith leave many pieces of the puzzle on the floor, and other theologians might argue that the way certain pieces are put together should have been done so differently. Theology is risky, something of a tightrope act. One might piece together two biblical-theological motifs and do so in ways that so overemphasize one motif that other motifs that deserve to be amplified are muted instead. We never get it entirely right. We inevitably produce theological visions that are incomplete. The hope is that we articulate something that is meaningful, more faithful than not to the deepest wellsprings of God's identify and purposes, and appropriate to the context to which we speak.

Salvation as Union with Christ/*Theosis*

It would be impossible to do justice to the rich and diverse theological history of reflection on the theme of *theosis* in both eastern and western theologies. One could write volumes upon volumes exploring the nuances of the thought of great Christian theologians from St. Irenaeus and St. Athanasius, to St. Augustine, to Gregory of Nyssa, to Maximus the Confessor, on to St. Thomas Aquinas in the west and Gregory Palamas in the east, Reformers such as John Calvin, and into the current theological scene. Inevitably, since this is one section of one chapter in a short book, this presentation will leave a lot out of the discussion and will inevitably oversimplify.

The Bible and a great cloud of Christian witnesses[2] have emphasized that, to speak very broadly, salvation involves union with God or participation in the life of the triune God. This notion has ancient roots in the patristic doctrine of *theosis*.[3]

Drawing upon St. Irenaeus, but consistent with the larger theological tradition, the starting point is that it is God who takes the initiative, in the

---

one another as reciprocal coefficients." What Kelsey is trying to say, by using this vague and abstract notion, is that at the root of theological positions, and how theologians draw upon Scripture, is an imaginative act in which the theologian tries to catch up in a single, synoptic, imaginative and metaphorical judgment what Christianity is all about, including a construal of how God is present and active in the common life and activities of ecclesial communities.

2. In the patristic era, the idea of *theosis* is found in Christian thinkers such as Origen, Maximus the Confessor, Cyril of Alexandria, St. Basil the Great of Caesarea, and even St. Augustine.

3. It is beyond the limits of this chapter to explore the magnitude of theological diversity and disagreement, the wide variety of understandings and models of *theosis*.

incarnation, to unite humanity with God's own life. When the word became flesh, the eternal Son of God united to himself human nature. When human nature was united with divinity in the person of Christ, the human nature united to Christ was healed and restored to the state for which God created humanity. According to St. Irenaeus, the incarnation made it possible for us to recover in Christ what humanity had lost in Adam: to be in the image and likeness of God. The union of divine and human natures in Jesus Christ made it possible for humans to be united with God. Irenaeus emphasized both the incarnation and the role of the Holy Spirit in God's work of uniting us to God:

> The Word, who existed in the beginning with God, by whom all things were made, who was also always present with mankind, was in these last days, according to the time appointed by the Father, united to His own workmanship, inasmuch as He became a man liable to suffering.[4]

> Since the Lord has thus redeemed us through His own blood, giving His soul for our souls, and His flesh for our flesh, and has also poured out the Spirit of the Father for the union and communion of God and man, imparting indeed God to men by means of the Spirit, and, on the other hand attaching man to God by His own incarnation.[5]

By uniting himself with human nature, Irenaeus argued, Christ "caused man to cleave to and to become one with God."[6] In this way, by virtue of the healing of human nature that takes place in Jesus's own body, the humanity of each of us can begin the process of being healed through union with Christ, through whom we are enabled by God to become "partakers of the divine nature" (2 Pet 1:4). According to Ben Blackwell, "The term *theosis* gave patristic writers a quick way to point to the nature and destiny of humanity in terms of being conformed to Jesus, participation in the Spirit, and union with the Father."[7]

St. Irenaeus affirmed that Christ became "what we are, that He might bring us to be even what He is Himself."[8] The language of *theosis*, which is often described as "divinization," is confusing. Protestants have often rejected the idea because the term sounds as if it humans cease to be human

---

4. Irenaeus, *Against Heresies* 3.18.1.
5. Irenaeus, *Against Heresies* 5.1.1.
6. Irenaeus, *Against Heresies* 3.18.7.
7. Blackwell, "You Become What You Worship," 17.
8. Irenaeus, *Against Heresies* 5.pref.

and actually become "gods." But this is not what the term actually means. *Theosis* does not obliterate the divine-human distinction.[9] Humans do not become gods or cease to be creatures. God is transcendent and infinite; there is an infinite distinction between God and finite creatures.

Rather, participation in the life of the triune God transforms believers into the likeness of God that is proper to humans as created in the divine image and likeness. Humans are transformed as the divine life, the divine "liveliness," and the divine moral attributes, such as love, justice, and generosity, permeate the being of human persons like leaven. One of the popular images used to describe the idea of participation in God's divine life and divine nature, the interpenetration of divine and human natures, was the analogy of a sword put in a fire: it remains a sword but gets very hot and starts to glow. As the sword takes on the attributes of light and heat like the fire, it never changes from being a sword to being itself fire. *Theosis* involves an elevation or even a change in our human nature, the transformation of the self (2 Cor 4:16), a reception of the character traits of God. In and through the Spirit, we are transformed into the likeness of Christ (Rom 8:29; 2 Cor 3:18; Phil 3:21) and have "the mind of Christ" (Phil 2:5; 1 Cor 15:49).[10]

At first glance, the motif of deification seems to be antithetical to robust concern about justice in this world. Eastern Orthodox theologian Aristotle Papanikolaou recognizes that *theosis* conjures up images of individual striving for a mystical, ahistorical, world-denying union with God. The monk escaped to the desert to avoid the messiness of politics, which was believed to distract attention from the spiritual aspiration for union with God.[11] However, *theosis* should not be construed as a turning to God that results in a turning away from love for the neighbor or from the practical life of discipleship. First, as Papanikolaou points out, the fullness of divine-human communion results in loving God with all of one's heart, soul, strength, and mind and also to love neighbor as self. To exist in this way is to exist in communion with God.[12] Second, St. Irenaeus links *theosis* with discipleship. For St. Irenaeus, union with God and the transformation of the self depends, first and foremost, upon what God has done to unite divinity with human nature in the incarnation. But we are progressively drawn into this union and transformed through the life of Christomorphic

---

9. Karkkainen, "Holy Spirit and Justification," 29. The key ideas of the idea of *theosis* are likeness to God and participation (*'methexis'*) in God.

10. Finían and Kharlamov, "Introduction," 1–3; Ciraulo, "Divinization as Christification," 479; Blackwell, "You Become What You Worship," 16–17.

11. Papanikolaou, *Mystical as Political*, 1.

12. Papanikolaou, *Mystical as Political*, 3.

"discipleship." The incarnation makes it possible for us to learn the things of God from Jesus's teachings and his actions. The eternal word of God becomes visible and audible and thereby makes it possible for us to become doers of his words and imitators of his words. Through this obedience and imitation, a relationship of communion with the eternal word is forged.[13]

Throughout the New Testament, salvation is portrayed as union with and participation in the life of the triune God. Language and imagery of union with or participation "in Christ" is pervasive in the Pauline corpus. J. Paul Sampley maintains that Paul viewed the Christian's relationship with God in terms of solidarity with, participation in, or belonging to Christ.[14] Salvation is the Christian's living union with the crucified and risen Christ. The expression "in Christ" occurs approximately 150 times in Paul's letters.[15] To be baptized into Christ is to be incorporated into Christ, to participate in Christ's death and resurrection (Rom 6:3–5). Paul tells the Corinthian Christians, "Your bodies are members of Christ himself" (1 Cor 6:15–16). The intimate sexual union in which husband and wife become one flesh is identified as a fitting analogy of the union between Christ and church (Eph 5:31–32).

The Gospel of John also gives powerful expression to this idea. Salvation involves connection to Jesus, as branches are connected to the grapevine. If the branch "abides" in the vine, it would receive nourishment and life from the vine and will bear fruit. To be severed from the true vine is to wither and die (15:1–8). Jesus promised to ask his Father to send the Spirit, who will "live with you and in you" (14:16–20). In 14:20, Jesus asserted, "I am in my Father, and you are in me, and I am in you." Christian unity is rooted in the indwelling and participation of believers in the life and unity of Father and Son (17:21–23).

But union with Christ is not merely a "spiritual" union that pertains to our interior relationship with God. Participation in the life of God involves the transformation of the self as the Holy Spirit draws us into a new pattern of living. Paul speaks of being crucified with Christ such that "it is no longer I who live, but Christ who lives in me" (Gal 2:20). Transformed existence involves the conformation of the self to Christ and a life patterned after Christ's self-offering for our sake and his cruciform generosity, which takes the form of radical concern for the well-being of others even when it is costly to oneself (Rom 8:29; 15:1–3, 7; 2 Cor 3:18; 8:7–12; Gal 6:1–2; Eph 4:32; 5:1–2; Col 3:10).

---

13. Irenaeus, *Against Heresies* 5.1.1; Loewe, *Lex Crucis*, 39–40.
14. Sampley, *Walking Between the Times*, 12.
15. Vanhoozer, "Wrighting the Wrongs of the Reformation?," 253.

In 1 John, we find a fascinating chain of connections drawn between union with Christ and the transformed self that is required for faithful Christian living. To know God *is* to walk in the light and live a life of love. Relationship with God, knowing God, means living a life of love, which is the same as "walking in the light." John makes this point in terms of union with God: to live in love is to live in God (4:17). This mutual indwelling is linked to the Holy Spirit (1 John 4:12–13). God living in us and we abiding in him takes the form of responding to humans in need (3:17) in a way patterned after Christ's love, manifested in his laying down his life for us (3:16).

It is beyond the parameters of this short segment of one chapter to discuss the diverse ways in which great Christian thinkers have understood and theorized *theosis*. One of the profound theological questions faced by various thinkers is that of how the ontological chasm between the transcendent God and the creature can be crossed without collapsing the distinction. How does the redeemed creature participate in the life of God without being absorbed into God and ceasing to be a creature?

In the fourteenth century, Gregory Palamas argued that humans cannot participate in God's essence, due to God's utter transcendence, but God's energies are bestowed in order to elevate and divinize human persons.[16] In this way, the Palamite tradition sought to safeguard the transcendence of God through a distinction between the divine essence and the divine energies.

Jonathan Ciraulo argues that the flaw in the Palamite approach is that *theosis* is construed as participation in the divine energies as shared equally by all of the divine persons rather than, first and foremost, sharing in what is particular and unique to the Son. Ciraulo follows twentieth-century Roman Catholic theologian Erich Przywara and twentieth- and twenty-first-century Orthodox theologian John Zizioulas, advocating for a hypostatic model of divinization. In the incarnation, God, in the person of the Son, has crossed the ontological chasm by uniting human nature to himself, opening the way of human participation in the life of God through union with Christ. A hypostatic conception of the incarnation stands in contrast to flawed conceptions of *theosis* that correspond to the christological heresies of Monophysitism, in which the humanity of Jesus is absorbed into the divine, and Nestorianism, in which the divine and human remain separated. Corresponding to these christological extremes are models of *theosis* as absorption into God's reality, such that the ontological distinction between

---

16. Ciraulo, "Divinization as Christification," 480.

God and the creature is breached, and *theosis* as a mere shorthand for moral transformation of the will that comes by imitating Christ.[17]

Ciraulo argues that in the hypostatic union the human and divine retain their respective natures, while the human is truly united to the Divine Person. Participation in the divine nature does not mean that we are God in the same sense that Father, Son, and Holy Spirit are God but in a manner fitting to our human nature, elevated by God's grace, according to our capacities as creatures. A human cannot become God in the way that Father, Son, and Spirit are God, but thanks to the incarnation, a human can become like Christ.[18] Our union with the triune God occurs in and through one person of the Trinity and not through an aspect of God's being that belongs to all three of the Trinitarian Persons, such as the divine energies. Our union with the Triune God is hypostatic, a union as a member of Christ.[19]

Theosis and Ecclesiology: Salvation is Incorporation into Christ/Christ's Body

Making the connections: *Theosis* is a living union with the triune God that is made possible by our incorporation into Christ. But union with Christ is simultaneously incorporation into Christ's body, the *ekklesia*.

Theologian Mark Medley correctly argues that the primary locus of participation in the divine life is not the individual's private devotional life. Rather, "the focal point of our participation in the life of God is the gathered people of God, the church."[20]

Incorporation into Christ is not merely a relationship between Christ and the *individual*. To be joined to Christ is simultaneously to be incorporated into Christ's body, the church (Rom 12:4–5; 1 Cor 12:4–31). This theme finds its most powerful expression in the Pauline corpus. There is no union of the individual with Christ that is prior to or disconnected from Christ's ecclesial body. In the church, we are one body in Christ and members of one another (Rom 12:5; Eph 4:25). The solidarity within this community is such that the suffering or celebration of any member is experienced by the rest of the community, which suffers or celebrates with the one member of the body (1 Cor 12:26).

Union with Christ includes both reconciliation with God (Rom 5:8; 2 Cor 5:14–15, 18–20; Eph 2:16) and reconciliation between previously

17. Ciraulo, "Divinization as Christification," 477–78, 481–82, 488–89, 494.
18. Ciraulo, "Divinization as Christification," 477–78, 488–91, 494.
19. Ciraulo, "Divinization as Christification," 492.
20. Medley, "'Do This,'" 385–86.

hostile and alienated persons and groups. The socio-economic, ethnic, or racial categories that function to divide persons through alienated relationships of domination, social stratification, enmity, and mechanisms of exclusion are meant to be overcome through the formation of this new and reconciled humanity "in Christ" (Gal 3:28; Col 3:10). In Eph 2:11–22, Christ's redemptive work on the cross is identified as that of reconciling Jews and gentiles by gathering and incorporating the gentiles into God's covenant people. This reconciliation is not a positive by-product of salvation but is itself the salvific goal of Christ's redemptive death, which was to bring into reality a new humanity, a new kind of human community in which those previously alienated from and hostile to one another are reconciled (Eph 2:11–22). Salvation is not incorporation into the life of God in a way that severs us from connections to other humans. Rather, this new humanity is "located" in Christ's broken, crucified, and risen body. If sin is that which destroys community, between God and humanity and among humans, then salvation takes concrete shape as a new kind of human community, characterized by union with God in Christ and the reconciliation of humans with one another. This radically new kind of human community is one in which the alienating and dividing power of the sinful social orders that characterize our fallen world has been broken. Sinful social orders produce forms of identity that divide and estrange humans from one another. But this new community is called by God to break down the barriers of race, ethnicity, gender, social class, and national identity, as well as any other perversely artificial barriers, when such identity markers function to divide human beings by categorizing some persons as superior and others as inferior, some as winners and some as losers, or some as insiders and others as outsiders. In Christ, the binary characterizations of humans as Jew and Greek, slave and free, male and female, "civilized" Greeks and "uncivilized" barbarians and Scythians (Gal 3:26–28; cf. Col 3:10–11) are deconstructed as socially constructed mechanisms of domination.

The relevance of this ecclesiological emphasis for the tragic ecclesial divisions produced by the long history of white supremacy we have inherited and perpetuated, wittingly or unwittingly, should be evident. That we have inherited and continue to live inside of the patterns of separation produced by this tragic history and present reality should be recognized as scandalous in relationship to the purposes of Christ. Given the tragic separations, slow and patient labor to heal and mend should be central to the ecclesial mission in this moment. I cannot prescribe what this task might mean for Christians who are non-white, but for those of us who are Christian, white, and American, the fact that dividing walls of hostility of "our" own collective making, past and present, exist calls us to repentance in humble conversation with other Christians. We will be called to listen rather than dictate solutions. We will be called to abstain from the fantasy of quick and easy reconciliation.

If we take a Johannine detour, we find a vision that is certainly consistent with Pauline ecclesiological insights. In what is cast in the Gospel of John as Jesus's farewell prayer, Jesus prays that all of his followers, then current and future, might be one, united in conformity to the unity of the Trinitarian life (John 17:21–23a). Jesus prayed that his followers might be brought to complete unity to let the world know that the Father sent Jesus (John 17:20–23). As Bruce Marshall argues, the very credibility of the gospel depends upon the unity of Christ's followers.[21]

That salvation is ecclesial is counterintuitive if one inhabits the dominant soteriological imagination. Church membership is seen as desirable as an aid to personal spiritual growth, but it is assumed that one can accept Jesus as one's personal savior and have a relationship with Christ all by oneself. However, if salvation is union with Christ, to be joined to Christ is, by definition, to be incorporated or baptized into Christ's body by the Holy Spirit (1 Cor 12:13, 27). There is no union of the individual with Christ that is prior to or disconnected from Christ's ecclesial body.

Salvation, then, is God's act of graciously including us in this new social reality, governed by the pattern of Jesus Christ, in which enemies are reconciled, the outcast welcomed, and the poor cared for. This new form of human community is simultaneously a divine gift and an ecclesial project. We are graciously invited to participate in the *missio Dei*, God's ecclesial and eschatological project of reconciling to himself all things by making peace through Christ's blood, shed on the cross (Col 1:20). The wholeness, unity, peace, holiness, and faithfulness of God's people is fully the work of the Holy Spirit and yet requires participation, work, and struggle on our part. Paul called the Roman Christians to make every effort to do what leads to peace and mutual edification (Rom 14:19; see also Eph 4:3). Unity, reconciliation, and mutual forgiveness are facets of an ecclesial project, but the human effort involved is by no means an autonomous human accomplishment, for which we might boast. Rather, our participation in God's work of creating and sustaining this new and reconciled kind of human community is always already the work of the Holy Spirit and, indeed, to the extent it is faithful, is human agency inside of God's agency and action.

---

21. Marshall, "Disunity of the Church," 78–89.

Section Three: A Soteriological Vision

The Transformation of the Self in Christ: Conformity to Christ and Ecclesial Selfhood

Making the connections: *Theosis* is transformative. That transformation is a conformation of the self to Christ. And since incorporation into Christ is incorporation into Christ's body, the transformed, Christomorphic self is an ecclesial self, transformed for participation in the new human community Christ died to bring into reality.

There is no union with Christ without the transformation of the self. To be "in Christ" is to have one's life conformed to the self-giving love enacted on the cross.[22] Paul speaks of being crucified with Christ and transformed such that the person who lives is no longer Paul but rather Christ living through him (Gal 2:20). Baptism into Christ's death is the event in which the old self, enslaved to sin, is crucified with Christ in order that we might be liberated from the tyranny of sin. To be alive to God in Christ is to be dead to sin (Rom 6:11). Throughout the Pauline corpus (Rom 8:5–14; Gal 5:16–26; Col 3), the sharpest antithesis is drawn between the former way of life, the practices of the old self, which is life according to the "flesh" or sinful nature, on the one hand, and transformed existence in Christ, on the other. This conformation of the self to Christ (Rom 8:29; 2 Cor 3:18; Col 3:10) involves living in accordance with the pattern of Christ's generosity, sacrificial self-offering to God "for us," and radical concern for the well-being of others, even if at great cost to himself (Rom 15:1–3, 7; 2 Cor 8:7–12; Gal 6:1–2; Eph 4:32; 5:1–2).

This transformation of the self is not a private and individual matter. Far too often, sanctification is construed as pertaining to the individual Christian and is not situated ecclesiologically. At most, the church is viewed as a crucial and indispensable aid to the individual's sanctification. However, in the Pauline corpus, the point of God's saving and reconciling work in Christ is that the church might become the righteousness of God, embodying in its *communal* life the reconciling love of Christ (2 Cor 5:21).[23] This transformation is explicitly connected to our status as members of one another (Rom 12:1–5).

The new self in Christ (Eph 4:24) is an ecclesial self, transformed for participation in this communal life of reconciliation and unity, mutual edification, and mutual responsibility (Rom 14:19; 1 Cor 10:23–33; Gal 6:1–2). The destructive vices of the old self destroy community: lying, theft, bitterness, wrath, anger, slander, and malice. The new and transformed

---

22. Hays, *Moral Vision of the New Testament*, 32.
23. Hays, *Moral Vision of the New Testament*, 24.

ecclesial self speaks words designed to edify, is kind, tender-hearted, forgiving, compassionate, and truthful because "we are members of one body" (Eph 4:22–5:2). The transformation of the self in Christ is for the purpose of participation in this communal life of reconciliation and unity (Eph 4:1–4), mutual edification, mutual responsibility, and "bearing one another's burdens" (Rom 14:19; 1 Cor 10:23–24; Gal 6:1–2). The basis for this communal way of life is conformation to the pattern of Christ's self-sacrificial love, obedience, and willingness to adopt the posture of a servant (Phil 2:1–11).

Spiritual growth is first and primarily a group ecclesial project. The purpose of spiritual gifts is to prepare God's people for works of service so that the body of Christ may be built up, with the goal being unity and growth together into the fullness of Christ (Eph 4:11–13).

The conformation of the self to Christ is "cruciform." The Christian life is both a present participation in Christ's eschatological, risen glory (2 Cor 3:18) and participation in Christ's crucifixion as we suffer with Christ in the present evil age (2 Cor 4). As Michael Gorman argues, "The core of Paul's soteriology is a vision of Spirit-enabled identification, participation in, and conformity to the incarnate, crucified, resurrected, and glorified Christ."[24]

Gorman contends that Phil 2:6–11 is Paul's "master story." This text portrays Christ as the "self-emptying" form of God, in contrast to Adam's quest to be equal with God and the Roman emperors' self-glorying, self-elevating ethos of asserting godlike status for themselves. Instead of "upward mobility," Jesus takes the path of downward mobility as he humbles himself to the status of a slave and the consequent death by crucifixion, reserved for slaves and others regarded by the empire as "garbage." All of this constituted "status degradation" in the Roman Empire.[25]

Paul tethers this master story to a call for the Philippian Christians to relinquish behavior driven by selfish ambition and instead to adopt a posture consistent with Christ's downward mobility by valuing others above themselves and caring about the well-being of others instead of living a life of self-preoccupation (Phil 2:1–5). In Rom 14:14–21, Paul points to his freedom to eat meat purchased in the marketplace even though the animal from which the meat was derived may have been sacrificed to a pagan deity. But if doing so in the presence of Christians of "weaker conscience" would lead them to emulate such behavior and then feel crushing guilt, the true exercise of Christian freedom is to relinquish what one is otherwise free to do for the sake of the brother or sister in Christ. Cruciformity means prioritizing the well-being of others instead of focusing first and primarily

---

24. Gorman, *Inhabiting the Cruciform God*, 6–8.
25. Gorman, *Inhabiting the Cruciform God*, 2–3, 16–17.

upon one's own rights and prerogatives. In 1 Corinthians 8, Paul points to his own relinquishment of his rights as an apostle to travel with a wife and to be supported by the Christian communities he served. But, as he states, he relinquished such rights and took the posture of a slave or servant, by supporting himself and adapting to the cultural mores of others, in order to share the gospel more effectively. For Paul, the primary orientation of love is not to seek its own interests or edification but rather that of others, (1 Cor 8:1; 13:5), which is the core meaning of conformity to Christ. This participation in Christ is participation in the one whose status of being equal to God was most truly and fully exercised, not in exploiting that status for selfish advantage but in the self-emptying that manifested itself in incarnation and crucifixion.[26]

However, I would argue that we must make an important qualification that is literally a matter of life and death. This message of imitation of the Christ who took on the form of a servant and sacrificed his own interests for the sake of others is abused if it is used against persons who are already vulnerable, abused, and exploited. Cruciform renunciation of power, status, and privileges should be performed by those persons who, in any situation, have power, status, and privilege. This message should be accentuated when persons have power and privilege vis-à-vis the others for whom self-giving occurs. However, this message of imitation of Jesus's self-sacrificial love has often been preached to persons who are exploited economically, subjected to domestic abuse, abusive workplaces, or oppressive social, political, and economic arrangements, as a call to docile acceptance of abuse and mistreatment. When the call to imitate Jesus is marshalled in the service of those who dominate to counsel submission to those who are dominated, those who preach this message are literally anti-christic. Jesus's self-sacrifice on the cross was not an instance of passive acquiescence to abuse and exploitation. Jesus's death on the cross occurred precisely because of his self-sacrificial solidarity with the abused and exploited and his resistance to the sources of their oppression and exploitation. Here, we must heed the voices of so many feminist and liberation theologians. While I would not agree with the entirety of the theological vision articulated by the authors, reflection on the meaning of Christ's death and discipleship as cruciform participation in and conformation of self to the crucified and risen Christ should pass through the crucible of the painful theological meditations offered by Rita Nakashima Brock and Rebecca Ann Parker. Brock and Parker rightly argue that suffering is not inherently redemptive and that this message has functioned to place women in situations of domestic abuse in even greater

---

26. Gorman, *Inhabiting the Cruciform God*, 23–25.

danger.[27] A victim of domestic violence should not be told that Christ-likeness means suffering meekly in a way that enables an abuser to inflict violence with impunity. Christ expended himself to heal desperate persons, to extend God's gracious hospitality to those the powerful regarded as beyond the pale of God's concern, and to resist the economic exploitation of the vulnerable by those engaged in predatory economic practices. Jesus did not die on the cross because he passively acquiesced to abuse and injustice. He knowingly risked his life to resist these exploitive powers for the sake of the victims of that power.

This means that cruciformity in many contexts should not take the form of renunciation of rights but rather a demand for justice for oneself and others. For example, during the American civil rights movement, cruciformity for white persons meant solidarity with African-Americans struggling for justice, even if such solidarity and participation in the movement meant loss of family approval, loss of social status, loss of a job, or, for persons like Violet Liuzzo and James Reeb, martyrdom. The goal was not to suffer because suffering is intrinsically redemptive. What was redemptive was the love that was willing to risk suffering. But the suffering itself was imposed by persons in the grip of the satanic power of white supremacy and racial hatred.

A paradigm of cruciformity for persons already without power and privilege was Fanie Lou Hamer, who resisted the racial caste system that consigned black citizens of Mississippi to lives of poverty and misery. Cruciformity, in this context, would not have consisted in passive acceptance of the denial of one's rights, such as the right to vote, but rather resistance to these denials. Hamer's battle was costly to herself as well as to other black Mississippians. She fought for freedom, empowerment, and the right to vote. But this was not a selfish assertion of her rights; it was for the sake of other oppressed persons, and it came with the sacrifice of safety. For the simple act of trying to register to vote, she was expelled from the tiny shack she occupied as a sharecropper because the owner knew he would face social pressure and consequences if he did not "keep his help in line."[28] When Hamer and others returned to Mississippi after she attended the SCLC's citizenship school in South Carolina, they were arrested and subjected to unspeakably brutal beatings and verbal humiliation (bitch, fatso, whore, and racial slurs) by the members of the sheriff's department in Winona,

---

27. Brock and Parker, *Proverbs of Ashes*.
28. Marsh, *God's Long Summer*, 13–16.

Mississippi. She was abused for the "crime" of being a black woman with a voice.[29]

The cruciform pattern of Hamer's struggle against racial injustice is evident when we recall that Jesus was crucified because he resisted injustice, the abuse of power, and the exploitation of vulnerable persons. Like Jesus, Hamer embraced her own cross because of her courage. The pattern of the cross is not passive acquiescence to suffering but the kind of active resistance that often provokes the powers to kill or inflict suffering in order to protect their unjust privileges. Though she had no power to fight back in the jail cell when she was being beaten so severely that she could have died, she spoke words of divine judgment to her torturers. After the beating, she and the others boldly sang a spiritual at the heart of the African-American struggle for freedom, *Go Down Moses*. A few days later, when she was escorted by one of the jailers who had helped carry out her beating just a few days earlier, she asked, "Do you people ever think or wonder how you'll feel when the time comes you'll have to meet God?"[30] As will be argued in an upcoming chapter, Hamer embodies the cruciformity of courageous witness to the truth and resistance to evil that is faithful to Jesus's own action that led to his crucifixion.

The Gift of the Holy (Eschatological) Spirit

Making Connections: The Holy Spirit incorporates us into Christ, making possible our union with God and our transformation through that union. The Holy Spirit incorporates us into Christ's body, the church, and is the transforming power of God that forms the new-self-in-Christ to be a Christomorphic, ecclesial self. The Holy Spirit is also the eschatological Spirit, the power of the age to come, through whom Jesus inaugurated the reign of God. This latter connection will be explored further in the next chapter.

In the Pauline corpus, salvation is the reception of the gift of new life in Christ through the gift of the Holy Spirit (Gal 3:11, 14). It is having the Spirit that defines and determines someone as being "in Christ" (Rom 8:9–10).[31] Therefore, we should expect to discover a link between the Spirit and the two soteriological motifs of incorporation into Christ and Christ's body and the conformation of the self to Christ. First Corinthians 12:13–27 affirms that we were baptized by one Spirit into the body of Christ. The Holy Spirit is the bond of unity and the basis for Christian fellowship (Eph

---

29. Marsh, *God's Long Summer*, 20–21.
30. Marsh, *God's Long Summer*, 20–21.
31. Dunn, *Theology of Paul the Apostle*, 414, 423.

4:3–4). The Spirit is also the agent of rebirth and renewal (Titus 3:5–7). We are saved through the "sanctifying work of the Holy Spirit" (2 Thess 2:13). Transformed existence is "living according to the Spirit" (Rom 8:5–13; Gal 5:16–18).

The Holy Spirit is the eschatological power of God. In the Synoptic Gospels, the Spirit is at work in Jesus's deeds of deliverance, which signal the in-breaking of God's eschatological reign (Matt 11:2–5; 12:28). Jesus's resurrection, as an act of the Spirit (Rom 1:3–4; 8:11; 1 Tim 3:1), signals the inauguration of the eschatological new creation in the midst of the present evil age of sin and death. Through our incorporation into Christ, by virtue of our participation in the Spirit, Christians are drawn into the sphere of eschatological new creation in the here and now (2 Cor 5:17). James Dunn characterizes the work of the Spirit as analogous to a bridge between the present and future, the already and the "not-yet." The gift of the Spirit, who attests to our adoption as children of God (e.g., Rom 8:23; 2 Cor 1:22, 5:5; Eph 1:14), is the beginning of the process that will reach its end with the resurrection of the body, the climactic saving act of the life-giving Spirit.[32] Frank Macchia notes that, for Paul, the resurrection is the ultimate form of pneumatic experience, in which mortality is swallowed up by life (1 Cor 15:44–46; 2 Cor 5:4). The indwelling of the Spirit in this age is the "down payment" or guarantee of the future resurrection in the coming age (Eph 1:14; Rom 8:11; 2 Cor 5:5). This process of eschatological transformation, in which we already participate, is ultimately fulfilled only when the Spirit fully duplicates in us, eschatologically, what the Spirit has already done in the resurrected Christ as the New Creation.[33]

---

32. Dunn, *Theology of Paul the Apostle*, 403, 469.

33. Macchia, "Justification as New Creation," 211–12; Macchia, *Justified in the Spirit*, 11; Sampley, *Walking Between the Times*, 21; Dabney, "Grace of the Spirit," 5–6.

CHAPTER EIGHT

A Soteriological Vison, Part 2
Salvation Is Incorporation into and Participation in the Eschatological New Creation

A Neglected New Testament Theme: Jesus's Enthronement and Authority

Jesus was turned over to the Roman authorities by the aristocratic elite of the temple-state. He was accused of "subverting our nation" and opposing the payment of taxes to Caesar. He was accused of claiming to be the Messiah and as such, the king of the Jews (Mark 15:2; Matt 27:11; Luke 23:2). The irony, of course, is that Jesus was indeed the Messiah, the true and rightful king of God's covenant people and of all humanity. In that sense, he was indeed guilty, not of sin before God but of being a destabilizing force whose words and deeds undermined the moral legitimacy of the Roman Empire.

Jesus was not guilty of being a conventional threat, a garden-variety zealot messiah pretender seeking to foment a violent revolution. But the movement he inaugurated was anti-imperial. The first commandment and Israel's core conviction regarding the sole sovereignty of Yahweh made it impossible to proclaim and inaugurate the kingdom of God as anything other than counter-imperial, an alternative social movement. The kingship of God is incompatible with Rome's claims to ultimate allegiance. The kingdom Jesus proclaimed and embodied was antithetical to Roman values such as conquest, humiliation of defeated peoples, social hierarchy, and the quest for social dominance, wealth, and economic exploitation. Jesus was indeed a threat to all that Rome held dear.

Jesus's crucifixion seemed to be a clear and decisive victory for Rome. Crucifixion was what Rome did to crush any semblance of resistance. We so easily forget how radical and, indeed, subversive it must have been for the early Christian movement to proclaim that a man the Roman authorities had judged to be a criminal, a threat to law and order, and to the security of the empire, is the true Lord and ruler of the cosmos. To proclaim Jesus to be the Lord was to repudiate the judgment of imperial Rome about Jesus.

Add to this the shame associated with crucifixion. To be crucified was to be decisively humiliated as a failure, a loser, and, literally, garbage. The only thing that could make sense of how explosive the Jesus movement was in its first thirty years is the conviction that God raised the crucified Jesus from the dead and, therefore, Jesus is not merely another martyr-hero but the living Lord.

What is the "theological significance" of the resurrection? The obvious answer is, of course, literally everything! But in particular, recall that many faithful Jews during the intertestamental period came to believe that God would, at the end of human history, raise the dead, judge every human who had ever lived, and reward and shame or punish. This idea is referred to as the "general resurrection." The hope for the resurrection pertained to the righteousness of God and the vindication of God's faithful people. If God is the God who blesses his covenant people, then the persecution, suffering, and martyrdom of those who experienced such suffering, because of their faithfulness to God, raised the question of God's righteousness. As J. R. Andrew Kirk points out, the development of hope for the resurrection meant that there is a sphere in which God can make good on his promises to his people and thus justify himself. This provided the hope that those who had been faithful to God throughout their lifetimes but failed to receive a reward for their work can look forward to resurrection life as the context for receiving God's promised blessings.[1] For the righteous, who would be blessed for their faithfulness, resurrection meant vindication.

The general resurrection meant that everyone would be resurrected at the same time at the end of history. But Jesus's first followers encountered the risen Christ three days after his crucifixion, before the messianic age and the general resurrection. If God raised Jesus first, before everyone else, these followers came to believe, then this must be God's validation of Jesus as the messiah, as the divine judge who will judge the living and the dead at

---

1. Kirk, *Unlocking Romans*, 10–11.

the end of the age. Jesus is described as "the firstborn from the dead" or the "first fruits of those who have died" (1 Cor 15:20; Col 1:18; Rev 1:4).

The conviction that Christ has risen is also linked with the conviction that Jesus has been enthroned as king as the right hand of God. The "right hand of God" is a figure of speech that refers to the place of supreme authority in the cosmos.[2] To proclaim that Jesus has been raised from the dead and enthroned at the right hand of God is to say that "Jesus is the Lord" and Caesar is not. The belief that Jesus is enthroned at the right hand of God the Father does not mean that the "location" of Jesus's kingdom is up in heaven and, therefore, is a spiritual kingdom without relevance for life on earth. After all, in Matt 28:18, the risen Jesus proclaims not only that all authority in heaven has been given to me but also that all authority on earth is his as well. This image of enthronement at the right hand of God is drawn from the royal enthronement psalm, associated with the coronation of a new king in Judah, in which God commands the new king to sit at God's right hand and invites the king to do so until God makes the king's enemies into the king's footstool (Ps 110:1). Both Psalm 2 and Psalm 110, which celebrate the coronation and enthronement of a new king in Judah, are interpreted throughout the New Testament to be ultimately fulfilled in Jesus Christ, now the occupant of the place of supreme authority in the cosmos.

Matthew Cox points out that the imagery of Psalm 2 is scattered throughout Matthew's Gospel as integral to its identification of Jesus Christ. In Psalm 2, the nations and kings of the earth plot and conspire, but in vain, against God's people and the Lord's anointed, the king of Judah. But God laughs at them and will defeat them. Throughout the Gospels, rulers conspire against Jesus, the ultimate anointed one of God. Herod tries to kill him while just a child (2:16). Pilate and the Jewish rulers conspire against Jesus and put him to death. Psalm 2:7 is referenced when Jesus is baptized and the voice from heaven identifies him as "my beloved Son" (3:17) as well as at the transfiguration, when the disciples hear the voice from heaven telling them, "This is my Son, the Beloved" (17:5).[3]

This idea of Christ's exaltation, supreme authority, and ultimate triumph over all of this world's oppressive rulers and powers was at the heart of the gospel proclaimed by the early church. In what is presented to us as the first post-resurrection "sermon," Peter proclaims that Christ is exalted at the right hand of God (Acts 2:33). In Acts 3, Peter proclaimed that the risen Jesus must remain in heaven until the time of universal restoration, which is, of course, the anticipated messianic age (3:20). One of the most

---

2. Wright, *What St. Paul Really Said*, 151.
3. Cox, "Gospel of Matthew and Resisting Imperial Theology," 33.

powerful assertions that Jesus has been enthroned at the right hand of God, and that his enthronement has political implications on earth, is found in Ephesians 1:20–23, which proclaims that Jesus is elevated above every human political authority. The implication of the claim and confession of Eph 1:20–23, combined with the conviction that Jesus is coming again to establish his reign on earth, is that he is the one who deserves our ultimate and complete allegiance as Lord and ruler. Christ's exaltation to the right hand of the Father and his ultimate authority in the cosmos is found in a wide variety of New Testament texts (Matt 22:44; 26:64; Mark 12:36; 14:62; Luke 20:42; 22:69; Acts 5:31; 7:55–56; Rom 8:34; Col 3:1; Heb 1; 8:1; 10:12–13; 12:2; 1 Pet 3:22; Rev 3:21).

Of course, if Jesus is the one in the place of supreme authority, then Caesar is not. To the risen Lord belongs ultimate allegiance. This is not a rule or reign in the spiritual domain, leaving the rulers in the social and political sphere unaffected. Rather, the ultimate outcome of Christ's rule is that the entire world comes into submission to Christ's Lordship. This is evident in Phil 2:6–11, where the one who humbled himself and submitted in obedience to God to the most horrible and humiliating death possible has been elevated to the highest place of authority in the cosmos and given the name of Lord that is above every name.

Matthew Bates calls attention to the close linkage of all of these ideas in Rom 1:1–5. Jesus, as a descendant of David, was, by means of his resurrection, appointed Son of God in Power. This connects Jesus's coronation as the seed of David, the messiah, with his resurrection and his ascension and enthronement at the right hand of God as the reigning Lord of heaven and earth. This means that our allegiance is owed to this Jesus who God has enthroned as king through his resurrection. Bates argues that the meaning of the biblical term "faith," *pistis* in Greek, is fidelity or allegiance to Jesus as king and cosmic Lord.[4]

This framework is also present in the book of Revelation. The Lamb who was slain is worthy of worship (Rev 5) and will ultimately defeat the oppressive imperial powers and the Satanic power behind imperial power (Rev 18–20). When he returns to establish the messianic reign on earth, the dead will be raised and judged, and then the New Jerusalem will descend and a renewed world of justice and peace, from which evil and death have been banished, will prevail (Rev 20–21).

---

4. Bates, *Salvation by Allegiance Alone*, 31–37.

Section Three: A Soteriological Vision

Incorporation into the Eschatological New Creation

Summary of this chapter and the previous chapter: If I had to put my soteriological vision into the proverbial nutshell, it would go something like this: Salvation is union with Christ, being incorporated into or joined to Christ and to Christ's body, by the Holy Spirit, through whom we are brought into communion with the triune God. But we must not abstract the New Testament theme of union with Christ and communion with the triune God, *theosis*, from the good news that Jesus is the Messiah, the bringer of the "eschatological new creation." As the Messiah, he is risen and enthroned as the true Lord of the cosmos, to whom our allegiance is due. To be joined to Christ is to be brought into the kingdom of God, not only in the future but in the here and now! We are saved to be participants in the invasion of God's new world into the present age.

Jesus is more than merely the messenger who teaches about the kingdom. He is the kingdom in the flesh. Origen correctly identified Jesus as the *autobasileia*.[5]

The Holy Spirit, who incorporates us into Christ, is the eschatological Spirit, the power of the age to come already breaking into our world. The Spirit's work is not to draw us out of creation but rather to deliver us from our entanglement with the sin and destruction of the present evil age so that we might begin to inhabit, however provisionally and imperfectly, the sphere of eschatological new creation and live a life appropriate to God's new order. In the Synoptic Gospels, the Holy Spirit is the eschatological power of God at work in Jesus's deeds of deliverance that inaugurate the reign of God and are the first fruits of a world put right. When we are joined to Christ, by virtue of our participation in the Spirit, Christians are not merely given a personal, individual relationship with God that is confined to our interior spiritual life. Rather, when we are joined to Christ by the Spirit, we are also drawn into the kingdom of God over which Jesus Messiah presides as Lord. We are drawn into the sphere of eschatological new creation in the here and now (2 Cor 5:17; Gal 6:15). As St. Paul proclaims the good news in Col 1:13, we are rescued from the present evil age, described as the dominion of darkness, and incorporated into the kingdom of God's beloved Son.

Salvation is both inclusion in the new social reality that God has brought into being "in Christ" and the correlative transformation required for such participation. Both the inclusion in God's new order and the transformation required for active and faithful participation in that new order are gifts of grace.

---

5. Origen, *Commentary on Matthew* 14.7.

A Soteriological Vison, Part 2

Contrary to popular Protestant understandings of St. Paul, justification by faith is not the only or even primary theme of Paul's writings. In fact, this issue is present only in the Epistles to the Romans and the Galatians. This does not mean that justification by faith is not an important theme. However, this theme has often been ripped away from its context within Paul's entire body of writings and thought, especially from the apocalyptic eschatology his writings assume. Paul's account of the justification of each Christian individual is not something he focuses upon in abstraction from God's rectification of creation by Jesus the Messiah. New Testament scholars such as N. T. Wright, Richard Hays, and J. Christian Beker, among others, emphasize that St. Paul's framework was also an apocalyptic eschatological vision of the inauguration of the reign of God in the midst of the old order, which has happened in a decisive way in the life, death, and resurrection of Jesus Christ. To be saved is to be rescued from the present evil age (Gal 1:4), from the dominion of darkness, and to be inserted into the kingdom of the Son (Col 1:13–14). Beker contends that the center of Paul's gospel is the proclamation that the death and resurrection of Jesus Christ has inaugurated the coming apocalyptic triumph of God. Paul's proclamation of Jesus Messiah expresses his conviction that, in his death and resurrection, the covenant God of Israel has confirmed and renewed his promises of salvation to Israel and the nations. These promises pertain to the expectation of the public manifestation of the reign of God, the visible presence of God among his people, the defeat of all his enemies, and the vindication of Israel in the gospel.[6] In similar fashion, Richard Hays argues that the Christian gospel involves the startling confession that God had raised a crucified man from the dead and thus initiated a new age in which the whole world is to be transformed. For Paul, the death and resurrection of Jesus was an apocalyptic event that signaled the end of the old age. Paul is an ambassador for Christ (2 Cor 5:20), announcing the apocalyptic message of the reconciliation of the world to God and proclaiming that a new world is bursting onto the scene. Salvation simply *is* incorporation into this eschatological new creation (2 Cor 5:17).[7]

As one example of how we miss this dimension of Paul's theology, Hays points out many translations, including the King James Version and the Revised Standard Version, individualize and thereby obscure the apocalyptic framework of 2 Corinthians 5 when 5:17 is translated "if any man is in Christ, he is a new creation" or "he is a new creature." This translation distorts Paul's meaning by making it seem as if he is describing the personal

---

6. Beker, *Paul's Apocalyptic Gospel*, 19, 30.
7. Hays, *Moral Vision of the New Testament*, 16, 19–20, 23–24.

transformation of the individual. As Hays points out, the language of new creation echoes Isa 65:17–19 and the thought world of Jewish apocalyptic. The sentence in Greek lacks both subject and verb. A literal translation would treat the words "new creation" as an exclamatory interjection: "If anyone is in Christ—new creation!" *Ktisis* (creation) refers to the whole created order (see Rom 8:18–25). When we hear 2 Cor 5:17 in the context of Isaiah's prophetic hope for the renewal of the world, Hays argues, we understand that Paul is proclaiming that the church has already entered the sphere of the eschatological new creation.[8] Inaugurated eschatology is not only the framework for understanding the Synoptic Gospels but also the framework Paul is working with as well.

If we connect all of the dots, we find that the eschatological process of healing, deliverance, and transformation into which we have been incorporated and, by God's grace, invited and empowered to participate, is ecclesial in character. The church is not the kingdom. But it is called to be the "location" where the eschatological reign of God is most concentrated. It is called to be God's new humanity. J. Louis Martyn has argued that Paul's "cosmological apocalyptic eschatology" features the conviction that the nations are enslaved to anti-God powers that include false gods, lords, the rulers of this age, and the principalities and powers. Christ's saving work includes the conquest of these powers and establishment of a new socio-political order, the church, through which we can be united with God in Christ.[9]

Ecclesial communities, though often broken and deeply flawed, nonetheless have been called to the holy mission of bearing witness to and embodying the quality of life characteristic of God's ultimate eschatological purposes for human wholeness. The gift of salvation is simultaneously an ecclesial group project. As Richard Hays argues, if the church is God's eschatological beachhead, the place where God's power has invaded the world, then the church's mission is to provide a sneak preview of God's ultimate redemption of the world.[10] Or in the words of the younger Jim Wallis, the mission of the church is to oppose empire by incarnating the new social order inaugurated by Jesus as the first fruit, the pilot project, the seed of the new order that God intends for the entire creation. The church is called to provide living proof that the oppressive and divisive realities of the world need not hold sway. For example, in a society that believes in the necessity of violence and an economic system that blesses greed and overconsumption, the church presents the world with another viable option,

---

8. Hays, *Moral Vision of the New Testament*, 20.
9. Martyn, *Theological Issues in the Letters of Paul*, 87.
10. Hays, *Moral Vision of the New Testament*, 24–27.

demonstrating that it is possible to share generously, relinquish violence, and reject the idols of security, money, and power.[11] As N. T. Wright notes, with respect to Paul's "theological vision":

> The united, multiethnic church is a sign of God's healing and remaking of the cosmos and also thereby a sign to Caesar and his followers that his attempted unification of the world is a blasphemous parody.[12]

Saved for Participation in Christ's World-Transforming Invasion, Part 1

Discipleship is a word that has been saddled with a wide and wild range of meanings in popular Christian discourse. Discipleship is all too often uncoupled from the narrative within which discipleship makes sense, from the life of the church, from the power of the Holy Spirit, and from the necessity of being drawn into the eschatological new creation inaugurated by Jesus. When the conventional understanding of salvation is in play, discipleship may be reduced to the cultivation of the Christian individual's "personal relationship with Jesus Christ." If the good news of salvation is reduced to a technique for getting to heaven by believing and saying the sinner's prayer, then discipleship and the Christian life are considered to be merely desirable ways to "follow up" on one's conversion experience as a way of expressing gratitude to God.

Theologically liberal Christianity can also sever discipleship from salvation. Discipleship can be reduced to the individual's efforts to follow Jesus by building a better world by aligning with and contributing to progressive social causes. But the uniqueness of Jesus as the inaugurator of the eschatological reign of God is often lost; instead, Jesus becomes merely an inspiration for our efforts to build a better future. Imitation of Jesus becomes a matter of heroic moral effort.

In order to sketch out a more faithful account of discipleship, we will need to link the themes we have presented in this chapter. Salvation means being drawn into union with Christ by the Holy Spirit and, since Christ is the way to the Father (John 14:1–7), union with Christ through the Holy Spirit is communion with the triune God. Since the risen Christ has been enthroned as Messiah and king, to be united with Christ is to be drawn into the kingdom he inaugurated. If the early church fathers are correct about

---

11. Wallis, *Call to Conversion*, xvi–xvii, 65, 72, 103, 107–8, 117, 129–33, 140–45.
12. Wright, "New Perspectives on Paul," 262.

theosis, union with God transforms us into the likeness of God's character, which is revealed to us most fully in the life, death, and resurrection of Jesus Christ. Therefore, union with God should result in Christlikeness. If this chain of reasoning is correct, we should expect to find an emphasis on the transformation of the self in Jesus Christ in the New Testament, which, as noted earlier in this chapter, we do indeed find throughout the New Testament, including the Pauline and Johannine corpus.

If our theology of salvation remains entangled within the conventional version of salvation and a conception of faith as interior passive believing that Jesus will save me if I ask, along with the sharp separation between justification and sanctification, much of what Jesus says in the Synoptic Gospels is confusing and unsettling. Jesus seems to be unaware of "the plan of salvation." As Matthew Bates points out, multiple passages in the Synoptic Gospels that address the question of how one attains "eternal life," that is, the life of the age to come, emphasize not faith alone but the necessity of right action. For example, the story of the Rich Young Man is an embarrassment to conventional Protestant accounts of salvation. When the young man asks what he must do to obtain or inherit "eternal life," Jesus's response involves action: keeping the commandments, selling all he has, giving it to the poor, and following Jesus.[13] In the last judgment scene of Matt 25:31–46, the criterion by which the nations are judged is not faith, in the sense of interior passive believing in Jesus, but their action, how they treated "the least of these."

In the well-known and loved parable of the Good Samaritan in Luke 10:25–37, a scribe asks Jesus, "What shall I do to inherit eternal life?" Literally translated, the term *zoen aionion* is "life of the ages," which was a way of speaking of the future messianic age. As Bates points out, the conventional account of how one "gets saved" would lead us to expect that Jesus to say something along the lines of "forget the commandments and have faith in me."[14] Instead, Jesus asked the scribe how he interpreted the law and what he believed to be the greatest commandment. Jesus affirmed the scribe's answer, that the greatest commandments are wholehearted and whole person love of God and loving the neighbor as one loves oneself, saying, "You have answered right; do this, and you will live."

After the scribe asked, in effect, "who counts as my neighbor?," Jesus told a story that cast a Samaritan as the hero of the story because the Samaritan took action to save the life of the man who had been severely beaten and left for dead by robbers on the road from Jerusalem to Jericho.

---

13. Bates, *Salvation by Allegiance Alone*, 10–12.
14. Bates, *Salvation by Allegiance Alone*, 10–12.

While this parable has long been loved by Christians, we often treat it as if Jesus is merely dispensing a bit of peripheral moral advice. But the framing question is the question of salvation. Inclusion and participation in the kingdom of God has to do with doing what is necessary to rescue people from what threatens death or extreme suffering.

However, we miss the point if we read the parable of the Good Samaritan through a hyper-Protestant lens that places faith, construed as passive believing or trusting, and action in opposition. The point is not that we love our neighbors by engaging in deeds of rescue and healing as a means to another end, as if love of neighbor and deeds corresponding to that love were hoops that must be jumped through to receive "something else," which we understand to be salvation. Rather, active love of neighbor through deeds of rescue and healing is itself the gift of salvation, the truly fulfilling way to live. It is *zoen aionion*, the quality of living of the age to come. This way of life is not something we do by our own human choices and abilities or by heroic effort. *This way of life is one that is lived inside of the gift of God's abundant love*, a gift that is given as and through the Holy Spirit!

The Gift of Salvation Includes Participation in the *Missio Dei*

If salvation means being drawn into the kingdom Jesus inaugurated, the future messianic age already arriving, what is the shape of life in this new social order? The best clue, of course, is the pattern of Jesus's own activity. The inclusion of the Gospels in the Christian canon represents the church's theological judgment that these particular narratives are indispensable for the church's identification of Jesus Christ. This requires us to integrate Pauline language of conformity to Christ with the Gospels' narrative portrayals of Jesus's words, deeds, and mission. These narratives are indispensable for our theological and practical discernment of what it means to be conformed to Christ.

Jesus heals. He places a premium upon deeds of compassion and deliverance for the poor and destitute, for persons who were social outcasts, on the margins, at great risk of death, destruction, suffering, or social exclusion. Jesus welcomed and embraced those persons who had been written off as "non-persons." Jesus affirmed their humanity, value, and worth. Jesus restored human persons to health and wholeness, to community, to a sense of their own worth and value. And Jesus pushed back and resisted the religious and political systems that functioned to dehumanize, exploit, impoverish, and marginalize people. He formed a different kind of community that modeled hospitality and welcome and mutual sharing and support.

Salvation means we have been delivered from the power of the present evil age, the dominion of darkness, and drawn into Christ's reign (Col 1:13). This kingdom is all about putting the world to rights. This was Jesus's mission. He had a healing and transformative impact on the humans he encountered. He told the truth and he resisted powers, spiritual and political, that inflicted misery, oppression, and death. He taught us to pray that God's Kingdom might come and God's will be done in this world and in this age (Matt 6:10).

We were saved for the purpose of being the people through whom God's kingdom continues to arrive and break into the present order of things. We were saved to be "doers of the eschatological reign of God," to paraphrase Jas 1:22. We were saved to be interrupters and disruptors of human institutions, social practices, and pervasive cultural assumptions when these "kill and steal and destroy" (John 10:10). Drawn into Christ and the kingdom by the Holy Spirit, we were saved to be the agents through whom the eschatological Spirit heals, transforms, communicates God's love and acceptance, convicts of sin and injustice, and upends the powers of death. We were saved to be the channels, the conduits, of God's insurrection against the powers of death and destruction and the conduits of God's creative, life-giving love. As God's people, we are called to "do heaven on earth." We have been called to offer a living performance of "another world" of reconciliation, peacemaking, generosity, love, and justice. This is what we were "saved for"!

CHAPTER NINE

Justification and "Personal Salvation"

BUT WHAT ABOUT THE doctrine of justification? After all, for Protestant theology in the magisterial Reformation tradition, the doctrine of justification has been considered the foundational doctrine of the Christian faith, the article by which the church stands or falls.[1]

Justification: Protestant and Catholic: A Really, Really Quick Historical Overview

From Origen to St. Augustine, into the medieval period and into the present, the Roman Catholic Church as well as Eastern Christianity, to the extent that the language of justification is used in Eastern Christianity, have understood justification to be the lifelong process of transformation of the self, made possible by God's grace at work in the life of the Christian. On this account, to be justified is to be transformed, to be made just, righteous, and holy, such that one begins to become a person whose moral character and patterns of activity are conformed to the pattern of Jesus Christ. Justification is a real transformation of the self.

Prior to St. Augustine, justification was not a central soteriological motif among the church fathers.[2] However, justification, as it appears within the writings of multiple church fathers, included two "phases." The initial phase of justification features God's acceptance and forgiveness as a gift bestowed through the sacrament of baptism, accompanied by personal faith

---

1. Bird, "Judgment and Justification in Paul," 299.
2. McGrath, *Iustitia Dei*, 1:38.

and repentance. Without any preceding merits or good works on our part, God forgives our sins and counts us as righteous.[3]

Once initial justification had taken place, believers were expected to be caught up into a transformative process of growth in grace, virtue, and good works.[4]

If the preceding paragraph was a complete summary of the patristic consensus on justification, there would be little disagreement between the magisterial Protestant Reformers and church fathers such as Origen, John Chrysostom, and, later, St. Augustine. However, the heart of the disagreement is that the tradition prior to the Protestant Reformation taught that our ultimate acceptance by God on judgment day depends upon whether, after baptism and initial justification, we lived lives of Christian faithfulness and obedience, producing good works and good fruit.

"Ambrosiaster"[5] follows this patristic pattern. Though our initial justification comes strictly through God's mercy, our progress in good works will determine whether we are ultimately justified or damned.[6] Origen also gives expression to this patristic consensus. Origen taught that baptism cleanses us of all previous sins. This is a free gift received through faith and not on account of one's merits. But, he insisted, this does not guarantee the non-imputation of the believer's future sins. If it did, the believer would have a license to sin, which is unthinkable. The one who is justified must now lead a good life. Jesus, the good and merciful Savior and Advocate is also Jesus the just Judge. One who confesses Jesus with his mouth (Rom 10:9) must subject himself or herself to Christ's lordship. To be "in Christ" is to be clothed with the virtues or moral attributes of Christ, whose very identity is his virtues and moral attributes. Few people, he argued, are saved without post-justification good works. The thief on the cross was an exception, not the rule. Faith is the foundation and beginning of salvation, but faith must be complemented by hope, which represents progress, growth, and love, which is the perfecting and summit of the whole.[7]

---

3. An excellent summary of this patristic account of "initial justification" and its compatibility with later Protestant accounts is found in Needham, "Justification in the Early Church Fathers," 25, 27–37, 41, 51.

4. Beilby and Eddy, "Justification in Historical Perspective," 16–17; Needham, "Justification in the Early Church Fathers," 48; Eno, "Some Patristic Views," 112, 127–28.

5. Ambrosiaster was the name given to the unknown author who wrote commentaries on Paul's epistles in the fourth century. These commentaries were once erroneously attributed to St. Ambrose.

6. Eno, "Some Patristic Views," 115–17.

7. Eno, "Some Patristic Views," 113–17; Scheck, *Origen and the History of Justification*, 28–29, 35–36, 232.

Justification and "Personal Salvation"

But it was St. Augustine who articulated this patristic pattern in a way that shaped the subsequent course of western theology and ecclesial practice. Justification for St. Augustine involves the transformation of the self. "For what else does the phrase 'being justified' signify than being made righteous—by Him, of course, who justifies the ungodly man, that he may become a godly one instead?"[8] A real change in the human person's being is envisaged in Augustine's understanding of justification. He or she is not merely treated as if he or she were righteous and a son of God. Augustine makes this assertion:

> Lest it should be thought that good works will be wanting in those who believe, he [St. Paul in the book of Ephesians] adds further: "For we are His workmanship, created in Christ Jesus unto good works, which God hath before ordained that we should walk in them." We shall be made truly free, then, when God fashions us, that is, forms and creates us anew, not as men—for He has done that already—but as good men, which His grace is now doing, that we may be a new creation in Christ Jesus, according as it is said: "Create in me a clean heart, O God."[9]

Augustine interprets St. Paul's language of justification by faith to mean that any role for human works done prior to justification is excluded. But Augustine interprets James's declaration that faith without works is dead to refer to the good works that must be done after the sinner comes to faith. If those once forgiven fail to persevere in the true faith or fail to produce appropriate works, they will be condemned as sinners. But for Augustine, this is not a matter of earning salvation by good works. The good we do is always the gift of God, not autonomous human achievement. The lifelong process of justification was understood to be the work of the Holy Spirit. For St. Augustine, the Holy Spirit is God's love shed abroad in our hearts, by which the human person is transformed. God must transform our will, replacing a heart of stone with a heart of flesh (Ezek 11:19), such that former sinners now delight in doing good. Our wills are able to will and do what is good only because God transforms the will and empowers us.[10]

---

8. Augustine, *Spirit and the Letter* 45 (361); McGrath, *Iustatia Dei*, 1:30–32; Beilby and Eddy, "Justification in Historical Perspective," 20.

9. Augustine, *Enchiridion* 31 (512).

10. Augustine, *Enchiridion* 117 (608); *On the Holy Trinity* 13.10.14 (358); 15.17.31 (451); *Treatise on Grace and Free Will* 13 (1229); 29 (1249); 32–33 (1253–56); Westerholm, *Perspectives Old and New on Paul*, 8, 12.

In the middle ages, there is a crucial shift as the focal point of the justification process comes to be centered upon the confessional, the sacrament of penance. Justification came to be situated within the continuous cycle through which the believer passes, from a state of grace, to sin, to the confession of sins, and the work of satisfaction or penance. The guilt of sin was removed by confession and absolution, through which the Christian is restored to a state of grace and thereby is drawn once again into the process of justification.[11] Nonetheless, most medieval theologians and church leaders believed that no one could know with absolute certainty whether he or she was in a state of grace. This uncertainty produced severe spiritual anxiety. Theological questions about the role of human free will and the required human contribution or effort were at the forefront of the theological agenda.

One of the most important medieval maxims, which later played a crucial role in precipitating the Protestant Reformation, was the claim that God does not deny his grace to the person who does his or her best (*facienti quod in se est Deus non denegat gratiam*).[12] Alister McGrath points out that this maxim was meant to be comforting. God is gracious toward repentant Christians genuinely seeking to amend their lives in accordance with the demands of the gospel.[13] In spite of the pastoral intentions of those who utilized this axiom to reassure troubled consciences, the axiom came to function in a manner diametrically opposed to that intention and thereby generated intense spiritual anxiety. How does any person know whether she or he has truly done his or her best in cooperation with God's transforming grace?

Of course, to the extent that this medieval maxim is interpreted as requiring maximum human exertion, there comes to be a strong emphasis on human agency and action as the decisive factor in determining whether or not a person is accepted by God and will be judged to be "justified" by God. A second decisive theological shift of emphasis also placed the accent upon human agency and action. Where St. Augustine, as well as the medieval theologian Peter Lombard, understood grace in terms of the Holy Spirit as God's transformative love poured into the Christian's heart, later

---

11. The guilt of sin was removed by confession and absolution. but a penalty remained, to be removed by the performance of prescribed acts of penance. Whatever of sin's penalty that is not removed by penance prior to death must be atoned for by the excruciating sufferings of purgatory before the Christian can enter heaven. Cameron, *European Reformation*, 79–80; McGrath, *Iustitia Dei*, 1:90, 95–96, 99–100.

12. Translated more literally, "God does not deny his grace to he who does what is in him."

13. McGrath, *Iustitia Dei*, 1:111.

medieval theology spoke of the infusion of the "habit" or disposition of grace as a kind of substance that God pours into our heart, mind, and soul to transform our very being from the inside out. The animating theological concern in this notion of habitual grace is that the transformation worked by grace becomes part of the very being of the justified person.[14] But when grace comes to be seen as something infused and thereby something that the Christian possesses, there is greater emphasis on human agency that cooperates with that grace instead of viewing human action as caught up in the preceding or prevenient transformative work of the Holy Spirit.

The soteriological pathology that is already present in medieval soteriology, long before the individualism of modernity, is that salvation becomes a matter of whether the individual attains a happy afterlife. This shapes the Christian life into one of intense preoccupation with "my" ultimate salvation. This means that deeds of compassion, service, and justice become means to the end of my own justification, my ultimate acceptability to God.

A doctrine of justification that taught Christians that one could never be certain of receiving a positive verdict on judgment day, and that this positive verdict was contingent upon a divine judgment regarding one's progress in holiness and production of good fruit in a life of good works and deeds of compassion, produced unbearable spiritual anxiety. This anxiety, combined with the deepening corruption surrounding indulgences and the sacrament of penance, which exploited that spiritual anxiety, produced the spiritual crisis that sparked the Protestant Reformation.

Protestants in the mainstream or magisterial Reformation tradition came to redefine "justification" as a forensic act, a divine legal verdict. God declares us to be righteous because Christ's perfect righteousness is imputed or credited to us. We are pardoned for all of our sin and our "legal standing" before God (*corum Deo*) changes from that of a condemned sinner deserving of death to that of a person considered by God to be entirely righteous.[15] Justification, on this definition, does not refer to the moral transformation of the self-in-Christ. It is an alien righteousness, not possessed or internal to my being. Justification is an act performed *extra nos* (outside of us).[16]

What is crucial to understand is that Luther's understanding of "justification by faith" does not mean that God justifies us in exchange for or in response to the human act of having faith. Justification, as God's act, is independent of all human cooperation. For the magisterial Reformers, there is nothing that human effort, including our faith, contributes to our

---

14. McGrath, *Iustitia Dei*, 1:96–98; Atsushi, "Textual Salvation 2.0," 42–44.
15. Campbell, *Quest for Paul's Gospel*, 34–35.
16. Campbell, *Quest for Paul's Gospel*, 34–35.

justification. It is entirely the work of Christ. It is a divine decree prior to any human act. The faith by which we believe and receive this gift of justification is something God gives to us. Faith is not something the human does by choosing to believe or trust God by our own capabilities.

For the magisterial Protestant theological tradition, sanctification is the life-long process of being made holy and transformed into a person whose character comes to resemble that of the generous, life-engendering love of Jesus Christ. Sanctification is construed as separate from and subsequent to justification. Sanctification requires our participation and effort, our active engagement to open our hearts and lives to allow God to transform us by participating in various practices of the Christian life, including prayer and worship, spiritual disciplines such as self-examination, and practices of compassion and service to those who are in need.

Because the Protestant Reformers wanted to emphasize that salvation is entirely God's work and, as such, is not contingent upon human choice and effort, sanctification was sharply distinguished from justification and, to some extent, de-emphasized. Sanctification was included in the "order of salvation" (*ordo salutis*), but because sanctification involves human participation, justification was considered to be that which is decisive when it comes to our ultimate acceptance by God.

While the Protestant Reformers sharply distinguished justification and sanctification, they endeavored not to sever the connection between the two. John Calvin believed that those who were truly elect, predestined, and therefore justified would make discernible progress in the journey of sanctification. Martin Luther believed that genuine faith is a divine and transforming gift that is given to the redeemed person by the Holy Spirit, who empowers and enables us to a life of love for God and neighbor. Good works do not justify. But a faith that produces no good works is not faith at all. It is a counterfeit faith. Similarly, Philip Melanchthon insisted that saving faith is always accompanied by good works, though it is not the good works that justify us.[17]

Post-Tridentine Catholic Doctrine

In 1547, the Council of Trent set forth the official Catholic doctrine in its Decree on Justification. This decree affirmed that justification is an unmerited gift but insisted that human cooperation is involved in the free

---

17. Westerholm, *Perspectives Old and New on Paul*, 34; Luther, *Lectures on Galatians*, 26:155; 27:30; *Preface to the Epistles of St. James and St. Jude*, 35:395–96; *Preface to the Three Epistles of St. John*, 35:393.

human acceptance of the gift. Unlike the forensic account of justification of the Protestant Reformers, Trent affirmed, in continuity with the patristic consensus, that justification consists of an inner renewal brought about by divine grace. Trent held that justification is not received by faith alone but by faith working in tandem with hope, love, and good works. Finally, Trent insisted that the justified, by performing good works, merit the reward of eternal life.[18]

Avery Cardinal Dulles suggested that there are at least two decisive points of contention between the Roman Catholic approach to justification and magisterial Protestant accounts. For the magisterial Protestant tradition, justification consists in the imputation of Christ's righteousness. Trent declared that justification consists in an interior renewal and sanctification of the self in Christ, whereas Lutherans, historically speaking, distinguish between justification and sanctification, making justification prior to sanctification. For Trent, what the Protestant tradition refers to as justification and sanctification are but two sides of the same proverbial coin. There is a basic continuity from Trent to Roman Catholic theology today. Justification is regarded as a process of becoming actually and intrinsically righteous. The first justification occurs at baptism, which eradicates both the guilt and corruption of original sin. Due entirely to God's grace, this initial justification infuses the habit or principle of grace into the recipient. By cooperating with this inherent grace, one merits an increase of grace and, one hopes, final justification. While initial justification is by grace alone, final justification depends on the works of the believer, which God graciously accepts as meritorious.[19]

Catholic theologians have long suspected that Protestant accounts of justification treat justification as a legal fiction; we are declared righteous when, in fact, no transformation has taken place. The Council of Trent condemned the view that our justification is only an imputation of Christ's righteousness. Protestants in the magisterial Reformation trajectory disagree with Catholic notions that after justification one can merit the increase of grace and the reward of eternal life, as was affirmed at Trent. The Catholic view is that our capacity to merit is itself God's gift, which is unmerited.[20]

---

18. Dulles, "Two Languages of Salvation," 25.

19. Catholic Church, *Catechism*, 482–83; Horton, "Traditional Reformed View," 85.

20. Dulles, "Two Languages of Salvation," 25, 28; *Canons and Decrees of the Council of Trent*, 29–42.

Section Three: A Soteriological Vision

Theosis as Remedy for Justification/Sanctification Binaries?

The hard distinction between justification and sanctification that originated in the magisterial Protestant Reformation has caused significant theological mischief. What if "justification" and "sanctification" are not seen as two separate stages in the order of salvation but are, instead, organically connected within our union with and participation in the life of the triune God?

On the one hand, what the Protestant tradition gets entirely correct is that we are accepted by God as God's beloved children apart from anything good that we bring to the proverbial table. This is a gift that precedes anything we could ever do. It is entirely unearned.

However, justification as God's gracious acceptance of human persons, in spite of their sin, is inseparable from the gift of being drawn into God's life. Being drawn into God's life is transformative. The Protestant tradition is correct in its concern to safeguard the theological truth that our righteousness is Christ's righteousness and not a matter of our own achievement. However, Christ's righteousness is not merely legally imputed but truly is a righteousness that begins to transform our hearts, our desires, our moral imagination, our actions, and our relationships.

The Protestant critique of the classical view of justification was that infused rather than imputed righteousness meant that the Christian person could claim this infused righteousness as his or her own rather than professing that Christ is our righteousness. However, if we understand infused righteousness not as the insertion of created grace but rather as ongoing union with God, then we could recognize that the transformative righteousness flowing into us through the Holy Spirit is never our own possession or achievement but is always a "constantly-given gift." With *theosis* taking soteriological primacy over the Protestant categories of justification and sanctification, without, however, entirely abandoning those categories, the bifurcation between the two can be healed without undermining some of the most important Protestant concerns. In particular, this account will seek to safeguard the classical Protestant conviction that justification, as God's gracious acceptance of us in spite of our sin, does indeed precede and make possible the rest of God's saving work within us.

The idea that salvation is *theosis*, being drawn into a saving union with the triune God, contains resources for avoiding any sharp split between justification and sanctification while preserving the best insights of the Protestant tradition. Both our justification and sanctification flow from our union with Christ.[21] To be joined to Christ and Christ's body by the Holy Spirit, to be drawn into union with the Father through Christ, is pure gift. We could never do anything to earn it or deserve it. But unlike the classical Protestant conception of justification, this unearned gift is not merely a divine legal verdict that takes place *extra nos* or "outside of us." Rather, God's gracious acceptance of us in Jesus Christ involves God drawing us into a union with God. That union is inevitably transformative. To truly be drawn into the eternal life of love and goodness that is the Trinity is to be transformed by that love and goodness. Being graciously accepted by God is not the result of anything we have done to deserve, earn, or merit God's love, forgiveness, and acceptance. But as we are drawn into God's very life, God's character traits flow into us and we are transformed. This transformation is also the work of God. It is not something we could achieve by autonomous human effort. That transformation is itself the gift since life in intimate union with God is the truly fulfilling way to be human, the only way to be fully alive.

A Better Way to Think About Salvation: The Gift of Salvation Is a Christ-Patterned Manner of Living

What does the Protestant tradition get right? God's love for us, God's forgiveness of our sins, and God's gracious acceptance of each of us as one of his children in Jesus Christ is entirely a gift. Everything in the Christian life that we may do or contribute, our faith and our deeds of love and obedience, are entirely dependent on God's prior action of accepting us, forgiving us, and drawing us into communion with God.

On the other hand, does not the Roman Catholic account of justification gets something fundamentally right as well? Does not salvation include the transformation of the self? Are we in any meaningful sense "saved" if we are merely acquitted but permitted to remain in bondage to sin in all of its destructive power in our lives? While the magisterial Reformation tradition includes sanctification in the *ordo salutis*, sanctification sometimes seems, in later Protestant thought, like something awkwardly tacked onto a soteriology in which justification as forensic declaration is the dominant motif.

Maybe there is another way to frame the issue. Classically, the disagreement over justification between the Protestant Reformers and the medieval Roman Catholic church was a disagreement over how each individual will

---

21. Kevin Vanhoozer argues that this was the position of John Calvin, who insisted that one cannot attain righteousness in Christ, justification, without participation in Christ's sanctification because Christ cannot be divided. Vanhoozer, "Wrighting the Wrongs of the Reformation?," 253; Calvin, *Institutes of the Christian Religion* 3.16.1.

be judged to be "in the right with God" and thereby be included in the happy side of the life to come. In popular jargon, the debate was over how to get to heaven. When framed in this way, the question of salvation is the question of the right means to the end of going to heaven.

If the entire question of salvation is centered upon how to get to heaven after I die, then the issue divides into these three options:

(1) For the classical perspective on justification as the lifelong transformation of the self that results in a life of good actions and good fruit, it would seem that living the way God wants us to live is the means to the end of getting to heaven. Even when we emphasize that the transformation of the Christian self, the good fruit and good deeds that transformed selves produce, is the work of the Spirit, divine acceptance on Judgment Day does seem to be a matter of how much "I" achieve. And the danger becomes, as the greatest Protestant thinkers of the sixteenth century duly noted, that of making my salvation more fundamentally dependent on me rather than upon what Christ did for me.

(2) The second possibility is the classical Reformation position that justification is a divine verdict to which our choices and actions contribute nothing. This position has the virtue of making my salvation entirely depend upon the work of Jesus Christ. The Reformers believed in the importance of sanctification, the transformation of the self, in the Christian life. However, since sanctification has nothing to do with our ultimate salvation, sanctification is neither an end, since the end or goal is going to heaven, nor is sanctification a means to any important end. It is merely an awkward appendage tacked onto the body of Christian belief. It has no significant importance for the question of salvation. The heart of the Christian life might be said to be that of resting in our own justification, or rather in God's gracious acceptance of us, and relinquishing any anxious striving to earn God's approval. It is indeed true that we should celebrate God's acceptance of us in justification as a sheer gift that frees us from anxiety about earning God's approval through our own performance. But the downside is that an emphasis on justification as "everything" when it comes to salvation is that the ethical concern for human well-being that was the pattern of Jesus's activity, and therefore a concern that should animate the Christian's life as disciple of Christ, becomes a peripheral matter, something beyond the range of concern of the central drama of salvation.

(3) The conventional version of the plan of salvation combines the worst of the first and second possibilities above. The transformation of the self, the conformation of the self to Christ, is relegated to an awkward appendage, a matter of peripheral concern. And, ironically, since faith is now understood as the human person's choice to accept Jesus as personal Savior,

Justification and "Personal Salvation"

the person's choice to accept Christ is more decisive in determining one's ultimate or eternal destiny than what Christ did for us.

But what if we reframed the issue of salvation? What if salvation is not, simplistically speaking, about who gets into heaven after death? What if the question of salvation is the question of how to be fully alive both now and in the life to come? What if the question of salvation is, first, the question of how to "live heaven" in the here and now?

Typically, Christians who belong to camps two and three are fond of citing the proclamation of Eph 2:8–9 that we are saved by grace through faith, not by works. Therefore, no one can boast. Our salvation is a gift of God. Obviously, we want to affirm the truth of this affirmation. But when we interpret the Bible, we are often oblivious to the ways we "edit" the Bible by what we highlight and what we do not highlight, what we bring to the foreground and what we relegate to the background. What is interesting is that in popular Christian usage of this text, we abruptly stop at the end of verse 9 and, in effect, pretend that verse 10 does not exist. In our "Bible verse quoting," we too often fail to ask why we choose the texts we choose and, by doing so, what we do not highlight and, indeed, what we effectively screen out or edit out of the Bible. Do many Christians who affirm loudly that they are Bible-believers excel in what they accuse others of doing: cherry-picking their favorite texts and ignoring others?

What difference might it make theologically if we highlight not Eph 2:8–9 but rather Eph 2:8–10? We would affirm *both* that we are saved by grace, as a gift of God, and that we are "saved for" good works. Clearly, we cannot earn God's favor such that we could "boast" in our own achievements or goodness. But nonetheless, what Eph 2:10 calls "good works" are central to salvation. How do we hold those two insights together?

The legacy of the Protestant Reformation, with its sharp distinction between justification and sanctification, has been a conception of grace as synonymous with mercy and pardon. But what if grace is not just pardon but divine power? St. Augustine famously stated:

> Neither the knowledge of God's law nor nature nor the mere remission of sins is that grace which is given to us through our Lord Jesus Christ; but it is this very grace that accomplishes the fulfillment of the law, and the liberation of nature, and the removal of the dominion of sin.[22]

A longstanding theological error is a conception of God's agency and human agency as in competition, as if God's agency and human agency

---

22. Augustine, *Treatise on Grace and Free Will* 27 (1247).

operated on the same imminent plane. This would mean that the more humans are active, the less God is active, and the more God is active, the more humans must be passive. Thus, Protestant theologians and church leaders have been prone to the view that if humans have any part to play at all in salvation, then God's role has been diminished and salvation is seen as the result of human action. But what if true human agency is entirely made possible by God's agency? What if an action is only authentically "mine" insofar that it is first and most fundamentally, God's action? When our will and our actions are rightly ordered, then human motives and action are themselves works of grace instead of autonomous human choices, rooted in human capabilities that we possess apart from participation in the life of God. And as humans, we are most fully ourselves not when we have seized the driver's wheel and are calling the shots, apart from God, but when our action is caught up in God's grace and love and thereby enabled. The more I am united with God, the more fully myself I am.[23]

This is the case because we were not created as self-possessing and self-governing entities, sovereign and in full and complete control of our choices. We are not in sovereign control over the ends to which we will direct our actions. This view of the self, shared by the "Pelagian imagination" and by much of modernity, assumes that humans are self-sustained and self-subsisting without reference to the reality that we are creatures created by God with a *telos*. In other words, the way in which human nature has been created and therefore "wired" by God is for God, for love of God and neighbor and to delight in the good, and in God, as the supreme good and in the goodness of love in all of our relationships. To make choices and exercise our agency in opposition to the way we were created by God is not to exercise our free will in determining who we will be. Rather, we are most fully ourselves when we act in ways consistent with how we were created for God and for love.[24] This is the source of our fulfillment, of being most fully ourselves. Sin is therefore more fundamentally bondage to enslaving powers that disorder our delights and desires and lead us to act in ways that diminish our being than it is a result of true "free will."

With all of this in mind, we might ask, "What if the gift of salvation is not, simplistically speaking, getting to heaven when one dies but rather being united with Christ and so powerfully drawn into God's life and love that one begins to live 'heaven' in the here and now?" In other words, what if the gift of salvation involves how we live, the things we do, and the ways in which we do what we do?

---

23. Hanby, *Augustine and Modernity*, 110, 232.
24. Hanby, *Augustine and Modernity*, 114–16.

Justification and "Personal Salvation"

The gift of salvation we receive is God's powerful action of drawing us into a Christ-shaped way of life. This is the way of living that is "fully alive" because it is a way of living that engenders life in others. We do not seek to live in this way as a means to the end of going to heaven or being rewarded in heaven. Rather, this Christ-patterned way of life is "heaven," it is the gift of salvation. It is itself the desired end we seek.

This way of living is not something we can accomplish by our own efforts, by heroic moral achievement. This way of living is only possible by the gift and power of the Holy Spirit. The gift is a way of living that 1 John 1:7 describes as "walking in the light." St. Paul speaks of this way of life as "walking in the Spirit" (Gal 5:16), and the Gospel of John speaks of it as the "abundant life" (John 10:10). Salvation is a quality of living, of being fully alive in God's love and goodness.

The goal is not merely to "get to heaven" but to be the conduit through which heaven flows into this world. To be saved is to be drawn into God's life and love such that one begins to "live heaven" already in the here and now. To be saved is to be drawn by God into the joyous way of life that is only possible if we are saturated with God's goodness and love. Being drawn into this way of life is not something we earn but rather is something God does for us. The gift of salvation is being so drawn into the life of God such that our lives begin to have a healing, life-giving, joy-communicating impact on others. The gift of salvation is the gift of being "fully alive."[25]

Is this a denial of life beyond this life? Of course not! But it might require us to imagine the life to come in a different way. Too often, we retain a superficial view of "heaven" as a kind of five-star luxury resort hotel in the sky featuring a way of being that looks a lot like self-indulgence and being pampered. In other words, it is the fantasy of aristocratic elites and colonial overlords of a life of being served. But if the gift of salvation is a way of living that is so saturated with God's love that our fundamental way of being is to engender life in others, then the life to come after death would be the perfection of this life of love that we've already been initiated into. First John 3:2b proclaims that when Christ appears, we will be like him. We will be drawn together into the perfection of the mutual love of a community of people who have been fully freed to love God and one another and give themselves away in love more fully than was ever possible in this life. The

---

25. On this account, our sin problem is not the problem of punishment. The problem of sin is the problem of a way of life that is death-dealing, a pale shadow of a life. We can't live life fully to extent that we are in bondage to selfishness, fear, hatred, insecurity, resentment, and to idolatries that entice us to seek true fulfillment in money or dominating power or fame or popularity or success or a belief in racial supremacy. What we need to be saved from, on this account, is bondage.

blessing of the life to come is that our self-expending love will be met by the self-expending love of others in a beautiful endless cycle of joy and endless creativity. What will make "heaven" heavenly is not opulent surroundings but rather the divine love into which we all will be fully drawn, enabling us to love God and one another without reservation. While our participation in this divine Trinitarian love falls short in this life as we are but beginning to learn the way of Christ and salvation, the salvation we experience here and participate in now is a way of living that will reach its completion in the life to come.

With this picture of what we are saved for now in place, we can interpret all that Jesus said, did, and commanded in a new light. The conventional version of the plan of salvation lacks the ability to make sense of Jesus's life, teaching, and example except as, perhaps, good practical advice or "principles for living." But if we are "saved for" a certain way of living, then what Jesus teaches and exemplifies is the fulfilling way of living that is life inside the reign of God.

A prime example is the story of Zaccheus narrated in Luke 19:1–10. On the conventional version of the plan of salvation, this story makes no sense. Jesus, in an ironic inversion of the usual form of hospitality, extends hospitality by inviting himself to Zaccheus's house. As a tax collector for the hated Roman imperial oppressors, Zaccheus was also hated. In the presence of Jesus, Zaccheus, who has up until that point lived a life of greed and dishonesty, has a radical change of heart. Zaccheus announces that he will make reparations for what he has taken fraudulently and he will give half of his possessions to the poor. In response, Jesus joyously proclaims that salvation has come to Zaccheus's house.

What is this gift of salvation that has arrived at Zacchaeus's house? Zacchaeus has been delivered from a way of life that is death-dealing. In his greed, Zacchaeus has harmed others by plunging persons into destitution. He has harmed himself because of the rejection he has deservedly experienced because of his own acts of injustice. But in turning to Jesus and the way of Jesus, Zacchaeus has been drawn into God's way, the eschatological new creation way of love, generosity, sharing, justice, and right relationships. As Zacchaeus relinquishes his wealth, he is delivered from an enslaving idol. In wealth, he had not found joy but rather loneliness. But in letting go of his wealth for the love and justice of the reign of God, he is now fully alive and able to know the truest joy of a life saturated with the love of God and his neighbors.[26]

---

26. In understanding the discovery of true life and joy, we might helpfully read the story of Zaccheus alongside Charles Dickens's *Christmas Carol*.

But . . . Salvation by Works?

The problem lies with the framing of the issue in terms of flawed understandings of "faith" and "works." It *is* most certainly true that salvation has nothing to do with works *if* by works we mean *our own human efforts to secure God's approval*, to earn God's favor or acceptance. This kind of "works" is a bad thing. But if we define works as action or activity that is in conformity with the pattern of life exemplified, embodied, and commanded by Jesus Christ, then salvation has everything to do with "works."

The Greek word *pistis*, translated into English as "faith," carries with it the idea of loyalty or faithfulness, not merely interior believing or trusting. This is the argument made by Matthew Bates, who points out that *pistis* has been inappropriately interpreted and nuanced to mean, with respect to the gospel, "trust in Jesus's righteousness alone" or "faith that Jesus's death covers my sins," rather than allegiance to King Jesus.[27] As such, faith is not just a cognitive act but a "whole person" response. Faith means turning toward Christ with one's entire self. As such, it is both a believing and an activity. To believe in Christ as Savior involves committing oneself to Christ as Lord because one pledges one's unconditional allegiance or loyalty to Jesus Christ as the true sovereign ruler of this world. This means committing oneself to a way of living in conformity with Christ's Lordship.

When Jesus called his first four disciples, all Galilean fishermen, with the words "follow me," the only way they could exercise faith was with their feet. It was impossible for them to have an interior and private experience of faith in Jesus while remaining on their boats. If faith is allegiance to Christ, it is a whole person (head, heart, hands, and feet) response to Christ. Faith means the total orientation of our lives, which includes our activity, toward Christ. Faith includes within itself obedience and service to Christ.

Of course, many Christians will object that this is "works righteousness." But this "doing" that is an indispensable component of believing most certainly does not earn God's favor, acceptance, or forgiveness. This obedient loyalty, the faith by which one commits oneself to Christ, is itself a gift from God. In the words of Oliver O'Donovan, the human response of faith-obedience is not grounded in human initiative outside the sphere of divine initiative and action,[28] but can only take place inside of the action of God's Spirit. The ability to "walk in the newness of life" (Rom 6:1–11) is the gift of the Holy Spirit. Our human action is entirely "inside of" and made possible by God's prior action of drawing us into union with the crucified and

---

27. Bates, *Salvation by Allegiance Alone*, 9.
28. O'Donovan, *Resurrection and Moral Order*, 102.

risen Christ by the Holy Spirit. And ironically, as such, this action is most truly human and most truly our own. As pointed out by Frank Macchia, our cooperation with the Spirit, with grace, only comes through the Spirit's embrace and indwelling.[29]

---

29. Macchia, *Justified in the Spirit*, 10.

SECTION FOUR

Sin and Atonement

CHAPTER TEN

What We Need Saving From
Or, We Are All in This Mess Together

IF THE CHRISTIAN FAITH is the good news of salvation in Jesus Christ, just what is it that we need to be saved from? What exactly is the nature of our predicament?

The correct answer is that "sin" is what we need to be saved from. Prior to Jesus's birth, the angel informed Joseph that Jesus will be the one who "will save his people from their sins" (Matt 1:21). But what, exactly, is our sin problem?

One of the most inane bits of humor I encountered during my childhood is this silly riddle: "Pete and Repeat were sitting on a fence. Pete fell off. Who was left?" If the hapless listener answers the question with the correct answer, "Repeat," the riddle is literally repeated and potentially could be "repeated" *ad infinitum*. While this riddle is an "epic fail" if the actual goal is to be funny but a success if the goal is to annoy, it does illustrate something important about human thought and language. The kinds of questions we ask and, especially, how we frame the issue or "set up the problem" to be solved determines the range of answers or solutions that can plausibly count as answers to the questions or solutions to the problem. If we turn to theology, the way we understand the human dilemma, our account of what we need to be saved from, is foundational for our understanding of salvation. Any account of salvation presupposes some understanding of the human predicament that we need to be saved from.

Earlier in this book, we described and critically evaluated what was labeled as "the conventional view of salvation." This picture of salvation "frames the issue" of sin and the human predicament in terms of the criminal court. What we need to be saved from, on this view, is divine punishment. Sin is understood strictly as a private and individual matter rather than something that also separates us from other humans. If this is the problem, then the solution must be an acquittal that exempts us from the punishment of eternal separation from God. One of the many problems with this way of framing the issue is that sin's destructive grip upon our lives is not seen as the real problem. The ways that sin disorders and damages every facet of our world and the human situation is pushed into the background so that the drama of salvation can be presented as if it were strictly a legal matter between the individual and God. Sin as bondage to destructive and enslaving powers and forces, and the ways we are tangled up in sin together as the human race, gets pushed to the background in this account of salvation.

This is not to deny that we are indeed guilty of wrongdoing, of disobedience against God. We do desperately need to be forgiven by God in order to be restored to a right relationship with God. But reducing our sin problem to guilt and punishment distorts the fuller meaning of salvation.

Many people have a negative visceral reaction to the word "sin." Due to negative experiences in the religious upbringing of many persons, sin is perceived to be a word designed to make us feel ashamed and guilty. In particular, the close connection between sin and sexuality in some popular religious discourse contributes to this situation. Therefore, many Christian persons, preachers, and churches shy away from the word or would evict it from the theological vocabulary altogether. But that would be a serious error. The crucial need is to clarify what the word really means and how it should function.

Whenever words like sin, sinful, and sinner function to label some persons as sinners as opposed to other persons who are allegedly not sinners, we have misunderstood the word. For example, the way in which the mantra "love the sin but hate the sinner" has deteriorated into a cliché that serves as code for a simplistic way of labeling LGBTQ persons as sinners has already framed the issue as if the person who loves the "sinner" must not be a sinner. But the word sin should be understood, first and foremost, as a designation for the situation we all find ourselves in together. Words like sin and sinner, if understood, for example, in light of St. Paul's description of the human predicament in Romans 1–3 and 5:12-21, are designed to prevent us from drawing a line that divides the good people from the sinners and placing ourselves on the side of the good and pointing a finger of condemnation at the people we, from our allegedly superior vantage point, locate on the other side of the line. Rather, we are all in this mess together.

Growing up Baptist in the South, I thought I knew exactly what sin was. Sin was engaging in forbidden behaviors, such as consuming alcohol, saying curse words, having extra-marital sex, smoking, using illegal drugs, and of course, those deeds explicitly forbidden by the Ten Commandments such as murder, adultery, and theft. There were some genuine positives in this way of thinking about sin. Many destructive, abusive, and cruel behaviors were rightly named as sinful, and many of the rules, even when they were legalistic, provided boundaries and guardrails that helped steer me and many others away from destructive behaviors and ways of living. But the most insightful Christians from my childhood often pointed out that the naughty behaviors we label as sins were manifestations of something deeper.

While sin is first and foremost a matter of our *dys-relation* to God, sin is not confined within a spiritual cubicle between each individual and God. Theologian Scot McKnight points out that we were created in God's image for union with God, communion with other humans, proper love of ourselves, and a relationship of wise care and stewardship of the non-human creation. When our relationship with God is distorted, so are these other relationships.[1] When we turn away from God, we turn against other people. We inflict damage on one another. Like kudzu in the American South, sin spreads everywhere and covers everything in its path.

Cornelius Plantinga describes sin as that which goes against "the way things are supposed to be," the way things were created, designed, and intended by God. As such, sin is a spoiler of creation,[2] something that damages, corrupts, distorts, disfigures, and destroys everything it touches. As Ian McFarland puts it, in a world that is marked by the realities of extreme poverty, environmental degradation, terrorism, torture, and war, it is difficult to deny that "things are not right in the world."[3]

Sin is not merely individual bad behavior. *Sin is the total, messed-up human situation in which we find ourselves trapped together.* Sin has a perverse and destructive life of its own. Individual human actions always take place within a situation already contaminated by sin. The sinful and destructive actions of any individual do not take place in isolation from other humans but ripple outward and are caught up with other sinful human actions to generate ever more destructive dynamics.

While sin often involves wrong choices made by humans, more fundamentally, sin has the character of bondage. We find ourselves in bondage to addictions, fears, insecurities, toxic relationships, and distorted desires that often lead us to behaviors that may be chosen but are far from rational,

1. McKnight, *Community Called Atonement*, 22–24.
2. Plantinga, *Not the Way It's Supposed to Be*, 5, 8, 13–16.
3. McFarland, *In Adam's Fall*, 3.

deliberative decisions. Humans often find themselves in bondage to external powers, such as unjust social and political systems, dysfunctional families, a racialized society, destructive social values, and expectations about what it means to be successful or beautiful. St. Paul speaks of sin as an alien and external power that has us in its dominion (Rom 5:21; 7:11, 20).

The Classical Version of the Doctrine of Original Sin

The classical version of the doctrine of original sin which came to prevail in western Christianity is associated with the anti-Pelagian writings of St. Augustine in the early fifth century. Prior to this point, a wide range of views about the universality of sin had been articulated by Christian thinkers. In sharp opposition to various forms of determinism in the Greco-Roman world, such as the belief that our lives and actions are determined by fate, Origen, Justin Martyr, St. Irenaeus, and Clement of Alexandria, along with other church fathers of the first three Christian centuries, emphasized "free will." But early Christian thinkers also recognized a problem. The universality of sin seemed to count against enthusiastic confidence in the capacities of free will. Whatever freedom and agency humans possess, it is clearly not sufficient to allow anyone to escape the magnetic force of the power of sin. Even though no one offered a carefully theorized account of "original sin" as St. Augustine was to do later, most church fathers also believed that there was some kind of negative impact or inclination toward sin due to the sin of Adam and Eve.[4]

The Pelagian controversy sets the stage. There has been much scholarly debate about the extent to which Pelagius fully subscribed to all of the views attributed to him, whether or not Pelagius was actually a "Pelagian." However, what was ultimately condemned as Pelagianism or the Pelagian heresy is the notion that human nature and the human person's moral freedom were not significantly impaired or incapacitated by "the fall" of humanity through the disobedience of Adam and Eve. The Pelagian heresy viewed Adam and Eve as merely bad examples for the rest of us. Their sin did not condemn all of humanity. Rather, the rest of us sin by imitating Adam and Eve. Our sinfulness is not the result of biological propagation. While Pelagius allowed some constriction of human nature by the weight of ignorance, past habits, social conventions, and the corruption of society, he deemed these to be but slight impediments that can be overcome with the exercise of willpower. According to Pelagius, the difference between good

---

4. Wiley, *Original Sin*, 40–45.

and bad persons was simply that some chose the good and some chose the bad.[5]

Pelagius, or at least Pelagius as represented by others, reasoned that moral responsibility implied complete moral freedom. For Pelagius, "ought implies can." If I truly ought to do something, if I have a moral duty to act in certain ways or a moral duty to abstain from certain actions, then surely I am capable of acting or not acting in the ways required by that moral duty. For this reason, St. Augustine's conviction that original sin rendered humans "incapable of not sinning" struck Pelagius as absurd. Pelagius's follower Coelestius expressed the sentiment in this way:

> He must be asked, who denies man's ability to live without sin, what every sort of sin is—is it such as can be avoided? Or is it avoidable? If it is unavoidable, then it is not sin; if it can be avoided, then a man can live without the sin which can be avoided. No reason or justice, he argued, permits us to designate as sin what cannot in any way be avoided.[6]

Pelagianism was a denial that the human situation is a matter of bondage. Humans are understood to be entirely free and self-determining creatures. In creating humans, God bestowed the privilege of being able to accomplish God's will by our own choice. God set before us the ways of life and death and commanded us to choose life but allowed the final decision to rest with each individual.[7] Therefore, all sin is ultimately the product of the self-governing human person's moral choices. The cure for sin is self-control. We can pull ourselves up by our own moral bootstraps. The power to change resides within ourselves.

Pelagius does not deny that, in fact, all humans have sinned. But since our nature and will are not themselves corrupted by sin, the grace we need is the grace that pardons us for past sin. We do not need grace to empower our will to resist sin and change our ways. There is no impediment in human nature itself to obedience to God's commands. This we can do all by ourselves if we "set our mind to it" and try a little harder. The transition to

---

5. Brown, *Augustine of Hippo*, 340–52, 367, 372; Gilson, *Christian Philosophy of St. Augustine*, 158; Pelagius, "Letter to Demetrias" 2–4, 8–9; Smith, "Justification and Merit," 195; McGrath, *Iustitia Dei*, 1:71–72.

6. Brown, *Augustine of Hippo*, 340–42, 367, 372; Gilson, *Christian Philosophy of St. Augustine*, 158; Pelagius, "Letter to Demetrias" 4, 8–9; McGrath, *Iustitia Dei*, 1:71–72; Coelestius quoted by Augustine, *Treatise Concerning Man's Perfection in Righteousness* 3 (497–98).

7. McGrath, *Iustitia Dei*, 1:71–72.

a life of moral integrity and obedience to God is something we must do by our own effort.[8]

A secularized Pelagianism is part of the DNA of American culture. We often teach children that if they dream big dreams and work hard, nothing can prevent them from realizing those dreams and aspirations. At the core of the American way of life is the Horatio Alger mythology that proclaims that anyone, through hard work and determination to succeed, can "pull themselves up by the bootstraps" and become wealthy. One of our cultural classics is the *Wizard of Oz*, which teaches that all of the resources we need for successful living and happiness lie within ourselves. To achieve our goals, we simply must have the strength of will to actualize our own potential for love, courage, intelligence, and resourcefulness.

St. Augustine's anti-Pelagian writings offer an analysis of the human condition designed to repudiate the Pelagian heresy. St. Augustine assumed that Adam and Eve were historical figures who were placed in the garden of Eden and equipped by God with every human excellence, including moral freedom of the will. However, for Augustine, only Adam and Eve, prior to their disobedience of God's command, possessed the moral freedom that Pelagius thought to belong of all humans. Because Adam and Eve disobeyed God in an incomprehensible act of blatant rebellion, all of their descendants inherit disastrous consequences. Adam's sin, Augustine contends, is the sin by which sin entered the world and the sin in which we all sinned.[9]

For St. Augustine, all of Adam's descendants were, quite literally, present in his seed when Adam disobeyed God. The tragic consequence, therefore, of Adam and Eve's fall is that God considers every human being, from the moment of birth, to be as guilty of rebellious disobedience as our first parents. Every human, from the moment of birth, is already guilty of original sin and stands condemned in the eyes of God unless God pardons and washes away that individual's sin through the waters of baptism. Indeed, Augustine followed the "logical implications" of this belief to their bitter conclusion: unbaptized children who die are condemned to hell, not for their own individual sins but for the guilt they inherit from our first parents.[10]

---

8. Smith, "Justification and Merit," 195; Pelagius, "Letter to Demetrias" 2–3, 8; Ferguson, *Pelagius*, 57–60; Brown, *Augustine of Hippo*, 340–52, 367, 372; McGrath, *Iustitia Dei*, 1:71–72; Augustine, *Treatise Concerning Man's Perfection in Righteousness* 3 (497–98).

9. Augustine, *City of God* 13.14 (581); *On Marriage and Concupiscence* 2.5.15 (830); *Treatise on the Merits and Forgiveness of Sins and the Baptism of Infants* 1.4 (120), 11 (128).

10. Augustine, *City of God*, 13.14 (581). In the Christian East, Augustine's notions

The second disastrous consequence is that, while Adam and Eve were originally created with a human nature that was healthy and inclined toward God and toward what is good, the rest of us inherit a human nature that is sick and disfigured, with an inclination toward sin and an inclination to turn away from God toward inordinate self-love. A vitiated human nature took the place of the original good nature, though that original nature as willed and created by God has not been completely destroyed. After Adam and Eve, fallen humans are *non capax non peccator* ("incapable of not sinning"). We cannot, by our own free choice, capacities for action, or initiative, seek God, exercise faith, or repent. We can only turn to God and come to Christ if God graciously takes the initiative and draws and attracts us to God.[11]

Reinterpreting the Doctrine of Original Sin

The classical doctrine of original sin offered a causal explanation of how Adam and Eve's sin was passed down from our first parents to each human person. But the classical form of the doctrine has fallen on hard times in light of compelling evidence about the evolutionary history of humankind and corresponding doubts about a literal, historical Adam and Eve.[12] If St.

---

about inherited guilt and the fate of unbaptized children were never accepted. Hart, *Doors of the Sea*, 32–34. Today, the Roman Catholic Church, influenced by St. Thomas Aquinas, seems to have rejected the notion of inherited guilt. The *Catechism of the Catholic Church* includes this statement: "Although it is proper to each individual, original sin does not have the character of a personal fault in any of Adam's descendants" (Catholic Church, *Catechism*, 405).

11. Gilson, *Christian Philosophy of St. Augustine*, 151–52. St. Augustine also shared in the consensus of most church fathers, such as St. Irenaeus and St. Athanasius, among so many others, that Adam and Eve's fall into sin also introduced death, the condition of mortality, into the world.

12. Though this is far beyond the parameters of what can be addressed in this chapter, theologians would do well to heed the advice of Oliver Crisp and exercise great care in seeking to interpret the human condition in relationship to evolutionary biology. If Christian theologians accept the validity of some form of evolutionary theory, care must be exercised about which versions of the theory might be compatible with Christian faith. Metaphysically naturalist accounts draw a conclusion that goes far beyond the parameters of science. Evolutionary biology affirms that humanity evolved by Darwinian natural section, involving genetic chance and environmental necessity. Naturalists, however, draw a metaphysical conclusion that this explanation excludes the possibility of divine involvement in creation. Christian theologians must, in order to affirm a theistic teleology within the evolutionary process, appropriate versions of the theory that are not inconsistent with a teleological theological understanding of evolutionary history. There are various versions of evolutionary history, various perorations upon it, some of which are not metaphysically naturalist in nature. Though the broad

Section Four: Sin and Atonement

Augustine's *causal explanation* of the doctrine is no longer plausible, must Christian theology simply relinquish the doctrine of original sin?

Ian McFarland has argued that the function of the doctrine of original sin is to offer a description of, rather than explanation for, the human condition apart from grace.[13] Following this basic intuition, many theologians, over the course of the past seventy to eighty years, have endeavored to reformulate the doctrine to safeguard what are regarded by any particular theologian as its indispensable theological truths.[14] I will argue that there are certain theological insights that must be safeguarded in a reformulated doctrine of original sin if the integrity of the Christian gospel is to be maintained. Included among these key affirmations and insights are:

1. We really do find ourselves trapped in an inability to avoid sinning.

2. Humanity is in this mess together. The mess is a tragic human solidarity in sin and death. Our sins impact each other and we drag each other down.

3. Even though we are caught up in sin before we ever made a conscious choice in the matter, we do eventually consent to sin ... while our free will is weakened and, from the very beginning, in some sense, inclined toward sin, we are guilty because we do, at some point, freely choose ways that we know are wrong and destructive.

4. We (individually and collectively) cannot rescue ourselves from this mess.

---

outline of human descent from earlier hominid groups is regarded by the consensus of the scientific community as a settled matter, which groups, how that evolution came about, when and where, are contested matters. Crisp, "On Original Sin," 252–66. Two very important contributions to Christian theological anthropology in relationship to evolutionary biology includes the collection of essays edited by Smith and Cavanaugh, *Evolution and the Fall*. The second is Cunningham, *Darwin's Pious Idea*.

13. McFarland, *In Adam's Fall*, 47–48.

14. Ian McFarland rightly cautions care in our contemporary reinterpretations of the doctrine of original sin. If there was no identifiable "original first couple," does that mean that there was no fall or inherited guilt or inherited disposition to sin? If we read the Genesis 3 story as mythological, by what criteria do we seek to identify the true insights of the mythological form of expression, or, to use a problematic metaphor, how do we separate the kernel, the core idea of the doctrine of original sin, while discarding the mythological husk? McFarland asks the crucial question, what assumptions about reality control the reinterpretation and from where are those assumptions derived? Are they derived from how we interpret the Bible as a whole, the larger Christian tradition, contemporary insights from the natural and the human sciences? McFarland, *In Adam's Fall*, 24–25. While I cannot address these questions with the methodological rigor they deserve in this short chapter, I will proceed to "theological performance" with the full recognition that my own interpretive decisions are open to scrutiny.

Sin as (Corporate) Bondage and Sin as a Group Project

However, a view of sin as willful, culpable, and free choice of a morally wrong course of action does not capture the full dimensions of our tragic situation. If individual guilt were the totality of our sin problem, all "I" would need is a "personal savior" to pay my penalty, pardon me for my sins, and exempt me from punishment. But if this is all that Jesus did for us, Jesus does not actually deliver us from sin. He simply delivers us from punishment. However, sin is intrinsically destructive and enslaving. It wreaks havoc. Therefore, we also need deliverance from the destructive grip and power of sin in our lives, not only as individuals but as the corporate body that is humanity as a whole.

The Bible also speaks of our sin situation in terms of bondage to an external power. In Paul's writings, our ability to master sin is called into question. Sin is an alien and malign power that has us in its grip. We cannot, apart from divine deliverance, overcome and escape it. Sin is a dominion under which humanity is enslaved (Rom 3:9). In Rom 7:20, Paul contends that our wills are divided, that when we sin, we do, in part, what we do not want to do. The reason is that sin, as a malign and alien power, dwells in us. Paul describes his state as that of a person enslaved to sin rather than as a sovereign chooser of sin (Rom 7:20, 25). Paul presents sin as a reality that presses on his agency with such force as to render him all but helpless to resist it. Paul's language partly decouples sin from intentionality. The power of sin seems to be a reality antecedent to any particular act a person might do.[15]

The shared intuition of St. Augustine's classical formulation of the doctrine of original sin, patristic descriptions of the human situation as one of bondage to Satan, and St. Paul's account of the universality of sin in Rom 5:12–21, is that we are all in this mess together. Sin is a "group project." The human race is inter-connected, and the disease of sin, like a deadly contagion, has infected each of us. Even though St. Paul did not explain how sin got from Adam to the rest of us, he does insist that all of humanity is bound up together with Adam in a tragic solidarity of sin, bondage, and death in which we are all trapped and entangled together. Adam Kotsko has presented a compelling argument that there is a social-relational ontology implicit within Christian soteriology, according to which all human beings are irreducibly related to one another and all of creation. Since the most important and original Christian reflection on sin and on the atonement, which includes figures such as Irenaeus, Gregory of Nyssa, and Anselm,

---

15. Cousar, *Theology of the Cross*, 38, 57; Rutledge, *Crucifixion*, 189–91; McFarland, *In Adam's Fall*, 8–9.

drew upon St. Paul's "first and second Adam" schema in Romans 5 and 1 Corinthians 15, a social and relational logic is the indispensable assumption that renders intelligible the conviction that it is possible for an agent at a particular nodal point in human history to act in ways that have cascading effects, whether negatively in the case of Adam or positively in the case of Christ, that touch the entirety of created reality.[16]

If we hold together (1) the Pauline insight that sin is an alien and malign power that has us in its grip and (2) Adam Kotso's insights regarding the social-relational ontology implicit within Christian soteriology, we might view sin as, most fundamentally, the one interconnected tapestry of destruction in which all humanity is entangled. Human life is lived in networks of relationships.[17] Every sinful action produces a ripple effect that catches others into the deadly chain reaction of sin. Because humans are inter-connected, human activity is always a social activity; therefore, we affect one another. Sin is like a horrible chain-reaction automobile accident in which the wreckage keeps piling up as each destructive act facilitates a destructive reaction. Or, to switch metaphors, sin is like a contagious disease that gets passed from person to person, with the bacteria becoming more deadly as it spreads.

Individual human actions always take place within the context of a situation already contaminated and disordered by sin. Each individual action gets caught up in and interacts with other sinful human activity to generate ever more destructive dynamics. The whole of humanity, extended through history, is caught up in the same tragic continuum in which the sins of each of us impinge destructively upon others. Together, the entire human race has "collaborated" through generations to produce a world that deals out misery, intense suffering, cruelty, and injustice. We have, together, disfigured God's good world such that it is now also the generative matrix for hunger and starvation, war, the physical and sexual abuse of children, everyday cruelty, bullying behavior, gossip, and the exclusion and rejection of persons for all kinds of reasons, from skin color to economic status to popularity based on attraction or personality. *This is what we need to be saved from!*

Sin produces more sin as persons who are damaged by the sin of others in turn inflict damage on further others. There are multiple ways this happens:

---

16. Kotsko, *Politics of Redemption*, 2–5. What Kotso identifies as a social-relational ontology is articulated in a very different register by Bonnie Badenoch, who points out that relational neuroscience is revealing the astonishing ways human lives are interwoven together. Badenoch, *Heart of Trauma*, xix.

17. Gunton, *Actuality of Atonement*, 69.

1. Oppression, abuse, and violence against persons or groups provoke violent reactions since those who have been mistreated harbor anger and resentments that are the breeding ground for future retaliation and counter-violence.

2. We are social creatures who desire the approval of others; therefore, we capitulate to "peer pressure" in our desires to belong and be accepted. In particular, we capitulate to peer pressure to support or acquiesce in the oppression, mistreatment, marginalization, or denigration of others.

3. Persons who have been traumatized by physical, sexual, or emotional abuse are often wounded such that the ability to trust others and enter into healthy relationships is seriously impaired.

4. Dysfunctional family dynamics, often connected to alcoholism and other addictions, adversely impact the next generation, and cycles of abuse and addiction are perpetuated for generations.

5. Unjust social, economic, and political structures as well as racism or sexism undermine human well-being in myriad ways.

As L. Gregory Jones puts matters, the crisis of the human condition is not simply my individual guilt but a universal situation of disaster—the evil, suffering, and brokenness that undermines *our* communion with God and one another.[18] An "always-already brokenness" is the fundamental condition of sin. Ted Peters characterizes the idea of original sin as an attempt to make sense of the already existing reality of sin in which we find ourselves. Part of the deep symbolic meaning of the Genesis 3 narrative, in which a voice external to Eve, the serpent, addresses her, is that there is a force of evil antecedent to our human action, but one into which we are quickly drawn. The world into which we are born is not morally neutral. As soon as we arrive, Peters suggests, we are issued the invitation to join the "party" of concupiscence, aggression, injustice, and violence. The pot of this world's misery is already filled with sin and its fruit, the suffering of innocent victims.[19]

This fundamental situation of brokenness also manifests itself in particular and specific sins, which include both the things humans do to one another, such as violence, adultery, lying, and racist actions, and things humans fail to do for one another, such as abandoning those who suffer, neglecting the physical or emotional needs of others, and refusing to act

---

18. Jones, *Embodying Forgiveness*, 117–18.
19. Peters, *Sin*, 22–27.

justly or truthfully. In either case, we diminish others and we diminish ourselves.[20]

Our individual and personal sin cannot be separated from the corporate sinfulness and bondage of the human race. For each person, however, sin's accumulation is experienced in different ways. Some persons, obviously, are born into more advantageous circumstances than others. Nevertheless, we all inherit life circumstances shaped by the sin of the past and present.

The sins of others, past and present, impinge upon us, deform our desires, and incline us toward destructive paths because, as humans, we are interdependent and interconnected. Our personal identity is irreducibly relational in that we are who we are by virtue of our relationships to other humans. As L. Gregory Jones argues, we are heirs and participants in histories and habits of sin and evil that make it difficult, if not impossible, to break out of cycles of violence and counter-violence, of diminishing others and being diminished ourselves.[21]

Jones asks two important questions about this universal catastrophe that is the human sin situation. How, he asks, do we become enmeshed with one another in these patterns of sin within our world? How do we find ourselves caught in the traps of these habits before we are even able to recognize them or decide whether or not we want to participate in them?[22]

The two suggestions that follow are my own attempts to answer Jones's questions. First, before we can make moral decisions, our identity is shaped and molded by our families, the society we live in, the languages we learn, and the worldviews, beliefs, and ethics of those around us. In other words, our identity, our sense of self, our sense of what is right and wrong, true and false, etc., is socially constructed. What precedes any particular moral choice are the moral coordinates a person has learned from his or her socialization by parents and the barrage of messages about what is right and wrong, good and bad, or true and false that come from one's total social environment. Our moral imagination has been thoroughly shaped and molded by our socialization, by our parents, our social order, and by the moral language we inherit, long before any one of us have the chance to make our own personal moral choices. Beyond our families, we absorb myriad messages from friends, movies, social media, and television commercials about attractiveness, what counts as cool, sexuality, body image, power, masculinity or femininity, success, happiness and the good life, and what we

---

20. Jones, *Embodying Forgiveness*, 42, 62, 114–15.
21. Jones, *Embodying Forgiveness*, 42, 62, 114–15.
22. Jones, *Embodying Forgiveness*, 72.

should purchase, consume, and wear. Social orders feature structures and mechanisms by which some persons are attributed superior status or value and worth, while other persons are denigrated. Examples include sexism and racism but also patterns of both language and behavior that inculcate contempt for certain persons and groups, such as the homeless and other persons in poverty, gay or lesbian persons, those who may be overweight or deemed unattractive. One thinks of the story told by Audre Lorde:

> I wheel my two-year-old daughter in a shopping cart through a supermarket in Eastchester in 1967, and a little white girl riding past in her mother's cart calls out excitedly, "Oh look, Mommy, a baby maid!" And your mother shushes you, but she does not correct you.[23]

While this little girl did not have malicious intentions, the environment from which her view of the world was derived had led her to assume that the natural order was one in which African Americans belonged, by definition, to the servant class. And, of course, the very notion that humans belong to distinct classes, some of which are superior and some inferior, is a social imaginary that is entangled in sin.

Second, the damage of sin does not merely fall upon the person who commits wrong and destructive actions. We also need deliverance and healing from the wounds inflicted upon us by the harmful actions of others. Asian theologians, including Andrew Sung Park, have introduced into the theological vocabulary the concept of *han*, which is the wound produced in the victim when we are sinned against. Deep, unhealed wounds fester as intense bitterness, helplessness, shame, hopelessness, or resignation at both individual and collective levels of those who are sinned against. When we are humiliated, abused, or made constantly afraid, we carry scars, and sometimes, from those scars, we may act harmfully toward others. We may react with violence or hostility because we carry within us rage due to shame or we react out of fear or resentment because of past wrongs done to us.[24]

Ronald Hecker Cram tells the tragic story of a man he identifies as "Karl." Until he was in the sixth grade, Karl had attended a Roman Catholic grade school in the late 1950s or early 1960s. His parents made the decision to send him to the local public school during his seventh grade year. Having worn a school uniform up until this point, the clothes his mother purchased for him for school were significantly different from those worn by most of the other children. This factor, plus his newcomer status, rendered

---

23. Lorde, "Uses of Anger," 124–33.
24. Park, *Triune Atonement*, 39–41.

Karl vulnerable. He became the target of bullies who daily intimidated and threatened him. Worst of all, Karl was alone. Karl told the story of the day in which he was on the playground and found himself surrounded by his entire class. Into the "ring" was forced the class "runt," who Karl was challenged to fight. Of course, this humiliation ritual was designed to be one he could not win. If he beat up the smallest boy in the class, he would be vilified for doing so. But if he didn't fight, he would be considered a coward, and it would confirm his status as a target to be excluded and rejected. Karl walked out of the ring to the taunts of his classmates. Many days, Karl would drink warm water and Alka Seltzer to induce himself to throw up so his mother would believe him to be sick and allow him to miss school. This happened for two entire school years. While he was occasionally attacked physically, his tormenters threatened him on a daily basis. He would walk home by alternate routes to avoid being found by the bullies. He was afraid to go alone to dances, department stores, or sporting events. He was also ashamed of being afraid, so he did not tell his parents. Though his teachers observed what was going on, during this period in history, it was too often assumed that bullying was part of the childhood experience and each child had to learn how to handle the problem on their own.[25]

He became the class outcast and a laughingstock to the girls, none of whom would come near him. His life was not much better at home since he suffered physical and emotional abuse from his father. In a desperate attempt to be cool and fit in, Karl began smoking, shoplifting records from department stores, and cursing. He tattooed the letter K onto his arm with India ink and a safety pin. When his father discovered the tattoo, his father's response was, "You asshole, you are going to wash dishes until that goddamn thing wears off." Karl attempted to rub the tattoo out with a brillo pad until it became infected and had to be surgically removed.[26]

Karl reached his breaking point one day when one of his tormenters whispered into his ear, "after school tonight." Karl grabbed him by the hair, slammed his head against the desk, dragged him across the room, and repeatedly smashed his face into the glass window. Karl hunted down and attacked each of the bullies. He admitted in the interview with Ronald Hecker Cram that he became a totally vicious person. Karl would attack classmates for the slightest provocation and touched girls inappropriately in full view of classmates. However, Karl's newfound violence meant that many girls now found him attractive. He beat up one girlfriend's father. When a boy simply said goodbye to Karl's girlfriend as they were leaving a high school

25. Cram, *Bullying*, 33–34
26. Cram, *Bullying*, 34.

dance, Karl beat him so badly he was hospitalized. After beating up his own father, shoplifting, and several violent attacks on others, Karl accumulated eight arrests. He dropped out of school and chose a tour of duty in Vietnam when offered the option of joining the military instead of serving four months at the state correctional facility.[27]

In this tragic story, we see that one of the ways sin produces more sin is through trauma. What Karl experienced as victim of the bullies was a level of fear, shame, and humiliation that produced a wound in the soul that became the breeding ground for his own future destructive behavior.

When we talk about sin, we need to go beyond the language of guilt and also include an understanding of the ways in which trauma damages human persons. If sin is not, first and foremost, a matter of assigning blame but is, instead, the total messed-up human situation, then we recognize that humanity's total sin situation includes, for example, both the guilt of persons who sexually abuse children and the trauma and emotional and spiritual damage done to the person who was abused. We do not tell the entire story of sin if we only focus upon the guilt of individuals who commit sin. Sin's damage includes the toxicity injected into us when we are mistreated. The person who has been violated is not to blame for horrendous evils done to them. But sin, as an enslaving and destructive power, is not just bondage to inclinations, habits, and addictions which we perpetrate on others. The total sin situation in which we, humanity, find ourselves includes the profound emotional suffering of persons who have been robbed by other people of the wholeness God intended for them. For example, a person who was sexually abused as a child may have issues and struggles throughout his or her life, such as an inability to trust, to achieve true intimacy with a partner, feelings of powerlessness, depression, and rage. The way in which she or he acts out of his or her wounds, his or her shame, fear, and rage, may in turn inflict harm upon others. But even when this is not the case, what has been unjustly inflicted upon a person steals their wholeness, their spiritual, emotional, and physical well-being. Trauma, shame, and humiliation wound the soul. Whatever else salvation may be, it must include deep healing of wounds and trauma or we are not, in fact, saved.

As Karl's story illustrates, there are some circumstances that are so toxic and destructive that all of the options available to a person are destructive. Karl was initially forced to become a violent person because he was placed within circumstances that he, as a twelve- and thirteen-year-old, lacked the mental, psychological, and emotional resources to handle in any kind of constructive or redemptive fashion. The ages of twelve and thirteen,

---

27. Cram, *Bullying*, 34–35.

even within primarily emotionally-healthy environments, is a time of emotional turmoil due to adolescence and the body's hormonal changes. Brain development at this age is far from complete. While Karl, at some point in his teenage years, became, to some extent, morally blameworthy for choosing to continue to be the kind of destructive and violent person he was initially forced to become, Karl's own responsibility for his sinfulness was preceded by a situation so destructive that he had no good options available to him. The total situation of sin and evil took him under before there was any possibility of a spiritually and emotionally healthy resistance to evil.

When we think about the transmission of sin and the deadly effects of sin, what we might learn from trauma studies is extremely important. Behavior that inflicts trauma on others is evil because it disrespects and disregards the integrity of persons and tears them apart physically, psychologically, relationally, and spiritually. Trauma encompasses many forms, intensities, and degrees of hurt. The deep wounds produced by trauma can occur on many levels: intellectual, emotional, physical, psychic, relational, or spiritual. Jeffrey Means and Mary Elise Nelson argue that our interactions with others as children form the matrix upon which a sense of personhood and sense of self develops. Drawing upon Object Relations theory, Means and Nelson argue that the primary motivation in life is not, as Freud claimed, to seek pleasure. Rather, we are creatures who are more basically motivated to seek relationships and connection to others. How any person understands and experiences himself or herself is bound up with the ways in which one "internalizes" relationships with others, especially those relationships that are central and primary in our lives as children. This internalized experience of oneself with others in the world provides the framework for the development of basic mental schemas, which serve as guides and interpretive filters by which we evaluate all succeeding experience. The person we become is to a large extent formed by the nature and quality of our early experiences with others and by the ways we are valued or not valued by people important to us. One's developing sense of self is greatly determined by how those around us respond to us. Even our religious and spiritual development and, in particular, our image of God is influenced by the nature and quality of our early interactions with caregivers. A child begins to develop her concept of the world and others, including God, by the nature in which she is physically and emotionally handled and responded to by the persons responsible for her care. Thus, a child usually develops a concept of the world and God as trustworthy and responsive when her parents respond promptly and comfortingly to her cries of distress. Children reared in abusive or neglectful environments often conceive of God as harsh, judgmental, and uncaring.[28]

Trauma disrupts the capacity to feel safe and to feel safe in the arms of another person.[29] If God is love and God's deepest purposes for humanity involve mutual love, then trauma inhibits a person's ability to receive and participate in the life and flow of love that is God and human life in its wholeness or *shalom*. Experiences of human-induced trauma and neglect significantly distort crucial interpersonal relationships and the interpersonal environments in which basic structures influencing one's attitudes and orientations to the world are formed. This disruption can severely damage one's developing concept of self, world, others, and God and has a continuing deleterious impact on a person's development and interactions with others.[30]

The effect of such abuse and neglect on children is especially devastating because a child's defenses are weak and in the early stages of formation, so they are less able to understand what is happening to them. In the face of anxiety, all humans resort naturally to defensive maneuvers in an attempt to safeguard our security and sense of self. The normal responses to the anxiety of living as a creature in an uncontrollable and unpredictable world is very different from the mortal fear, terror, and maladaptive ways of being and thinking in the world developed by persons subjected to evil in the form of human-induced trauma. Human-induced trauma propels persons into a state of social isolation from others and psychological isolation from themselves as persons cut themselves off emotionally and psychically from others and from themselves. The more this state of disconnection approaches a state of radical disconnection, the more likely the results will be blatant psychopathology, pathological or sociopathic behavior, moral decline, and radical evil that treats others as objects to be used for the person's selfish needs that mirrors the radical evil done to the person who was initially abused or neglected.[31] In other words, persons who have been traumatized are most vulnerable to distorted emotional and psychological development that leads such persons to harm others in ways similar to how they themselves were harmed by others.

Stephen Porges contends that humans are wired for connection with others as integral to our health and well-being. It is a sense of safety that allows us to open up toward and welcome others. The state of feeling safe

---

28. Means and Nelson, *Trauma and Evil*, 1, 23–24, 38–39, 52–55.
29. Porges, "Foreword," ix.
30. Means and Nelson, *Trauma and Evil*, 24–25.
31. Means and Nelson, *Trauma and Evil*, 24–25.

functionally transforms the individual from a solitary to a social being. Evolution equipped humans to perceive danger and respond with fight or flight behaviors and to detect and respond to cues of safety. Defensive strategies are crucial survival mechanisms in the face of threats, but these strategies evolved for short-term fixes, not for chronic use. Trauma tends to lock a person into a more permanent mode of defensive behavioral and psychological strategies, leading either to aggression or withdrawal and inhibiting feelings of trust and love. And being functionally stuck in a "neural platform" optimized for defense compromises all aspects of human health and well-being. The neural demands of maintaining this state of optimized defense manifest in the autonomic nervous system, disposing a person to an array of mental disorders, such as anxiety, depression, and post-traumatic stress disorder, and physical disorders, such as hypertension, irritable bowel syndrome, fibromyalgia, dysautonomia, and migraine headaches. These conditions are all manifestations of the chronic recruitment of the autonomic nervous system to support defensive strategies.[32]

Social isolation is a powerful disruptor of human behavior and physiological health. Other forms of social marginalization, such as bullying, are interpreted by our nervous system similarly to isolation, which triggers feelings of despair that are captured by a nervous system, signaling its viscera to initially become aggressive and then subsequently to shut down and appear to be dormant. These responses and this sequence are encoded in our genes. Functionally, the survivor's nervous system resists being coaxed into a state of safety. It is a nervous system that obstinately refuses to dismiss its responsibility to protect and defend. These neurobiological features are independent of volitions, desires, and even explicit cognitive narratives. Survivors of trauma may have thoughts and mental images of welcoming others in a warm embrace, but their bodies are hyper-vigilant and resist engagement to protect and defend.[33]

The impact of trauma is powerfully described in the stories told by Johann Hari. Hari interviewed therapist Gabor Mate, who worked with heroin addicts in the Downtown Eastside of Vancouver, BC. What most of the addicts had in common were horribly disturbed childhoods that featured violence, sexual abuse, or both. What many articulated was the extent to which they had been made to feel ashamed and disgusting all their lives and only their drug took these feelings away. One example was a man named Carl, who had spent his childhood being moved from one foster home to another. He experienced a profound sense of being unwanted. One set of foster parents reacted to his bouts of hyperactivity by tying him to a chair in

32. Porges, "Foreword," x–xii.
33. Porges, "Foreword," x–xii.

a dark room. When he swore, they poured dishwashing detergent into his mouth. He learned that he could not express anger without being punished; therefore, in his adulthood, he would cut his own foot with a knife when he felt anger.[34]

Mate's ideas were reinforced by several studies about Adverse Childhood Experiences[35] that explored the long-term effects of childhood trauma. One study tracked a large number of persons who had suffered horrible childhood experiences, such as the death of a parent, physical, emotional, or sexual abuse, parental neglect, and parental divorce in order to study how those experiences shape a person over the course of a lifetime. It was discovered that the correlation between childhood trauma and various forms of addiction in adolescence and adulthood was extremely high. Adolescents who used drugs frequently, as opposed to merely experimenting, tended to be maladjusted, showing a personality syndrome characterized by interpersonal alienation, poor impulse control, and profound emotional distress. Jonathan Shedler and Jack Block argued that psychological differences between frequent drug users, experimenters, and abstainers were traceable to the quality of parenting received in the earliest years of childhood. In their long-term study, which followed the lives of children from the ages of five to eighteen, the scientists observed parent-child interaction when the children were still small. The children were given tasks to accomplish with their parents, such as working with building blocks. The researchers observed the parent-child interaction and made meticulous notes regarding which children had loving and supportive parents and which children had parents who were either disengaged or even cruel. Those whose parents were indifferent or nasty and cruel turned out, once they reached adolescence, to be dramatically more likely to abuse drugs. Due to negative experiences with

---

34. Hari, *Chasing the Scream*, 158–60.

35. The Centers for Disease Control–Kaiser Permanente Adverse Childhood Experiences (ACE) Study is one of the largest investigations of the relationship between childhood abuse and neglect and later health outcomes over the course of a lifetime. The original ACE Study was conducted at Kaiser Permanente from 1995 to 1997. Over 17,000 Health Maintenance Organization members from Southern California receiving physical exams completed confidential surveys regarding their childhood experiences and current health status and behaviors. The ACE score, a total sum of the different categories of ACEs reported by participants, is used to assess cumulative childhood stress. Study findings repeatedly reveal a clear connection between ACEs and negative health and well-being outcomes across the life course. As the number of ACEs increases so does the risk for alcoholism, illicit drug use, early initiation of smoking, depression, suicide attempts, poor academic achievement, poor work performance, financial stress, a wide variety of physical health issues, risk for intimate partner violence, early initiation of sexual activity, multiple sex partners, unintended pregnancies and sexually transmitted diseases. CDC, "About the CDC-Kaiser ACE Study."

parents, they had been less able to form loving relationships and, therefore, felt more angry, distressed, and impulsive more of the time. The conclusion drawn from the data was that drug use is a symptom, not a cause, of personal and social maladjustment.[36]

The Sinful Perpetuation of Sin in our Remedies for Sin

When it comes to criminal justice, American society is characterized by the false belief that the remedy for the crimes of the socially "disrespectable" is harsh, punitive measures. For example, the war on drugs was fought with the premise that drug addicts and users are criminals who deserve punishment, repression, shame, and coercion. But if drug addicts are typically persons coping with trauma, these measures simply wound, damage, and further traumatize already traumatized persons, thereby perpetuating addiction.[37]

From the very beginning, in the 1910s, efforts to criminalize drug use were bound up with racial prejudice. Harry Anslinger, head of the Federal Bureau of Narcotics in 1914, originally believed that marijuana was neither addictive nor a cause of violent crime until he came to believe that the two most feared groups in America, African Americans and Mexican immigrants, used the drug at a rate higher than white persons. In public presentations, he associated the use of marijuana with the jazz scene and castigated jazz as "musical anarchy," evidence of the allegedly primitive impulses that lurk in black people just below the surface and are just waiting to emerge. In testimony to the House Committee on Appropriations, Anslinger told "lurid tales" that he "had been told" of marijuana use and "colored students" at the University of Minnesota partying with white female students, leading to pregnancies.[38]

Subsequent phases of the war on drugs were also racially motivated. John Ehrlichman, White House counsel during the Nixon Administration, acknowledged that the intensification of the war on drugs in the late 1960s was motivated by racial animus and retaliation against political opposition by the anti-Vietnam war movement, the "hippies." In an interview with Dan Baum, Ehrlichman bluntly stated:

---

36. Shedler and Block, "Adolescent Drug Use and Psychological Health," 612–30; Hari, *Chasing the Scream*, 159–60.

37. Hari, *Chasing the Scream*, 1–2.

38. Hari, *Chasing the Scream*, 15–18.

> The Nixon campaign in 1968, and the Nixon White House after that, had two enemies: the antiwar left and black people.... We knew we couldn't make it illegal to be either against the war or black, but by getting the public to associate the hippies with marijuana and blacks with heroin, and then criminalizing both heavily, we could disrupt those communities. We could arrest their leaders, raid their homes, break up their meetings, and vilify them night after night on the evening news. Did we know we were lying about the drugs? Of course we did.[39]

A harsh and punitive criminal justice system is a poor remedy for sin since it is itself entangled with sins of self-righteousness, scapegoating, past and present racism and racial biases, and self-deception. By demonizing criminals as the entirely evil "other," we imagine ourselves to be "the right kind of people," the innocent and pure. When a society incarcerates racial minorities at astronomical levels, the scapegoating has a pernicious racist dimension as well. By stereotyping African American and Hispanic persons as criminals, it is easy to blame "them," to draw a hard line dividing good and evil, and to imagine "us," the supposedly good and law-abiding white folks in the so-called "silent majority," as innocent and pure. This strategy goes hand-in-hand with angry resistance to any claim that our society still features systemic racism and economic injustice. The result is a reinforcement of the belief, on the part of those claiming the moral authority to condemn, in their own innocence and purity.

Concluding Reflections

Sin disorders and distorts everything. Sin is simultaneously individual and personal and social and systemic. Often, these two dimensions of sin are seen as incompatible theologies of sin, as if an emphasis on the social and systemic reality of sin is a denial that sin also involves individual culpability and the moral disordering of individual human persons. If we recognize that sin is the total "messed-up" or disordered human situation, we have a theology of sin that fits a theology of salvation as God's eschatological and present work of rectifying all things. Putting all things right means both individual healing and forgiveness and reordering systems. The next chapter situates a theology of the atonement in relationship to the long "chain-reaction" that is the human history of sin *and* the need for individual forgiveness and transformation.

---

39. Baum, "Legalize It All."

CHAPTER ELEVEN

The Grammar of Atonement
Apocalyptic Recapitulation, Forgiveness, and Rectification

ONCE UPON A TIME, standard treatments of the atonement featured a simple classification scheme with three major families of atonement doctrine: Satisfaction, *Christus Victor*, and Subjective or Moral Influence. A major problem with this approach, as Michael Gorman points out, is that atonement models morph into theories designed to explain the mechanics of the cross and, as such, tend to be isolated from other doctrinal themes integral to the meaning of salvation, such as pneumatology, ethics, and ecclesiology.[1] And, I would add, such abstract atonement models also become severed from the gospel narratives.

This chapter endeavors to avoid these pitfalls by situating atonement theology within the broader soteriological framework we have introduced in earlier chapters. Salvation is bound up with Christ's inauguration of the eschatological new creation within human history. This involves deliverance from the enslaving powers that have fallen humanity in their grip and the rectification of a fallen creation. Part and parcel of this work of salvation is the forgiveness of sin and the transformation of human persons through their incorporation, by the Holy Spirit, into Christ and the community that is Christ's body. The cosmic and eschatological scope of salvation and "personal salvation" are not to be set in opposition to each other. This calls for

---

1. A previous version of this chapter was published as Richard D. Crane, "Rethinking the Grammar of Atonement: Forgiveness, Judgment, and Apocalyptic Recapitulation," *Perspectives in Religious Studies* 46 (2019) 55–78. Used with permission. Gorman, *Death of the Messiah*, 19–21.

an atonement theology that holds together two motifs that are often pried apart: the cross as a victory over and deliverance from those powers that enslave humans and the cross as a sacrifice through which Christ bears our sins away, forgives sin, and reconciles humans to God and to one another.[2]

I will take my initial bearings from what might seem like a surprising starting point. Martin Luther King Jr.'s leadership of the American civil rights movement was a profound theological performance.[3] King's actions and writings are saturated with insights for the construction of an atonement theology that is faithful to Scripture and the best wisdom of the Christian theological tradition. While King did not devote much attention to the task of articulating a formal atonement theology,[4] his reflections and practices provide an illuminating angle of vision for interpreting the meaning of Christ's death. His written reflections and activism embodied a "grammar of atonement." King offers some salient insights for interpreting more faithfully what St. Paul identified as a matter of "first importance," that Christ died for our sins "according to the scriptures" (1 Cor 15:3).

Dr. Martin Luther King Jr. and the Patterns and Grammar of Atonement

While Martin Luther King Jr. was deeply influenced by liberal Protestant theology, numerous King scholars have argued that the African-American church exercised a much more profound impact upon his theological imagination. Lewis Baldwin points to the rich theological reservoir in the language, hymns, history, and tradition of the black church upon which King drew. Like his forebears, King drew upon the experiences of Moses and the Israelites in Egyptian slavery as evidence that God's justice ultimately triumphs.[5]

---

2. As will become clear, I reject penal substitutionary accounts of the cross, but do not jettison the motif of sacrifice.

3. Of course, the success of the American civil rights movement was due to the participation, moral courage and integrity of countless men and women. Dr. Martin Luther King Jr. was not a lone heroic individual. The civil rights movement also included such courageous and faithful persons as Fannie Lou Hamer, Fred Shuttlesworth, Joanne Gibson Robinson, James Bevill, and so many others. And the civil rights movement was possible because the biblical story was faithfully preached, taught, and embodied by generations of men and women in churches in the African-American tradition.

4. A written reflection on this theme from his days as a student was a characteristically liberal Protestant appropriation of an Abelardian interpretation of the cross as a revelation and symbol of God's love, designed to draw humans into fellowship with the divine. King, "View of the Cross," 263–67.

5. Lischer, *Preacher King*, 5–8; Baldwin, "Martin Luther King Jr.," 98–103; Cone,

Section Four: Sin and Atonement

In this portion of the essay, I will explore four motifs in King's reflections. These motifs will provide a lens for thinking about the soteriological meaning of Christ's crucifixion in relation to classical atonement themes and our earlier chapters on the apocalyptic intrusion of the reign of God.

The first of these is love, especially enemy love. God's love for enemies is at the heart of the grammar of the atonement (Rom 5:8). Enemy love was foundational to King's principled non-violence, which he described as a refusal to hate and inflict violence on adversaries. He insisted that the goal of his campaigns was not to defeat or to humiliate white people. After his house was bombed in Montgomery, an angry crowd of supporters, many of whom were armed, gathered around his residence. King defused a situation that could have turned violent by proclaiming, "We must love our white brothers. . . . Jesus still cries out in words that echo through the centuries: 'Love your enemies'. . . . We must meet hate with love."[6]

Second, the ultimate goal of King's work was reconciliation. He knew that non-violence would not win every heart, but he insisted that non-violence leaves the door open for future reconciliation, whereas violence destroys the possibility. One finds in King the hope that reconciliation across boundaries of race, social class, and gender is possible for the entire human family. In his "I Have a Dream" speech, he gives voice to his hope that "even in Alabama, white and black children will be able to join hands as sisters and brothers, that in Georgia, sons of former slaves and sons of former slave owners will be able to sit down together at the table of brotherhood."[7] These visions of "beloved community" also echo the profound anticipation of African-American Christians of an eschatological future of reconciliation and peace when "God's gonna bring together the nations."[8]

Third, however, the goal of reconciliation does not sanction acquiescence to injustice because justice is the precondition for reconciliation.[9]

"Theology of Martin Luther King Jr.," 21–22; "Martin Luther King Jr., Black Theology," 413.

6. Cone, *Martin and Malcolm and America*, 125; King, "Nonviolence and Racial Justice," 165–67.

7. King, "I Have a Dream," 217–20.

8. James Cone links this dream to the black church tradition, which has extended offers of reconciliation and forgiveness to the white community for brutality during slavery, lynching, and ongoing economic oppression. Cone, "Martin Luther King Jr., Black Theology," 416, 419; Lischer, *Preacher King*, 87–88, 94–95.

9. Writing almost fifty years later, theologian Willie James Jennings makes this point in a powerful way in response to premature calls for racial reconciliation. "The concept of reconciliation is not irretrievable, but I am convinced that before we theologians can interpret the depths of divine action of reconciliation, we must first articulate the profound deformities of Christian intimacy and identity in modernity. Until we

King's goal, as well as that of the civil rights movement as a whole, was not merely reconciliation but the rectification of what is wrong. A conversation during the Montgomery Bus Boycott illustrates this tight linkage between justice and reconciliation, which King described in terms of "brotherhood":

> One of the white citizens came to me one day and said . . . that in Montgomery for all of these years we have been such a peaceful community . . . and then you people have started this movement and boycott, and it has done so much to disturb race relations, and we just don't love the Negro like we used to love him. . . . And I said to him . . . we have never had peace in Montgomery, Alabama, we have never had peace in the South. We have had a negative peace . . . in which the Negro patiently accepted his situation and his plight, but we've never had a true kind of peace. . . . True peace is not merely the absence of tension, but it is the presence of justice and brotherhood.[10]

King refused to sever connections between love, power, and justice. Power without love, he argued, is reckless and abusive, but love without power is sentimental and anemic. Power at its best is love implementing the demands of justice and justice at its best is power correcting everything that stands against love.[11]

Fourth is what might be characterized as the effort to orchestrate a collision with oppressive powers. In a broken world of injustice and oppression, the privileged do not give up unjust privileges voluntarily.[12] Therefore, justice as rectification requires resistance to unjust and oppressive systems of power and domination.

In order to make sense of this conflictual dimension of the civil rights movement, it is helpful to take what seems to be a strange detour from the twentieth century to the second century in order to connect King's non-violent civil disobedience to the mythological imagination of St. Irenaeus's account of Christ's defeat of Satan. Irenaeus described Christ's victory over Satan as a triumph of non-violence. Though Satan used deception and violence to snatch away what was not his own, that is, humanity, God used

---

do, all theological discussions of reconciliation will be exactly what they tend to be: (a) ideological tools for facilitating the negotiations of power; or (b) socially exhausted idealist claims masquerading as serious theological accounts. In truth, it is not at all clear that most Christians are ready to imagine reconciliation" (Jennings, *Christian Imagination*, 10).

10. King, "Love, Law, and Civil Disobedience," 50–51.

11. King, "Where Do We Go From Here?," 247; "Address at Mass Meeting, December 5, 1955," cited by Garrow, "Intellectual Development of Martin Luther King Jr.," 15.

12. King, "Letter From the Birmingham Jail," 290–95.

persuasion rather than violence so as not to infringe upon justice. Interpreting the story of Adam, Eve, and the serpent in the garden of Eden as Satan's act of taking humanity into bondage, Irenaeus maintained that Satan's power over humanity was based on a lie, a false promise of immortality. Christ's victory consists in exposing Satan *in his true colors as a liar*. This left Satan bound with the same fetters with which he had bound humanity: judgment as a sinner by the word of God. Paradoxically, however, Irenaeus employed violent imagery to describe this non-violent victory. Christ wages war against the enemy, crushing him, and trampling upon his head.[13]

There is a profound insight articulated by Irenaeus in quasi-mythological form. What is it that destroys Satan? What is it that can defeat systems of unjust power and privilege? It is *truth*, uttered and performed, that possesses the power to liberate from bondage and break the spell that mesmerizes those who had capitulated to oppressive powers. However, a performance of truth that exposes evil for what it is and breaks its power by revealing it in its "true colors" requires such an aggressive and disruptive collision with systems and powers that only violent imagery will be able to give adequate expression to its impact.

King wrote in a 1966 essay of the need to dramatize the evils of our society in such a way that pressure is brought to bear against those evils by the forces of goodwill in the community. But in this essay, King connected the need to "exert pressure" and the language of performance or dramatization with explicitly martial imagery. Non-violent resistance involves "fighting back," putting one's life and safety at risk. One must be willing to break the chain of evil with one's own body, aggressively colliding with unjust systems. King wrote:

> It is always amusing to me when a Negro man says that he can't demonstrate with us because if someone hit him he would fight back. Here is a man whose children are being plagued by rats and roaches, whose wife is robbed daily at overpriced ghetto food stores, who himself is working for about two-thirds the pay of a white person doing a similar job and with similar skills, and in spite of all this daily suffering, it takes someone spitting on him and calling him a [racial epithet] to make him want to fight. Conditions are such for Negroes in America that all Negroes ought to be fighting aggressively.[14]

---

13. Irenaeus, *Against Heresies* 3.23.1 (1146); 5.1.1 (1301); 5.23.1, 3 (1352–1354); Loewe, "Irenaeus's Soteriology," 6–8; Boersma, *Violence, Hospitality, and the Cross*, 188.

14. King, "Nonviolence, the Only Road to Freedom," 54–61.

Irenaeus's mythological language of exposing Satan in his true colors finds an intriguing parallel in King's efforts to strip the façade of moral legitimacy from systems of segregation, racism, and economic injustice and expose these systems in all of their moral ugliness. Boycotts, sit-ins, and marches were events of conflict-laden truth-telling and as such, performances of judgment. These actions were provocations and as such, "collisions" with sinful systems, designed to force the white establishment either to repent and rectify the injustices or use force to stop the demonstrators, thereby exposing the raw violence undergirding the entire system of segregation. In the Birmingham letter, King wrote:

> Nonviolent direct action seeks to create such a crisis and foster such a tension that a community which has constantly refused to negotiate is forced to confront the issue. It seeks so to dramatize the issue that it can no longer be ignored. . . . Like a boil that can never be cured so long as it is covered up but must be opened with all its ugliness to the natural medicines of air and light, injustice must be exposed, with all the tension its exposure creates, to the light of human conscience and the air of national opinion before it can be cured.[15]

When the powers-that-be in Birmingham used fire-hoses, mass arrests, and police dogs against persons acting non-violently, the guardians of the segregated order were exposed in their "true colors." The oft-repeated claim that white and black people were happy with the racial *status quo* was exposed as a lie when African Americans, no longer intimidated, took to the streets and forced the ruling powers to display the raw violence that had always supported the unjust order. In Birmingham in 1963, this collision with an evil system undermined its moral legitimacy as its violence was out in the open, leading to its defeat.

Yet, this conflictual dimension of the civil rights movement was intended to be a modality of love. Through aggressive resistance, not with weapons but with words and performances of judgment, one risks the violence of persons and systems that do not wish to be challenged, opposed, and exposed. But this resistance is not retributive. It seeks the well-being not only of victims but also of the perpetrators and beneficiaries enmeshed within unjust systems. The goal is both reconciliation and the construction of just social and political arrangements. King insisted that love is the only answer to humankind's problems. But he made clear that he was not

---

15. King, "Letter from the Birmingham Jail," 290–95.

speaking of love as "sentimental bosh," but as strong and demanding,[16] holding persons accountable. King wrote:

> There are three ways that oppressed people have generally dealt with their oppression. One way is the method of acquiescence, the method of surrender; that is, the individuals will somehow adjust themselves to oppression.... The other method that has been used in history is that of rising up against the oppressor with corroding hatred and physical violence.... But there is a weakness in this method because it ends up creating many more social problems than it solves. And I am convinced that if the Negro succumbs to the temptation of using violence in his struggle from freedom and justice, unborn generations will be the recipients of a long and desolate night of bitterness.[17]

The third way, affirmed by King, is non-violent direct action.[18] But non-violent direct action is not exactly placid and non-threatening. It is an aggressive collision that is designed to destabilize and undermine unjust systems, ideologies, and powers and to do so in ways that are sufficiently threatening as to provoke a violent backlash.

There are two crucial insights to be gleaned from King's reflections and lived theology. The first is that sin and evil are not defeated by revenge and counter-violence, which perpetuate chains of sin and evil. Neither is evil defeated by passivity. This includes "forgiveness" in its popular Christian expressions as well as popular cultural versions, tantamount to a kind of "blanket amnesty." Forgiveness imagined in this way offers no resistance to abuse and injustice. This version of forgiveness is not healing or transformative, but merely enabling. Instead, King teaches us that evil is defeated by resistance and truth-telling that is willing to collide with the evil powers, systems, and persons who perpetuate such systems. Obviously, this is an insight that resonates with what has been described as the *christus victor* motif.

Second, if we take King's theological performance as a plausible interpretive lens for appropriating insights from the church's theological tradition, we may be able to discern an interesting pattern. The cross is not about forgiveness alone[19] but is bound up with the justice that is God's transformation of the self in Christ, which in turn is bound up with the justice that

16. King, "Where Do We Go from Here?," 250.
17. King, "Love, Law, and Civil Disobedience," 44; "Where Do We Go from Here?," 245.
18. King, "Showdown for Nonviolence," 65.
19. Volf, *Exclusion and Embrace*, 275–306.

is God's eschatological rectification of the cosmos. When we turn to two important voices in the Christian tradition, those of St. Irenaeus and St. Anselm, we will discover an emphasis on the work of Christ on the cross as that of the rectification of all that is wrong rather than merely securing pardon.

Atonement Theology in Crisis

During the past thirty years, atonement theology has been subject to sharp criticisms. First, for many feminist, womanist, and other theologians, atonement doctrine valorizes suffering as inherently redemptive,[20] the troubling implication of which has been the notion that victims of abuse and political oppression imitate Jesus by forgiving oppressors and abusers in ways that include passive acceptance of mistreatment. Second, the notion that the innocent Son dies to appease the wrath of the divine Father or even, following Abelardian moral influence models, to demonstrate God's love for the world, inscribes divine violence and child abuse at the heart of the gospel, since, as J. Denny Weaver argues, it is ultimately God who arranges and inflicts suffering and death upon the Son.[21]

These two lines of criticism have often been accompanied by calls to jettison entirely any notion that Christ's death has soteriological significance. Marit Trelstad reports, as the consensus of a collection of essays for which she served as editor, the conviction that the cross was strictly the result of state-sponsored violence. The notion that the cross was planned or caused by God for the world's redemption, she notes, was not seriously entertained by the authors of the essays.[22] In order to avoid implicating God in the violence of the cross, J. Denny Weaver contends that God neither willed nor needed Jesus's death. He states, "The cross adds nothing to, nor was it necessary for, our salvation."[23]

My proposal takes these concerns seriously, but emphatically rejects the theological maneuver of evacuating the cross of soteriological significance as the best way to deal with these two problems. This chapter will set forth an atonement theology that holds together the conviction that Christ's death liberates humans from the myriad powers that hold us in bondage and the conviction that Christ bears our sins away and forgives us. The key is an interpretation of the cross in relationship to God's eschatological

20. For what may be the clearest statement of this line of criticism, see Brown and Parker, "For God So Loved the World?," 1–29.

21. Weaver, *Nonviolent Atonement*, 3–6, 132; "Narrative *Christus Victor*," 5.

22. Trelstad, "Introduction," 1–15.

23. Weaver, *Nonviolent Atonement*, 45, 72, 132, 211.

purposes of bringing about both justice and reconciliation. This essay will seek to do justice to the fascinating juxtaposition of the apocalyptic motifs of deliverance from evil powers and incorporation into the eschatological reign of God, and that of forgiveness of sin found in two pivotal texts from Colossians, 1:13–14 and 2:13–15. In these texts, the cross is seamlessly linked to rescue from powers of darkness, incorporation into the reign of God, defeat of the powers, and forgiveness of sin.

Re-Framing the Anselmian Motif of Satisfaction and the Biblical Theme of Sacrifice

Reading St. Anselm's *Cur Deus Homo* informed by King's lived theology of reconciliation and justice might lead us to a renewed appreciation for Anselm's refusal to sever divine forgiveness from justice. The crucial question he posed is whether it is fitting for God to remit sins by mercy alone, without any reparations for the honor taken from God. Anselm argued that if God remits sin by mercy alone, then God presides over an unjust cosmos. Without punishment or reparations for sin, sinners are subject to no law. This would be an unjust moral order in which persons can act with impunity.[24]

Anselm is harshly criticized, often by those who care most about matters of societal justice, for portraying God as one who demands innocent blood as compensation for his offended honor. But this criticism misses the mark. For Anselm, sin disrupts the *rectitudio*, the good order and beauty of the cosmos.

However, if we seek to appropriate Anselm's insights beyond his medieval context and, therefore, perhaps think about Anselm in a different key or register, we might ask, "Is not social injustice a dimension of a morally disordered cosmos?" Anselm's conception of satisfaction, while certainly vulnerable to critique, is nonetheless more akin to restorative than retributive models of justice. Satisfaction means making amends through reparations in order to put right what has been thrown out of kilter by sin.[25]

Criticism of Anselm's language regarding Christ's death as providing to God satisfaction that makes amends for the obedience humans owed but failed to render is based upon a picture of God as demanding compensation for the human failure to perform the obedience we owe. The picture, against which many contemporary theologians have expressed offense, echoing medieval theologian Abelard, is one of a harsh God who demands

---

24. Anselm, *Cur Deus Homo?* 1.12 (203).
25. Anselm, *Cur Deus Homo?* 1.11 (202).

the blood of the innocent as compensation for his offended honor. Ironically, it is David Bentley Hart, an Eastern Orthodox theologian, who points out that for Anselm it is not God but humanity who suffers as a result of sin. God is not diminished by our disobedience and does not need Jesus's blood to compensate God for something taken from God by human sin. Rather, for Anselm, God is motivated by the divine will that his good purposes for humanity, who Anselm describes as very precious to God, not be thwarted by sin. By sinning and thereby allowing ourselves to be taken away from God and vanquished by the devil, what humankind took from God was the blessedness God intended for us. For Anselm, God's honor is inseparable from his goodness, which imparts life, harmony, and rectitude to his creation. To dishonor God is to reject the *rectitudio* of creation upon which our flourishing depends. Since it is contrary to God's goodness and honor that he should abandon his creature to destruction, honor returned to God is for the sake of the repair of human nature deprived of its original beauty and goodness. Redemption transforms human persons by restoring *rectitudio*, which includes the ability to will and perform the good that God desires and thereby achieve the end for which we were created.[26]

The question will be whether we might appropriate some of Anselm's insights while understanding the "satisfaction" offered to God by Jesus Christ was a life of unreserved love for God and human persons. God did not require Christ to suffer a brutal death to satisfy God. Rather, the "satisfaction" of a life of unreserved love and obedience, in a fallen world, requires the kinds of resistance to the powers that oppress and destroy that will provoke those powers to lash out against every threat.

The New Testament Language of "Sacrifice" and the Non-Necessity of a Penal Interpretation of that Language

One line of interpretation of biblical language of sacrifice, penal substitutionary theory, is flawed due to a retributive conception of justice, which requires wrong to be rectified by compensatory violence, with the scales of justice balanced by inflicting pain or penalty upon the offender. Though most penal substitutionary theories endeavor to accentuate God's love and mercy, penal models are nevertheless predicated on the assumption that the prerequisite for divine pardon is retributive punishment, an externally imposed penalty. But this "remedy" for sin only adds more misery to a world already saturated with suffering and bloodshed. For penal substitution, our

---

26. Anselm, *Cur Deus Homo?* 1.4 (189), 15 (207); 2.4 (234); Hart, "Gift Every Debt Exceeding," 336, 342; Gunton, *Actuality of Atonement*, 91–96.

primary need is not deliverance from bondage to the power of sin or from sinful systems and histories that draw humans into webs of destruction. Salvation is instead pictured as deliverance from the punishment, external to sin itself, that God will inflict. Ultimately, on this model, God saves us from God.

Penal substitutionary models also tend to reduce the soteriological import of the cross to that of securing forgiveness and, in doing so, either marginalize justice as rectification by relegating it to an entirely different and secondary compartment of Christian life or jettisoning the notion entirely. Christ frees us from the penalty of sin we deserve, making it possible for us to be pardoned by God. Penal models tend to be yoked to one unfortunate legacy of the Protestant Reformation: a soteriology that depends upon an overly sharp distinction and separation between justification and sanctification. The cross secures justification, construed as our "legal status" before the divine judge. Pardoned for our sins, we stand before God as if we were entirely righteous. On this account, sanctification, the transformation of the self in Christ by the power of the Holy Spirit, is relegated to a different compartment of Christian life and is tenuously, if at all, connected to the work of redemption on the cross.

However, penal substitution is not the only way to "theorize" the biblical language of sacrifice. And rejection of penal substitution does not exempt us from the requirement to make interpretative sense of the sheer volume of New Testament texts that resonate with the imagery of sacrifice and substitution. That Christ died "for our sins" (ὑπὲρ τῶν ἁμαρτιῶν) was described by St. Paul as being a matter of primary importance for the faith. ὑπέρ can mean "on behalf of," which would indicate that Christ's death had a representative character, or "in the place of." Charles Cousar argues that in several instances in the New Testament, this preposition clearly denotes a replacement of one party for another and thus a vicarious death (Gal 3:13; 2 Cor 5:21; probably 2 Cor 5:14).[27] The identification of Jesus by John the Baptist as the Lamb of God who takes away the sin of the world (John 1:29) echoes across two thousand years of Christian liturgical practice.[28] According to Eph 5:2, Christ gave himself up for us as a fragrant offering and sacrifice. Christ redeemed from the curse of the law by becoming a curse for us (Gal 3:13). He "bore our sins" in his body on the cross (1 Pet 2:24). The language of Christ as a lamb without blemish or defect who redeemed us

---

27. Cousar, *Theology of the Cross*, 44, 55–56.

28. The image of Jesus as sacrificial lamb connects with the paschal lamb of the Passover narrative. The book of Exodus' description of God's deliverance of Israel from Egypt as redemption provides a crucial part of the background for the New Testament's language of ransom and redemption.

by his blood draws upon Passover imagery. Christ the great high priest who offers himself as sacrifice (Heb 9:23–26). Jesus is the Lamb who was slain, by whose blood the redeemed have been cleansed (Rev 5:6–7). Motifs of exchange and substitution are explicit in 1 Pet 3:17–18.

Part of the difficulty of making sense of this language is its multivalent nature and the unsystematic character. Sacrificial and substitutionary imagery is not tethered to any carefully theorized account of the atonement. Paul Fiddes identifies two distinct dimensions of this sacrificial language. First, sacrifices are gifts offered to God. The "whole burnt offering" in ancient Israel was an extravagant expression of praise, thanksgiving, and obedience. Second, Fiddes maintains that there is also another, more objective dimension of sacrifice. The sin offerings of Leviticus were an act through which God overcame the human predicament of estrangement from God and removed guilt. The Hebrew word is *kippur*, referring to the cover of the ark of the covenant, the mercy seat, which was sprinkled with blood on the Day of Atonement. Most New Testament references to Christ's death as a sacrifice draw from this sacrificial imagery, especially from the annual ritual of the Day of Atonement, when the blood of a bull was offered for the sins of the priests and the blood of a goat for the sins of the people. Sacrifice in this sense had a strongly objective aspect, accomplishing expiation or the wiping out of offenses.[29]

Romans 3:25 proclaims that God presented Christ as a *hilasterion*, which refers back to the Day of Atonement. How to translate this term has been a hermeneutical battlefield. If translated as "propitiation," the emphasis is upon Christ's death as an event whereby God's righteous anger was appeased or satisfied. This tends to yield a penal understanding of the atonement. Translated as "expiation," the emphasis is upon Christ's death as a purification of sin whereby our sin is removed from us.[30]

Understood as expiation, what is offered is something precious to God, the blood, which is life given. The offering of something precious is an act of love. First Peter 4:8, which is a pivotal text for this line of interpretation, proclaims that love covers a multitude of sins. Already in the book of Hebrews, Peter Schiechen argues, we find the idea that Jesus's obedience was the true sacrifice through which Christ became pioneer and perfecter of the new humanity. One prominent motif within the western theological tradition is the idea that what purifies from sin is Jesus's love and obedience. St. Thomas Aquinas affirmed that Christ's sacrifice is received by God as

---

29. Fiddes, *Past Event and Present Salvation*, 62–66; Rutledge, *Crucifixion*, 244.
30. Rutledge, *Crucifixion*, 278–79; Cousar, *Theology of the Cross*, 62–63.

sufficient for the sins of the world because it is offered in pure love.[31] Aquinas's thought is in continuity with that of St. Anselm because, for Anselm, what Christ offers is not the payment of a penalty but rather the love and obedience that humans owed but failed to render.

Sacrifice and Collision: Mixing Together Insights from Anselm and King

For Anselm, what Christ offers to God is a human performance of love and obedience that is so abundant and excessive that it more than makes amends for the bad performance on the part of humanity as a whole. What would happen if we were to seek to hold together this Anselmian inflection on the meaning of sacrifice with: (1) the insight appropriated from King's lived atonement theology that sin and evil are defeated by resistance and truth-telling that is willing to collide with the evil powers, systems, and persons who perpetuate such systems, and (2) David Bentley Hart's suggestion that for Anselm, the restoration of honor to God accomplished by Christ's death is for the sake of the rectification of a disordered cosmos and the restoration of human persons to right relationship with God?

Jesus's death was a sacrifice, a total offering of himself in love to God. But the point of Jesus's sacrifice was not to appease God's anger or to effectuate a *quid pro quo* whereby God gets something, a pound of flesh, in exchange for the bestowal of pardon. Rather, Jesus's obedience was a life of unreserved love for God as a life of love for and solidarity with sinful humanity, who, Anselm points out, is very precious to God. Jesus's self-offering to God means giving himself entirely to God's project to rectify the human situation, to reclaim humans for God. This means that he lived his life with the purpose of breaking the shackles that hold humans in bondage and resisting the powers that harm and destroy human life. If we draw upon the core insight gained by our consideration of King's lived theology, we might speak of Jesus's obedience as that of bearing the divine mission to collide with the powers of evil in order to break their stranglehold on human life. He did not die on the cross because suffering is itself intrinsically redemptive or atoning. Rather, he had to collide with those powers that mangle bodies and dehumanize persons in order to defeat them. Contrary to Weaver's claim that Jesus's death on the cross was not God's will, I would argue that the cross was God's will, not because God needed to punish someone in our place but because God willed that the powers of evil be

---

31. Aquinas, *Salvation*, 244; Schmiechen, *Saving Power*, 45–47.

broken in the location, in first-century Palestine, where sin and evil were most intensely concentrated.[32]

Collison Course: Apocalyptic Eschatology and Soteriology, the Reign of God and the Idolatrous Imperial Powers that Rule This Present Evil Age

We must situate this collision in relation to the soteriological narrative configuration we have already presented earlier in this book. As God's people faced a world dominated by idolatrous and oppressive imperial powers, many Old Testament prophets began to articulate hope for a glorious future in which Yahweh's kingship would be established and made manifest for the entire world to see (Zech 14:9; Isa 45:23). In this future envisioned in numerous prophetic oracles in our book of Isaiah, the knowledge of the Lord will cover the earth as the waters cover the sea, swords will be beaten to plowshares, tears wiped away from every eye, captives set free, the Jubilee year of economic justice is proclaimed, and healing of physical impediments will happen (Isa 2:2-4; 11:9; 25:8; 45:5-6; 61:1-2).

This vision of a world put right is rooted in Israel's foundational conviction that God is a God of justice, especially for the vulnerable who are deprived of justice. If God is the world's true sovereign Lord, eventually everything in creation must be brought into alignment with God's purposes. But a crucial prerequisite is the destruction of idolatrous empires and kingdoms that seek to usurp God's rightful rule by claiming ultimate allegiance for themselves. Since Yahweh is the world's true sovereign, God is on a collision course with the powers and principalities that idolatrously claim ultimate allegiance, rule abusively, and disfigure God's world. We see this notion in the prophetic theme of the "day of the Lord," in apocalyptic anticipations of a day in which God will judge the nations that have abused his people Israel in Zechariah 9-14, and in the book of Daniel, which anticipates a coming day when Yahweh's reign crushes and replaces the imperial powers that have ruled through violence and oppression (e.g., Dan 7).

---

32. Christopher Marshall also makes a powerful case against Weaver's contention that God did not will Jesus's death on the cross. This claim cannot accommodate the weight of New Testament evidence that Christ's death was in accordance with the plans and purposes of God (Acts 2:23; 3:17-18; Col 1:19-22; Eph 2:13), that God sent Christ to die for us (Rom 8:3). In the garden of Gethsemane, Jesus yielded to his Father's will for him to drink the cup of death on the cross. The Synoptic Gospels present Jesus going to Jerusalem in the knowledge that he would be killed but doing so in obedience to God. In Romans, Paul asserts that the Father gave up his son for us (4:25; 8:32) and in 2 Corinthians (5:21). Marshall, "Atonement, Violence, and the Will of God," 81-89.

The Messiah, by definition, is the inaugurator of this eschatological new creation. However, the Synoptic Gospels offer an interesting plot twist: the messianic age is inaugurated prior to the end of the present evil age. Through Jesus's life, death, and resurrection, the kingdom that is yet to come in its fullness invades or intrudes, in Jesus's own ministry, into the present age. This new order of reality will inevitably come into conflict with persons and systems of power that have a stake in the maintenance of the arrangements of the present age.

The dominion of the Evil One, in first-century Palestinian Jewish imagination, was not locked inside of a spiritual realm with no tangible reality in the real world of political systems but rather included all social, political, religious, cultural, and economic systems and institutions that crush and disfigure human life. Demon expulsions and Jesus's conflicts with Pharisees, scribes, and rulers of synagogues, whose ritual-purity driven interpretation of Torah burdened and condemned those struggling to survive, were part and parcel of the same apocalyptic battle against the powers that disorder God's good creation and destroy human lives. Jesus's mission, as the personal presence of the reign of God he proclaimed, was to attack the kingdom of the evil one, to bind up the strong man, and set human persons free from all of the powers that enslave and inflict suffering (Matt 12:22–29).

This battle reaches its climax in Jesus's resistance to the exploitation bound up with the collaboration of the temple leadership with Roman imperial oppression and the temple's pivotal role in a predatory lending economy that had dispossessed Judean and Galilean peasants. Reading the Gospels with a lens informed by American civil rights movement, we might recognize that Jesus sought to defeat these oppressive powers by truth spoken and publicly dramatized. He condemned the temple as a den of thieves after he disrupted commercial activity in the outer court of the temple. He publicly criticized the institution that devoured widows' houses (Mark 11:15–17; 12:40). He forced the hand of the temple establishment by publicly calling into question their spiritual and moral legitimacy, and they responded by killing him.

Of course, Jesus's execution would seem to be not the victory of God but the victory of imperial injustice. The conventional understanding was that the cross makes a humiliating public spectacle out of the person who is crucified. But Col 2:15 presents us with a startling critical inversion. On the cross, Jesus disarmed the powers and principalities and made a public spectacle that discredited them. St. Paul may be alluding to the victory parades in Rome, in which conquered kings and prisoners of war were paraded through the streets in ceremonies which were public spectacles celebrating

Rome's victories and rituals of public humiliation of conquered peoples.[33] But Paul flips the metaphor and interprets the cross as the decisive event that exposed the Roman *imperium* in its true character as wicked and idolatrous, in opposition to Rome's imperial propaganda as the bringer of peace and prosperity. Rome's pretensions of benevolence were exposed in their "true colors" as deceptive propaganda.

The cross of Christ is not merely the collision of one courageous individual with one particularly powerful and entrenched system of oppression. The universal significance of the cross is to be found in the conviction definitive of Christian faith: Jesus is the one in whom the fullness of deity dwells bodily (Col 2:9). Jesus's crucifixion is *the* decisive confrontation between God and the principalities and powers that seek to usurp God's rule. On the cross, the final eschatological judgment has proleptically occurred, even if the final defeat and elimination of these regimes remains a future event. The cross is an event of judgment on this world's systems of power and domination (John 12:31–32). The "prince of this world," the power behind imperial and all other oppressions, is driven out by Christ's death (John 12:31–32; see also John 16:11). The rulers of this age, in other words, the imperial powers who crucified Christ, are doomed to perish (1 Cor 2:6–8).[34]

For those who understand what it means to believe in Jesus Messiah, the idolatrous pretensions of this world's ruling powers are exposed as lies. Their power to deal death, which this world's rulers falsely believe to be the supreme power in the cosmos, is revealed to be a parody of the true and ultimate power, God's power to give life, to raise the dead. As soon as people cease to fear death, the source of empire's power is extinguished because the power of empire is the power to kill or otherwise harm all who do not comply. This power is named by Heb 2:14–15 as the power of death possessed by "the Devil." To be redeemed is to participate in Jesus's resurrection victory over powers that reign by violence and terror. Participation in Christ's crucifixion and resurrection through union with Christ liberates from the paralyzing fear of death, such that we are empowered to speak and live truthfully even when the powers that be inflict sanctions upon us.

The martyrs are those who have been divinely empowered to embody this divine victory most fully in their faithful witness in spite of death and suffering. Most recently, this power has been manifested in lives such as that of Dietrich Bonhoeffer, Oscar Romero, Fanie Lou Hamer, Martin Luther King Jr., Alexei Navalny, and others, many unknown to us, who have been

---

33. Horsley, *Jesus and Empire*, 26–27.
34. Jennings, *Transforming Atonement*, 17–18, 41–42.

willing to stand against unjust power without a weapon in their hand but that of truth.

The Chain Is Decisively Broken and a Counter-History Inaugurated: Recapitulation Revisited

The apocalyptic soteriology proposed in this book finds its center in the conviction that salvation means rectification. Christ's work as the Messiah, and therefore the inaugurator of the eschatological reign of God, is to put the world to rights. The theme of rectification is obviously bound up with the theme of victory since the disordered powers must be defeated and, as Mary proclaimed, the mighty must be taken down from their thrones (Luke 1:52). Disordering powers certainly include governments, rulers, and institutions that abuse their power, but these powers also include everything that harms human life. The disordering powers include disease, toxic social ideologies such as white supremacy or the belief that a person's value is reducible to their personal wealth, bullying, and all of the ways humans seek power by dehumanizing others because of perceived deficiencies of attractiveness or simply not belonging to the popular group or clique. Putting things right means overcoming all of these forces and powers that "kill and steal and destroy" (John 10:10).

Origen rightly described Jesus as the *autobaselia*,[35] the one who simply *is* the kingdom he proclaimed. And, of course, the reign of God is where God's will is done on earth as it is in heaven. Christ is the "location" in which the world has been put right. The idea that Jesus is the *autobaselia*, and as such, the "location" in creation where the world has already been put right, finds an echo in an insight of St. Irenaeus that theologians have described with the term "recapitulation." Irenaeus developed St. Paul's portrayal of Christ as the second Adam (Rom 5:12–21), who inaugurates and therefore is the head of a new human race. For Irenaeus, Christ, as second Adam, re-traces the course of human life and systematically undoes what Adam did. Where Adam got it wrong, Christ gets it right. Where Adam was disobedient and yielded to Satan's lie, Jesus obeyed God and overcame Satan's lies and temptations by speaking truth from God's word. As Adam corrupted all of humanity by eating the fruit from a tree, Christ's death upon the wood of a tree is the obedience that cancels Adam's disobedience and restores human nature to wholeness:[36]

---

35. Origen, *Commentary on Matthew* 14.7 (793).
36. Boersma, *Violence, Hospitality, and the Cross*, 187.

> [Christ] was in these last days, according to the time appointed by the Father, united to His own workmanship, inasmuch as He became a man liable to suffering.... He commenced afresh the long line of human beings, and furnished us, in a brief, comprehensive manner, with salvation; so that what we had lost in Adam—namely, to be according to the image and likeness of God—that we might recover in Christ Jesus.[37]

By living a fully human life and retracing Adam's steps and getting the task of being human right, Jesus rectified the human situation from within, thereby inaugurating a new beginning for the human race. Jesus's life, his story as narrated in Scripture, and his body, crucified and now risen, is the "space" or "place" within human history where the world has already been rectified.

Salvation as union with Christ means that humans can be joined to or incorporated into that space where the world has been put right. The healing and restoration of each individual's fallen human nature takes place through union with the triune God, made possible by the incarnation. Just as the eternal word of God united himself with human nature, so he "caused man to cleave to and to become one with God."[38]

Union with Christ means that our lives come to be rectified by the communion with Christ through which the self is conformed to Christ. "The word became visible and audible that, having become imitators of His works as well as doers of His words, we may have communion with him."[39] For Irenaeus, William Loewe points out, knowledge of the Father comes through the life of discipleship, acting as Christ acts and doing what he bids. In other words, we grow in knowledge and union with God through following Christ in the path of obedient discipleship. But this is not a human achievement. Humans are empowered as they receive an *augmentum*, a donation of the Holy Spirit to forge the union and communion with God that is experienced in and through following and imitating Christ.[40] In summary, for Irenaeus, when persons are joined to the risen Christ, that union with the divine begins the process of the healing of the human nature of each person so joined to Christ.

But putting the world right in order to inaugurate the eschatological new creation requires a social, historical, and material location where the chain reaction of sin, as described in the last chapter, has been decisively

---

37. Irenaeus, *Against Heresies* 3.18.1.
38. Irenaeus, *Against Heresies* 3.18.7; 5.1.1.
39. Loewe, "Irenaeus's Soteriology," 4; Irenaeus, *Against Heresies* 5.1.1.
40. Loewe, "Irenaeus's Soteriology," 4.

broken. Irenaeus insisted that only God can overcome the powers that hold humans in bondage[41] while simultaneously maintaining that the human situation must be rectified from within:

> For unless man had overcome the enemy of man, the enemy would not have been legitimately vanquished. And again: unless it had been God who had freely given salvation, we could never have possessed it securely. . . . For it behooved Him who was to destroy sin, and redeem man under the power of death, that He should Himself be made that very same thing which he was, that is, man; who had been drawn by sin into bondage, but was held by death, so that sin should be destroyed by man, and man should go forth from death.[42]

Anselm's classical question was *"Cur Deus Homo?"* An answer to Anselm's question, inspired by St. Irenaeus, would go something like this: because he is human, he can break the chain of sin and death from within human history. Because he is divine, what he does has universal significance as *God's* invasion and deliverance of the cosmos in bondage.

In order to break the chain reaction of sin and death at one crucial nodal point in human history and to inaugurate a new chain reaction of reconciliation, restoration, and the rectification of all things, Jesus, in an act of excessive and abundant love for God and sinful humanity, became the sacrificial victim of the mess we have made of things. It is "our" sins he bears because it is the world we have collectively damaged and disfigured that crucifies, abuses, oppresses, and forges systems of domination. Jesus absorbed the brunt of humanity's collective evil where it was most intensely concentrated in his place and time in history. Our corporate sin, which includes the human fear that cooperates or capitulates to empires and allows them to thrive, has produced or enabled such destructive powers as an oppressive empire dedicated to self-preservation and domination at all costs. If the human history of sin and death is one, if we exist together "in Adam" in one tragic corporate solidarity, each of us has perpetuated the one chain reaction of this one tragic history, whether, for example, we feed the chain reaction through gossip, exclusion of others, or the knowing or unknowing purchase of products made with slave labor. It is in this sense that the sins of each one of us crucified Jesus.

If sin has a self-perpetuating dynamic within which we are entrapped, which we perpetuate by revenge, enabling passivity, or quests to dominate others or to protect ourselves at the expense of others, then the inauguration

---

41. Boersma, *Violence, Hospitality, and the Cross*, 122–23.
42. Irenaeus, *Against Heresies* 3.18.7

of a new humanity requires someone to step into the chain reaction and absorb its violent impact without passing sin and evil on to others. With reference to Simone Weil, Rowan Williams suggests that the transmission of destructive forces is only halted when someone absorbs the destructiveness instead of conveying it to others.[43] At one crucial point in human history, a life was lived that was not drawn into the chain reaction of sin. Jesus breaks the chain reaction because, as Rowan Williams argues, he is perfectly obedient to the Father and, as such, he does not oppress, do violence, exclude, or diminish others. As sinless, he alone is pure victim, the lamb who bears the sins of the world.[44]

For this reason, the classical metaphor of victory is illuminating. Jesus is victor because he does not capitulate to sin's enticements, either to fear of dominative power or to the lust for dominative power that so captivates and enslaves humans. By doing so, Jesus broke the stranglehold of sin at one location in human history. In his resurrected body, to which we may be united by the Holy Spirit, a new chain reaction of love, generosity, forgiveness, and reconciliation has been inaugurated within human history. This new chain reaction is, of course, the eschatological new creation which is both "not yet" and yet has already irrupted into the present.

The Cross and Forgiveness

Is an interpretation of the cross as victory over the powers of evil a soteriological model incompatible with an interpretation of the cross as decisive for the forgiveness of sin? These two motifs can be integrated if we understand both in terms of God's eschatological mission to put all things right. After all, if sins are not forgiven, if damaged relationships are not repaired, and if estranged parties are not reconciled, the alienation and hostility that disfigures God's world remains and the world is not put right.

Forgiveness is a truly creative and innovative gesture.[45] To forgive involves, at minimum, bearing the destructive consequences of someone else's wrongdoing without retaliating and doing so in a way designed to offer a new beginning and restored relationship to the offender. When seriously wronged, the easiest course of action is to "save face," either through revenge or by severing the relationship and abandoning the perpetrator. To forgive is to "turn toward" rather than "turning away" or "turning against" those who have wronged us in order to contribute to the mending of the

---

43. Weil, *Intimations of Christianity*, 60; Williams, *Resurrection*, 14–15.
44. Williams, *Resurrection*, 14–15.
45. Jones, *Embodying Forgiveness*, 118–26.

relationship, to find a creative way forward for the perpetrator to be restored to right relationship.

What might it mean for God to forgive? God forgives as the one who, in the mystery that we speak of in theological language as the incarnation, entered into human history and willingly suffered the horrible things humans have done to one another. For this reason, divine forgiveness is not a transcendent impersonal legal verdict delivered from on high. Rather, divine forgiveness happens as an ongoing event within human history.

In ordinary human affairs, the prerequisite for forgiving someone is having been wronged by that person. If Stan steals your bicycle, I have no right to pardon Stan. On one level, of course, God can forgive sin because all sin, by definition, is against God. God is the generous Creator who gave us life. To sin is to live at cross purposes with God's good purposes. To sin is to cause harm to others who God loves and to oneself, also treasured by God.

Therefore, it can be argued that God may indeed remit sin by a verdict rendered from on high, by mercy alone. But a better, "Anselmian" question is not what God is sovereignly capable of doing but instead the question of what is "fitting." And, of course, the question of what is fitting is not an independent human determination but rather a question tethered to what God has done in the life, death, and resurrection of Christ.

A divine pardon dispensed from on high might successfully establish a vertical relationship between God and discrete individuals. But if God's purposes involve the repair and transformation of the total human situation, God's forgiveness must happen from "within" the human situation. A world put right requires reconciliation with God but also reconciliation and right relationships between human persons. Therefore, being forgiven by God must draw us into the patterns and processes of forgiving and being reconciled both to God and to one another.

In Christ, God was wronged on the stage of human history. Therefore, God does not forgive from a safe transcendent "location" above the fray. God in Christ has also suffered[46] the horrible things that humans do to one another. If God calls us to the vocation of mutual forgiveness, it is because Christ also forgave on the same historical stage or terrain, within the same historical continuum, that we also inhabit. By doing so, Christ inaugurated and made possible our participation in patterns and practices of mutual forgiveness, reconciliation, and justice-making.

---

46. Depending on how one interprets classical notions of divine "impassibility," this claim does not require a complete rejection of this notion. See, for example, Hart, "No Shadow of Turning"; Gavrilyuk, *Suffering of the Impassible God*.

The incarnation and crucifixion embody the divine love that turns toward rather than turning against or away from, and thereby abandoning, sinful humanity. Christ was "made sin" (2 Cor 5:21) in the sense that he allied himself with us in our farthest extremity as both sufferers of the sins of others and by bearing the shame and humiliation that sinners deserve.

To make sense of this, we must remember that crucifixion was the mode of torture and death reserved for slaves and the lowest classes in the Roman Empire. Fleming Rutledge compares the sheer horror of crucifixion to another form of the slave's death. Untold thousands of African men and women, abducted and placed on filthy crowded ships for the middle passage across the Atlantic, died during the journey. Those who abducted them did not know their names or their individual stories. They were all treated as non-persons. The bodies of those who died were thrown into the ocean as if they were garbage. Roman crucifixion likewise functioned to deny its victims any vestige of humanity. Victims of crucifixion were tortured, stripped naked, and crucified on public roadways, and their bodies were often left on the cross to be eaten by birds or wild animals. Those who were crucified were abandoned, officially consigned to the status of non-human, unworthy of any human compassion or sympathy. Rutledge writes:

> Crucifixion was a form of entertainment; the specific role of passersby was to mock and jeer, to exacerbate the dehumanization and degradation of the victim. Crucifixion was cleverly and diabolically designed to be a theatrical enactment of the sadistic and inhumane impulses that lie within human beings. The Son of God voluntarily and purposefully absorbed all of that, drawing it into himself.[47]

The horrible irony, Rutledge points out, is that when persons are tortured, abused, and degraded, it is the victims who are enveloped in shame, not as a result of their own misdeeds but due to the ways in which their perpetrators exert power over their bodies and exercise the power of judges, who condemn them as if they were guilty and deserving of suffering and shame. God in Christ meets us here, in solidarity with the nameless and forgotten, the shamed, rejected, and humiliated.[48]

The horrible irony is this: the deepest depth of sin is to treat another person as garbage, as a non-person. The diabolical lie that is integral to sin's reality is this perverse inversion, according to which those with the power to torture, to inflict suffering and humiliation, are able to represent themselves as the paragons of goodness, honor, and respectability. But those who treat

---

47. Rutledge, *Crucifixion*, 92–93.
48. Rutledge, *Crucifixion*, 75–79, 103.

other persons like garbage are the guiltiest of all and the most deserving of condemnation, shame, and abandonment. As Jesus taught, it is the person who seeks to dehumanize and degrade another person, who calls someone a fool, a worthless person, who puts himself or herself at risk of deserving the judgment of being cast into *gehenna*, the garbage dump (Matt 5:22). But the miracle is that God does not will to abandon even the perpetrators of this sin. Jesus absorbed what wicked persons deserve: to be shamed and treated with the inhumanity with which they treated their victims. In this way, God entered into our deepest degradation. And while most humans may not directly torture or kill, we are guilty participants in a multiplicity of modes of harm, destruction, humiliation, and dehumanization of others. Gossip, bullying, intentional exclusion of others due to skin color, social status, or lack of popularity are also modes of treating persons as non-persons. To the extent to which we, by our words, actions, and our inaction, reinforce destructive and oppressive opinions and values within our social order, we support a plurality of forms of dehumanization of others.

As the victim of those who are guilty, Jesus Christ can forgive the guilty from within the human situation. By entering this space, he also stands in solidarity with humans who are abused and mistreated and vindicates them by unmasking the lie that defines some persons as deserving abuse and mistreatment by the powerful. By entering the space of our guilt, shame, cruelty, and degradation, he engages in the creative act that makes something radically new possible, turning toward us rather than against us in order to restore the relationship we have destroyed.

But once again we must insist that this divine forgiveness is not passive forgiveness that tolerates and enables abusive behavior. The offer of forgiveness is inseparable from the divine judgment that collides with what is evil, destructive, and wrong. The violence inflicted upon Jesus was the inevitable outcome not of passive acquiescence to violence but of Jesus's aggressive resistance, truth telling, and performance of divine judgment against all that destroys human lives. This performance of judgment on Jesus's part is manifest in the Gospel narratives of his conflicts with religious leaders for callous indifference to the suffering of others, and in his acts of resistance in the temple during the final week of his life.

In popular discourse and often in preaching about forgiveness, it is often assumed that forgiveness is the opposite of judgment and justice-seeking. Forgiveness is often pictured as a private and subjective act of releasing one's personal bad feelings toward an offender. But this superficial theology reduces forgiveness, in effect, to sweeping an offense under the proverbial rug, pretending in public that it never happened or that it was "not a big deal."

To be faithful to the deep logic of the gospel, it is imperative, recalling Martin Luther King Jr.'s performed grammar of atonement, that forgiveness not be severed from the necessity of justice, of making things right. Otherwise, forgiveness can be a weapon used against victims of abuse, wrong, and injustice, and function as a way to allow perpetrators of wrong to get off the hook without accountability. There may be times in which forgiveness should be deferred and not granted too quickly.[49]

Therefore, true forgiveness must not be reduced to a private and interior action. It is an interpersonal event that includes the act of passing judgment. Judgment is part and parcel of true forgiveness. To forgive is to render the judgment that something sufficiently wrong and harmful was done that needs to be forgiven. True forgiveness identifies a wrong as wrong and brings this into the light. Forgiveness is not antithetical to but includes, as part of its inner structure and logic, the invitation to repent, to change one's behavior, and often, depending upon situational discernment, to make some kind of amends to rectify damage in order to heal and restore a broken relationship.[50]

Judgment and justice are not opposites of forgiveness. While human forms of justice in a fallen world may be retributive, God's judgment is oriented toward purification and healing. If God is for us and for our salvation, God must be against all that would threaten or destroy that purpose.[51] God's judgment is not the opposite of God's mercy but part and parcel of it. We cannot be whole and flourish apart from coming to terms with our own distortion, self-deception, and self-righteous judgment of others.[52] The divine judgment that exposes and challenges our self-deception and self-righteousness is meant to enable the repentance that opens our lives to communion with God and right relationships with other humans possible. God's judgment is for the sake of God's love, mercy, and justice.

One could speak of the cross, the final week of Jesus's life, and indeed of Jesus's many conflicts with religious authorities as an anticipatory performance of eschatological judgment, which has cascading effects that take in all of human history. This judgment is embedded in the word of the cross, which calls us out as sinners and is inextricably linked to the call to repent, which is to allow oneself to be opened to Christ and the Spirit to be transformed and thereby put right. This word of judgment is an offer of the gift of life! To be forgiven is not merely to be pardoned. Rather,

---

49. Fortune, "Forgiveness."
50. Fortune, "Forgiveness."
51. Rutledge, *Crucifixion*, 317.
52. Jones, *Embodying Forgiveness*, 54–59; Williams, *Resurrection*, 12.

God's forgiveness is the foundation of God's salvific purpose of making each person right again and putting the web of relationships that is the human situation right again.

Rowan Williams helps us tie the threads of forgiveness, judgment, and justice together. He insists that God does not shoulder aside the victim to pronounce a formal acquittal to oppressors and brutalizers. God forgives in such a way that requires a repentance on the part of victimizers. This repentance involves a turning to their victims to seek forgiveness and reconciliation[53] and, I would add, to make amends for wrongs done. A paradigmatic example of this is Zaccheus's commitment to make amends for his past tax theft (Luke 19:1–10).

Therefore, forgiveness is not a divine verdict from on high that allows offenders to get off the hook. As Christ entered into solidarity with all who have been wronged, abused, and victimized, Christ's gracious forgiveness can only be received by the repentance that encounters Christ at the site of his solidarity with those we have wronged. Forgiveness inaugurates a new beginning, but this new beginning is only entered into as we are joined to Christ and drawn by the Spirit into God's work of rectifying all things by making amends and repairing the damage sin has caused.

---

53. Williams, *Resurrection*, 16–22.

SECTION FIVE

The Struggle for Justice as Participation in the Eschatological New Creation

CHAPTER TWELVE

The Politics of Salvation as Participation in God's Eschatological/Apocalyptic Intrusion

THE ISSUES OF "CHRIST and Culture,"[1] or church and society, are often treated as matters of social ethics, a concern regarded as at least one step removed from "doctrinal" matters that we group into the categories of Christology, soteriology ("the person and work of Christ"), and eschatological hope. In this chapter, it will be argued that faithful social and political engagement, on the part of Christians and ecclesial communities, is a mode of participation in the eschatological new creation and, as such, integral to the meaning of the gift of salvation.

The Current Playing Field

As D. Stephen Long and Karen Guth have argued in recent books, there seem to be three major trajectories within American Christian theological ethics when it comes to the intersection of ecclesiology and "social ethics." These three trajectories are:

1. A broad array of approaches that claim Augustinian inspiration, which includes twenty-first century neo-Augustinians as well as theologians working within the trajectory of Christian Realism associated with Reinhold Niebuhr;

---

1. Of course, to frame the issue as that of "Christ and Culture" is an echo of H. Richard Niebuhr's classic, *Christ and Culture*.

Section Five: Justice as Participation in the Eschatological New Creation

2. The Liberationist tradition, for which the true agenda of Christian theology is to be of service to struggles to liberate the poor and marginalized from the yokes of oppression and injustice; and

3. Neo-Anabaptist approaches, which tend to have some affinity for the ecclesiology and ethics of Stanley Hauerwas. Long describes this group as "ecclesial ethicists," while Guth speaks of "witness theologians."[2]

Certainly, these approaches do not exhaust the field. There is also the Religious Right, new Roman Catholic Natural Law approaches, and, of course, a wide plurality of approaches to political engagement on the part of African-American churches, some of which fit into a liberationist paradigm and some of which do not.

Realists, Neo-Augustinians, and Liberationists have emphasized Christian engagement in extra-ecclesial politics. Neo-Augustinians have tended to be more reformist in temperament, often, though not always, affirming classical liberal democratic norms of American society and emphasizing conventional political activity. Liberationists, on the other hand, which include feminist theologies, black theologies, as well as a plurality of Hispanic/Latino/Latina/Latinx, Asian, and LGBTQ theologies, have reflected upon American society from a stance as outsiders and have advocated for much more radical social change and forms of action that are revolutionary in spirit. Liberationist analyses have resulted in a construal of American society as profoundly diseased, disordered, and oppressive, endemically racist, sexist, heterosexist, and economically unjust in ways that require a much more radical disruption of the *status quo*.

This chapter is inspired by appreciation of some of the features of each of these three major strands but will not fit comfortably within any "camp."

Stephen Long identifies one of the salient questions that divide ecclesial ethicists from realists in the Niebuhrian tradition as the question of whether ethics is an ecclesial or national project.[3] The danger of the latter is reducing Christianity's "public role" to that of sub-system or merely one more part of civil society whose primary purpose is to serve the well-being of the nation. The primary "public" project is not the faithfulness of the life of the church itself as God's people but rather service to America, seen as the larger, more important, and all-encompassing reality. The danger is

---

2. Long, *Augustinian and Ecclesial Ethics*; Guth, *Christian Ethics at the Boundary*. All of these categorizations, as the two authors acknowledge, are inadequate and often, particular theologians do not fit neatly or completely into any category. Long focuses almost exclusively on Neo-Anabaptists and Neo-Augustinians. Guth discusses the liberationist trajectory through one of its variations: feminist theologies.

3. Long, *Augustinian and Ecclesial Ethics*, 156.

the reduction of the significance of the communal life of the church to its contribution to the civic and political life of the nation. Stanley Hauerwas refers to this tendency in his complaint that the subject of Christian ethics in America has long been America and how to sustain the moral resources of American society.[4]

Christian theologians in the ecclesial ethicist trajectory maintain that Christian ethics is first and foremost an ecclesial rather than a national project. The church is in its own life a *polis*, a political body whose task is to embody, and thereby bear witness to, God's new political order. Of all other human communities and institutions, only the church is the body of Christ. Only the church, it is argued, has been drawn into God's eschatological new creation.[5] One of Stanley Hauerwas's theological aphorisms is that the first social ethical task of the church is to be the church.[6] This sensibility leads not merely to a strong sense of the church-world distinction but also to a heightened sense of the conflict between the way of Christ and the church against the ruling powers or dominant cultural *ethos*. To utilize imprecise but different and significantly overlapping theological categorizations, ecclesial ethicists, postliberals, and neo-Anabaptists accentuate the tension between the way of Christ and the modern liberal and secular nation-state, militarism, and capitalism.[7]

Christian realists have accused those in the neo-Anabaptist trajectory of encouraging withdrawal from social and political engagement into a counter-cultural ecclesial "ghetto," thereby abdicating the responsibility to engage in struggles for social justice and in opposition to racism and economic injustice.[8] Even though these accusations of sectarian withdrawal have often caricatured thinkers within this trajectory, especially Stanley Hauerwas,[9] there are strong tendencies within ecclesiological sensibilities

---

4. Hauerwas, *Against the Nations*, 36.

5. Rasmusson, "Ecclesiology and Ethics," 184–86, 188–89; Long, *Augustinian and Ecclesial Ethics*, 127–28, 155; Guth, *Christian Ethics at the Boundary*, 9–10, 40.

6. Hauerwas, *Peaceable Kingdom*, 99.

7. Long, *Augustinian and Ecclesial Ethics*, xxi–xxii; Guth, *Christian Ethics at the Boundary*, 39, 42.

8. Gustafson, "Sectarian Temptation," 83–94; Guth, *Christian Ethics at the Boundary*, 39–40; Lovin, "Religion and American Public Life," 18–19.

9. Sometimes, Hauerwas's rhetorical excesses, such as his description of the church as "resident aliens" inhabiting "the Christian colony," shed more heat than light and therefore, render him vulnerable to this critique. These rhetorical flourishes often obscure his more nuanced position. Hauerwas and Willimon, *Resident Aliens*, 38, 47; Hauerwas, *Against the Nations*, 1.

There are multiple statements scattered throughout his massive corpus in which Hauerwas denies that it is his intention that Christians give up working for justice.

that presume such an extremely sharp antithesis between church and world and therefore make it difficult to conceptualize how the church might have a positive and creative impact on the cultures and social orders in which it finds itself.

Nevertheless, there are emphases characteristic of postliberal or neo-Anabaptist theologians that will be appropriated in this chapter. The ecclesial or witness theologians are those who have been strongly influenced by John Howard Yoder and Stanley Hauerwas and include James McClendon, William Cavanaugh, Michael Baxter, and Daniel Bell, among many others. Theologians in this trajectory are correct to argue that the salvation Christ brings is ecclesial in character. It involves the formation of a radically new kind of human community, called to embody, in its own life together, a counter-imperial alternative to pervasive practices, values, and ways of life promoted by the powerful and which are at odds with the gospel. This community is called to "do together" the life of discipleship, which entails love of enemies, hospitality, and generosity in response to human suffering and human need. This community is called to be a visible and living repudiation of the fallen world's ways of domination, quests for power that involve placing oneself above others on various status hierarchies, and fear and exclusion of the "other." This alternative way of life requires intensive catechesis or formation of character and identity in order to cultivate a "sociologically sectarian" people[10] willing to be a cognitively dissonant minority in at least some significant respects.

Theologians within this neo-Anabaptist trajectory sometimes share some common ground with many theologians in the liberationist trajectory. Both see profound incompatibility between Christian faith and the dominant social order. In both theological camps, one finds a profound critique of political liberalism, capitalism, indifference to the poor, war-making, and the concentration of power in the hands of the wealthiest and most well-connected.

However, theologians within the neo-Anabaptist trajectory have sometimes been criticized for a "tone-deafness" on matters of race and racial justice. Emphasis on the cultivation of ecclesial communities of character have, for the most part, failed to address the magnitude of ecclesial

---

For example, he insists that the kinds of ecclesial communities he advocates "can participate in secular movements against war, against hunger, and against other forms of inhumanity as part of the church's necessary proclamatory action.... I have no interest in legitimating ... a withdrawal of Christians or the church from social or political affairs. I simply want them to be there as Christians and as church" (Hauerwas, *Peaceable Kingdom*, 100–101; *After Christendom?*, 68).

10. Lindbeck, "Sectarian Future of the Church," 226–43.

malformation and unfaithfulness to the gospel on the part of white ecclesial communities as sources of the tragic brokenness and alienation along racial lines within North American Christianity. As Kristopher Norris has recently argued, racial injustice is not a matter of ecclesial complicity and capitulation to cultural evils "outside" the church. Rather, the injustice is endemic to our ecclesial lives as white Christians in the United States.

Neo-Anabaptists and Fellow Travelers: An Apocalyptic Soteriological and Ecclesiological Imagination

An apocalyptic theological vision privileges the life, death, and resurrection of Jesus as the eschatological interruption into history of God's new political order.[11] The gospel, Douglas Harink maintains, echoing J. Louis Martyn, is the good news of God's radical and decisive invasion, in Jesus Christ and the outpouring of the Holy Spirit, of a *kosmos* in bondage. Salvation involves rescue from idolatry and the "principalities and powers," which include unjust social structures, dominant cultural values and ideologies, and idolatrous allegiances to one's nation or ethnic group. Salvation is the inauguration of the "age to come" in the midst of the present order. Harink contends that the establishment of a new socio-political order, the church, is part of the good news. Christ's Lordship over the powers and the liberation of God's people from their dominion is embodied in communities that practice hospitality, feed the hungry, and reject violence and through ecclesial communal practices in which racial and economic differences are surmounted and every person, regardless of social status in the wider society, is valued and included. A further implication of an apocalyptic imagination is the expectation of significant discontinuity between the reign of God and dominant social orders, economic systems, and institutions of governance in any context. Every nation, Harink asserts, is, in the first instance, "a power that enslaves human beings and makes us serve its ends," "an idolatrous regime from which God comes to set his people free." The cruciform church is the sociopolitical space where the new creation breaks into the present and inevitably conflicts with the dominant order as the church exposes the powers' pretensions to ultimate allegiance.[12]

For the neo-Anabaptist trajectory, ethics is an ecclesial project. Karen Guth describes this approach as one that stresses the primacy of revelation, the role of biblical narrative and church practices for the moral formation

11. Long, *Augustinian and Ecclesial Ethics*, xxi.

12. Harink, *Paul among the Postliberals*, 17–18, 22–23, 37, 60–61, 68, 110, 116–17, 126, 256–59; "Response to Jim Wallis's *God's Politics*."

of Christian disciples, and the nature of the church as a distinctive *polis* that witnesses to the world. Ecclesiology and the call to resist cultural accommodation takes precedence over engagement in extra-ecclesial politics.[13] One of Hauerwas's most well-known mantras is that "the church does not have a social ethic, the church is a social ethic."[14] The first task of Christian social ethics, Hauerwas argues, "is not to make the 'world' better or more just, but to help Christian people form communities consistent with their conviction that the story of Christ is a truthful account of our existence."[15] Hauerwas asserts that "the church does not exist to provide an ethos for democracy or any other form of social organization, but stands as a political alternative to every nation."[16]

Suspicion of all ruling powers will be a general tendency of a theological imagination informed by the category of apocalyptic. If the interruptive character and eschatological novelty of God's reign are emphasized, discontinuity between the church and any human social order will be accentuated. For example, Michael Baxter argues that Christians should identify themselves most fundamentally as citizens of another *patria*, as strangers and aliens in this and all other nation-states through which they pass on their pilgrim journey.[17]

As Stephen Long points out, neo-Anabaptists or ecclesial ethicists view the modern nation-state and the current global economy as the principalities and powers, rulers and authorities opposed to Christ. These powers are judged harshly as having rejected what was central to Jesus: the love for enemies that requires a refusal of lethal violence or at least such a strong presumption against it that only the strictest application of just war theory would be permissible.[18] For example, Michael Budde argues that what states do is "exercise lethal force in the pursuit of various objectives—order, justice, prosperity, self-preservation, elite security . . . *Pax Romana*, or *Pax Americana*, or any other kind of peace purchased by state power, is one in which killing for some social good is legitimate and inevitable."[19]

William T. Cavanaugh sets forth a similar critique of modern liberalism and capitalism. In opposition to the Thomistic sensibility regarding the "naturalness" of the state, Cavanaugh argues that the origins of the modern,

---

13. Guth, *Christian Ethics at the Boundary*, 9–10.
14. Hauerwas, *Peaceable Kingdom*, 99.
15. Hauerwas, *Community of Character*, 10.
16. Hauerwas, *Community of Character*, 12.
17. Baxter, "Review Essay," 254–55.
18. Long, *Augustinian and Ecclesial Ethics*, xxi.
19. Budde, *(Magic) Kingdom of God*, 145.

centralized, bureaucratized, and sovereign nation-state was hardly an expression of human sociality. Rather, the historical emergence of the modern nation-state was inseparable from the desire of rulers for greater efficiency in the extraction of tax revenue from the population for the sake of military might and war-making. Writing polemically against public theologians like Charles Curran and others who have tried to rehabilitate the notion of "the common good" as a central feature of a renewed American public philosophy, Cavanaugh articulates his complete skepticism regarding the potential of the nation-state to be the promoter and defender of the common good. He argues that the foundational anthropology of Lockean liberalism imagines the sovereign individual to be the natural condition of humankind. Liberalism cannot, he argues, produce a political philosophy in which the state's role is to secure the common good. Locke's "commonwealth" is a society constituted for the procuring, preserving, and advancing of individual interests: life, liberty, and material possessions. The *telos* of this state is strictly to secure the non-interference of individuals with each other.[20]

Critiques of Liberalism from Postliberal, Neo-Anabaptist, and Radical Orthodox Theologians

Theologians who might be placed into the neo-Anabaptist, postliberal, and radical orthodoxy trajectories often agree with one another in their harsh critique of "political liberalism." "Political liberalism" refers to modern ideals of equality, liberty, and freedom that may take a wide variety of institutional forms but are characterized by "limited government, individual rights, the consent of the governed, constitutionalism, and the rule of law."[21] What is most unique to modern liberalism is that it is a political philosophy that seeks social peace and stability in the absence of shared conceptions of the common good, substantive visions of justice, or any consensus regarding the good life or the ultimate purposes and ends of human existence. In the absence of consensus on these matters, often due to religious and other forms of pluralism, political liberalism seeks to organize a society that is indifferent to the ultimate goals and purposes of citizens, so long as they respect the laws and tasks necessary for the operation of responsible government.[22]

---

20. Cavanaugh, "Killing for the Telephone Company," 245–49, 253–54, 258, 265. See also Cavanaugh, "Fire Strong Enough to Consume the House," 398–409.

21. Gregory and Clair, "Augustinianisms and Thomisms," 176.

22. Hovey, "Liberalism and Democracy," 197; Gregory and Clair, "Augustinianisms and Thomisms," 176.

Section Five: Justice as Participation in the Eschatological New Creation

The Aristotelian-Thomist conception of politics was centered upon the discovery and pursuit of shared goods and human purposes tethered to conceptions of the human *telos* along with a conception of society as ordered to the production of virtuous citizens capable of attaining those purposes. St. Thomas conceived of the highest ends for humanity as beatitude and friendship with God. In contrast, liberalism tends toward a conception of the state as merely the preserver of the public peace and protector of individual human rights to life, liberty, and property.

In addition to concerns about a society that eschews any consensus about the ultimate purposes of human existence and the nature of the common good, theologians in the neo-Anabaptist trajectory are especially concerned about the idolatrous imagination of the modern nation-state as savior and peacemaker. Craig Hovey argues that Thomas Hobbes's sovereign state plays a salvific role for originally autonomous, free-associating individuals. According to Hobbes's famous argument, without society, life is a constant state of war with every individual against everyone else, hence "solitary, poor, nasty, brutish, and short."[23]

Finally, postliberal, neo-Anabaptist, and radical orthodoxy criticize modern liberalism for its de-politicization of the church through the imagination and fabrication of an autonomous and neutral secular realm. John Milbank, in *Theology and Social Theory*,[24] and William Cavanaugh, in a ground-breaking 1995 essay in *Modern Theology*,[25] provide extensive accounts of these developments. Lash identifies the birth of the modern state in sixteenth-century Europe as the victory of secular over ecclesiastical authority, which led to the eventual elimination of the church from the public sphere. With the emergence of the state as the sole agency of governance and public power, ecclesiastical authority was evicted from this realm and confined to what is now redefined as "spiritual" territory, i.e., to the inside of the private, Cartesian self.[26]

Therefore, these theologians are sharply critical of those modern public and political theologies that have sought a rapprochement with the Enlightenment and its politics, in particular the modern account of freedom as individual autonomy and liberty. They are sharply critical of the notion that the state and public sphere are secular, neutral vis-à-vis all substantive conceptions of the human *telos* and the comprehensive accounts of life's meaning and purpose provided by religious faiths. On this account,

---

23. Hovey, "Liberalism and Democracy," 198.
24. Milbank, *Theology and Social Theory*.
25. Cavanaugh, "Fire Strong Enough to Consume the House," 397–420.
26. Lash, "Church in the State We're In," 123.

theology's "public role," vis-à-vis the neutral and secular public realm, is to serve the national project as the custodian of values, ideals, and perhaps a cultural ethos or spirit that should inform, inspire, and animate action in the secular political realm amidst secular political options.[27]

Is This a Moment to "Dial Back" the Anti-Liberal Rhetoric?

As noted by Michael Quirk, the Augustinian conviction that the church is the only true polity implies that any social order will be, in some measure, deficient from a Christian point of view.[28] With this consideration in mind, this might be the moment, to employ a colloquial figure of speech, to "dial back" some of the anti-liberal rhetoric in light of the assault upon American institutions, elections, and checks upon executive power during and after the Trump administration. In this bizarre cultural moment, authoritarian Prime Minister Victor Orbán, who has systematically dismantled Hungary's democratic institutions and has undermined freedom of the press, is being championed by some on the American political right as a model for American political conservatives. After Orbán gave a speech in which he stated that Hungary must not become a "mixed-race" country, pointing to other nations in Europe with large immigrant populations, one of Orbán's top aides resigned, noting that Orbán's speech sounded as if it were given by a "Nazi." Two weeks after he made these comments, Orbán was enthusiastically received when he spoke at the Conservative Political Action Committee meeting.[29] At this particular moment, anti-liberal rhetoric is in danger of serving primarily to strengthen the authoritarian populism and its marriage to [white] Christian nationalism.

William Cavanaugh articulates a harsh critique of liberalism, especially its celebration of the freedom of the market, which leaves individuals free to choose their own ends and thereby elevates choice itself as the highest value to which a liberal social order is ordered. But Cavanaugh acknowledges the dilemma introduced by his hard critique of political liberalism and its construal of freedom as uninhibited freedom of choice. Who is authorized to decide what conception of the human *telos* should provide the ends around which the social order is to be organized?[30]

27. Bell, "Postliberalism and Radical Orthodoxy," 115–16.

28. Quirk, "Stanley Hauerwas's *Against the Nations*," 78–86.

29. Beauchamp, "It Happened There"; Allison and Johnson, "Orbán Gets Warm CPAC Reception."

30. Cavanaugh, *Being Consumed*, 1–15.

Section Five: Justice as Participation in the Eschatological New Creation

At this present moment, there are certainly those who would joyously organize the US social order around a substantive Christian vision of human life. However, it is not so certain that the version of the Christian faith that might prevail is a good or faithful account of the Christian religion. At the present moment, those who would take the country in the direction of a Christian nationalism should give us pause with respect to the harshest theological critiques of liberalism. As noted in the introduction, Christian nationalism was found to be a powerful predictor of intolerance toward immigrants, racial minorities, and interracial families as well as opposition to gay rights, support for harsher punishment for criminals, including the death penalty, support for authoritarian measures of social control, justification for use of excessive force against black Americans in law enforcement, and support for traditionalist, patriarchal gender ideology.[31]

A prime example of this kind of Christian nationalism is found in Rev. Baily Smith's sermon "The Sin that Seems So Nice." In this sermon, he articulates his contempt for those he considers "others" and antithetical to his vision of "Christian America." Smith expresses disgust that the New York Police Department conducted what he called "sensitivity training" to promote respectful treatment of transgender and gender non-conforming persons. He then moved through his King James Bible, listing all the times God had commanded his people to commit genocide. If they had followed God's orders, the evangelist suggested, the people we now know as "Arabs" wouldn't be around today to fly planes into buildings.[32]

"Why are we not allowed to have America anymore?" Smith asked.

> Now, I know we can't have the Walton America or the Andy Griffith America. That day will never exist anymore. And I'm sad about that. Because we had a right to have that kind of America, and it's amazing how many of the Muslims and the other countries love to come here and enjoy the country the children of God built.[33]

Surely, Smith is not oblivious to the fact that Walton America and Andy Griffith America are "lily white." At minimum, the depth of racial injustice of the culture of the time period in which his beloved shows were situated did not register with him as a problem. His conception of the "America the children of God built" is, at best, entirely tone deaf to the reality of racial injustice.

---

31. Baker et al., "Keep America Christian (and White)," 275–76.
32. Smith, "Sin that Seems So Nice"; Bean, "Are We Finally Ready to Learn?"
33. Smith, "Sin that Seems So Nice."

Politics of Salvation as Participation in God's Eschatological/Apocalyptic Intrusion

If political liberalism is repudiated in its entirety, whose vision of human flourishing and ultimate human purposes prevails? While classical Lockean political liberalism is deeply flawed, the danger at this present moment is that those with Christian nationalist theocratic aspirations, coopted by an even harsher illiberal authoritarianism, might gain the power to order the social order around their particular vision of the human good. And while this vision of a society organized around a substantive vision of human purposes and human flourishing is one which explicitly claims allegiance to the God of Jesus Christ, this theological vision is far from faithful to the actual way of Jesus Christ. This vision, no less than free-market liberalism, may be in thrall to disordered desires, especially if what is desired is cultural dominance and power, including the power to dominate and exclude those who do not fit their vision of an ideal America!

Another matter that deserves more reflection than can be provided here is whether the United States and its governing institutions constitute anything even remotely close to a pure liberal social order or government. Certainly, the disestablishment clause of the United States Constitution and at least some trajectories of First Amendment jurisprudence suggest a secular society and a secular public realm. But the United States is hardly a coherent social and political order. The actual organization and functioning of the political institutions of American society is so multi-faceted and unwieldy that it defies any simple categorization. The modern bureaucratic state, with the proliferation of federal agencies, an extremely complex apparatus of federal and state law, and a dysfunctional two-party system, result in a chaotic plurality of voices and visions. Undergirding political preferences, policies, and regulations are latent but far more substantive moral aspirations than one might expect in a society that approached a purer liberal individualism and secular neutrality. These visions, some good and others perhaps not so good, shape political policies, whether we speak of battles over what should be taught in high school history classes, local municipal ordinances pertaining to building safety, or perennial concerns about the impact of economic realities upon citizens.

The political history of the United States reveals that Lockean individualism, on the one hand, and a politics animated by the quest to achieve some more substantive vision of "the common good" and shared values and social objectives exist in creative, and sometimes destructive, tension in American political debate and policies. The Americans with Disabilities Act, social safety nets, environmental regulations, and Title VII of the Civil Rights Act of 1964, which pertains to employment discrimination on the basis of race or national origin, sex, or religion, are not entirely consonant with Lockean liberalism and, paradoxically, include both concern for the common good and liberal individual rights considerations. These tensions provide openings for Christians to engage the political process in ways that resist "confinement" within the logic of forms of political liberalism that would endeavor to restrict Christian faith to the private sphere.

The Pitfalls of (Some) Public Theologies

In the last quarter of the twentieth century, numerous American theologians sought to address the privatization of religion in modern, secular society by articulating "public theologies." There are risks associated with any effort to group together such a wide range of thinkers. Those who understood themselves in these terms were a diverse lot, theologically and politically.

Public theologians, in contrast to the polemic against liberalism prevalent in neo-Anabaptist or ecclesial ethics approaches, tended to assume a fundamental compatibility between the church's mission and the American political order as well as the project of liberal and secular democracy. This was true of those in the mainline liberal Protestant trajectory and of the Americanist tradition, indebted to John Courtney Murray, in American Catholicism.[34]

This fundamental compatibility with the United States political system and secular, liberal democracy might be justified from either a Thomist or Augustinian sensibility. Speaking from a Thomist sensibility, Michael and Kenneth Himes assert that the "benign view of human nature in Catholic theology" leads to a benign view of human society, assumed to be a harmonious system of interaction and cooperation. The state, they argue, "arises naturally from the interaction of persons who create a variety of organizational mechanisms so that shared activities are encouraged and shared goods can be obtained."[35]

In contrast, an Augustinian sensibility sees worldly government as a *post-lapsum* reality that is permitted by God to restrain evil. On this account,

---

34. Hessel and Hudnut-Beumler, "Public Church in Retrospect and Prospect," 301–2. See Murray, *We Hold These Truths*. While most public theologians represented a left-progressive variation on this theme, it can also be articulated with a more politically conservative sensibility. For example, Richard John Neuhaus famously asserted that "on the balance and considering the alternatives, America has been and is an influence for good in the world" (Neuhaus, *Naked Public Square*, 72).

35. Himes and Himes, *Fullness of Faith*, 23–25, 38. According to Richard P. McBrien, "Society is a gathering of various communities that are ordered for cooperation and communication so as to enhance human well-being. Society is composed of many different and diverse communities and groups: families, voluntary associations, colleges/universities, small businesses, corporations, labor unions, religious organizations, and even governmental agencies" (McBrien, *Caesar's Coin*, 25).

Politics of Salvation as Participation in God's Eschatological/Apocalyptic Intrusion

politics is not natural but rather a stop-gap measure in a fallen world.[36] Reinhold Niebuhr drew upon St. Augustine's account of the lust for power or *libido dominandi* in worldly governance as a perennial threat. Niebuhr argued that groups have a tendency to degenerate into intolerant organizations that aim for political advantage to the detriment of other groups and individuals. Niebuhr's theology of sin emphasized group egoism, leading him to insist that justice requires a balance of power to check the ability of any group to achieve dominance. This served as a powerful defense of American democracy and the ideal of checks and balances to control the will-to-power of any group.[37]

The danger of this long trajectory of American Christian social ethics is that the primary public project becomes not the embodiment and participation in the in-breaking of the eschatological new creation, God's new social order, but rather the instrumentalist role of serving the civic and political life of the nation. It is the nation that is treated as if it were the larger, more all-embracing project. But this means that ecclesial communities are "positioned" as smaller sub-systems whose function is to serve the larger project of a better America, the health of American civil society, or the public life of the nation. For example, Michael and Kenneth Himes assert that every part of society is responsible for fostering the common good. The state and other components of society, including the churches, each have their role to play in achieving the common good.[38] Similarly, Richard Bernstein expresses the hope that churches might play a crucial role in the service of American democracy. Religious communities, Bernstein believes, provide the vestiges of community that are capable of fostering the type of public life of deliberation and debate needed for a democracy.[39]

Public theology's inclination to see the public and civic life of the nation as the primary "public" project is also manifest in the tendency of public church social ethics to seek to articulate an ethic for society. For example, Max Stackhouse identifies the church's "public role" as the responsibility to represent and advocate a public theology as the normative basis for society and its institutions.[40] Michael and Kenneth Himes situate their project in continuity with John Courtney Murray's efforts to rehabilitate a shared consensus among Catholics, Protestants, Jews, and secularists on the

---

36. Long, *Augustinian and Ecclesial Ethics*, 21–23.

37. See chapter 12 in Niebuhr, *Reflections on the End of an Era*; Long, *Ecclesial Ethics*, 10–12.

38. Himes and Himes, *Fullness of Faith*, 20, 23.

39. Bernstein, "Meaning of Public Life," 44, 47. See also Coleman, "Possible Role for Biblical Religion," 701–6; Lovin, "Resources for a Public Theology," 707–10.

40. Stackhouse, "Public Theology," 65, 74, 78, 82.

foundational truths and values of the American experiment and thereby to contribute to a public philosophy for the nation.[41] Richard John Neuhaus said much the same when he argued that the Christian religion's public role is to construct a moral philosophy, a religiously inspired but publicly accessible language of political discourse in the service of the American experiment in republican democracy.[42] Ron Stone describes Reinhold Niebuhr and Paul Tillich, two of the most influential theologians from the 1940s into the 1960s, as public theologians because their message was directed to policy makers in public ways and not exclusively to the church. Their words were as much to politicians with the church overhearing them as they were to the church with politicians overhearing them.[43]

One of the problems with this strand of public theology is that it paradoxically keeps "religion" confined to the private sphere. Religion and religious experience remain private, with its primary location within the "Cartesian" self, but through a mighty leap effectuated by a project of translation, Christianity's reservoir of values and symbols of community, human interdependence, and love might provide resources for a moral vision in service of American society.[44] But the implicit rules regarding what may and may not be transported across the translational bridge indicate that what is distinctively Christian must remain confined to the private and personal realm. Christian social ethics in this vein seeks to serve as a mediating language which allows the translation of Christian convictions into secular philosophical language that, as Joseph Cardinal Bernardin argued, "can be accepted by a religiously pluralistic society as the moral foundation of public policy positions."[45] Others argued that appeals to Christian beliefs and symbols are appropriate in public conversation if arguments can be constructed in such a way that non-religious persons can accept a theologian's public proposals without acceptance of his or her religious premises. For example, David Tracy argued that even though classic religious texts and symbols are "non-public" and non-shareable in their origins, their effects can be public if they disclose new ways of being-in-the-world or transformative possibilities for human existence.[46] The assumption, Kathryn Tanner argues, is that Christians and non-Christians can share general humanistic understandings

---

41. Himes and Himes, *Fullness of Faith*, 11.

42. Neuhaus, "Catholic Moment," 46.

43. Stone, "Tillich and Niebuhr as Allied Public Theologians," 504.

44. Hollenbach, "Editor's Conclusion," 713.

45. Hehir, "Perennial Need for Philosophical Discourse," 711; Bernardin, "Address at Georgetown University," 343.

46. Tracy, "Particular Classics, Public Religion," 118–23, 126–29.

of the significance of Christian beliefs and symbols. However, Tanner cautions, if the public recommendations of theologians are presented in such a way that the most distinctive features of the Christian religion are minimized or bracketed so that someone who is not religious can make them as well, this strategy is indistinguishable from the position that religious arguments should be kept out of public debate altogether.[47]

The Necessity of a "Neo-Anabaptist Ecclesial Moment or Dimension"

According to James Gustafson's "sectarian accusation," theological accounts of the church as a political entity in its own right promote principled withdrawal of the church from "the larger society" into a counter-cultural ecclesial ghetto.[48] In his critique of Stanley Hauerwas, Jeffrey Stout expresses the fear that when an apocalyptic ecclesiology is combined with a sharp polemic against liberalism, "the secular," and democracy, theologians are calling for total rejection of American society on the part of Christians.[49]

The recognition of the element of discontinuity and conflict between the eschatological new creation and the ruling powers or dominant cultural *ethos* is a strength, though it can become a weakness if it legitimates withdrawal into an ecclesial enclave. Lacking this sensibility often leads to the worst forms of accommodation to destructive cultural patterns and oppressive social arrangements.

It is of utmost importance to safeguard and maintain another crucially important emphasis of the witness or ecclesial theologians. Theologians and ethicists in this trajectory have strongly accentuated the distinctive role of the church in forming and shaping members in the *ethos* and way of life of the household of faith, with its distinctive patterns of feeling, thinking, and acting. The indispensable task is the production of disciples who are equipped for this unique role to which God has called the church, which is to be a distinctive *polis* that displays clearly God's new order. A distinctively Christian ethical moral vision, embedded in the whole network of Christian convictions, practices, rituals, and dispositions, is a prerequisite for faithful Christian discernment which seeks to interpret the world rightly, resist accommodation to cultural values and ways of living at odds with the

---

47. Tanner, "Public Theology," 83–84.
48. Gustafson, "Sectarian Temptation," 83–94.
49. Stout, *Democracy and Tradition*, 140, 147–48.

Christian faith,[50] and, I would add, act faithfully in the quest to be agents of transformation within the social order.

The centrality of this task is illuminated by Dan Compier's criticism of David Cunningham. In the early 1990s, both Compier and Cunningham wrote important books about the importance of the discipline of rhetoric for the theologian's task.[51] Though his overall evaluation of Cunningham's *Faithful Persuasion* was positive, Compier's central criticism of the book was that Cunningham's primary agenda was to provide "a catechetical instrument by which persons may be fully persuaded to adopt the Christian faith and lifestyle." Compier wrote:

> I am aiming at a different public.... Cunningham addresses the church ... and uses rhetoric to re-conceptualize theology as a catechetical and evangelizing activity. These activities certainly express key components of the church's mission. But the people of God are also called to *diakonia* on behalf of victims. A focus on the conversion of persons to Christianity does not necessarily entail the changes in behavior stressed so often by classical orators.... This different yet related duty involves addressing a different case to a different audience.... I aim to address my work to Tracy's third public, namely, society at large.[52]

But why should we frame the issue in this way? Why should the ecclesial activities of evangelization and catechesis be seen as unconnected to *diakonia* to victims if, as Compier rightly insists, it is precisely the people of God who are called to this task? And if practices of evangelization and Christian formation are not producing desirable behavioral changes, as Compier also rightly points out, then something has gone terribly wrong. Either churches are engaging in forms of evangelism tethered to defective soteriological understandings, leading to a truncated understanding of conversion, or churches are failing in the task of catechesis if catechetical practices either impede or fail to facilitate the formation of Christians who understand *diakonia* on behalf of victims as integral to the way of life to

---

50. Rasmusson, "Ecclesiology and Ethics," 184–86, 188–89; Guth, *Christian Ethics at the Boundary*, 40.

51. Cunningham, *Faithful Persuasion*; Compier, *What Is Rhetorical Theology?*

52. Compier, *What Is Rhetorical Theology?*, 23–24. This way of framing the issue regarding the audience of the theologian is derived from David Tracy's proposal that different theological specialties are addressed to different primary audiences. According to Tracy, the primary public addressed by fundamental theology is the academy. Systematic theology is addressed to the church. Practical theologies, concerned with social justice and public policy matters, speak to society at large. Tracy, *Analogical Imagination*.

which they have been converted. This was Jim Wallis's point over forty years ago, when he lamented the mal-formation of American Christians who frequently speak Jesus's name while ignoring the content of his teaching and life. Wallis offered an analysis of the problem, with which Compier is also rightly concerned, of conversions of persons to Christianity without changes in behavior consistent with the way of Jesus Christ. Wallis identified the problem as the reduction of the gospel to personal salvation and the neglect in evangelistic preaching of the kingdom of God. Merely registering "decisions for Christ" produces a disastrous result: "saved" individuals who fit comfortably into the old order instead of a more authentic conversion that produces Christians whose lives and values are at odds with American racism, militarism, and consumerism.[53]

Concern for societal justice and *diakonia* to victims calls for significant theological attention to the task of forming the mind of the church. This theological task requires the evaluation and repair of defective soteriological understandings or deficient practices of catechesis. Without such formation, Christians will derive their political values and beliefs from other sources, especially from voices in our society that are the loudest, most assertive, and most hostile to those who are the most vulnerable among us.

Tragically, this has happened. Though professing to embrace a religion that has valued hospitality to strangers and delivering compassion for persons in need, white evangelical hostility toward immigrants and refugees is higher than other demographics in American society. White evangelicals "are more opposed to immigration reform, and have more negative views about immigrants, than any other religious demographic."[54] 68 percent of white evangelicals claim that America has no responsibility to take in refugees. As Tara Isabella Burton asks, "How did a religious group whose foundational sacred text explicitly mandates care for the poor, the sick, and the stranger become a reliable anti-refugee, anti-immigrant voting bloc?"[55]

---

53. Wallis, *Call to Conversion*, xii–xiii, xviii, 18–20, 24–29, 32–36, 41–42, 87.

54. Cooper et al., "How Americans View Immigrants"; Du Mez, "Understanding White Evangelical Views on Immigration."

55. Burton, "Bible Says to Welcome Immigrants"; Stroop, "White Evangelicals Have Turned on Refugees."

Section Five: Justice as Participation in the Eschatological New Creation

Ecclesial Witness: Extra-Ecclesial Politics as Participation in the Intrusion of the Reign of God

Critics of Neo-Anabaptists such as Robin Lovin, whose project is situated in the Niebuhrian Christian realist trajectory, have charged that the formation of an alternative community is not sufficient. Lovin rightly argues:

> For the African-American woman ordered to the back of the crowded bus, Sunday's sermon about one's freedom as a child of God will not suffice. For the laborer who works a ten-hour shift in an unsafe factory, the generosity and sharing of resources within the church community are not enough. The achievement of racial and economic justice demand changes in social, political, and economic policies and structures.[56]

Karen Guth offers a very important "re-framing of the issue" when she asks how we might think about participation in the political life of our society, in "extra-ecclesial politics," in a way that is itself an ecclesial practice.[57] Following Guth's suggestion, I would argue that a Christian theology of political engagement should be bigger in its aspirations that either an ecclesial or a national project. Rather, it should be an eschatological project, with an ecclesial starting point but one which seeks to move, in union with Christ and the Spirit, into spaces in which destructive powers inflict harm in order to be agents of deliverance and conduits of divine love and justice.

At the heart of God's covenant relationship with Israel and at the heart of the Christian movement, in faithful continuity, is the revelation that God's deepest purpose is human flourishing. God is opposed to all oppressive and destructive powers and social arrangements that inflict unjust suffering and destroy human lives and communities. Jesus's own ministry and mission reinforce this core theological conviction about the identity and character of God. If salvation means being drawn into union with Christ, and if union with Christ the Messiah means being drawn into the sphere of the eschatological new creation, then the gift of salvation is a participation in the arriving and invasion of this present age by the reign of God.

A theology of Christian social and political engagement might find its bearings in a text that, at first glance, has nothing to do with struggles for social and political justice. In Matt 12:22–29, Jesus expels an evil spirit that has made a man blind and mute. This evil spirit is a life-stealing destructive power that has caused this man to be cut off from communication and interaction with others. Jesus interprets this deed of deliverance for his

---

56. Lovin, "Religion and American Public Life," 18–19.
57. Guth, *Christian Ethics at the Boundary*, 53.

Politics of Salvation as Participation in God's Eschatological/Apocalyptic Intrusion

audience by situating it within an apocalyptic eschatological framework. Jesus declares that if he casts out evil spirits by the power of the Holy Spirit, then the kingdom of God is present, in the midst of the present age, in and through the power of the Holy Spirit at work in setting humans free to flourish. But Jesus goes further and interprets the arrival of the reign of God as an act of aggression in which Jesus breaks the stranglehold of the Evil One in order to set persons free from its death grip (Matt 12:22–29).

The Evil One's power is broken when persons are delivered from bondage to any reality that harms and destroys life. As Ched Myers points out, the kingdom of Satan, within this apocalyptic imagination, is a symbolic accentuation of the negative experiences of earthly rule.[58] The expulsion of the evil spirits, who identify themselves as "Legion," from the man who lived in the tombs in the region of Gedara, suggest the connection between Jesus's battle against evil spirits and the realities of political oppression and trauma. The events narrated as demon expulsions in the Synoptic Gospels set persons free from physical ailments that make life painful and burdensome and lead the persons so afflicted into social spaces of exclusion and economic deprivation. The dominion of Satan is not confined to a "spiritual realm," but is life-crushing social systems, structures, and economic arrangements. This means that we should see Jesus's expulsions of evil spirits and Jesus's confrontations with various segments of the ruling elite of his day as episodes in the same battle between the intrusion of the eschatological new creation and the powers of sin, death, and oppression. As the personal presence of the reign of God, Jesus entered into conflict with all of the powers, practices, and institutions that enslaved, oppressed, and dehumanized human persons.

If being saved means being drawn into union with Christ, and thereby into the eschatological new creation in its ongoing invasion and intrusion of the present evil age, then being saved means being drawn into the conflict with every power and force that kills, maims, and destroys, whether physically or emotionally. We are drawn into conflict with whatever inflicts trauma and dehumanizes or diminishes human persons.

Being drawn into union with Christ is indeed being drawn into the body of Christ. But this ecclesial space is no insulated enclave of "resident aliens" if that metaphor is read to entail insulation from the wider society. There is no pure space upon which to construct an insulated and pure enclave of heaven. The ecclesial community, drawn into the intruding eschatological new creation, has no other terrain to inhabit except contested terrain, currently possessed by the enslaving powers. The church's "inner"

---

58. Myers, *Binding the Strong Man*, 165.

Section Five: Justice as Participation in the Eschatological New Creation

life is already situated on the playing field occupied by the principalities and powers. Christians are inextricably entangled in destructive dynamics in their daily lives of buying, selling, and being employed. The candy bar we eat likely includes child slave labor in its supply chain. Even if we are conscientious shoppers, at least some of our clothes were produced in sweatshops where the conditions are dangerous and dehumanizing, including mandatory work weeks of eighty or ninety hours and wages that keep the workers in poverty in spite of how many hours they work. Christians are already implicated in economic and social forces that have shaped our ongoing residential segregation and the injustices of school funding that offer incredible educational opportunities to students in affluent districts and a school-to-prison pipeline to students in the poorest districts.

Shaping an ecclesial sociopolitical life in conformity with the shape of God's reign also finds its pattern in Jesus's own aggressive opposition to the economic exploitation of the temple establishment. This means we are called to participate in an intrusion into the world in bondage to destructive powers in order to resist their destructive grip upon human lives.

The politics of the kingdom of God calls us to cultivate communities that embody Christian virtue within the church's own "internal" life together. But if our conception of Christian virtue takes its cues from the practices of Jesus as narrated in the Gospels, that "internal" life is always already "on the go," to the ends of the earth. There is no clear boundary line between the internal life of the people of God and the call to be "on the go" in the *missio Dei*. We are called to make disciples, baptizing them in the Trinitarian name, and to do so by teaching the disciples to do everything Jesus commanded. Integral to what Jesus commanded was that his followers welcome, include, and exercise delivering compassion for the sick, the poor and destitute, the marginalized, those who suffer, the hungry, and persons whose lives were destroyed by predatory economic arrangements (e.g., Matt 25:31–46; Luke 10:25–37; 14:12–14). Jesus healed and delivered. He affirmed the dignity of those who were degraded. He made it a point to welcome and show hospitality to the persons that his society considered to be the losers. The politics of the kingdom requires us to place a premium on human well-being and to engage in delivering compassion and resistance when humans are abused and violated.

The politics of the kingdom is neither a nationalist project nor an ecclesial project, narrowly defined. The political engagement that flows from incorporation in the eschatological new creation, in its irruption into a world still in bondage to enslaving and destructive powers, is one that is oriented toward human wholeness or *shalom*. In sync with Jesus's Isaianic mission statement in Luke 4:17–21, the political goal of God's people should be neither a better America nor the cultivation of a community of virtue insulated from the larger social order; rather, it is resisting what is oppressive and abusive and creatively contributing to the construction of institutions and arrangements that are more conducive to justice, peace, and healthy communities.

One might say that Christian political engagement should be instigated by the encounter with the human person in distress, as Jesus indicated in the Parable of the Good Samaritan. When persons are threatened with destruction, stigmatization, and therefore dehumanization and degrading treatment, this should draw Christians into action in hopes of being the conduit of God's healing and delivering and transforming power.

A Paradigm of the Politics of the Reign of God: Care for the Vulnerable Refugee or Undocumented Immigrant

Christian ethicist Luke Bretherton describes the widespread phenomenon, throughout the world, of refugees labelled, stigmatized, and made scapegoats such that empathy towards them is diminished.[59] Such dehumanizing processes facilitate the tragic inversion whereby the humanness, the vulnerability, and powerlessness of refugees, asylum seekers, and economically-desperate, unauthorized migrants becomes the basis for viewing such persons as dirt or pollution, as threats of contamination. Georgio Agamben has argued that both the Jewish people under Nazi rule and contemporary refugees have been reduced to the status signified in ancient Roman law's legal category of *homo sacer*. The *homo sacer* was someone, such as a slave, who could be killed with impunity. The *homo sacer* was "bare life," someone who exists in a social space without protection, exposed to death, and excluded or banned from participation in the human community.[60] A paradigmatic example was the Supreme Court decision in the 1994 case *Sale v. Haitian Centers Council*. The court held that it was neither a violation of US domestic law nor of international law to interdict Haitian boats filled with asylum seekers before they reached US territorial waters and to return them to Haiti without assessment of their asylum claims.[61] While the United States government did not kill these asylum seekers from Haiti, they were regarded as persons to whom the government had no obligation to welcome or protect. Therefore, they were returned to a life-threatening situation.

59. Bretherton, "Duty of Care to Refugees," 50–51.
60. Agamben, *Homo Sacer*.
61. *Sale v. Haitian Centers Council, Inc.*, 509 US 155 (1993).

Both unofficial rhetoric and US policy toward undocumented immigrants from Mexico are another example of regarding some lives as outside the pale of compassionate human concern. Border security and a legal process by which persons seeking entry into the nation are documented is a legitimate concern. However, US immigration policy is driven not simply by this legitimate concern but by a vicious dehumanization of persons who cross the border illegally.

Physician and cultural anthropologist Seth Holmes spent a significant amount of time in community with undocumented migrants from among the Triqui people, an indigenous people from the mountains of Oaxaca, Mexico. He did so in order to study the realities of illegal border crossing. These persons, he argues, are forced to migrate out of sheer desperation, in order for themselves and their families merely to survive. It would be riskier, Holmes argues, to stay in their hometown of San Miguel without work, money, or food. As one Triqui man put it, "There is no other option left for us."[62]

In the case of undocumented migrant farmworkers, it is difficult to imagine anyone making the "choice" to work twelve hours a day, bent over picking berries, exposed to pesticides, and suffering severe back, knee, and joint pain and permanent injury. Due to their vulnerability, undocumented immigrants "face high rates of substandard wages, wage theft, disproportionately unsafe working conditions, sexual harassment, and death and injury on the job." Undocumented workers in factories, food services, and agriculture frequently report denial of access to bathrooms or bathroom breaks, lack of allowances for tending to emergencies, and illegal discrimination due to pregnancy. Fear of reprisals, especially family separation due to deportation and fear of being terminated from a job, effectively deters any resistance to poor treatment, unjust conditions, and rampant wage theft.[63]

Holmes contends that our framing of the issue of crossing the border illegally as a choice legitimates contempt for undocumented immigrants as willful lawbreakers and therefore justifies a lack of concern for those who die. By labeling persons as illegal, undocumented immigrants are categorized as simply criminals. Once this rhetorical maneuver has been made, such persons are deemed to be deserving of punitive measures. Nevins points to the language employed by Senator Alan Simpson, who stated, in praise of the Senate's passage of the Immigration and Financial Responsibility Act of

---

62. Holmes, *Fresh Fruit, Broken Bodies*, 21–30.

63. Holmes, *Fresh Fruit, Broken Bodies*, 21–30; Heyer, *Kinship across Borders*, 12; Nevins, *Operation Gatekeeper and Beyond*, 153, 167, 187–88.

1996, "We have stuff in there that has everything but the rack and screws for people who are violating the laws of the United States."[64]

The treatment of undocumented immigrants from Mexico and other nations in Central America as *homo sacer* is manifested in US immigration policy, which, since 1994, has channeled the flow of unauthorized migrants away from heavily populated areas to more sparsely inhabited ones, where it is more difficult to cross. Border Patrol and US public officials initially expected that a simple cost-benefit analysis would lead migrants to decide to forego the risks and remain in Mexico. However, the effort to deter illegal border crossing by making it more difficult has not succeeded. There has been no significant impact on the propensity of would-be migrants to attempt the journey. Even after recognizing that few were deterred, the United States continued policies and strategies of border enforcement that led desperate people to take death-defying risks. Since the early 1990s, thousands of persons have died crossing the US-Mexican border because of the US Border Patrol strategy of rerouting immigrants toward the most dangerous terrains.[65] Since the mid-1990s, deaths of border crossers have occurred at a rate of at least one every twenty-four hours.[66]

When humans suffer on this scale, Christians should recognize, as participants in the in-breaking reign of God, that we are called to resist the powers that create this suffering and to participate in deeds of deliverance. We should mirror the moral passion of persons like Joseph Nevins, an Associate Professor of Geography at Vassar College. In the course of his research for his book *Operation Gatekeeper and Beyond*, he was riding along with Border Patrol agents in eastern New Mexico. In the pre-dawn hours, they apprehended a Mexican family who had crossed the border illegally, not for the purposes of residing in the United States but to scavenge in a garbage dump in order to bring materials back to their hometown in Ciudad Juarez to sell. After seeing the family arrested and herded into the van, Nevins shared his sense of the cruelty of it all when he wrote, "It pained me to witness the arrest of these seven human beings—for the crime of trying to survive poverty."[67] I do not know whether Nevins would identify himself as religious or as Christian. However, his moral vision, at least in this respect, is much more aligned with that of Jesus than many self-identified Christians. Nevins asserts that (undocumented) "immigrants are first and

64. Holmes, *Fresh Fruit, Broken Bodies*, 21–30; Heyer, *Kinship across Borders*, 136; Nevins, *Operation Gatekeeper and Beyond*, 177–78.

65. Nevins, *Operation Gatekeeper and Beyond*, 160, 174, 200; Heyer, *Kinship across Borders*, 8–9; Cade, "Water Is Life!," 261.

66. Holmes, *Fresh Fruit, Broken Bodies*, 8–9.

67. Nevins, *Operation Gatekeeper and Beyond*, 216–17.

foremost human beings who—regardless of their legal status—deserve our respect and solidarity, rather than poverty wages, or a potential death sentence."[68] Nevins speaks of a transformation of vision whereby we come to see people from the other side of the border as our neighbors rather than constructing them in our fearful imagination as faceless masses to be feared and repelled.

"No More Deaths" (No Mas Muertes)

The Spirit and the spirit[69] Jesus poured out into the world has spread far beyond sanctuary walls. A paradigmatic example of the incursion of the reign of God is, ironically, the efforts of "No More Deaths" (No Mas Muertes). This organization was formed to respond to the humanitarian crisis caused by US immigration policy. In this organization's political activism and service to undocumented immigrants, one cannot fail to hear the echo of Matt 25:31–46 and the parable of the Good Samaritan.

"No More Deaths" is an official ministry of the Unitarian Universalist Church of Tucson, Arizona. While I affirm Nicene orthodoxy, "No More Deaths" may be significantly more faithful than many Christians who fail to grasp the implications of professing the full divinity and humanity of Jesus Christ. Hans Frei argued that christological doctrine should function as a heuristic aid that serves the Christian community best when it thrusts readers back into the stories themselves.[70] If Jesus is fully divine, he reveals *God's* character and purposes. The Jesus who is also fully human reveals God's will and purposes *for human life*. The Jesus who is the savior is the one who saves by inaugurating the reign of God that puts all things right. If salvation is participation in this eschatological new creation, already arriving, intruding, and conflicting with the powers of death and destruction, then No More Deaths is shaped by the way of Jesus Christ, even if the more faithful doctrinal affirmation is lacking. The actions of this group conform to the shape of participation in the reign of God, which is indicated in texts

---

68. Nevins, *Operation Gatekeeper and Beyond*, 216–17.

69. By spirit (lower case), I refer to the ethos or the moral vision that inspires a multitude of human persons, whether explicitly Christian or not, to show compassion for human need and desperation. While Christian history includes horrendous episodes of cruelty and support for injustice, many Christians through the ages also carried and enacted a beautiful ideal of love, compassion, and action for the vulnerable. This ideal has influenced persons throughout the world who may not yet profess faith in Christ, but who nonetheless, are drawn by the Holy Spirit to do the kinds of deeds that are the work of God's reign.

70. Frei, *Types of Christian Theology*, 126.

like Matt 25:31–46 and Luke 10:25–37. Here we see courageous men and women who have given drink to the thirsty, food to the hungry, clothes to the poorly shod, hospitality to strangers, and have visited those in prison. As such, they have done what Jesus said to do.

Recalling the parable of the good Samaritan, the remote corridors where undocumented immigrants have been funneled into the desert regions of Arizona is a contemporary "Jericho Road" where travelers are vulnerable to thieves and to the natural elements that are equally deadly. Undocumented immigrants would not traverse these dangerous spaces unless they were desperate economically or threatened in other ways in their home countries in Central America. In the desert, there is lack of access to potable water for hours or days at a time and an inability to carry enough water to survive during remote and prolonged travel. The result is often dehydration and death or illnesses associated with dehydration. Often, these persons drink contaminated water in remote areas from sources such as ponds and cattle tanks. There is a lack of access to food, sometimes for days at a time. There is the reality of rattlesnake bites and scorpion stings. These persons face extreme temperature and temperature variations. Exposure to prolonged high heat and direct sunlight during the day intensifies the risk of dehydration and heat-related illnesses. Exposure to prolonged cold temperature at night, rain, snow, and severe storm conditions, results in cold related illnesses. Sprains, strains, fractures, blisters, muscle cramping, musculoskeletal soreness and pain, head, neck, and back pain, or injury are not merely sources of physical discomfort. Any of these injuries can result in an inability to stay up with the group with which one is traveling and the survival resources the group may be transporting. All of these situations, resulting in medical distress, are exacerbated by the lack of access to medical care. Undocumented immigrants face the threat of death and destruction because they are also vulnerable to physical and/or sexual assault by human traffickers, civilian militias, Border Patrol agents, and financial demands by organized crime circuits that may be reinforced by death threats to persons and family members.[71]

"No More Deaths" is best known for placing water in the Arizona desert. Volunteers leave water, food, socks, blankets, and other supplies. Under the direction of the medical team, volunteers provide emergency first-aid treatment to individuals in distress. No More Deaths aligns its relief work in accordance with the International Committee of the Red Cross's principle that "relief aid must strive to reduce future vulnerabilities to disaster as well

---

71. No More Deaths, "Foundations of Borderlands Humanitarian Relief"; Holmes, *Fresh Fruit, Broken Bodies*, 8–9.

as meeting basic needs." The organization is based upon the core conviction that everyone who crosses the southern border is a human being, deserving of basic dignity. In accordance with the principles of humanity, neutrality, impartiality, and independence, No More Deaths seeks to uphold the United Nations OCHA mandate that all humanitarian action be provided independent from political and military objectives.[72]

The organization also seeks to document abuses committed by governmental and nongovernmental actors. Legal resources are made available, including information about the requirements for asylum or visas, access to immigration attorneys, and information about the process of immigration arrest and detention.[73]

Conflicts with the powers that deal death, in this case, US immigration policy, have resulted. No More Deaths volunteers have been arrested, though they have escaped prosecution thus far. Border Patrol agents arrested Scott Warren on the basis of an erroneous claim that he was helping migrants evade custody. Prosecutors charged Warren with two counts of harboring undocumented immigrants and one count of conspiracy to harbor and transport.[74] But all Warren had actually done was provide lifesaving aid. In other words, Scott Warren was arrested for doing what Jesus called all Christians to do: follow the paradigmatic example of the Good Samaritan, who took action to save life when a person was at grave risk of dying after being beaten and left for dead. Warren provided shelter, food, and first aid to migrants who could have died in the Arizona desert.

---

72. No More Deaths, "Foundations of Borderlands Humanitarian Relief."
73. No More Deaths, "Foundations of Borderlands Humanitarian Relief."
74. Carroll, "Eight Activists Helping Migrants Cross Brutal Desert"; Aguilera, "Humanitarian Scott Warren Found Not Guilty"; Aguilera, "They Tried to Save the Lives of Immigrants."

Thankfully, No More Deaths volunteers have not yet been subjected to serious criminal penalties. In 2017, a federal judge reversed the convictions of four members of the organization, finding that members were exercising "sincere religious beliefs," in accordance with the Religious Freedom Restoration act of 1993, when they placed water and food for migrants in Arizona's protected Cabeza Prieta National Wildlife Refuge, an area of desert wilderness where people frequently die of dehydration and exposure in the summer heat. Ingram, "Judge Reverses Convictions."

Apocalyptic Discontinuity Is Not Stark Antithesis: Seeking First the Kingdom of God and Its Righteousness and the Good of the Nation

If resources for a better vision of ecclesial faithfulness are to be found within an apocalyptic theological imagination, we must qualify and "nuance" the metaphorical imagery of "intrusion" or "invasion" by the kingdom of God. God's reign is indeed a disruptive invasion of the world in its bondage to death-dealing powers. God's reign arrives to break the power of evil and set persons free. This language is indispensable. However, we must also guard against the power of this imaginative language to create a picture of total rupture, total discontinuity, and stark antithesis between human cultures and societies and the reign of God. A corresponding ecclesiological model would indeed be a "sectarian" practice that seeks, as much as is possible, to escape from human society or an aggressive stance of sharp and relentless opposition and denunciation.

However, radical apocalyptic discontinuity is not stark antithesis. There is a sharp antithesis is between the reign of God and the enslaving powers. But there is not a sharp antithesis between the reign of God and all that belongs to human societies and cultures. As Miroslav Volf has argued, we cannot describe the church-world relationship in terms of either fundamental commensurability or principled incommensurability of value systems.[75] Barry Harvey points to Dietrich Bonhoeffer's categories of the "natural" as those practices and products of the "earthly city" which, after the Fall, remain open to Christ and the messianic reign of God, and the "unnatural" as those aspects of human societies and institutions that are refusals of Christ and the reign of God. Of course, the natural and the unnatural, creational goodness and sin, are so intertwined that they cannot be neatly or tidily differentiated.[76] Kathryn Tanner has called attention to the reality that cultures and societies are not self-enclosed, monolithic, and internally self-consistent "systems" of beliefs and values but rather sites of contestation.[77]

Christians in the United States would be wise to avoid two positions that would disfigure the ecclesial witness to Christ and his reign. Efforts to achieve cultural and political dominance, to "impose" a singular Christian vision upon a pluralistic society, will not result in transformation. On the other hand, too much rapprochement with modernity's privatization of

---

75. Volf, "Soft Difference," 26–29.
76. Harvey, "Preserving the World for Christ," 64–82.
77. Tanner, *Theories of Culture*.

religion, resulting in the church positioning itself as a sub-system and the civic and political life of the nation construed as the "real" public project, prevents the way of the reign of God from presenting itself in its distinctive character. On this approach, another project and agenda takes precedence; the reign of God is kept in a place of subservience to the project and agenda of the nation.

But if the ecclesial communions that belong to the body of Christ seek first God's reign, the agenda is, first and foremost, human flourishing. This means that the political agenda of a faithful ecclesial community is neither Republican nor Democratic, neither America First nor a liberal and progressive America. Rather, there is a place for exerting influence and pressure on political leaders and seeking to influence the moral imagination of persons in our society in order to nudge the needle closer to policies and outcomes that are more rather than less compatible with God's purposes for human wholeness as opposed to policies that are dramatically inconsistent with a deep Christian moral vision. This means that we might advocate for more humane immigration policies and more compassionate treatment for asylum seekers, an end to mass incarceration, stronger safety nets for the working poor, etc. If we advocate for political policies and outcomes, the goal should not be to be good liberals or progressives but rather the care of human beings in distress or threatened with misery or death.

If we approach these issues with an apocalyptic soteriological imagination, and if we look to Jesus as portrayed in the Gospels to discern the shape and agenda of the reign of God, it also crucial that we also think about these issues in a pneumatological key. The Spirit is not confined to the life of the Christian community. D. Lyle Dabney calls for a recognition of the Spirit's ubiquitous and mysterious presence and activity throughout creation and human existence. He argues that the Bible bears witness to the wider work of the Holy Spirit, including activity of the Spirit that "precedes" and prepares for the word of God. From the Spirit's hovering over the waters in preparation for the utterance of God's creative word (Gen 1:1–3), to the Spirit's activity in the ministry of the prophets, to Jesus's conception by the Spirit, the Spirit's presence and activity is presupposed by the utterance of the Word. Jesus's messianic mission was dependent on his anointing by the Holy Spirit (Luke 3:21–22; 4:16–21).[78] If the Holy Spirit is the eschatological Spirit, in whose power Jesus the Messiah performs and embodies the reign of God, it is also important to bear in mind the Johannine affirmation that

---

78. D. Lyle Dabney argues that the western theological tradition has been marked by a pronounced tendency to subordinate pneumatology to Christology and, consequently, to limit the Spirit's role to the subjective appropriation in faith of the objective work of Christ. Dabney, "Justified by the Spirit," 46–68.

Politics of Salvation as Participation in God's Eschatological/Apocalyptic Intrusion

the Spirit's activity in the world is that of convicting of sin and drawing the world toward Christ (John 15:25; 16:8–15). If the Spirit's work is to draw to Christ, the Spirit's work is, by definition, that of drawing the world in the direction of eschatological transformation. Therefore, we should be open to the possibility that eschatological novelty and transformation may erupt unexpectedly from within the interstices of the world beyond the boundaries of the church. This is not the organic unfolding or development of possibilities latent within the old order of things, which is, as St. Paul points out, passing away (1 Cor 7:31). Rather, it is the transfiguration of the old as the Spirit makes possible unanticipated transformations within our world. This indicates that there are possibilities of eschatological transformation at multiple points of intersection between ecclesial communions and the wide varieties of social orders inhabited by God's people. The Spirit—who, like the wind, blows where the Spirit wishes, beyond human control or confinement—is the eschatological power of God, confined neither to the church nor to the inner life of Christians. Rather, when genuinely positive transformation happens in human history, it is to be attributed to the power of the Holy Spirit, opening up new possibilities for human flourishing, reconciliation of enemies, peace, justice, food for the hungry, healing for the sick, and fragments of social justice.

The Unpredictability of Apocalyptic Irruptions

Political theorist Sheldon Wolin provides a helpful way of imagining the "potentially" apocalyptic character of social action that is oriented toward human well-being and resistance to injustices that harm. Wolin argues that neither the United States nor other modern liberal democracies are truly democratic or genuinely responsive to the citizenry. The state lacks sufficient autonomy to tame the worst excesses of the market or to serve as our primary hope for alleviating grotesque economic inequalities and other social injustices. This is because the politics of a liberal society allow those who control economic power to promote corporate interests through the political process.[79]

Real democracy, he argues, lies not with the orchestrated performances of the American electoral process, which are contests between candidates who have curried the most favor from powerful and wealthy interests. Wolin argues that "real democracy" has a certain "fugitive" character, laden with certain quasi-apocalyptic possibilities whenever people come together

---

79. Wolin, "Fugitive Democracy," 13–14, 18–19, 22–23; *Politics and Vision*, 401, 526, 564–65, 578, 600–603; Villegas, "Fugitive Democracy."

Section Five: Justice as Participation in the Eschatological New Creation

temporarily in acts of resistance against particular injustices. The possibility of renewal rests in the fact that ordinary individuals are capable of creating new cultural patterns of commonality at any moment. Individuals who concert their powers for low-income housing, worker ownership of factories, better schools, better health care, safer water, controls over toxic waste disposals, and a thousand other common concerns of ordinary lives experience a democratic moment and contribute to the discovery, care, and tending of a commonality of shared concerns. When people come together and discover shared grievances or needs, local democratic movements might explode into a wildfire that spreads to the centers of power and exerts pressure on the ruling powers. Sometimes the unanticipated and "unanticipatable" happens: an "apocalyptic spark" generates profound transformation, as happened in the abolitionist and civil rights movements, the Populist and agrarian revolts of the nineteenth century, and the struggles for autonomous trade unions and women's rights.[80]

Could there be some overlap or convergence, albeit imperfect, in some circumstances, between what Wolin described as the fugitive character of democracy, which he characterized as an apocalyptic spark that cannot be managed or controlled, and the work of the Holy Spirit in human history? The *missio Dei* is to go and make disciples, teaching them to do all that Jesus commanded. What Jesus commanded is to feed the hungry, to resist oppressive powers that crush and dehumanize, to rescue persons at risk of death and destruction, and to deliver humans from the powers that inflict suffering and dehumanize human persons. When we are faithful to this mission, we cannot control all of the outcomes. Our task is to be faithful in the struggle in order that we might be conduits, in the Spirit, of the transformative work of the Spirit as the eschatological power of God. Sometimes, struggles seem to bear little fruit beyond temporary relief to human persons crushed under the wheels of oppressive systems and powers. But sometimes, faithfulness in the struggle is the conduit through which transformation erupts suddenly and unpredictably.

Fifty to sixty years later, we narrate the American civil rights movement as a triumphant success, a breakthrough in American social and political life. In spite of the ongoing pervasive realities of racial discrimination and systemic racial injustices, the civil rights movement resulted nonetheless in true transformation. But it is easy to forget all of the years of slow, meticulous labor that preceded the most prominent victories of the civil rights movement. While Dr. Martin Luther King Jr. deserves the respect and admiration he has received for his courageous leadership role in

---

80. Wolin, "Fugitive Democracy," 23–24, 39; Villegas, "Fugitive Democracy."

several major campaigns of the movement, he was not alone. For example, the Montgomery Bus Boycott happened because of the slow and patient labors of women like JoAnn Gibson Robinson, a professor at Alabama State University and a member of the Women's Political Council ("WPC"), a civic organization composed of African-American professional women. Five years before Rosa Parks's courageous refusal to relinquish her seat on a Montgomery bus, Robinson had been verbally attacked by a city bus driver for sitting in the "whites only" section of the bus. The WPC complained to Montgomery city leaders about the unfair seating arrangements on city buses and abusive driver conduct. After these concerns were repeatedly dismissed, Robinson and the organization started patiently laying plans for a bus boycott. It was because of their quiet preparatory labors over the course of several years that the African-American community had the organizational and communication infrastructure to spring into action in 1955 after Rosa Parks's arrest. Robinson and the WPC copied tens of thousands of leaflets and distributed them across the city, calling for a one-day boycott. The success of the one day boycott gave rise to the establishment of the Montgomery Improvement Association ("MIA") and the selection of Dr. Martin Luther King Jr. as the MIA's president.[81]

In 1955, a bus boycott in a small southern city would not have seemed promising as a movement with potential to impact the nation with respect to racial justice. The objectives of the movement were incredibly modest: to achieve a fair system of bus seating arrangements. Indeed, initially, the Montgomery Bus Boycott did not request an end to segregated seating. It merely asked that African Americans seated in the African-American section of the bus not have to relinquish their seats to white riders when the bus was crowded. But the faithfulness in this small, local, and, at first glance, insignificant struggle for basic human dignity was a tiny spark that was caught up within an apocalyptic intrusion of the Spirit and ignited a much larger, transformative fire, even if the struggle for racial justice is far from complete.

---

81. "Jo Ann Robinson."

CHAPTER THIRTEEN

Eschatological Hope, Apocalyptic Soteriology, and the Struggle for Justice and Human Dignity and Flourishing

Anamnestic Solidarity, the Longing for the Wholly Other, and the Redemption of the Past

Christian hope for the life to come is often placed in opposition to passionate struggle and engagement on behalf of justice and goodness in this world. Both Christians and non-Christians can fall prey to this binary. In his famous statement, "[Religion] is the opium of the people," Marx's point was that religion exists as a mode of illusory happiness, but as such, it gives expression to a protest against real oppression. Marx's brief comments conveyed his belief that the abolition of the conditions, that is, the economic injustices that produced suffering, would lead to the end of the need for religion's illusions.[1] While Marx did not directly claim that eschatological hope inhibited commitment to a just world "here on earth," others have, including one of the most famous utopian anthems of the previous generation.

Christian eschatological hope has indeed sometimes functioned to undermine commitment to the struggle for a more humane world and to facilitate indifference to human misery. However, I will argue that it should have the opposite effect.

One need not be Marxist, as I am not, to appreciate the profundity of the ways in which Walter Benjamin and Max Horkheimer, associated

---

1. Marx, "Contribution to the Critique of Hegel's Philosophy of Right."

in different ways with the Frankfurt School, wrestled with the theme of "anamnestic solidarity." Marx was deeply critical of the English and French revolutions for seeking legitimacy by donning the mantles of their historical predecessors.[2] Max Horkheimer, Theodor Adorno, and Walter Benjamin departed from Karl Marx's rejection of memory as a resource for radical social action and instead sought to uphold the importance of past generations that struggled for liberation and, as a consequence, suffered persecution, torture, and death.[3] Horkheimer, Adorno, and Benjamin, while unable to profess a belief in God, also seemed unable to relinquish both the question of God and the longing for God.

Horkheimer pointed out that even if a better society were to overcome the present social disorder and injustice, it would not make good past misery.[4] On the one hand, Horkheimer believed that history is closed. The dead are dead and there is nothing that can undo what has happened to them.[5] But, he suggested, it would be horrendous ingratitude to forget the dead. The correct relationship with the dead requires remembrance of their sufferings, their hopes of redemption, and their happiness, which was destroyed due to the same powers of domination and destruction that distort and destroy the lives of people today. Their memory is kept alive by a social praxis of hope for the "Other," a better, happier, and more humane future society.[6]

Walter Benjamin was also concerned with this solidarity with generations of the oppressed. Benjamin feared that in its anxiety to liberate the grandchildren, progressivist ideology risks alienating us from the sufferings, and the memory of the sufferings, of our downtrodden ancestors, who cannot be liberated but at least can be remembered.[7]

Christian Lenhardt has identified the paradox of anamnestic solidarity.[8] If the future liberated generation, through remembrance, pays its debt to past generations and keeps solidarity with the "innocently annihilated," how can this liberated future be truly happy? The future liberated generation is acutely aware of its inability to redeem the past and make a difference for those who have been irretrievably lost to death and failed to live to see

---

2. Clements, "Marxism and the God Question," 22.
3. Simpson, "*Theologia Crucis* and the Forensically Fraught World," 177–78.
4. Horkheimer, *Die Sehnsucht*, cited by Moltmann, *Crucified God*, 224.
5. Ott, "Max Horkheimer's Critical Theory of Religion," 115.
6. Horkheimer and Adorno, *Dialectic of Enlightenment*, 215; Ott, "Max Horkheimer's Critical Theory of Religion," 115–16.
7. Beiner, "Walter Benjamin's Philosophy of History," 429; Simpson, "*Theologia Crucis* and the Forensically Fraught World," 177.
8. Lenhardt, "Anamnestic Solidarity," 133–54.

Section Five: Justice as Participation in the Eschatological New Creation

the glorious future. Genuine anamnestic solidarity will lead to a profound sorrow for those who are irretrievably lost. But if, in order to preserve happiness, this future generation forgets the past, innocently-annihilated generation, it is not truly liberated because it has severed its solidarity with past generations through its self-induced amnesia.[9]

Neither Horkheimer nor Benjamin could arrive at the place of confession of belief in God, but they also could not relinquish the question of God or the longing for God. Horkheimer argued that while there is no theistic answer to the question of suffering and injustice, there is simultaneously no atheistic possibility of being content with the world. He believed it impossible to believe in the existence of an omnipotent and all-gracious God because of the pervasiveness of suffering and injustice. But he insisted that it is also impossible not to long for truth and righteousness and for that which provides them. Horkheimer spoke of the longing for the "Wholly Other," which he never quite defined, but he linked this phrase to the ideal of a perfectly just, human, and humane world. Horkheimer stated that the quintessence of his critical theory of society was religious and theological in character: the longing that the murderer should not triumph over his innocent victim, at least not ultimately.[10] For Horkheimer, the very possibility of the struggle for a more just and humane world is a "non-scientific wish," the hope that earthly horror does not possess the last word.[11] Adorno and Horkheimer argued that the historical struggle for a better future society is based on the human hope and longing for the "Totally Other," that injustice and horror will not have the last word; that there will be a "Judgment Day" in which the innocent victims will have their day in court. Horkheimer acknowledges that this hope is a religious statement of indictment of the oppressive injustice of the social world, an "unscientific longing" that this injustice will ultimately be overcome by a "Totally Other."[12]

Walter Benjamin also addressed the longing to redeem the past. In thesis IX of his *Theses on the Philosophy of History*, Benjamin reimagines a Klee painting entitled *Angelus Novus*, which portrays an angel looking intensely at something, his mouth open and his wings spread. Benjamin states that this is how he pictures the angel of history. He gaze is transfixed on the past. What we see as a chain of events, the angel sees as one single

---

9. Simpson, "*Theologia Crucis* and the Forensically Fraught World," 177–78; Lenhardt, "Anamnestic Solidarity," 133–54; Peukert, *Science, Action, and Fundamental Theology*, 187, 208–9.

10. Horkheimer, *Die Sehnsucht*, 56–58, cited by Moltmann, *Crucified God*, 223–25, and Siebert et al., "Critical Theory of Religion," 39.

11. Horkheimer, "Foreword," xi–xii.

12. Horkheimer and Adorno, *Dialectic of Enlightenment*, 225.

catastrophe in which wreckage piles up upon wreckage. This angel, Benjamin imaginatively suggests, would like to awaken the dead and make whole that which has been smashed. But the wind has forced his wings open and he cannot close them as the wind propels him into the future. He can only watch as the wreckage continues to accumulate.[13]

On Not Relinquishing Eschatological Hope

Under the pressures of modernity, some Christians have jettisoned hope for life beyond our deaths and have often appropriated a modern narrative of inevitable progress, hoping to be "on the right side of history" and riding the wave of progress into the future by building the kingdom of God on earth. Some, though certainly not all, liberationist projects have adopted a similar stance. Marit Trelstad describes this theological sensibility in many of the essays in a book she edited about the atonement. In these essays, she points out, salvation is conceived in social categories rather than primarily emphasizing the salvation of individual souls for an afterlife. Salvation is construed as this-worldly liberation from injustice and oppression. "Even as Jesus was resurrected, oppressed people can be assured that repressive economic systems and tyrannical governments do not have the last word."[14]

If this trajectory is followed all the way and salvation is construed exclusively as this-worldly liberation from oppression, as opposed to any genuine eschatological hope, the implications are significant. In light of a long human history of injustice and oppression, which "progressive" forces in history have yet to dislodge, interpreting the resurrection as a powerful symbol offering hope and assurance to oppressed people that repressive economic systems and tyrannical governments do not have the last word seems no less utopian, no less "pie in the bye and bye," than does hope for a life to come in which all things are rectified.

The first danger of jettisoning eschatological hope under the pressures of modernity is that building a just and humane world depends in its entirety upon humanity. The God who cannot raise the dead is, at most, merely a cosmic cheerleader for our entirely human project. For example, Richard Hays is sharply critical of the "non-apocalyptic Jesus" produced by the scholarship of Robert Funk, Marcus Borg, and their fellow travelers. Hays points out that this Jesus offers no hope beyond the grave, no promise of an eschatological rescue of humanity from death and injustice. But the

---

13. Benjamin, "Theses on the Philosophy of History," 257–58.
14. Trelstad, "Introduction," 15.

Section Five: Justice as Participation in the Eschatological New Creation

implication is that the fate of the human race lies in our own hands. Given human history, this should not inspire confidence.[15]

Second, as noted in the previous section, anamnestic solidarity means that even if a just and peaceful social order is truly achieved in the future, that just society cannot redeem the sufferings of the past or deliver justice and life to those who died as victims of injustice. The price of happiness in such a utopian future means "abandoning" the dead by forgetting them and their sufferings. This severs human solidarity and is a failure to love as the dead are consigned to nothingness.

While Horkheimer, Benjamin, Adorno, and Lenhardt could not embrace a belief in a God who will bring about an eschatological justice, Christians should not relinquish our eschatological hope in the God who raised Jesus. Otherwise, there is not much left in the Christian faith that is worth bothering over. If the only hope is for what is humanly achievable, God-talk is merely decoration and makes no real difference. St. Paul made a similar, even if not identical, point in 1 Cor 15:17–19. Absent eschatological hope, if Christianity is but a symbol system inspiring progressive social action, what is left that is worth bothering over?

The challenge is to find a way to maintain eschatological hope, to inhabit and navigate the "already-not yet tension" in ways that underwrite rather than undermine commitment to struggles for justice, for a better world in the present age.

First we must eschew the notion that we have been given, via divine revelation, a blueprint that explains the relationship of human history to the eschatological culmination of all things. Both narratives of inevitable decline and narratives of progress represent efforts to impose an intelligible pattern upon the course of human history. For example, Pre-Millenial Dispensationalism is linked with a declension narrative that treats efforts for social change as equivalent to repairing the furniture on the Titanic. To the extent that Pre-Millenial Dispensationalists have embraced political engagement, as is the case with the American religious right, the agenda has been cultural and political dominance rather than justice and compassion for the poor and destitute.

---

15. Hays acerbically adds, "It is no accident that these new scholarly visions of a non-eschatological Jesus have found their most enthusiastic reception in their natural sociological and theological home: a dwindling but affluent liberal Protestant church in North America seeking some way to reconnect with a kinder, gentler Jesus who will offer them new spiritual stimulation without threatening them with God's final judgment" (Hays, "Why Do You Stand Looking Up," 121–22).

Optimistic narratives of inevitable human progress also break down if we simply recognize the persistence of radical evil in human history.[16] The twentieth century began with the hope that it would be "the Christian century," in which human progress coalesced with efforts to build the kingdom of God on earth. The next 123 years saw two world wars, the Nazi Holocaust, Stalin's murder of millions of Ukrainians by famine in the early 1930s, Mao's cultural revolution, genocides in Rwanda, Sudan, Croatia, Cambodia, Myanamar, and in the present, Russia's invasion of Ukraine.

Therefore, it is important to insist upon a kind of apophatic reserve, to insist that we know precious little about what the Christian tradition has referred to as "the second coming of Jesus Christ." Jesus refused to answer the disciples' questions as to when he would restore the kingdom to Israel (Acts 1:1–8). The disciples were not asking the wrong question. It was merely a question that God has chosen not to answer. God has not given us any comprehensive blueprint as to the unfolding of human history. We are, literally, inside of a story. Its present and future unfolding and its overarching trajectory are far from fully comprehensible.

There is another way in which we often "imagine" the life to come that is "disabling." It is easy to imagine a return of Christ in which, magically, as it were, everything is instantly put right. This might imply that all human action and struggle for a just world within human history, prior to this eschatological culminating event, are ultimately irrelevant. On this picture, it is as if all of our efforts to show compassion and kindness, to be agents of repair, healing, and transformation are, when Christ returns, washed away like sandcastles on the beach. On this picture, our actions within the present life have no ultimate or eschatological purchase.

N. T. Wright has argued that the Christian calling is not to "build the kingdom of God," but to "build for" the kingdom of God. Wright points to St. Paul's encouragement to the Christians in Corinth to excel in their work for the Lord. Then he adds the observation that "your labor in the Lord is not in vain" (1 Cor 15:58). Ironically, this word of encouragement follows a lengthy discussion of Christian hope for a future beyond death, the

---

16. The poplar rhetorical trope about being "on the right side of history" illustrates the persistence of this progressivist imagination regarding inevitable progress. But if there is no inevitable progress, the judgment of any future generation on the past and its own present is not necessarily a more enlightened moral perspective. From a Christian perspective, "the right side of history" is ultimately a matter of God's eschatological judgment on human history. Of course, within the flow of history, "we" must make moral assessments about right and wrong, but must do so with a humility that acknowledges our limited vantage point and our vulnerabilities to our individual and group pride, self-interests, and group self-righteousness, all of which distort our judgments.

resurrection of our bodies. Instead of concluding this section on our future hope with an admonition to turn our attention from earth to heaven, Paul encourages the Corinthians to be engaged in God's work in the here and now. Wright argues that God's future purposes do not wipe away the work we do in the present for God's cause. Rather, he argues that whatever we do out of love for God in Christ and for the sake of the neighbor, whether it is feeding the hungry, working for a more just and equitable educational system, the end of mass incarceration, or the mentoring of an at-risk child, will last into eternity, will find its way into the New Jerusalem.[17]

Perhaps our struggles to be conduits of God's reign of love and justice in the present, beyond our ability to comprehend from where we currently stand within the unfinished story, contributes to God's final victory, to Christ's completion of the new world of eschatological justice, love, and peace. This image of "building for" the kingdom of God provides a powerful incentive to struggle as if what we do has an eternal significance we cannot yet discern. Somehow, God takes our contributions throughout history and weaves them into the new world Christ will bring about. The basis for this hope is our incorporation, by the Spirit, into Christ who is the *autobasileia*. If we have already been drawn into the reign of God, then our Spirit-enabled human efforts and action are already situated inside of the rectification of the world that has already been initiated by Jesus Christ.

A Paradigm for Reflection on Salvation as God's Intrusion on the Old Order

Salvation is ultimately the rectification of all things when all things are brought into subjection to Christ and all things are brought into union with Christ. But if this is salvation, we must remember that Christ inaugurated the "arriving" of this eschatological new creation as an intrusion into the present age, in all of its disjointed brokenness and oppression, death, and suffering. If the anticipated messianic age is all things put right, then the intrusion of the eschatological new creation into the present, and our participation in that intrusion, must involve the struggle to put things right in the present.

We are called, in a profoundly cruciform fashion, to inhabit spaces where humans have been abandoned. In these spaces, mere hope may seem utopian. To struggle for precious human beings in these spaces requires some kind of hope for apocalyptic transformation that involves a breakthrough that is, humanly speaking, barely anticipatable or, perhaps better

17. Wright, *Surprised by Hope*, 207–15.

stated, not anticipatable for as far as is visible on the imminent horizon. But if we have the audacity to believe that God raised Jesus from the dead, then we believe that the power of the eschatological age to come has invaded the present evil age of suffering and death. This power, if unleashed into the present, is infinitely greater than our constricted imaginations with respect to what is possible. To believe that Jesus inaugurated the eschatological new creation is to believe in the possibility of the irruption of the eschatologically novel when we least expect or anticipate it.

In their powerful essay "Redeeming Justice," Rachel López, Terrell Carter, and Kempis Songster articulate a powerful argument that all humans have a "right to redemption," expressed as political opposition to sentences of life in prison without the possibility of parole.[18] They argue that no one is irredeemable; therefore, no one should be written off as beyond redemption through a life sentence without the possibility of parole. Lopez, Carter, and Songster argue that all humans have the capacity to forgive and be forgiven, to transform and to be transformed, and therefore all humans have a "right to redemption."[19]

Lopez is Associate Professor of Law at the Thomas R. Kline School of Law at Drexel University. Both Carter and Songster had been sentenced to life in prison without the possibility of parole. Songster served thirty years in prison before being resentenced and finally released, thanks to the Supreme Court's decision in *Miller v. Alabama*, 567 US 460 (2012), which held that mandatory life sentences for juveniles violate the Eighth Amendment.[20] Because Carter was a "young adult" when he committed his crime, he remains in prison, serving the thirtieth year of what is in fact a sentence of "death-by-incarceration."[21]

In West Philadelphia, Songster joined a street gang, selling drugs out of a crack house. One night, Songster killed someone during a fight. Even though he was only fifteen years old, he was tried as an adult and sentenced to life in a maximum security prison without the possibility of parole.[22] While in prison, Songster engaged in a spiritual struggle to come to terms with his action of taking another life. Songster asserts that he had blood on his hands that the next thirty years could never wash off. When he was released from prison, Songster searched for ways to atone for what years of scholarship, prayer, and meditation had enabled him to recognize as "the

18. Carter et al., "Redeeming Justice," 315–82.
19. Carter et al., "Redeeming Justice," 315–82; Brooks, "Lifers Speak Out."
20. *Miller v. Alabama*, 567 US 460 (2012).
21. Carter et al., "Redeeming Justice," 315.
22. Brooks, "Lifers Speak Out."

cosmic implications" of what he had done. He married and became a father. He started to work as an organizer for The Amistad Law Project, a West Philadelphia public interest law center working to end mass incarceration. Currently, he is the Program Director of Healing Futures, a restorative justice diversion program that helps youth in the criminal justice system ameliorate the harms they have caused through dialogue with their victims.[23]

The Right to Redemption Committee was formed in Graterford, one of Pennsylvania's State Correctional Institutions outside Philadelphia, by Terrell Carter and others sentenced to life in prison without the possibility of parole. Adopting a human rights framework, the Committee has claimed that there is a "right to redemption" because this capacity for transformation is something at the core of what it means to be a human person, something therefore belonging to all humans. The men on the committee sought to enable each other to reach redemption through accepting personal responsibility for the harms they caused and by making amends for their wrongs.[24]

The men on the committee assert that their own lives are illustrations of the fact of the human capacity for transformation. Through a collective process, the members of the committee struggled to come to terms with their past wrongs in order to find a path to redemption, in spite of the legal system's verdict that they were, in effect, beyond redemption.[25] For example, Carter has committed his life to becoming the best version of himself. He graduated from Villanova University and is working on a Master's degree in Creative Writing in order to tell his story in ways that may have a redemptive impact on others. He has also used his position as chairman of the Right to Redemption Committee to mentor young men in prison and to provide hospice care to those with terminal illnesses. "To help as many people as possible" is that which Carter identifies as his purpose in life. In spite of this personal transformation, the great tragedy is that the state has no meaningful mechanism to modify his sentence to reflect these changes simply because he was over the age of eighteen at the time of his crime.[26]

The Right to Redemption Committee's mission is to challenge the legal damnation of humans rooted in the denial of capacity for change. Of course, not everyone will change. But the implication of the right to redemption is that if someone does redeem himself or herself, then he or she should be considered for release. In *Miller v. Alabama*, the Supreme Court held that mandatory life sentences for juvenile offenders is cruel and

---

23. Brooks, "Lifers Speak Out."
24. Carter et al., "Redeeming Justice," 318.
25. Carter et al., "Redeeming Justice," 318.
26. Brooks, "Lifers Speak Out"; Carter et al., "Redeeming Justice," 320.

unusual punishment.[27] The Committee has argued for a need to go one step further and recognize that a sentence of life without the possibility of parole ("LWOP") is cruel and unusual punishment.[28]

Kempis Ghani Songster points out that he was once deemed so dangerous that he could never be free. But his life illustrates the possibility of redemption. The overwhelming majority of persons originally sentenced to life without the possibility of parole but released in Philadelphia after the decision in *Miller v. Alabama* have never committed another crime. A 2020 study conducted by researchers at Montclair State University found that only 1.14 percent of the 174 people released in Philadelphia post-*Miller* have committed crimes since their release. The state's judgment that these offenders were beyond redemption was wrong nearly 99 percent of the time. This study undermines fixed understandings of the dangerousness of "violent offenders" for the rest of their lives and raises serious doubts about the state's aptitude to make accurate determinations about future dangerousness at the time of sentencing.[29]

Through the Lens of an Apocalyptic Soteriology

In the late twentieth century public policymakers in the United States opted for a campaign of mass incarceration. Today, more than 200,000 persons are incarcerated for life, five times more persons than were serving life sentences in 1984. The exponential increase in life imprisonment was the result of changes in sentencing, which were the result of the rise of a much more punitive regime in criminal justice. This occurred, ironically, during a time in which violence in America was declining significantly. These policies were a response to public fears about crime, exacerbated by sensationalized media stories.[30]

Deep systemic injustice is baked into the criminal "justice" system. Racial and ethnic disparities shape outcomes from arrest to conviction to the sentencing process. One in five black men in prison is serving a life sentence. More than two-thirds of the persons serving a life sentence are African-American or Hispanic. On the whole, there are harsher sentencing outcomes when the person is black or Hispanic.[31] Mass incarceration

---

27. *Miller v. Alabama*, 567 US 460, at 490.
28. Carter et al., "Redeeming Justice," 321–22. Right to Redemption's Mission Statement is found at https://www.right2redemption.com.
29. Carter et al., "Redeeming Justice," 319.
30. Nellis, "No End in Sight"; Brooks, "Lifers Speak Out."
31. Nellis, "No End in Sight."

and our harshly retributive criminal justice system are powers destroying lives and communities and, disproportionately, African-American lives and communities. Racial biases, fears, and inequalities have driven the political powers to make this nation into a carceral state that imprisons 2.3 million people.[32]

The racial injustices built into the system are illustrated by the story of Michael Phillips, a thirty-two year old African-American man who pled guilty to the rape of a sixteen-year-old white girl at a motel in Dallas, Texas. Phillips was innocent. He was exonerated twenty-four years later by DNA evidence. But he pled guilty because his public defender, who did not investigate the charges against Phillips, advised him to take the plea deal instead of going to trial. He told Phillips that he would likely receive a life sentence because "no jury would believe a Black man over a white girl." Out of fear, Phillips took a plea bargain that reduced his sentence to twelve years in prison. He later expressed the sense of futility of insisting upon his innocence in the face of state institutions and actors convinced of his guilt: "The deck was stacked against me."[33]

To be sentenced to life in prison without the possibility of parole is to be deemed "irredeemable."[34] The "state," through its criminal justice system, "plays God" when it renders a verdict that is perilously close to an ultimate eschatological judgment upon a human person. A legal determination that a person is irredeemable transgresses the boundaries of law into the theological domain. If the foundational Christian confession is that Christ alone is qualified to be the eschatological judge of the living and the dead, then the judgment that another human is irredeemable is not ours to make.

This way of "playing God" is diametrically opposed to the way that God is God and the way that God deals with wayward humanity. God reveals Godself by breaking into the present evil age, which is a cruel dominion of closed systems of death and despair. God acts to break the shackles of evil into which precious human persons have been enslaved.

The powers of the present evil age are driven by a logic of domination, undergirded by the power to inflict death. Pontius Pilate gave expression to the "nothingness" upon which domination rests: the power to kill or otherwise diminish life. Pilate's last attempt to intimidate Jesus was his invocation of his power to kill Jesus (John 19:10). The men at Graterford Prison who

---

32. Sawyer and Wagner, "Mass Incarceration," cited by Carter et al., "Redeeming Justice," 322–23.

33. Bragg, "On Condemning Whom We Do Not Know," 317.

34. Carter et al., "Redeeming Justice," 322–23.

formed the Right to Redemption Committee gave expression to the despair of being condemned by these powers of death:

> There was this unspoken truth that we all shared. We knew that if nothing changed in the near future regarding our condition, then we would all have to face the bleak reality of dying alone in prison, without ever having the opportunity to try to make up for the harm that we caused. We all knew that it was only a matter of time before each and every one of us would be taking that sightless ride on a penitentiary gurney.[35]

The men in the Right to Redemption Committee recognized the perverse logic of the closed system of death and condemnation in the language used to justify the confinement of incarcerated persons. Words like criminals, convicted felons, and super-predators functioned to define these men as entirely sub-human, entirely beyond redemption, and left no space for alternative narratives, for the novelty that is the transformation of the self:

> No matter how much we transformed, no matter the determination that we had to be the best versions of ourselves, no matter the certificates, the degrees, and the lives that we affected in positive ways, we would always be chained and shackled to the worst moments of our lives.[36]

It is tragically ironic that many Christians in the United States are the strongest supporters of a harsh and punitive criminal regime. These Christians have forgotten their own elementary grammar or perhaps hold the "oxymoronic" belief that grace is for those who are "less undeserving" and not for those who are judged to be "more undeserving."

Holding Together Salvation as Justification, Transformation, and Eschatological Rectification of All Things

The doctrine of justification is construed narrowly as a divine verdict of acquittal that is restricted to the individual's spiritual relationship to God, as if what is true *corum Dei* has no further implications than one's interior assurance that one is right with God and confidence in a happy eschatological verdict. Belief in God's "acquitting" grace is rarely seen to be applicable to political support for a criminal justice system that would incorporate

---

35. Carter et al., "Redeeming Justice," 326.
36. Carter et al., "Redeeming Justice," 327.

the logic of grace and offer opportunities for repentance and redemption. Instead, many Christians, who, with their right theological hand wax eloquent about amazing grace, use their left theological hand to oppose grace for those deemed to be "other." Obviously, implicit assumptions about who is "deserving of grace" in the spiritual realm and who is undeserving of grace in relation to the criminal justice system are shaped by racial fears and biases. A faith that celebrates God's grace for the undeserving while simultaneously supporting a harshly punitive criminal justice regime in order to close the portals of hope for incarcerated persons is theologically incoherent. If we are all truly undeserving, then the lines our systems of death draw that effectively define some persons as worse than undeserving entirely undermines the logic of grace.

The powerful story Paul tells in Romans is of a human race trapped together in a tragic solidarity of sin and death from which we cannot extricate ourselves. Sin is not confined to a certain class of human beings but rather is something in which we are all entangled. God's word of judgment applies to us when we assume our own superior righteousness and engage in condemnation of other humans as irredeemably evil (Rom 2:1–3). Judgment, the indictment of humanity as guilty, trapped into a closed system of sin, death, and domination, is, however, God's penultimate word. The whole point of Romans is that God has acted in Christ to rescue us, to recreate and transform us, and to offer a word of justification that redefines us as God's beloved children in solidarity with Christ.

Romans 4 gives expression to the identity and character of God as the God who breaks into the closed circle of sin, death, and condemnation to engender life where there was no hope whatsoever with respect to human possibilities. This is the God who raises the dead and calls into being things that did not exist. Paul points to the birth of Isaac as a miracle of this magnitude: from Sarah's dead womb, life was conceived and the impossible became possible. Paul links new life to the dead to the justification of the person who was previously defined as "sinner." The common denominator is the God who opens new possibilities where all human possibilities had reached their end.

Politically speaking, transformations of the United States criminal justice system seem impossible. "Getting tough on crime" remains politically popular. However, getting tough on crime is sin's own failed attempts to remedy sin. Getting tough on crime does not actually prevent and reduce crime but rather is driven by the fear of the racial "other" and the fear of death, which results in more death. When the criminal justice system is driven not by what actually deters crime but by retributive and punitive motives tethered to the fear of death, it is an enslaving power of the present evil age. God's eschatological reign came to break open enslaving powers to set human persons free.

Romans 3–6 should inspire Christians who believe in a God who transforms persons and situations. If we believe in a God who justifies, transforms, and rectifies, legally codified condemnation stands opposed to all we believe in. The Right to Redemption Committee has not argued for parole for persons sentenced to life in prison if there is no evidence of transformation and if there is evidence that the person remains a danger to society. However, the Right to Redemption Committee is arguing that transformation is possible. The Right to Redemption Committee is making the case that a good society does not condemn persons as beyond redemption. And above all, the Right to Redemption Committee's vision is, at minimum, congruent with the core Christian conviction that God's purposes are not condemnation (John 3:16–17) but to open a future, both within the present age and into the eschatological future.

If Christ identified with all of us on the cross in the state of condemnation in order to open up another verdict, that of God's gracious acceptance and forgiveness, to destroy the power of death, and to make human transformation possible, then as Christians, the identification with those who have been condemned is not extreme political radicalism. It is Christomorphic. It is participation in the incursion of the eschatological future. And it is the hope that there will be an eschatological future where all will be rectified that inspires the ongoing struggle to put things right in the here and now in the teeth of closed horizons of hopelessness. The men who formed the Right to Redemption Committee provide a paradigm, perhaps a secular or not-so-secular parable, of the kind of hope and struggle for transformation and justice in which those who believe in the eschatological rectification of all things should be engaged. Whatever the religious beliefs of the men who came together to form the Right to Redemption Committee, there is something here that is attributable to the stirrings of the eschatological Spirit, groaning for redemption and liberation, which drove them into a struggle to put right what was wrong. They struggled to rectify a situation that was, politically speaking, hopeless, in the hope against hope that one day, persons condemned to death and hopelessness might find new life and possibilities.

Christ came that we might have life abundantly. God's purposes are, in the final analysis, life for all. To be drawn into the eschatological new creation in Christ is to join the *missio Dei*, which is nothing other than the in-breaking eschatological reign of God, whose breadth is nothing less than all things put to rights in Christ. We are saved to be conduits of healing and transformation. This is what we were saved to do. Social transformations that will set persons free will not be our own human achievement. But we are called to step forth and act in congruence with God's deepest purposes in the faith that it is God who is at work in our struggles for justice, for reconciliation, and for human wholeness and to pin our hopes in apocalyptic breakthroughs that are always, even though through our efforts, the work of the God who makes all things new!

Conclusion

ONE OF THE REASONS I wrote this book was to offer an alternative for ex-evangelicals who begin by "deconstructing" their evangelical faith and finding that nothing is left that is "worth bothering over." This was mentioned in the "Preface" but was not made explicit in the book's chapters. My observations are based, in part, upon twenty years of teaching undergraduate students, most of whom were from conservative evangelical churches. My impression, based upon multiple conversations with both undergraduate students and with groups of adult ex-evangelicals as well, is: (1) these persons operated with a deep, visceral assumption that their inherited versions of the Christian faith simply were the normative versions of the Christian faith; (2) after the credibility of their inherited version broke down, often because they found the faith they inherited to be toxic, they did not find a compelling alternative vision of the meaning and point of the Christian faith.

The word *du jour* is "deconstruction." As this term is used, it bears little resemblance to anything derived from French post-structuralism. Rather, the term, as used in popular parlance, seems to mean simply dismantling.[1]

This book represents what I hope will be one small contribution to the task of "re-construction." The goal is to provide an account of the Bible, Christian discipleship, and an ecclesial construal of the *missio Dei* that is beautiful, powerful, and persuasive. No doubt, my contribution is meager and, thankfully, I am not the only theologian or church leader engaged in this task. Hopefully, the weaknesses and deficiencies of my own theological account will be supplemented by other voices in the body of Christ, situated very differently than me racially, culturally, and otherwise, with critiques, corrections, and insight that might aid in the continual development of the theological vision set forth in these pages.

---

1. Perhaps ex-evangelical deconstruction might actually be more constructive if it at least passed through something akin to a post-structuralist deconstructive moment of recognizing that the complexity of language makes possible plural interpretations.

One of the deepest visceral intuitions present in persons raised in at least some conservative evangelical contexts[2] is the deep sense, like a popular Freudian super-ego, that inherited versions of Christianity simply are "the voice of God," simply the normative and biblically-based version of the Christian faith. This means that for many evangelicals, once the received version of the Christian faith starts to unravel, it is difficult to imagine the possibility that another construal of the faith might be more faithful to Scripture. Because evangelical Christian groups have so loudly proclaimed themselves to be based on "the" Bible, bolstered by theories about the Bible, such as inerrancy, and a thick web of conventional interpretations of the Bible, rejecting evangelical interpretations of the Bible is sometimes experienced as rejecting *the* Bible. Hence, once one starts down the road of this version of "deconstruction," the outcome is far too often the unraveling of everything.

In my undergraduate theology courses, I tried, perhaps sometimes successfully, to help students arrive at the recognition that there is a distinction between "the" Bible and "my" or any Christian group's understanding and interpretation of the Bible. Neither white conservative evangelicals nor anyone else owns the Bible, nor are they authorized by God to serve as the supreme court of biblical interpretation. To employ a crude metaphor, evangelical pastors and theologians, especially those who deem themselves to be gatekeepers authorized to determine who is in and who is out, may own local franchises, but they are not CEO's of the entire "corporation."

Over the years, I have become convinced that in many conservative evangelical circles, the claim to be "Bible-believing" is a substitute for actual deep engagement with the Bible in its real depth and complexity. Often, those who claim to be "Bible-believing" in fact have a very thin *de facto* canon and screen out huge chunks of the biblical witness. Claiming to believe "all of the Bible" and actually engaging the Bible in its broad canonical scope and complexity are not the same. Of course, this book has been a sustained argument for an alternative way to put the canonical pieces together to craft a theological account of salvation. But this account is what many evangelical readings of Scripture unwittingly or wittingly screen out.

This book represents an effort to linger long over Scripture in order to sketch another way of reading the Bible. What if the meaning of salvation in the Bible is not afterlife insurance, but God entering his creation to reclaim it and rectify it? What if we were saved to participate in that *missio Dei*

---

2. The real world is messier than any simple characterization or categorization. I seek to qualify my language with words like "often" and "many" in recognition that I am inevitably painting with a broad brush and my critiques do not fit everything that falls under the categories of white conservative evangelical or conservative evangelical.

during our lives in the present age? What if the truly fulfilling way of living, what we were "saved for," is God's work of reclaiming human persons from the grip and stranglehold of what is destructive? What if what we are saved from is not God and punishment but bondage to what is enslaving and destructive? What if what we were saved for is a life lived inside God's love, goodness, and justice, resulting in a shared life together of mutual edification and a mission of "engendering life in others"?

Second, as pointed out in the "Introduction," the years 2016 through 2023 have exposed the deep racial fault lines in American society and the church. White Christian support for Donald Trump and angry efforts to push back against any claims that the nation is not innocent on matters of racial justice have exposed, once again, the diseased nature of western and American Christian life and theology. This calls for an even more thorough reckoning than I am capable of providing. This book is only a start.

However, the need to look unflinchingly at soteriological deformations and rethink soteriology is one of the urgent theological tasks required for this reckoning. To return to Katie Cannon's statement with which I began the "Introduction," our inherited soteriologies have functioned to deny that the gospel has anything to do with the eradication of affliction, despair, and systems of injustice.

The breeding ground for this quarantining of salvation from any imperative to participate in deliverance of human persons from abuse, injustice, and suffering has been, in part, the overly sharp separation between justification and sanctification that characterized the Protestant Reformation. This separation was not initially designed to legitimate chattel slavery and colonial conquest and domination but rather as a theological weapon against medieval Roman Catholic abuses. Nevertheless, as noted earlier in the book, it provided a resource, after chattel slavery became economically beneficial, to locate economic relationships and the exploitation of human beings outside the scope of gospel concerns.

Therefore, the urgent reparative and reconstructive task is to go "back to the Bible" and recover a soteriological vision that calls us into God's eschatological and present purposes of rectifying all things. We are not saved *by* our efforts to eradicate affliction, despair, and systems of injustice, but this mode of action is precisely what we were saved *for*! We lack sufficient power to put anything right. But we are called to participate, "in Christ," in the power of the eschatological Spirit at work in the world, in God's work and purposes.

Finally, it is crucial to resist interpretations of this project as merely white liberal Protestant Christianity that is nothing more than a call to find inspiration in Jesus for progressive do-goodism, as if the answer is human efforts to build a better world. While my early chapters were deeply critical of presentations of the gospel oriented toward saying a prayer in order to be forgiven and be assured of going to heaven, this project does not jettison the centrality of conversion to Christ.

Because we are so deeply entangled in sin, both social and systemic sin and the brokenness manifested in our deep fears, insecurities, wounds, hatreds, as well as personal and collective forms of self-deception, we are incapable of building a better world by human effort alone. We are in need of healing, transformation, love, and divine empowerment that only comes through being drawn into the current of the life of God. This requires prevenient divine action. The intrusion of the eschatological new creation is God's action in the life, death, and resurrection of Jesus Christ. We can only participate as we are drawn by the Spirit into the life of God. This soteriological project depends upon the core conviction that Jesus of Nazareth, the prophet, preacher, teacher of parables, healer, resistance activist, martyr, sacrifice, and the resurrected one, is the location where creation has been rectified. To be saved is to be drawn into God's insurrection against the powers of destruction which Jesus inaugurated. He is the space and location of the eschatological new creation. We are saved to participate in that insurrection by embracing God's cause, which is human flourishing, joy, right relationships, justice, goodness, and love!

Bibliography

Abramsky, Sasha. *The American Way of Poverty: How the Other Half Still Lives*. New York: Nation, 2013.

Agamben, Georgio. *Homo Sacer: Sovereign Power and Bare Life*. Translated by Daniel Heller-Roazen. Stanford: Stanford University Press, 1998.

Aguilera, Jasmine. "Humanitarian Scott Warren Found Not Guilty After Retrial for Helping Migrants at Mexican Border." *Time*, November 20, 2019. https://time.com/5732485/scott-warren-trial-not-guilty.

———. "They Tried to Save the Lives of Immigrants Fleeing Danger. Now They're Facing Prosecution." *Time*, November 11, 2019. https://time.com/5713732/scott-warren-retrial.

Albertz, Rainer. *From the Exile to the Maccabees*. Vol. 2 of *History of Israelite Religion in the Old Testament Period*. Translated by John Bowden. 1st American ed. Louisville, KY: Westminster John Knox, 1994.

Alexander VI. "Inter Caetera: Division of the Undiscovered World Between Spain and Portugal." May 4, 1493. https://www.papalencyclicals.net/alex06/alex06inter.htm.

Allison, Natalie, and Lamar Johnson. "Orbán Gets Warm CPAC Reception After 'Mixed Race' Speech Blowback." *Politico*, August 4, 2022. https://www.politico.com/news/2022/08/04/viktor-orban-cpac-00049935.

Anselm. *Cur Deus Homo?* In *Proslogium, Monologium, An Appendix on Behalf of the Fool by Gaunilon, and Cur Deus Homo*, by Anselm, 171–288. Translated by Sidney Norton Deane. Reprint, Chicago: Open Court, 1926.

Aquinas, Thomas. *On the Truth of the Catholic Faith: Summa Contra Gentiles, Book Four: Salvation*. Translated by Charles J. O'Neil. Garden City: Image, 1957.

Asad, Talal. *Genealogies of Religion: Discipline and Reasons of Power in Christianity and Islam*. Baltimore: Johns Hopkins University Press, 1993.

Atsushi, Iguchi. "Textual Salvation 2.0: Literacy, Vernacular Theology, and the Place of *facere quod in se est* in Late-Medieval England." *Hiyoshi Review of English Studies* 71 (2019) 39–53.

Augustine. *The City of God*. In *Nicene and Post-Nicene Fathers*, Series 1, Volume 2, edited by Philip Schaff and translated by Marcus Dods. Grand Rapids: Eerdmans, 1956.

———. *The Enchiridion*. In *Nicene and Post-Nicene Fathers*, Series 1, Volume 3, edited by Philip Schaff and translated by J. F. Shaw. Grand Rapids: Eerdmans, 1956.

———. *On the Holy Trinity*. In *Nicene and Post-Nicene Fathers*, Series 1, Volume 3, edited by Philip Schaff and translated by Arthur West Haddon. Grand Rapids: Eerdmans, 1956.

———. *On Marriage and Concupiscence*. In *Nicene and Post-Nicene Fathers*, Series 1, Volume 5, edited by Philip Schaff and translated by Peter Holmes and Robert Ernest Wallis. Grand Rapids: Eerdmans, 1956.

———. *The Spirit and the Letter*. In *Nicene and Post-Nicene Fathers*, Series 1, Volume 5, edited by Philip Schaff and translated by Peter Holmes and Robert Ernest Wallis. Grand Rapids: Eerdmans, 1956.

———. *A Treatise Concerning Man's Perfection in Righteousness*. In *Nicene and Post-Nicene Fathers*, Series 1, Volume 5, edited by Philip Schaff and translated by Peter Holmes and Robert Ernest Wallis. Grand Rapids: Eerdmans, 1956.

———. *A Treatise on Grace and Free Will*. In *Nicene and Post-Nicene Fathers*, Series 1, Volume 5, edited by Philip Schaff and translated by Peter Holmes and Robert Ernest Wallis. Grand Rapids: Eerdmans, 1956.

———. *A Treatise on the Merits and Forgiveness of Sins and the Baptism of Infants*. In *Nicene and Post-Nicene Fathers*, Series 1, Volume 5, edited by Philip Schaff and translated by Peter Holmes and Robert Ernest Wallis. Grand Rapids: Eerdmans, 1956.

Badenoch, Bonnie. *The Heart of Trauma: Healing the Embodied Brain in the Context of Relationships*. New York: Norton, 2018.

Baker, Joseph O., et al. "Keep America Christian (and White): Christian Nationalism, Fear of Ethnoracial Outsiders, and Intention to Vote for Donald Trump in the 2020 Presidential Election." *Sociology of Religion: A Quarterly Review* 81 (2020) 272–93.

Baker, Peter, et al. "How Trump's Idea for a Photo Op Led to Havoc in a Park." *New York Times*, June 2, 2020. https://www.nytimes.com/2020/06/02/us/politics/trump-walk-lafayette-square.html.

Baldwin, Lewis V. "Martin Luther King Jr., the Black Church, and the Black Messianic Vision." *Journal of the Interdenominational Theological Center* 12 (1984–1985) 98–103.

Barna Research Group. "Black Practicing Christians Are Twice as Likely as Their White Peers to See a Race Problem." *Barna*, June 17, 2020. https://www.barna.com/research/problems-solutions-racism.

———. "White Christians Have Become Even Less Motivated to Address Racial Injustice." *Barna*, September 15, 2020. https://www.barna.com/research/american-christians-race-problem.

Barrera, Albino. *Biblical Economic Ethics: Sacred Scripture's Teaching on Economic Life*. Blue Ridge Summit: Lexington, 2015.

Barth, Karl. "The Strange New World within the Bible." In *The Word of God and the Word of Man*, by Karl Barth, 28–50. Translated by Douglas Horton. New York: Harper & Row, 1957.

Bates, Matthew. *Salvation by Allegiance Alone: Rethinking Faith, Works, and the Gospel of King Jesus*. Grand Rapids: Baker Academic, 2017.

Baum, Dan. "Legalize It All: How to Win the War on Drugs." *Harper's Magazine*, March 24, 2016. https://harpers.org/archive/2016/04/legalize-it-all.

Baxter, Michael J. "Review Essay: The Non-Catholic Character of the 'Public Church.'" *Modern Theology* 11 (1995) 243–58.

Bean, Alan. "Are We Finally Ready to Learn from Glenn Hinson, One of Our Baptist Prophets?" *Baptist News*, November 19, 2019. https://baptistnews.com/article/are-we-finally-ready-to-learn-from-glenn-hinson-one-of-our-baptist-prophets.

Beaton, Richard. "Messiah and Justice: A Key to Matthew's Use of Isaiah 42:1–4." *Journal for the Study of the New Testament* 75 (1999) 5–23.

Beauchamp, Zack. "It Happened There: How Democracy Died in Hungary." *Vox*, September 13, 2018. https://www.vox.com/policy-and-politics/2018/9/13/17823488/hungary-democracy-authoritarianism-trump.

Beilby, John, and Paul Eddy. "Justification in Historical Perspective." In *Justification: Five Views*, edited by John Beilby and Paul Eddy, 13–52. Spectrum Multiview Book Series. Downers Grove, IL: InterVarsity, 2011.

Beiner, Ronald. "Walter Benjamin's Philosophy of History." *Political Theory* 12 (1984) 423–34.

Beker, J. Christiaan. *Paul's Apocalyptic Gospel: The Coming Triumph of God*. Philadelphia: Fortress, 1982.

Bell, Daniel M., Jr. "Postliberalism and Radical Orthodoxy." In *The Cambridge Companion to Christian Political Theology*, edited by Craig Hovey and Elizabeth Phillips, 110–32. New York: Cambridge University Press, 2015.

Benjamin, Walter. "Theses on the Philosophy of History." In *Illuminations*, edited by Hannah Arendt, 253–64. New York: Schocken, 1968.

Bernardin, Joseph Cardinal. "Address at Georgetown University." *Origins* 14 (1984) 343.

Bernstein, Richard. "The Meaning of Public Life." In *Religion and American Public Life: Interpretations and Explorations*, edited by Robin Lovin, 36–48. Mahweh: Paulist, 1986.

Birch, Bruce C. *What Does the Lord Require?: The Old Testament Call to Social Witness*. Philadelphia: Westminster, 1985.

Bird, Michael. "An Invasive Story: Paul's Theology Between Messianic Event and Salvation History." Lecture delivered at Lanier Theological Library, February 6, 2016. https://www.laniertheologicallibrary.org/messages/an-invasive-story-paul-s-theology-between-messianic-event-and-salvation-history.

———. "Judgment and Justification in Paul: A Review Article." *Bulletin for Biblical Research* 18 (2008) 299–313.

Blackwell, Benjamin C. "You Become What You Worship: *Theosis* and the Story of the Bible." *Ex Auditu* 33 (2017) 1–20.

Blackwell, Benjamin C., et al. "Paul and the Apocalyptic Imagination: An Introduction." In *Paul and the Apocalyptic Imagination*, edited by Benjamin C. Blackwell et al., 3–21. Minneapolis: Fortress, 2016.

Blanden, Jo, et al. "Intergenerational Mobility in Europe and the North America." London School of Economics Centre for Economic Performance, April 2005. http://www.cep.lse.ac.uk/about/news/IntergenerationalMobility.pdf.

Bloom, Harold. *The American Religion: The Emergence of a Post-Christian Nation*. New York: Simon and Schuster, 1992.

Boer, Martinus C. de. "Apocalyptic as God's Eschatological Activity in Paul's Theology." In *Paul and the Apocalyptic Imagination*, edited by Ben C. Blackwell et al., 45–63. Minneapolis: Fortress, 2016.

Boersma, Hans. *Violence, Hospitality, and the Cross: Reappropriating the Atonement Tradition*. Grand Rapids: Baker Academic, 2004.

Booker, Brakkton. "White Defendant Allegedly Used Racial Slur After Killing Ahmaud Arbery." *NPR*, June 4, 2020. https://www.npr.org/2020/06/04/869938461/white-defendant-allegedly-used-racial-slur-after-killing-ahmaud-arbery.

Bibliography

Booth, Wayne. *The Company We Keep: An Ethics of Fiction.* Berkeley: University of California Press, 1988.

Bourdieu, Pierre. *Outline of a Theory of Practice.* Translated by Richard Nice. Cambridge: Cambridge University Press, 1977.

Boyle, Greg, SJ. "On Radical Compassion." July 28, 2017. https://www.youtube.com/watch?v=4rLTkgkTTao.

———. "One of the Most Inspirational Speeches from Gangsters." January 25, 2019. https://www.youtube.com/watch?v=zk—XN4ozr8.

———. *Tattoos on the Heart: The Power of Boundless Compassion.* New York: Free Press, 2011.

Bragg, Hunter. "On Condemning Whom We Do Not Know: Confession of Sins, Plea Bargains, and Apophatic Anthropology." *Political Theology* 23 (2022) 317–34.

Bretherton, Luke. "The Duty of Care to Refugees, Christian Cosmopolitanism, and the Hallowing of Bare Life." *Studies in Christian Ethics* 19 (2006) 50–51.

Broadway, Mikael N. "Practicing What We Preach: Churches Confessing the Whole Gospel." *Perspectives in Religious Studies* 29 (2002) 381–400.

Brooks, Cheri. "Lifers Speak Out on Right to Redemption." *Drexel Magazine* (Winter/Spring 2022). https://drexelmagazine.org/2022/lifers-speak-out-on-right-to-redemption/?fbclid=IwAR3Chwk9ozPvJMcGi7Ba8hkdYVUluq3no1orfNov5neRyL5pZMpscYHROFk.

Brown, Joanne Carlson, and Rebecca Parker. "For God So Loved the World?" In *Christianity, Patriarchy, and Abuse*, edited by Joanne Carlson Brown and Carole R. Bohn, 1–29. New York: Pilgrim, 1989.

Brown, Peter. *Augustine of Hippo: A Biography.* Berkeley: University of California Press, 1967.

Brueggemann, Walter. *Isaiah.* Westminster Bible Companion. Louisville, KY: Westminster John Knox, 1998.

———. *Texts Under Negotiation: The Bible and Postmodern Imagination.* Minneapolis: Fortress, 1993.

———. *Theology of the Old Testament: Testimony, Dispute, Advocacy.* Minneapolis: Fortress, 2012.

Buchanan, Larry, et al. "Black Lives Matter May Be the Largest Movement in US History." *New York Times*, July 3, 2020. https://www.nytimes.com/interactive/2020/07/03/us/george-floyd-protests-crowd-size.html.

Budde, Michael. *The (Magic) Kingdom of God: Christianity and Global Culture Industries.* Boulder, CO: Westview, 1997.

Burge, Ryan P. "The 2020 Vote for President by Religious Groups—Christians." *Religion in Public* (blog), March 29, 2021. Updated January 12, 2023. https://religioninpublic.blog/2021/03/29/the-2020-vote-for-president-by-religious-groups-christians.

Burns, J. Patout. "The Economy of Salvation: Two Patristic Traditions." *Theological Studies* 37 (1976) 598–619.

Butler, Anthea. *White Evangelical Racism: The Politics of Morality in America.* Chapel Hill: University of North Carolina Press, 2021.

Cade, Jason A. "Water Is Life!" (and Speech!): Death, Dissent, and Democracy in the Borderlands." *Indiana Law Journal* 96 (2020) 261–311.

Calvin, John. *Institutes of the Christian Religion.* Edited by John McNeill. Library of Christian Classics. Philadelphia: Westminister, 1960.

Bibliography

Cameron, Euon. *The European Reformation*. Oxford: Clarendon, 1991.

Campbell, Douglas A. *The Quest for Paul's Gospel: A Suggested Strategy*. London: T&T Clark, 2005.

Cannon, Katie G. *Black Womanist Ethics*. Eugene, OR: Wipf & Stock, 1988.

Carroll, Rory. "Eight Activists Helping Migrants Cross Brutal Desert Charged by US Government." *Guardian*, January 24, 2018. https://www.theguardian.com/us-news/2018/jan/24/us-immigration-activists-arizona-no-more-deaths-charged.

Carter, J. Kameron. *Race: A Theological Account*. Oxford: Oxford University Press, 2008.

Carter, Terrell, et al. "Redeeming Justice." *Northwestern University Law Review* 116 (2021) 315–82.

Carter, Warren. *Matthew and Empire: Initial Explorations*. Harrisburg: Trinity, 2001.

Catholic Church. *Catechism of the Catholic Church*. London: Geoffrey Chapman, 1994.

Cavanaugh, William T. *Being Consumed: Economics and Christian Desire*. Grand Rapids: Eerdmans, 2008.

———. "'A Fire Strong Enough to Consume the House': The Wars of Religion and the Rise of the State." *Modern Theology* 11 (1995) 398–420.

———. "Killing for the Telephone Company: Why the Nation-State Is Not the Keeper of the Common Good." *Modern Theology* 20 (2004) 243–74.

Centers for Disease Control and Prevention (CDC). "About the CDC–Kaiser ACE Study." *CDC.gov*, April 6, 2021. https://www.cdc.gov/violenceprevention/aces/about.html.

Ciraulo, Jonathan M. "Divinization as Christification in Erich Przywara and John Zizioulas." *Modern Theology* 32 (2016) 479–503.

Clapp, Rodney. "Why the Devil Takes Visa: A Christian Response to the Triumph of Consumerism." *Christianity Today* 40 (1996) 18–33.

Clements, Rob. "Marxism and the God Question: Perspectives from the Frankfurt School." *The Other Journal: An Intersection of Theology and Culture* 22 (2013). https://theotherjournal.com/2013/07/22/marxism-and-the-god-question-perspectives-from-the-frankfurt-school.

Coleman, John A., SJ. "A Possible Role for Biblical Religion in Public Life." *Theological Studies* 40 (1979) 701–6.

Collins, John J. *The Apocalyptic Imagination: An Introduction to Jewish Apocalyptic Literature*. 1st ed. New York: Crossroad, 1984.

———. *The Apocalyptic Imagination: An Introduction to Jewish Apocalyptic Literature*. 2nd ed. Biblical Resource Series. Grand Rapids: Eerdmans, 1998.

———. "From Prophecy to Apocalypticism: The Expectation of the End." In *The Origins of Apocalypticism in Judaism and Christianity*, edited by John J. Collins, 129–61. Vol. 1 of *Encyclopedia of Apocalypticism*. New York: Continuum, 1998.

———. *The Scepter and the Star: Messianism in Light of the Dead Sea Scrolls*. Grand Rapids: Eerdmans, 2010.

Compier, Don H. *What is Rhetorical Theology?: Textual Practice and Public Discourse*. Harrisburg: Trinity, 1999.

Cone, James H. *The Cross and the Lynching Tree*. Maryknoll, NY: Orbis, 2012.

———. *Martin and Malcolm and America: A Dream or a Nightmare*. Maryknoll, NY: Orbis, 1991.

———. "Martin Luther King Jr., Black Theology—Black Church." *Theology Today* 40 (1984) 409–20.

Bibliography

———. "The Theology of Martin Luther King Jr." *Union Seminary Quarterly Review* 40 (1986) 21–39.

———. "Theology's Great Sin: Silence in the Face of White Supremacy." *Black Theology: An International Journal* 2 (2004) 139–52.

Cooper, Betsy, et al. "How Americans View Immigrants, and What They Want from Immigration Reform: Findings from the 2015 American Values Atlas." *Public Religion Research Institute (PRRI)*, March 29, 2016. https://www.prri.org/research/poll-immigration-reform-views-on-immigrants.

Copan, Paul. *Is God a Moral Monster?: Making Sense of the Old Testament God*. Grand Rapids: Baker, 2011.

Copeland, M. Shawn. *Enfleshing Freedom: Body, Race, and Being*. Minneapolis: Fortress, 2010.

Cousar, Charles. *A Theology of the Cross: The Death of Jesus in the Pauline Letters*. Minneapolis: Fortress, 1990.

Cox, D. Michael. "The Gospel of Matthew and Resisting Imperial Theology." *Perspectives in Religious Studies* 36 (2009) 25–48.

Cox, Daniel, et al. "Beyond Economics: Fears of Cultural Displacement Pushed the White Working Class to Trump." *Public Religion Research Institute (PRRI)*, May 9, 2017. https://www.prri.org/research/white-working-class-attitudes-economy-trade-immigration-election-donald-trump.

Cram, Ronald Hecker. *Bullying: A Spiritual Crisis*. St. Louis: Chalice, 2003.

Creach, Jerome F. D. *Violence in Scripture*. Louisville, KY: Westminster John Knox, 2013.

Crisp, Oliver D. "On Original Sin" *International Journal of Systematic Theology* 17 (2015) 252–66.

Cunningham, Conor. *Darwin's Pious Idea: Why the Ultra-Darwinists and Creationists Both Get It Wrong*. Grand Rapids: Eerdmans, 2010.

Cunningham, David. *Faithful Persuasion: In Aid of a Rhetoric of Christian Theology*. Notre Dame, IN: University of Notre Dame Press, 1991.

Dabney, D. Lyle. "The Grace of the Spirit: Towards a Soteriology of the Spirit of Grace." Unpublished lecture delivered in Canberra, Australia, April 1999.

———. "Naming the Spirit: Towards a Pneumatology of the Cross." Unpublished lecture delivered in Canberra, Australia, April 1999.

———. "Nature of the Spirit." Unpublished lecture delivered in Canberra, Australia, April 1999.

———. "Staring the Spirit." Unpublished lecture delivered in Canberra, Australia, April 1999.

David, Joshua B. "The Challenge of Apocalyptic to Modern Theology." In *Apocalyptic and the Future of Theology*, edited by Joshua B. Davis and Douglas Harink, 1–48. Eugene, OR: Cascade, 2012.

Dittenberger, Wilhelm, ed. *Sylloge Inscriptionum Graecarum*. 3rd ed. Leipzig: Hirzel, 1915–1924.

Dougherty, Kevin D., et al. *The Values and Beliefs of the American Public: Wave III of the Baylor Religion Survey*. Waco, TX: Baylor University, 2011. https://baylorreligionsurvey.research.baylor.edu/sites/g/files/ecbvkj1931/files/2023-09/wave_3_2010_the_values_and_beliefs_of_the_american_public.pdf.

Douglas, Frederick. *Narrative of the Life of Frederick Douglas: An American Slave: Written by Himself*. Boston: Anti-Slavery Office, 1845.

Bibliography

Douglas, Kelly Brown. *Stand Your Ground: Black Bodies and the Justice of God.* Maryknoll, NY: Orbis, 2015.

Douglas, Mary. *Purity and Danger: An Analysis of the Concept of Pollution and Taboo.* London: Routledge and Kegan Paul, 1966.

Du Mez, Kristen Kobez. *Jesus and John Wayne: How White Evangelicals Corrupted a Faith and Fractured a Nation.* New York: Liveright, 2020.

———. "Os Guinness, Eric Metaxis, and Their Dangerous Myths of American History." *Anxious Bench* (blog), July 23, 2020. https://www.patheos.com/blogs/anxiousbench/2020/07/os-guinness-eric-metaxas-and-their-dangerous-myths-of-american-history.

———. "Understanding White Evangelical Views on Immigration." *Harvard Divinity Bulletin* 46 (2018). https://bulletin.hds.harvard.edu/articles/springsummer2018/understanding-white-evangelical-views-immigration.

Dulles, Avery. "Two Languages of Salvation: The Lutheran-Catholic Joint Declaration." *First Things* 98 (1999) 25–30.

Dunn, James D. G. *The Theology of Paul the Apostle.* Grand Rapids: Eerdmans, 1996.

Elliot, Neil. *The Arrogance of Nations: Reading Romans in the Shadow of Empire.* Minneapolis: Fortress, 2008.

Emerson, Michael O., and Christian Smith. *Divided by Faith: Evangelical Religion and the Problem of Race in America.* New York: Oxford University Press, 2000.

Engel v. Vitale, 370 US 421 (1962). *Justia.* https://supreme.justia.com/cases/federal/us/370/421.

Eno, Robert. "Some Patristic Views on the Relationship of Faith and Works in Justification." In *Justification by Faith: Lutherans and Catholics in Dialogue VII*, edited by H. George Anderson et al., 111–20. Minneapolis: Augsburg, 1985.

Equal Justice Initiative (EJI). *Cruel and Unusual: Sentencing 13- and 14-year-old Children to Die in Prison.* Montgomery, AL: Equal Justice Initiative, 2008. https://eji.org/wp-content/uploads/2019/10/cruel-and-unusual.pdf.

Femia, Joseph. *Gramsci's Political Thought: Hegemony, Consciousness, and the Revolutionary Process.* Oxford: Oxford University Press, 1981.

Ferguson, John. *Pelagius: A Historical and Theological Study.* Cambridge: Heffer and Sons, 1956.

Fiddes, Paul S. *Past Event and Present Salvation: The Christian Idea of Atonement.* Louisville, KY: Westminster John Knox, 1989.

Finlan, Stephen, and Vladimir Kharlamov. "Introduction." In *Theosis: Deification in the Christian Tradition*, edited by Stephen Finlan and Vladimir Karlamov, 1–15. Eugene, OR: Pickwick, 2006.

Fishbane, Michael. *Biblical Interpretation in Ancient Israel.* Oxford: Clarendon, 1985.

Fletcher, Jeanine Hill. *The Sin of White Supremacy: Christianity, Racism, and Religious Diversity in America.* Maryknoll, NY: Orbis, 2017.

Fortune, Marie M. "Forgiveness: The Last Step." In *Violence Against Women and Children: A Christian Theological Sourcebook*, edited by Carol J. Adams and Marie M. Fortune, 201–6. New York: Continuum, 1995.

Frei, Hans W. *The Identity of Jesus Christ.* Philadelphia: Westminster, 1975.

———. *Types of Christian Theology.* Edited by George Hunsinger and William C. Placher. New Haven, CT: Yale University Press, 1992.

Friedrich, Gerhard. "*euangelion*." In *Theological Dictionary of the New Testament*, edited by Gerhard Kittel et al., 2:722–25. Grand Rapids: Eerdmans, 1964.

Bibliography

Froese, Paul. "How Your View of God Shapes Your View of the Economy." *Religion and Politics*, June 13, 2012. http://religionandpolitics.org/2012/06/13/how-your-view-of-god-shapes-your-view-of-the-economy.

Garrow, David J. "The Intellectual Development of Martin Luther King Jr.: Influences and Commentaries." *Union Seminary Quarterly Review* 40 (1986) 5–20.

Gavrilyuk, Paul. *The Suffering of the Impassible God: The Dialectics of Patristic Thought.* Oxford: Oxford University Press, 2006.

Georgi, Dieter. *Theocracy in Paul's Praxis and Theology.* Minneapolis: Fortress, 1991.

Gilson, Etienne. *The Christian Philosophy of St. Augustine.* Translated by L. E. M. Lynch. New York: Random House, 1960.

Goldingay, John E. *Daniel.* Word Biblical Commentary 30. Dallas: Word, 1989.

Goodman, Martin. *The Ruling Class of Judea: the Origins of the Jewish Revolt Against Rome, AD 66–70.* Cambridge: Cambridge University Press, 1987.

Gorman, Michael J. *The Death of the Messiah and the Birth of the New Covenant: A (Not So) New Model of the Atonement.* Eugene, OR: Cascade, 2014.

———. *Inhabiting the Cruciform God: Kenosis, Justification, and Theosis in Paul's Narrative Soteriology.* Grand Rapids: Eerdmans, 2009.

Gottwald, Norman K. *The Tribes of Yahweh: A Sociology of the Religion of Liberated Israel, 1250–1050 BC.* Maryknoll, NY: Orbis, 1979.

Graham, Billy "Americanism." Radio Address, September 16, 1956. https://billygraham.org/audio/americanism.

Gregory, Eric, and Joseph Clair. "Augustinianisms and Thomisms." In *The Cambridge Companion to Christian Political Theology*, edited by Craig Hovey and Elizabeth Phillips, 176–95. New York: Cambridge University Press, 2015.

Grenz, Stanley. *Theology for the Community of God.* Nashville: Broadman & Holman, 1994.

Grimes, Nathaniel P. "The Racial Ideology of Rapture." *Perspectives in Religious Studies* 43 (2016) 211–21.

Grimsrud, Ted. *Instead of Atonement.* Eugene, OR: Cascade, 2013.

Gunton, Colin E. *The Actuality of Atonement: A Study of Metaphor, Rationality, and the Christian Tradition.* Grand Rapids: Eerdmans, 1989.

Gushee, David P. "Jesus and the Sinner's Prayer: What Jesus Says Doesn't Match What We Usually Say." *Christianity Today* 51 (2007) 72.

Gustafson, James. "The Sectarian Temptation: Reflections on Theology, the Church, and the University." *Proceedings of the Catholic Theological Society of America* 40 (1985) 83–94.

Guth, Karen V. *Christian Ethics at the Boundary: Feminism and Theologies of Public Life.* Minneapolis: Fortress, 2015.

Hanby, Michael. *Augustine and Modernity.* New York: Routledge, 2003.

Hanson, Paul D. *The Dawn of Apocalyptic.* Rev. ed. Philadelphia: Fortress, 1979.

———. *The Political History of the Bible in America.* Louisville, KY: Westminster John Knox, 2015.

Hari, Johann. *Chasing the Scream: The First and Last Days of the War on Drugs.* New York: Bloomsbury, 2015.

Harink, Douglas. *Paul among the Postliberals: Pauline Theology Beyond Christendom and Modernity.* Grand Rapids: Brazos, 2003.

Bibliography

———. "Response to Jim Wallis' *God's Politics: A New Vision for Faith and Politics in America.*" Unpublished paper delivered in the Theology and Religious Reflection Section, American Academy of Religion, Washington, DC, November 2006.

Harper, Victoria. "Henry A. Giroux: Neoliberalism, Democracy and the University as a Public Sphere." *Truthout*, April 22, 2014. http://www.truth-out.org/opinion/item/23156-henry-a-giroux-neoliberalism-democracy-and-the-university-as-a-public-sphere.

Hart, David Bentley. *The Doors of the Sea: Where Was God in the Tsunami?* Grand Rapids: Eerdmans, 2005.

———. "A Gift Every Debt Exceeding: An Eastern Orthodox Appreciation of Anselm's *Cur Deus Homo.*" *Pro Ecclesia* 7 (1998) 333–49.

———. "No Shadow of Turning: On Divine Impassibility." *Pro Ecclesia* XI (2002) 184–206.

Harvey, Barry. *Can These Bones Live?: A Catholic Baptist Engagement with Ecclesiology, Hermeneutics, and Social Theory.* Grand Rapids: Brazos, 2008.

———. "Into Lands as Yet Unknown: The Church's Vocation of Not Belonging." *Perspectives in Religious Studies* 41 (2014) 297–309.

———. "Preserving the World for Christ: Toward a Theological Engagement with the 'Secular.'" *Scottish Journal of Theology* 61 (2008) 64–82.

Hauerwas, Stanley. *After Christendom?: How the Church Is to Behave If Freedom, Justice, and a Christian Nation Are Bad Ideas.* Nashville: Abingdon, 1991.

———. *Against the Nations: War and Survival in a Liberal Society.* Minneapolis: Winston, 1985.

———. *A Community of Character: Toward a Constructive Christian Social Ethic.* Notre Dame, IN: University of Notre Dame Press, 1988.

———. *The Peaceable Kingdom: A Primer in Christian Ethics.* Notre Dame, IN: University of Notre Dame Press, 1983.

Hauerwas, Stanley, and William H. Willimon. *Resident Aliens: A Provocative Assessment of Culture and Ministry for People Who Know That Something Is Wrong.* Nashville: Abingdon, 1989.

Hays, Richard B. "Can Narrative Criticism Recover the Theological Unity of Scripture?" *Journal of Theological Interpretation* 2 (2008) 193–211.

———. *The Moral Vision of the New Testament.* San Francisco: HarperCollins, 1996.

———. "Why Do You Stand Looking Up Toward Heaven?: New Testament Eschatology at the Turn of the Millenium." *Modern Theology* 16 (2000) 115–35.

Hehir, J. Bryan. "The Perennial Need for Philosophical Discourse." *Theological Studies* 40 (1979) 710–13.

Heim, Karl. *The Nature of Protestantism.* Translated by John Schmidt. Philadelphia: Fortress, 1963.

Helwys, Thomas. *A Short Declaration of the Mystery of Iniquity.* Edited by Richard Groves. Macon, GA: Mercer University Press, 1998.

Herzog, William R., II. *Jesus, Justice, and the Reign of God: A Ministry of Liberation.* Louisville, KY: Westminster John Knox, 2000.

Hessel, Dieter T., and James Hudnut-Beumler. "The Public Church in Retrospect and Prospect." In *The Church's Public Role: Retrospect and Prospect*, edited by Dieter T. Hessel, 297–309. Grand Rapids: Eerdmans, 1993.

Heyer, Christine. *Kinship across Borders: A Christian Ethic of Immigration.* Washington, DC: Georgetown University Press, 2012.

Bibliography

Hill, Charles E. *Regnum Caelorum: Patterns of Future Hope in Early Christianity*. Oxford: Clarendon, 1992.

Hill, Wesley. "After Boomer Religion." *Commonweal*, April 29, 2019. https://www.commonwealmagazine.org/after-boomer-religion.

Himes, Michael J., and Kenneth R. Himes, OFM. *The Fullness of Faith: The Public Significance of Theology*. Mahwah: Paulist, 1993.

Hinton, Anthony Ray. *The Sun Does Shine: How I Found Life and Freedom on Death Row*. New York: St. Martin's, 2018.

Hinze, Bradford E. "The End of Salvation History." *Horizons* 18 (1991) 227–45.

Hollenbach, David, SJ. "Editor's Conclusion." *Theological Studies* 40 (1979) 713–15.

Holmes, Seth M. *Fresh Fruit, Broken Bodies: Migrant Farmworkers in the United States*. Berkeley: University of California Press, 2013.

Hopkins, Dwight N. "The Construction of the Black Male Body: Eroticism and Religion." In *Sexuality and the Sacred: Sources for Theological Reflection*, edited by Marvin M. Ellison and Kelly Brown Douglas, 205–19. Louisville, KY: Westminster John Knox, 2010.

Horkheimer, Max. *Die Sehnsucht nach dem ganz Anderen:Ein Interview mit Kommentar von Helmut Gumnior*. Hamburg: Furdie-Verlag H. Renneb, 1970.

———. "Foreword." In *The Dialectical Imagination: A History of the Frankfurt School and the Institute of Social Research, 1923–1950*, by Martin Jay, xxv–xxvi. Boston: Little, Brown, and Co., 1973.

Horkheimer, Max, and Theodor W. Adorno. *Dialectic of Enlightenment*. New York: Seabury, 1969.

Horsley, Richard A. *Covenant Economics: A Biblical Vision of Justice for All*. Louisville, KY: Westminster John Knox, 2009.

———. "General Introduction." In *Paul and Empire: Religion and Power in Roman Imperial Society*, edited by Richard A. Horsley, 1–8. Harrisburg: Trinity, 1997.

———. *Jesus and Empire: The Kingdom of God and the New World Disorder*. Minneapolis: Fortress, 2003.

———. *Jesus and the Powers: Conflict, Covenant, and the Hope of the Poor*. Minneapolis: Fortress, 2015.

———. *Jesus and the Spiral of Violence: Popular Jewish Resistance in Roman Palestine*. 1st ed. San Francisco: Harper & Row, 1987.

Horton, Michael S. "Traditional Reformed View." In *Justification: Five Views*, edited by John Beilby and Paul Eddy, 83–111. Downers Grove, IL: InterVarsity, 2011.

Hovey, Craig. "Liberalism and Democracy." In *The Cambridge Companion to Christian Political Theology*, edited by Craig Hovey and Elizabeth Phillips, 197–217. New York: Cambridge University Press, 2015.

Hughes, Richard. *Myths America Lives By: White Supremacy and the Stories That Give Us Meaning*. 2nd ed. Urbana: University of Illinois Press, 2018.

Ingram, Paul. "Judge Reverses Convictions of Four No More Deaths Volunteers." *Tucson Sentinel*, February 3, 2020. https://www.tucsonsentinel.com/local/report/020320_no_more_deaths/judge-reverses-convictions-4-no-more-deaths-volunteers.

Ireneaus. *Against Heresies*. In *Ante-Nicene Fathers*, Volume 1: *The Apostolic Fathers, Justin Martyr and Irenaeus*, edited by Philip Schaff and translated by Alexander Roberts and William Rambaut. Grand Rapids: Eerdmans, 1950.

Jackson, David. "Donald Trump's Call for Banning Muslims from Entering US Draws Condemnation." *USA Today*, December 7, 2015. https://www.usatoday.com/story/news/politics/elections/2015/12/07/donald-trump-muslims-united-states/76942932/.

James, William. *The Varieties of Religious Experience*. New York: Longmans, Green, 1916.

Jennings, Theodore W. *Transforming Atonement: A Political Theology of the Cross*. Minneapolis: Fortress, 2009.

Jennings, Willie James. *The Christian Imagination: Theology and the Origins of Race*. New Haven, CT: Yale University Press, 2011.

"Jo Ann Robinson: A Heroine of the Montgomery Bus Boycott." *National Museum of African-American History and Culture*. https://nmaahc.si.edu/explore/stories/jo-ann-robinson-heroine-montgomery-bus-boycott.

Jones, L. Gregory. *Embodying Forgiveness: A Theological Analysis*. Grand Rapids: Eerdmans, 1995.

Jones, Robert. *The End of White Christian America*. New York: Simon and Schuster, 2016.

———. "Racism among White Christians Is Higher than among the Nonreligious. That's No Coincidence." *NBC News*, July 27, 2020. https://www.nbcnews.com/think/opinion/racism-among-white-christians-higher-among-nonreligious-s-no-coincidence-ncna1235045.

———. *White Too Long: The Legacy of White Supremacy in American Christianity*. New York: Simon & Schuster, 2020.

Karkkainen, Veli-Matti. "The Holy Spirit and Justification: The Ecumenical Significance of Luther's Doctrine of Salvation." *Pneuma* 24 (2002) 26–39.

Kelly, Christopher. *The Roman Empire: A Very Short Introduction*. Oxford: Oxford University Press, 2006.

Kelsey, David. *The Uses of Scripture in Recent Theology*. Philadelphia, Fortress, 1975.

King, Martin Luther, Jr. "I Have a Dream." In *A Testament of Hope: The Essential Writings of Martin Luther King Jr.*, edited by James Melvin Washington, 217–20. San Francisco: Harper & Row, 1986.

———. "Letter from Birmingham Jail." In *A Testament of Hope: The Essential Writings of Martin Luther King Jr.*, edited by James Melvin Washington, 289–302. San Francisco: Harper & Row, 1986.

———. "Love, Law, and Civil Disobedience." In *A Testament of Hope: The Essential Writings of Martin Luther King Jr.*, edited by James Melvin Washington, 43–53. San Francisco: Harper & Row, 1986.

———. "Nonviolence, the Only Road to Freedom." In *A Testament of Hope: The Essential Writings of Martin Luther King Jr.*, edited by James Melvin Washington, 54–61. San Francisco: Harper & Row, 1986.

———. "Nonviolence and Racial Justice." *The Christian Century* 74 (1957) 165–67.

———. "Showdown for Nonviolence." In *A Testament of Hope: The Essential Writings of Martin Luther King Jr.*, edited by James Melvin Washington, 64–74. San Francisco: Harper & Row, 1986.

———. "A View of the Cross Possessing Biblical and Spiritual Justification." In *Called to Serve, January 1929–June 1951*, edited by Clayborne Carson et al., 263–67. Vol. 1 of *The Papers of Martin Luther King Jr*. Berkeley; Los Angeles: University of California Press, 1992.

———. "Where Do We Go From Here." In *A Testament of Hope: The Essential Writings of Martin Luther King Jr.*, edited by James Melvin Washington, 245–52. San Francisco: Harper & Row, 1986.

Kirk, J. R. Daniel. *Jesus Have I Loved, but Paul?: A Narrative Approach to the Problem of Pauline Christianity*. Grand Rapids: Baker Academic, 2011.

———. *Unlocking Romans: Resurrection and the Justification of God*. Grand Rapids: Eerdmans, 2008.

Kotsko, Adam. *The Politics of Redemption: The Social Logic of Salvation*. Edinburgh: T&T Clark, 2010.

Kraybill, Donald B. *The Upside-Down Kingdom*. Scottdale, PA: Herald, 1990.

Kristof, Nicholas. "Reverend, You Say the Virgin Birth Is a 'Bizarre Claim?'" *New York Times*, April 20, 2019. https://www.nytimes.com/2019/04/20/opinion/sunday/christian-easter-serene-jones.html.

Lash, Nicholas. "The Church in the State We're In." *Modern Theology* 13 (1997) 121–37.

Lee, Michelle Ye Hee. "Fact Checker: Donald Trump's False Comments Connecting Mexican Immigrants and Crime." *Washington Post*, July 8, 2015. https://www.washingtonpost.com/news/fact-checker/wp/2015/07/08/donald-trumps-false-comments-connecting-mexican-immigrants-and-crime.

Lenhardt, Christian. "Anamnestic Solidarity." *Telos* 25 (1975) 133–54.

Lindbeck, George. "The Sectarian Future of the Church." In *The God Experience*, edited by Joseph P. Whelen, 226–43. New York: Newman, 1971.

Lipka, Michael. "Many US Congregations Are Still Racially Segregated, but Things Are Changing." *Pew Research Center*, December 8, 2014. https://www.pewresearch.org/short-reads/2014/12/08/many-u-s-congregations-are-still-racially-segregated-but-things-are-changing-2.

Lischer, Richard. *The Preacher King: Martin Luther King Jr. and the Word That Moved America*. Oxford: Oxford University Press, 1995.

Loewe, William P. "Irenaeus' Soteriology: *Christus Victor* Revisited." *Anglican Theological Review* 67 (1985) 1–15.

———. *Lex Crucis:Soteriology and the Stages of Meaning*. Minneapolis: Fortress, 2016.

Lohfink, Gerhard. *Does God Need the Church?: Toward a Theology of the People of God*. Collegeville, MN: Liturgical, 1999.

Long, D. Stephen. *Augustinian and Ecclesial Christian Ethics: On Loving Enemies*. Minneapolis: Fortress, 2018.

Lopez, Davina C. *Apostle to the Conquered: Reimagining Paul's Mission*. Minneapolis: Fortress, 2008.

Lorde, Audre. "The Uses of Anger: Women Responding to Racism." *Sister Outsider: Essays and Speeches by Audre Lorde*, edited by Nancy K. Bereano, 124–33. Berkeley: Crossing, 2007.

Lovin, Robin. "Religion and American Public Life: Three Relationships." In *Religion and American Public Life: Interpretations and Explorations*, edited by Robin Lovin, 7–28. Mahwah: Paulist, 1986.

———. "Resources for a Public Theology." *Theological Studies* 40 (1979) 707–10.

Luther, Martin. *Lectures on Galatians, 1535, Chapters 1–4*. In *Luther's Works*, Volume 26, edited by Jaroslav Pelikan and Walter A. Hansen. St. Louis: Concordia, 1963.

———. *Lectures on Galatians, 1535, Chapters 5–6*. In *Luther's Works*, Volume 27, edited by Jaroslav Pelikan and Walter A. Hansen. St. Louis: Concordia, 1964.

Bibliography

———. *Preface to the Epistles of St. James and St. Jude*. In *Luther's Works*, Volume 35, edited by E. Theodore Bachman and Helmut T. Lehmann. Philadelphia: Muhlenberg, 1960.

———. *Preface to the Three Epistles of St John*. In *Luther's Works*, Volume 35, edited by E. Theodore Bachman and Helmut T. Lehmann. Philadelphia: Muhlenberg, 1960.

———. "Temporal Authority: To What Extent It Should Be Obeyed." In *Luther: Selected Political Writings*, edited and with an Introduction by J. M. Porter, 51–63. Philadelphia: Fortress, 1974.

Luu, Phuc. *Jesus of the East: Reclaiming the Gospel for the Wounded*. Harrisonburg: Herald, 2020.

Macchia, Frank D. "Justification Through New Creation: The Holy Spirit and the Doctrine by Which the Church Stands or Falls." *Theology Today* 58 (2001) 202–17.

———. *Justified in the Spirit: Creation, Redemption, and the Triune God*. Grand Rapids: Eerdmans, 2010.

MacMullen, Ramsey. *Roman Social Relations: 50 BC to AD 284*. 1st ed. New Haven, CT: Yale University Press, 1974.

Malick, David E. "The Poor Widow Who Gave at the Temple: Narrative Logic in Mark 12:41–44." *Priscilla Papers* 33 (2019) 8–12.

Malina, Bruce J. *The New Testament World: Insights from Cultural Anthropology*. Atlanta: John Knox, 1982.

Marsh, Charles. *God's Long Summer: Stories of Faith and Civil Rights*. Princeton: Princeton University Press, 1997.

Marshall, Bruce. "The Disunity of the Church and the Credibility of the Gospel." *Theology Today* 50 (1993) 78–89.

Marshall, Christopher D. "Atonement, Violence and the Will of God: A Sympathetic Response to J. Denny Weaver's *The Nonviolent Atonement*." *The Mennonite Quarterly Review* 77 (2003) 69–92.

Martin, William. *A Prophet with Honor: The Billy Graham Story*. Rev. ed. Grand Rapids: Zondervan, 2018.

Martinez, Jessica, and Gregory A. Smith. "How the Faithful Voted: A Preliminary 2016 Analysis." *Pew Research Center*, November 9, 2016. https://www.pewresearch.org/fact-tank/2016/11/09/how-the-faithful-voted-a-preliminary-2016-analysis.

Marty, Martin E. *The Public Church: Mainline, Evangelical, Catholic*. New York: Crossroad, 1981.

Martyn, Louis. "Events in Galatia: Modified Covenantal Nomism versus God's Invasion of the Cosmos in the Singular Gospel: A Response to J. D. G. Dunn and B. R. Gaventa." In *Thessalonians, Philippians, Galatians, Philemon*, edited by Jouette M. Bassler, 160–79. Vol. 1 of *Pauline Theology*. Minneapolis: Fortress, 1991.

———. *Galatians: A New Translation with Introduction and Commentary*. New York: Doubleday, 1997.

———. *Theological Issues in the Letters of Paul*. Nashville: Abingdon 1997.

Marx, Karl. "A Contribution to the Critique of Hegel's Philosophy of Right." 1844. Edited by Andy Blunden and Matthew Carmody. *Marxists.org*, 2009. https://www.marxists.org/archive/marx/works/1843/critique-hpr/intro.htm.

Massingale, Bryan. "Black Catholics Are Leaving the Church. Why?" *US Catholic* 86 (2021) 40–41.

McBride, Jennifer M. *Radical Discipleship: A Liturgical Politics of the Gospel*. Minneapolis: Fortress, 2017.

Bibliography

McBrien, Richard P. *Caesar's Coin: Religion and Politics in America*. New York: Macmillan, 1987.

McCarraher, Eugene. "'The Most Intolerable of Insults': Remarks to Christian Infidels in the American Empire." In *Anxious About Empire: Theological Essays on the New Global Realities*, edited by Wes Avram, 103–15. Grand Rapids: Brazos, 2004.

McElwee, Sean, and Jason McDaniel. "Economic Anxiety Didn't Make People Vote Trump, Racism Did." *Nation*, May 8, 2017. https://www.thenation.com/article/archive/economic-anxiety-didnt-make-people-vote-trump-racism-did.

McFarland, Ian. *In Adam's Fall: A Meditation on the Christian Doctrine of Original Sin*. Oxford: Wiley-Blackwell, 2010.

McGrath, Alasdair E. *Iustitia Dei: From the Beginnings to 1500*. 1st ed. Cambridge: Cambridge University Press, 1986.

McKnight, Scot M. *A Community Called Atonement*. Nashville: Abingdon, 2007.

Means, Jeffrey, and Mary Elise Nelson. *Trauma and Evil: Healing the Wounded Soul*. Minneapolis: Fortress, 2000.

Medley, Mark. "'Do This': The Eucharist and Ecclesial Selfhood." *Review and Expositor* 100 (2003) 383–401.

Mendenhall, G. E. *Law and Covenant in Israel and the Ancient Near East*. Pittsburgh: Biblical Colloquium, 1955.

Milbank, John. *Theology and Social Theory: Beyond Secular Reason*, Oxford: Blackwell, 1990.

Miller, Amanda C. "Wrestling with Rome: Imperial Violence and Its Legacy in the Synoptic Gospels." *Perspectives in Religious Studies* 42 (2015) 283–94.

Miller, Daniel. "The Limits of Dominance." In *Domination and Resistance*, edited by Daniel Miller et al., 63–79, London: Unwin Hyman, 1989.

Miller, Robert D., OFS. "Dragon Myths and Biblical Theology." *Theological Studies* 80 (2019) 37–56.

Miller v. Alabama, 567 US 460 (2012). *Justia*. https://supreme.justia.com/cases/federal/us/567/460.

Mitchell, Timothy. "Everyday Metaphors of Power." *Theory and Society* 19 (1990) 545–77.

Moltmann, Jürgen. *The Crucified God: The Cross of Christ as the Foundation and Criticism of Christian Theology*. New York: Harper & Row, 1974.

Murphy, Frederick J. *Apocalypticism in the Bible and Its World: A Comprehensive Introduction*. Grand Rapids: Baker Academic, 2012.

Murray, John Courtney. *We Hold These Truths*. New York: Sheed and Ward, 1960.

Mutz, Diana C. "Status Threat, Not Economic Hardship, Explains the 2016 Presidential Vote." *Proceedings of the National Academy of Sciences* 115.19 (2018) E4330–E4339. https://www.pnas.org/doi/full/10.1073/pnas.1718155115.

Myers, Ched. *Binding the Strong Man: A Political Reading of Mark's Story of Jesus*. Maryknoll, NY: Orbis, 1988.

Nakashima Brock, Rita, and Rebecca Ann Parker. *Proverbs of Ashes: Violence, Redemptive Suffering, and the Search for What Saves Us*. Boston: Beacon, 2002.

Needham, Nick. "Justification in the Early Church Fathers." In *Justification in Perspective: Historical Developments and Contemporary Challenges*, edited by Bruce L. McCormack, 25–53. Grand Rapids: Baker Academic, 2006.

Nellis, Ashley. "The Lives of Juvenile Lifers: Findings from a National Survey." *Sentencing Project*, March 1, 2012. https://www.sentencingproject.org/publications/the-lives-of-juvenile-lifers-findings-from-a-national-survey.

———. "No End in Sight: America's Enduring Reliance on Life Imprisonment." *Sentencing Project*, February 17, 2021. https://www.sentencingproject.org/publications/no-end-in-sight-americas-enduring-reliance-on-life-imprisonment.

Neuhaus, Richard John. "The Catholic Moment." *National Review*, November 7, 1986. 46.

———. *The Naked Public Square: Religion and Democracy in America*. Grand Rapids: Eerdmans, 1984.

Nevins, Joseph. *Operation Gatekeeper and Beyond: The War on "Illegals" and the Remaking of the US–Mexico Boundary*. 2nd ed. New York: Routledge, 2010.

Newport, Frank. "Religious Group Voting and the 2020 Election." *Gallup*, November 13, 2020. https://news.gallup.com/opinion/polling-matters/324410/religious-group-voting-2020-election.aspx.

Neyrey, Jerome H. "The Idea of Purity in Mark's Gospel." In *Social-Scientific Criticism of the New Testament and its Social World*, edited by John H. Elliot, 91–128. Decatur: Scholar's, 1986. https://www3.nd.edu/~jneyrey1/Purity-Mark.html.

Nicholas V. "Bull Romanus Pontifex: Granting the Portuguese a perpetual monopoly in trade with Africa." January 8, 1455. https://www.papalencyclicals.net/nichol05/romanus-pontifex.htm.

Nichols, Terence. *Death and Afterlife: A Theological Introduction*. Grand Rapids: Brazos, 2010.

Nickelsburg, George W. E. "Apocalyptic and Myth in 1 Enoch 6–11." *Journal of Biblical Literature* 96 (1977) 383–405.

———. "Judgment, Life-After-Death, and Resurrection in the Apocrypha and the Non-Apocalyptic Pseudepigrapha." In *Judaism in Late Antiquity*, edited by Alan J. Avery-Peck and Jacob Neusner, 4:141–62. Leiden: Brill, 2000.

Niebuhr, H. Richard. *Christ and Culture*. New York: Harper, 1951.

———. *The Social Sources of Denominationalism*. Reprint, Gloucester: Peter Smith, 1987.

Niebuhr, Reinhold. *Reflections on the End of an Era*. New York: Scribner's, 1934.

No More Deaths. "Foundations of Borderlands Humanitarian Relief." https://nomoredeaths.org/about-no-more-deaths.

Noll, Mark, et al. *The Gospel in America*. Grand Rapids: Zondervan, 1979.

Norris, Kristopher. *Witnessing Whiteness: Confronting White Supremacy in the American Church*. New York: Oxford University Press, 2020.

O'Donovan, Oliver. *Resurrection and Moral Order: An Outline for Evangelical Ethics*. Grand Rapids: Eerdmans, 1994.

Origen. *Commentary on the Epistle to the Romans. Books 1–5*. Edited by Thomas P. Scheck. Washington: Catholic University of America Press, 2001.

———. *Commentary on the Epistle to the Romans. Books 6–10*. Edited by Thomas P. Scheck. Washington: Catholic University of America Press, 2002.

———. *Commentary on Matthew*. In *Ante-Nicene Fathers*, Volume 9, edited by Philip Schaff et al., 640–818. Grand Rapids: Eerdmans, 1885.

Ormerod, Neil. *Creation, Grace, and Redemption*. Maryknoll, NY: Orbis, 2007.

Bibliography

Ott, Michael R. "Max Horkheimer's Critical Theory of Religion: The Meaning of Religion in the Struggle for Human Emancipation." Phd diss., Western Michigan University, 1998. https://scholarworks.wmich.edu/dissertations/1579.

Papanikolaou, Aristotle. *The Mystical as Political: Democracy and Non-Radical Orthodoxy*. South Bend: University of Notre Dame Press, 2012.

Park, Andrew Sung. *Triune Atonement: Christ's Healing for Sinners, Victims, and the Whole Creation*. Louisville, KY: Westminster John Knox, 2009.

Pelagius. "Letter [to Demetrias] from Pelagius (413)." *Epistolæ: Medieval Women's Letters*. https://epistolae.ctl.columbia.edu/letter/1296.html.

Peters, Ted. *Sin: Radical Evil in Soul and Society*. Grand Rapids: Eerdmans, 1994.

Peukert, Helmet. *Science, Action, and Fundamental Theology: Toward a Theology of Communicative Action*. Cambridge, MA: MIT Press.

Pierce, Yolanda. "Watching 81 Percent of My White Brothers and Sisters Vote for Trump Has Broken Something in Me." *Religion Dispatches*, November 15, 2016. http://religiondispatches.org/watching-8fs1-of-my-white-brothers-and-sisters-vote-for-trump-has-broken-something-in-me.

Plantinga, Cornelius. *Not the Way It's Supposed to Be: A Breviary of Sin*. Grand Rapids: Eerdmans, 1995.

Porges, Stephen W. "Foreword." In *The Heart of Trauma: Healing the Embodied Brain in the Context of Relationships*, by Bonnie Badenoch. New York: Norton, 2018.

Portier-Young, Anathea. *Apocalypse Against Empire: Theologies of Resistance in Early Judaism*. Reprint, Grand Rapids: Eerdmans, 2014.

Quirk, Michael. "Stanley Hauerwas's *Against the Nations*: Beyond Sectarianism." *Theology Today* 44 (1987) 78–86.

Rasmusson, Arne. "Ecclesiology and Ethics: The Difficulties of Ecclesial Moral Reflection." *Ecumenical Review* 52 (2000) 180–94.

Robertson, Pat. *The New World Order*. Dallas: Word, 1991.

Roe v. Wade, 410 US 113 (1973). *Justia*. https://supreme.justia.com/cases/federal/us/410/113.

Rose, Anton. "Paul, Christ, and Time: An Investigation of Apocalyptic and Salvation-Historical Themes in the Undisputed Pauline Epistles." MA thesis, Durham University, 2015. http://etheses.dur.ac.uk/11351.

Rothstein, Richard. *The Color of Law: The Forgotten History of How Our Government Segregated America*. New York: Liveright, 2017.

Rovner, Josh. "Juvenile Life without Parole: An Overview." *Sentencing Project*, May 24, 2021. https://www.sentencingproject.org/publications/juvenile-life-without-parole.

Russell, D. S. *Divine Disclosure: An Introduction to Jewish Apocalyptic*. Minneapolis: Fortress, 1992.

Rutledge, Fleming. *The Crucifixion: Understanding the Death of Jesus Christ*. Grand Rapids: Eerdmans, 2015.

Sachs, Jeffrey. *The Price of Civilization: Reawakening American Virtue and Prosperity*. New York: Random House, 2012.

Said, Edward W. *Culture and Imperialism*. New York: Knopf, 1993.

Sale v. Haitian Centers Council, Inc., 509 US 155 (1993). *Justia*. https://supreme.justia.com/cases/federal/us/509/155.

Sampley, J. Paul. *Walking Between the Times: Paul's Method of Moral Reasoning*. Minneapolis: Fortress, 1991.

Bibliography

Santa Ana, Otto. *Brown Tide Rising: Metaphors of Latinos in Contemporary American Public Discourse.* Austin: University of Texas Press, 2002.

Sawyer, Wendy, and Peter Wagner. "Mass Incarceration: The Whole Pie 2022." *Prison Policy Institute*, March 14, 2022. https://www.prisonpolicy.org/reports/pie2022.html.

Scheck, Thomas P. *Origen and the History of Justification: The Legacy of Origen's Commentary on Romans.* Notre Dame, IN: University of Notre Dame Press, 2008.

Schillebeeckx, Edward. *Jesus: An Experiment in Christology.* New York: Crossroad, 1979.

Schleiermacher, F. D. E. *The Christian Faith.* Translated by H. R. Mackintosh and J. S. Stewart. Edinburgh: T&T Clark, 1928.

Schmiechen, Peter. *Saving Power: Theories of Atonement and Forms of the Church.* Grand Rapids: Eerdmans, 2005.

Schultz, Thom, and Joani Schultz. *The One Thing: What Everyone Craves—That Your Church Can Deliver.* Loveland, CO: Group, 2004.

Scott, James C. *Domination and the Arts of Resistance: Hidden Transcripts.* New Haven, CT: Yale University Press, 1992.

Seibert, Eric. *Disturbing Divine Behavior: Troubling Old Testament Images of God.* Minneapolis: Fortress, 2009.

Shedler, Jonathan, and Jack Block. "Adolescent Drug Use and Psychological Health: A Longitudinal Study." *American Psychologist* 45 (1990) 612–30.

Shelton, Jason E., and Michael O. Emerson. *Black and Whites in Christian America: How Racial Discrimination Shapes Religious Convictions.* New York: New York University Press, 2012.

Shipler, David K. *The Working Poor: Invisible in America.* New York: Knopf, 2004.

Sider, Ron. *The Scandal of the Evangelical Conscience: Why Are Christians Living Just Like the Rest of the World.* Grand Rapids: Baker, 2005.

Siebert, Rudolf J., et al. "The Critical Theory of Religion: From Having to Being." *Critical Research on Religion* 1 (2013) 33–42.

Simpson, Gary M. "*Theologia Crucis* and the Forensically Fraught World: Engaging Helmut Peukert and Jürgen Habermas." In *Habermas, Modernity, and Public Theology*, edited by Don S. Browning and Francis Schüssler Fiorenza, 173–205. New York: Crossroad, 1992.

Smietana, Bob. "Taylor Professor Julie Moore Cited Jemar Tisby on Her Syllabus. Then She Lost Her Job." *Religious News Service*, May 3, 2023. https://religionnews.com/2023/05/03/taylor-english-professor-julie-moore-cited-jemar-tisby-on-her-syllabus-then-she-lost-her-job.

Smith, Bailey. "The Sin that Seems So Nice." *Fairview Baptist Edmond*, September 18, 2016. https://www.fairviewbaptistedmond.org/messages-list/the-sin-that-seems-so-nice.

Smith, J. Warren. "Justification and Merit Before the Pelagian Controversy: The Case of Ambrose of Milan." *Pro Ecclesia* 16 (2007) 195–217.

Smith, James K. A., and William Cavanaugh. *Evolution and the Fall.* Grand Rapids: Eerdmans, 2017.

Sprunt, Barbara. "The History Behind 'When the Looting Starts, the Shooting Starts.'" *NPR*, May 20, 2020. https://www.npr.org/2020/05/29/864818368/the-history-behind-when-the-looting-starts-the-shooting-starts.

Bibliography

Stackhouse, Max. "Public Theology and the Future of Democratic Society." In *The Church's Public Role: Retrospect and Prospect*, edited by Dieter T. Hessel, 63–83. Grand Rapids: Eerdmans, 1993.

Stafford, Tim. "Good Morning Evangelicals!: Meet Ted Haggard, the NAE's Optimistic Champion of Ecumenical Evangelism and Free-Market Faith." *Christianity Today* 49 (2005) 40–45.

Stevenson, Bryan. *Just Mercy: A Story of Justice and Redemption*. New York: Spiegel and Grau, 2014.

Stone, Ron. "Tillich and Niebuhr as Allied Public Theologians." *Political Theology* 9 (2008) 503–11.

Storkey, Alan. *Jesus and Politics: Confronting the Powers*. Grand Rapids: Baker Academic, 2005.

Stout, Jeffrey. *Democracy and Tradition*. Princeton: Princeton University Press, 2004.

Tacitus. *Annals*. Translated by Alfred John Church and William Jackson Brodribb. Internet Classics Archive. http://classics.mit.edu/Tacitus/annals.html.

———. *Life of Cnaeus Julius Agricola*. Translated by Alfred John Church and William Jackson Brodribb. Ancient History Sourcebook. https://sourcebooks.fordham.edu/ancient/tacitus-agricola.asp.

Tanner, Kathryn. "Public Theology and the Character of Public Debate." In *The Annual of the Society of Christian Ethics*, edited by Harlan Beckley, 79–101. Washington, DC: Society of Christian Ethics, 1996.

———. *Theories of Culture: A New Agenda for Theology*. Minneapolis: Augsburg Fortress, 1997.

Tillig, Chris. "Paul, 'Apocalyptic' and 'Salvation-History Approaches, and Barth." *Chrisendom* (blog), December 4, 2007. http://blog.christilling.de/2007/12/paul-apocalyptic-and-salvation-history_04.html.

Tisby, Jemar. *The Color of Compromise: The Truth About the American Church's Complicity in Racism*. Grand Rapids: Zondervan, 2019.

Tracy, David. *The Analogical Imagination: Christian Theology and the Culture of Pluralism*. New York: Crossroad, 1981.

———. "Particular Classics, Public Religion, and the American Tradition." In *Religion and American Public Life: Interpretations and Explorations*, edited by Robin Lovin, 115–31. Mahweh: Paulist, 1986.

Tran, Jonathan. *Asian Americans and the Spirit of Racial Capitalism*. AAR Reflection and Theory in the Study of Religion. Oxford: Oxford University Press, 2021.

Trelstad, Marit. "Introduction: The Cross in Context." In *Cross Examinations: Readings on the Meaning of the Cross*, edited by Marit Trelstad, 1–17. Minneapolis: Fortress, 2006.

Van Driel, Edwin Christiaan. "Climax of the Covenant vs Apocalyptic Invasion: A Theological Analysis of a Contemporary Debate in Pauline Exegesis." *International Journal of Systematic Theology* 17 (2015) 6–25.

Vanhoozer, Kevin J. "Wrighting the Wrongs of the Reformation?: The State of the Union with Christ and St. Paul in Protestant Theology." In *Jesus, Paul, and the People of God: A Theological Dialogue with N. T. Wright*, edited by Richard B. Hays and Nicholas Perrin, 235–59. Wheaton Theology Conference Series. Downers Grove, IL: IVP Academic, 2011.

Verhey, Allen. *Remembering Jesus: Christian Community, Scripture, and the Moral Life*. Grand Rapids: Eerdmans, 2002.

Bibliography

Villegas, Isaac. "Fugitive Democracy: Sheldon Wolin and Contemplating the Local." *Rusty Parts*, April 25, 2006. http://www.rustyparts.com/wp/2006/04/25/fugitive-democracy-sheldon-wolin-and-contemplating-the-local/#more-214.

Volf, Miroslav. *Exclusion and Embrace: A Theological Exploration of Identity, Otherness, and Reconciliation*. Nashville: Abingdon, 1996.

———. "Soft Difference: Theological Reflections on the Relation Between Church and Culture in 1 Peter." *Ex Auditu* 10 (1994) 15–30.

Wallis, Jim. *The Call to Conversion*. San Francisco: Harper & Row, 1981.

Watson, Kathryn. "Trump Questions Why US Welcomes People from "Sh*thole" Countries." *CBS News*, January 11, 2018. https://www.cbsnews.com/news/trump-asks-why-u-s-welcomes-people-from-shole-countries-report.

Weaver, J. Denny. "Narrative *Christus Victor*: The Answer to Anselmian Atonement Violence." In *Atonement and Violence: A Theological Conversation*, edited by John Sanders, 1–32. Nashville: Abingdon, 2006.

———. *The Nonviolent Atonement*. Grand Rapids: Eerdmans, 2001.

Weil, Simone. *Intimations of Christianity among the Ancient Greeks*. London: Routledge Kegan Paul, 1957.

Westerholm, Stephen. *Perspectives Old and New on Paul: The "Lutheran" Paul and His Critics*. Grand Rapids: Eerdmans, 2003.

Whitehead, Andrew, and Samuel Perry. *Taking America Back for God: Christian Nationalism in the United States*. Oxford: Oxford University Press, 2020.

Wiley, Tatha. *Original Sin: Origins, Developments, Contemporary Meaning*. New York: Paulist, 2002.

Williams, Dolores. "Black Women's Surrogacy Experience and the Christian Notion of Redemption." In *Cross Examinations: Readings on the Meaning of the Cross*, edited by Marit Trelstad, 19–32. Minneapolis: Fortress, 2006.

Williams, Rowan. *Resurrection: Interpreting the Easter Gospel*. London: Darton Longman & Todd, 2014.

Wink, Walter. *Engaging the Powers: Discernment and Resistance in a World of Domination*. Minneapolis: Fortress, 1992.

———. *When Powers Fall: Reconciliation in the Healing of the Nations*. Minneapolis: Fortress, 1998.

Wolin, Sheldon S. "Fugitive Democracy." *Constellations* 1 (1994) 11–25.

———. *Politics and Vision: Continuity and Innovation in Western Political Thought*. Exp. ed. Princeton: Princeton University Press, 2004.

Wright, N. T. *Justification: God's Plan, Paul's Vision*. Downers Grove, IL: IVP Academic, 2016.

———. "New Perspectives on Paul." In *Justification in Perspective: Historical Developments and Contemporary Challenges*, edited by Bruce L. McCormack, 243–64. Grand Rapids: Baker Academic, 2006.

———. *Paul and the Faithfulness of God*. Minneapolis: Fortress, 2013.

———. *Surprised by Hope: Rethinking Heaven, the Resurrection, and the Mission of the Church*. New York: HarperOne, 2008.

———. *What St. Paul Really Said: Was Paul of Tarsus the Real Founder of Christianity?* Grand Rapids: Eerdmans, 1997.

Yeago, David. "A Christian Holy People: Martin Luther on Salvation and the Church." *Modern Theology* 13 (1997) 101–20.

www.ingramcontent.com/pod-product-compliance
Lightning Source LLC
Chambersburg PA
CBHW031433230426
43668CB00007B/523